THE LONG AND WINDING ROAD

LIONEL BARRY HARRIS

THE LONG AND WINDING ROAD

ReadersMagnet, LLC

The Long and Winding Road
Copyright © 2021 by Lionel Barry Harris

Published in the United States of America
ISBN Paperback: 978-1-955603-42-3
ISBN eBook: 978-1-955603-41-6

All rights reserved. No part of this publication may be reproduced, stored in a retrieval system or transmitted in any way by any means, electronic, mechanical, photocopy, recording or otherwise without the prior permission of the author except as provided by USA copyright law.

The opinions expressed by the author are not necessarily those of ReadersMagnet, LLC.

ReadersMagnet, LLC
10620 Treena Street, Suite 230 | San Diego, California, 92131 USA
1.619.354.2643 | www.readersmagnet.com

Book design copyright © 2021 by ReadersMagnet, LLC. All rights reserved.
Cover design by Ericka Obando
Interior design by Mary Mae Romero

CONTENTS

Chapter 1	Out of the Blue	1
Chapter 2	The Power of Beer-Guzzling	7
Chapter 3	Grieving in Private	14
Chapter 4	Clearing the Air	19
Chapter 5	A Farewell to Chi-town	26
Chapter 6	A House Made of Tin	34
Chapter 7	A Volatile Storm	39
Chapter 8	In Defiance of a Tyrant	51
Chapter 9	An Unequal Punishment	60
Chapter 10	Brotherly Love	69
Chapter 11	Wounds that Won't Heal	78
Chapter 12	Twenty-One Dollars and Change	88
Chapter 13	Grief in Black and White	94
Chapter 14	An Audacious Behavior	101
Chapter 15	Fear Of The Unknown	105
Chapter 16	The House That Jack Built	114
Chapter 17	Circle Of Friends	131
Chapter 18	God's Book Of Life	143
Chapter 19	Life With The Fellows	156
Chapter 20	Envy And Jealousy	169
Chapter 21	Love Is In The Air	182
Chapter 22	For Love Of Family	190

Chapter 23	Unforgettable Characters	201
Chapter 24	America's Unsung Heroes	214
Chapter 25	Home - Sweet Home	229
Chapter 26	A Gathering of Brothers	245
Chapter 27	The Hands-Down Loser	260
Chapter 28	Birds Of A Feather	276
Chapter 29	In Lieu Of Diplomacy	291
Chapter 30	Grin And Bear It	310
Chapter 31	My World Is A Better Place	326
Chapter 32	Abnormal, But Congenial	344
Chapter 33	The Deep South	355
Chapter 34	A Topsy-Turvy Event	372
Chapter 35	The Awful November	384
Chapter 36	Bright Tomorrows	396
Chapter 37	A Storybook Life	407
Chapter 38	Love and Marriage	414
Chapter 39	A Friendship Beyond Compare	423
Chapter 40	The Same Old Story	433
Chapter 41	A Bit of Mother-Wit	444
Chapter 42	The Winds of Change	454
Chapter 43	Some Things Never Change	464
Chapter 44	Deja Vu In Spades	473
Chapter 45	The High Price Of Lust	482

Epilogue 495

"EVERYTIME SOMEONE DIES, THEY TAKE A PART OF ME WITH THEM."

Lionel B. Harris

DEDICATED TO THE PRECIOUS MEMORY OF:

My mother, RUBY (who understood me),
My uncle, BILL (who stood by me),
& My wife, GLORIA (who stood alongside me).

"I thank the living GOD for graciously ushering the three of them into my life."

THIS book is essentially true and rather candid. However, since it depicts events that transpired over fifty-five (55) years ago, the applied dialogue (although, sometimes, raw and blunt) captures the gist of the actual words that were spoken. In addition, the numerous characters who are cited in its pages are basically real and not composites or caricatures. However, since the author was not particularly interested in exalting or demeaning any individual portrayed in it (either living or deceased), he felt it was appropriate to use some pseudo names. Still, there are authentic names that grace the story line and they, too, were inserted without any semblance of begrudgment, malice or adoration. For the most part, the author applauds their very memory.

WITHOUT apparent rhyme or reason, a young black army corporal is assigned the somber task of escorting the body of a fellow African-American soldier to Chicago, Illinois. Stationed in San Antonio, Texas (specifically, Fort Sam Houston), the corporal neither knows the deceased soldier, and nor is he, himself, a native of Chicago. Therefore, the selected escort is immediately taken aback by the venture. Personally, he considers himself inadequate and altogether miscast in the endeavor. However, upon being privy to an in-depth view of the corporal's foregoing and current life, he could very well be underestimating himself. The distinct path that was travelled by the reluctant escort, replete with numerous peaks and valleys, might have groomed and well-prepared him for his mission. To say the very least, however, for the corporal - it was a LONG AND WINDING ROAD.

CHAPTER ONE

OUT OF THE BLUE

In the autumn of 1964, I was a twenty-year-old black corporal in the United States Army. Stationed at Fort Sam Houston, Texas, I was proficient in field operations when I dealt with the 250th General Hospital (which was my home station) and just as adept when I worked at Brooke General Hospital's Registrar office. In essence, they were coexisting positions. At Camp Bullis (the designated site where the 250th implemented and simulated field operations), I oversaw every facet of hospital "admissions" and "dispositions" and, similarly, at the Registrar office on post, I was skilled at every administrative task I was assigned. I was prized by, both, 250th General's commanding officer and the "Registrar" himself, a bird colonel named Simpson. In fact, I was deemed a valuable asset, and so much so that when I volunteered to go to Korea and then, to Vietnam, I was turned down on each occasion.

It may very well sound like I'm tooting my own horn or patting myself on the back, but, honestly, I am not that vain or braggadocious. Instead, I'm searching for a certain perspective, a sensible and rational explanation for a major happening during my young military life, but one that still plagues me to this very day. In my estimation, it was a life-altering event and I eventually came to relish it. However, when it transpired, I was awash with wonder and anxiety.

When the fall of sixty-four came on the scene (again, the onset of the happening), I was reconciled to a solid, unwavering fact. After enlisting in the army in June of 1962 and, subsequently, being shipped to my permanent duty station in San Antonio, Texas in December of that same year, I felt I was destined to spend the remainder of my military tour stateside. With less than eight months left (I was slated to muster out in June of 1965), I gave up all hope of going overseas. Although I was on the verge a snaring a sergeant's stripe and was assigned my very own cadre room, I was still somewhat sorrowful and disenchanted.

However, at the height of my despair, even as I contemplated my two-year anniversary at Fort Sam Houston, something happened out of the blue. After being summoned to the headquarters building at 250th General by my rather stoic commanding officer (CO), I was given an official, but very unusual assignment. Targeting the upcoming Monday afternoon, I was told to pack a ten-day supply of clothing and, at 1400 hours, be ready at my barracks to be picked up by jeep.

I, of course, asked what was going on. I was certain I hadn't committed a crime or had did anything wrong, so I then fretted that something had gone awry in St. Louis, Missouri, my hometown. That naturally led me to inquire about my immediate family and that's when the truth finally came out. Although I was instantly relieved and simultaneously awestruck, my CO seemed quite pleased with himself.

"You are being given a rare honor, Cpl. Harris," the officer explained. "I personally recommended you for this assignment and I'm more than confident you're the best soldier for it. And your associates, Lieutenants Morrison and Sanders, agreed with me." Still, I was in the dark. "But, Sir, just what assignment are we talking about here?" I asked.

"Well, sadly, and my heart goes out to the kid's family, but a young soldier died in the M.T.C. area recently. He was around your age, Corporal, and a colored boy, just like you, and he's from the city of Chicago, Illinois. It was brought to my attention that your father lives there. So-o, I figured you could escort the body there, comfort his family somewhat and spend some quality time with your dad. Then, after the funeral is over, you can catch a train to St. Louis, spend a little time there also. It'll be like a ten-day furlough, but a notch better, I'd say. Cause Uncle Sam will be footing the bill. Everything - Hotel fee, food, taxi fare, the whole smear. You'll be representing the United States army and I'm sure you'll make us all proud. In fact, I'd bet on it. So, what do you say, Cpl. Harris? Are you up to the task? We're kinda counting on you, young fellow."

In light of the colonel's enthusiasm and spirited praise, I wasn't about to say "No." I really didn't know if I could turn the assignment down at that point. Therefore, I said "Yes," thanked my CO for the "honor" and vowed to do a good job. It wasn't until after I shook the officer's hand, rendered him a salute and departed the headquarters building that I entertained misgivings and began to analyze the entire affair. I felt I was the wrong soldier for the endeavor (I perceived myself as much too emotional for it) and I seriously asked myself, "Why me?" I didn't quite buy into the colonel's explanation. I was estranged from my father, I only occasionally corresponded with the man and I hadn't seen him in years.

It was two years prior to my high school graduation, actually. Plus, I hardly ever talked about him to others, and especially to white associates. So what, I asked myself, really brought the impending happening to the forefront? I knew my work performance was exemplary, I was even awarded two letters of commendation during that very year, but could simple merit explain it all? I was resolved to do my level best, but, still, I didn't understand any of it.

A little while later, after I became reconciled to the fact that I'd pursue the mission, I was guilty of jumping to an "educated" conclusion. It was derived from my dual-headed position at the Registrar's office and it made perfect sense to me. In addition to taking verbal statements from military personnel and, then, converting them into "Line of duty affidavits" (which pertained to various injuries of soldier victims), I was also an assistant to an air force liaison. With Kelly, Lackland and Randolph fields being all located in San Antonio. I frequently arranged or had input in "air evacuations."

In essence, I was privy to the itinerary of numerous military flights (commonly called "hops") and I was in a position to secure airplane rides for uniformed personnel. So, naturally, I believed that my journey to Illinois would be by military transport.

I was plainly wrong. Except for the jeep that transported me and my duffel bag to San Antonio's commercial airport, I never saw another military conveyance during most of my trip. In fact, if I wasn't wearing my army attire (since it was a relatively warm November day, I dressed in my khaki uniform), I could have just as well been regarded as a civilian. The casket bearing the body of the young soldier was already loaded onto the plane, so all I had to do was to check my duffel bag in and then climb aboard it.

Earlier, when I was picked up by my jeep chauffeur, I was handed a packet of papers. The driver suggested that I read the instructions aboard the plane and assured me that I'd be apprised of everything I needed to know about my mission. I was relieved somewhat and took quiet refuge in having those instructions. After all, I didn't know what the hell I was doing.

The instructions were very precise and very informative. They told me what was expected of me, how to conduct myself military-wise and supplied me with a list of "help-oriented" telephone numbers. The packet also contained a hodgepodge of military vouchers; some for food, taxicab rides and even hotel lodging. Seemingly, every facet of my rather somber undertaking was thoroughly covered by the army.

For the first time since I agreed to my assignment, I felt momentarily good about it. It was a rather difficult and heart-tugging mission but death, too, was a part of life, I reasoned. In addition, I perceived myself as a person of deep compassion and I thought, that maybe, I'd turn out to be an asset in the affair. Perhaps I was the ideal soldier for the job after all.

My upsurge in confidence was short-lived, however. The information package also contained a sealed envelope, one that was labelled "Personal and Confidential," and when I opened it and read its contents, I emerged downright depressed. My optimism took a sudden nose dive.

I was made aware of the deceased soldier's name and learned other things about him. I was apprised of his age, his rank, his service number and even his unit designation. I knew the name of the boy's mother, along with the names of his two surviving, younger brothers and their exact address in Chicago proper. However, something practically leaped out at me, a revelation that mentally and physically startled me. I must have jumped because my seat partner, an elderly white woman, asked me if I was alright.

I smiled, assured the lady that I was fine, and then went on to scrutinize the information that had managed to unnerve me. The young soldier had died from spinal meningitis, the highly contagious kind. Actually, it was a strain so contagious that it could be contracted from the dead body itself. And that was why, the document went on to convey, that the "remains" were hermetically sealed in glass. And due to that particular factor, I was instructed to check the coffin ever so often, making sure it remained secure and intact. Admittedly, I remained somewhat shakened. However, I dutifully brought myself to check on the state of the body a couple of times during the flight. It was a stipulated facet of my ongoing assignment.

CHAPTER TWO
THE POWER OF BEER-GUZZLING

From the very moment I committed myself to my mission to Chicago, I figured it would be plagued with one problem after another. Basically, it was an assignment that was well on the outskirts of normalcy. However, the initial problem was my own darn fault. When my plane took off from San Antonio, it was a pleasant 72 degrees outside. That was why I was wearing my dress khakis. Although I packed some winter clothing (my overcoat, included), they were in my duffel bag. I guess in my anticipation of the trip, I was rendered stupid. And I paid dearly for my stupidity.

When the airplane touched down at Chicago's O'Hare Airport, it was 18 degrees outdoors. I knew I was expected to stand at attention, render a prolonged salute when the casket was being unloaded from the plane and, then, see it placed securely inside the waiting hearse. I did that right on cue and tried desperately to keep my teeth from chattering. The frigid wind was literally whipping across the airfield. And I was damn cold, so cold, in fact, that large tears were rolling down my cheeks.

Then, about fifteen minutes later, as the military protocol finally came to a close, I climbed into the passenger side of the 'warm' vehicle and sighed in sheer relief. Apparently, the funeral director, who happened to be a smallish black woman, had observed my tearful state. She attempted to comfort me, speaking in a very sympathetic and soft tone.

"I know it's extremely hard for you, Cpl. Harris," she stated, "but I assure you - your buddy is now in a much better place. I can't tell you not to grieve for him, but he's alright. And you'll get through this just fine, we all will."

As I looked at the sympathetic lady, I almost hated to tell her the truth. "I wish I had known Donald," I said (that was the deceased soldier's name), "but I never had the pleasure of meeting him, Miss Turner. I'm just cold, ma'am."

The mortician was instantly shocked. She was so taken aback, in fact, she stopped the vehicle before we left the airport lot. "Oh, you mustn't tell Donnie's family that!" she urged me. "That'll further break their hearts. Just for pretense, Cpl. Harris, please tell 'em you knew their Donnie. It'll make them feel so good. Please, corporal, it'll be our little secret."

"But . . . but they'll know, Miss Turner," I frowningly responded. "I don't want to make the situation worse, by lying to the family."

"Believe me, you won't be making things worse," the woman countered. "I knew Donnie all his life and I'll tell you a few things about him. Please, Cpl. Harris, don't tell his people you guys were total strangers."

The funeral director looked so distressed that I didn't have the heart to debate her further. I reluctantly agreed to her unorthodox request (meaning I would lie) and she proceeded to do exactly what she said she'd do. Before I parted company with her that evening, I learned a great deal about the life of the deceased soldier. However, I didn't know it at the time but it would eventually wax detrimental to me.

～

As it turned out, I didn't meet Donald Cain's family until the following day, which was Tuesday. My maiden day in the city of Chicago saw me telephoning my father, thereby surprising the hell out of him (I didn't even inform him I was coming) and then, thanks to the Turner woman, being shuttled over to the old man's apartment building on Prairie Avenue. With my duffel bag in two, I had the utmost intentions of checking in at a reputable hotel or motel later on. As my CO put it, "Uncle Sam would be footing the bill."

The last time I saw my father, Melvin V. Harris, was when my oldest brother, Gary (I had three other brothers under me) issued him a stern challenge. Both, Gary and I were sophomores in high school at that time and Gary (whose actual name was Melvin 'Gary') didn't welcome Dad's pop-in visit. Moreover, since our absentee father was terribly abusive to Gary when he was a child, Gary was downright hostile to him. Showcasing an impressive physique, my eldest brother spoke rather gruffly to our dad, asking, "Hey, old man, remember how you used to knock me around when I was a kid? Well, try knocking me around now."

I especially remembered that incident because, alternately, Dad left our house in a state of tears. I could not help feeling sorry for him. Coincidentally, when I stepped over the threshold of the old man's Prairie Avenue apartment, it was like deja vu. Upon reaching out and firmly embracing me, my father started to heavily weep. Then, when I rather awkwardly returned his hug, he verbally professed he loved me. Calling me "Duke" (that was my nickname), he sounded sincere but I was a mite skeptical.

Then, minutes later, after introducing me to, both, his present wife, Reba (in reality, I had seen the lady before) and his wife's younger brother, Alvin, the old man started yearning for his youngest son, Keith. He continually told me how glad his little boy would be to finally meet his 'big brother' and soon sent his brother-in-law out to find the boy. Meantime, after toting my duffel into the apartment and making small-talk with his wife (she was pleasant enough), I took a seat and started filling my father in about my rather bizarre journey to Chi-town.

Suddenly, though, my verbal account was interrupted. The front door was pushed open and there stood the returning Alvin and a pint-sized little boy. Keith was around ten or eleven at the time and, in spite of hardly ever interacting with the youngster until that particular day, I was overjoyed upon seeing the little guy. And although I can't explain it till this very day, I instantly fell in love with him. I was certainly unsure of how the boy felt about me, but I tried to convey my sincere affection for him with a robust hug. For, to me, it was plain and simple. Keith was my kid-brother and I automatically loved him. Naturally, I hoped Keith would someday feel likewise towards me (and his other four brothers as well).

However, to be perfectly frank, during my flight to Chicago, I entertained the thought of 'not' visiting my dad at all. I contemplated just checking into a hotel, tending to the solemn mission at hand and, then, catching that train to Saint Louis. Although I, sometimes, communicated with my father by letter writing, I wasn't so sure I wanted to actually see him. Nor was I anxious to see his wife or his little boy. Intermittently, I found myself beset with a whole slew of vivid and very painful childhood memories.

As it turned out though, I was glad I chose to take the high road. It wasn't my nature to be begrudging or vindictive. And since the old man was so gracious and so utterly pleased to have me within arm's reach, I was happy I had made the decision to be with him. I deemed it a prime time for healing old wounds and silently wondered, too, if God was at work. Precisely, I couldn't refrain from thinking that, maybe, that was the divine motivation behind my out of the blue journey. And whether I was right on target or altogether wrong, I felt blessed.

As I stated, my father seemed as if he was in seventh heaven. Smiling widely, he insisted that I drink a beer with him and then asked his wife to fix me some food. I ate, drank several more cans of beer and then asked him to recommend a good hotel to me. Now, what did I do that for? You would have thought I had said, "Slavery has just been reinstated!"

"Aw, naw, you're not going to no damn hotel," my dad snapped. "You're staying right here, Duke, with us. So, put that hotel stuff out of your mind."

"Yeah, that's right," chimed in Dad's wife. "You're staying here."

I was momentarily dumbfounded and at a loss for a response. I looked around, the apartment wasn't that large! Then, I glanced out the adjacent rear window. I sought the window because I periodically heard the sound of the passing by "el" trains. The el's tracks seemed less than 25 yards away!

"Look, Dad, I appreciate your offer," I argued, "but the army's allowing me - carte blanche. They're paying the bills for everything; hotels, cabs, food, all of it." Via my old man's expression, I wasn't making a dent. So, I added, "Plus, I couldn't get any sleep with that el continually passing by. Besides, where would I sleep?"

Before my father could offer up a rebuttal, the bystanding Alvin inserted a remark that made me laugh out loud. (Up until that moment, he was silent and busily indulging in an alcohol mixture). "Donchu go giving up my bed to him, Melvin," he rather pitifully insisted. "Duke, don't come here takin' my bed."

I wanted to comfort Alvin, assure him I wouldn't think of taking his bed, but I couldn't. Observing the seriousness in his expression, I could not immediately squelch my laughter. My dad, on the other hand, was slightly upset. But even he fought off amusement when he decided to speak.

"Boy, shut your drunk ass up!" he scolded Alvin. "Ain't nobody giving your damn bed away. Me and Duke can sleep on the let-out sofa together, ya' damn fool! Why don't you just take your crazy ass somewhere?"

I finally regained my composure. "You see what you got started?" I teased my dad. "You almost started World War 3. Now, do you see why I need to check into a hotel or motel?"

"No, I don't - and that's all settled," the old man replied. "You're stayin' right here with us, Duke, and that's it - case closed. We wouldn't have it any other way. You're my son, and I love you."

I, then, gave up, surrendered. I was much too tired to put forth a worthy fight. Instead, I resumed my beer-drinking, discussed a whole gamut of topics with my dad and, finally, opted to retire for the night. Reba fixed up the sofa's let-out bed for her husband and me. However, before I was able to give way to sleep (both, Reba and little Keith had already gone to bed), my father and I heard someone fumbling with the front door lock. Of course, it was Dad's returning brother-in-law. And that's when the old man "whisperingly" urged me to do something nutty. He coerced me to jump into Alvin's bed and pretend that I was fast asleep.

I was a little reluctant but I didn't have enough time to talk myself out of the idea. Actually, I didn't try that hard to dissuade myself. When Alvin finally entered the apartment, I had just laid flat on his bed and closed my eyes.

"I knew it, I knew it!" Alvin complained, real tears rolling down his face. "Melvin, I knew you was gonna give my bed to Duke! It ain't fair and you know it!"

Although I realized it was actually Alvin's whiskey talking, I couldn't control my laughter. I apologized to the guy as I climbed out of his bed and I was sincere. "Look, man, we're just messin' with you, yankin' your chain," I stated. "There is no way I'd really take your bed. That wouldn't be cool and I am sorry."

"Don't worry about that boy, Duke," Dad laughingly insisted. "Alvin, take your drunk ass to bed. Nigga ain't worth a quarter."

With that, I made my way back to the couch. I had a big day ahead of me the next day, one that I deduced would be trying and challenging and I had to get some shut-eye. Plus, I was feeling the effects of my beer-guzzling. Funny thing though, when I finally succumbed to sleep, I never did hear the sounds of the rolling el trains outside.

CHAPTER THREE
GRIEVING IN PRIVATE

My second day in Chicago found me, again, dressed in military garb (this time, in dress greens instead of khakis) and patiently waiting around at my father's south side apartment. Originally, Alma Turner, the very personable funeral director, was scheduled to pick me up at twelve noon and then drive me to her mortuary, which was located on Chicago's west side. She and I had agreed to that before parting company last evening.

However, when I spoke to Miss Turner around ten a.m. and informed her of my whereabouts (she was pleased I was staying with my father), she apprised me of a slight change. Instead of her showing up, she told me that Donald Cain's younger brother, Frank, had volunteered to come and get me. "Frankie was looking forward to meeting me," she added. I said okay, told her I'd be ready at the set time and then hung up the phone. To be honest, I wasn't too thrilled about the change. For I was still wrestling with the premise of lying.

Frank Cain was about 18 years old (right away he insisted that I call him "Frankie") and he was instantly friendly. In fact, the minute I opened up the apartment's front door, he stepped forward and hugged me! I was surprised as hell, but I forced myself to return his embrace just as my dad (who was standing in the background) waved at him. "Frankie" side-stepped me at that point, walked over and briskly offered his hand to Dad.

"You gots to be Lonnie's pop!" he marveled, shaking the old man's hand. (Apparently, Miss Turner had divulged my first name to the boy, which was actually "Lionel"). "You two cats look like brothers! I'm glad to meet you, Mr. Harris."

"Same here, young man," my father replied. "And I am so very sorry about your brother. You have my sincere condolences."

Almost instantly, the teenager's facial expression changed. His smile turned into sheer anguish. "Yeah, that is something, ain't it?" he mused. "I feel so sorry for my mother. She's taking it so hard, real hard."

For a prolonged moment, an awkward hush fell over the apartment. As Frank Cain almost beseechingly looked my way, I forced myself to break the silence. "Well, I guess we best get to moving, Frankie," I spoke. "We're due at the funeral parlor by one o'clock."

"Yeah, you're right about that," the boy agreed. "My mom's probably already there. And, Benny, he's there too. He's my baby brother, but I'm sure Donnie talked to you about him. Right, Lonnie? And by the way, is it alright for me to call you that?"

"I really prefer that to Lionel," I replied. "But, Frankie, Donnie talked about both of his brothers. So much so, that I feel like I already know you two guys. Let me grab my overcoat and we can split."

⁂

When Frank Cain stated that his mother and little brother were probably already at "Turner's Mortuary," he was correct. When he and I entered the funeral facility through the side door, both of them, along with Alma Turner and three additional members of the Cain family (one male and two females), were standing in front of the flag-draped coffin of PFC Donald M. Cain. I immediately walked forward to introduce myself but since I wasn't certain which woman was the mother, I halted and glanced back at Frankie. However, Miss Turner quickly snared the floor at that juncture.

"Jenny, this is the nice soldier I've been going on and on about," she stated, addressing the tallest woman in the bunch. "He requested the honor of bringing our Donnie home to us. Cpl. Harris, this is Jennifer Cain and . . ."

I was aware that Alma Turner was trying to add Mrs. Cain's youngest son to her introduction speech, but she was somewhat stifled. With a face that was still moist from heavy sobbing, Jennifer Cain stepped forward and embraced me tightly.

"Thank you so much for your wonderful kindness, young man," the woman spoke. "It's so very good of you to bring my boy home. But what . . . what is your name again? I am sorry. Alma sure told it to me - but I haven't been thinking straight lately. Please try and bare with me."

"It's perfectly understandable, ma'am," I softly replied, returning her affectionate hold. "I only wish I could have met you folks under happy circumstances. It's Lionel Harris, Mrs. Cain. My real name's Lionel, but you can call me 'Lonnie,' like your son, Frankie, does. Then, as I glanced downward, I added, "And this must be your other little boy. I've heard a lot about him."

"Yeah, he's the baby of the family," the lady smiled gently. "Benny, say hello to your brother, Donnie's, good friend. Ben was absolutely crazy about his big brother."

When I went to shake the little kid's hand (he had to be around six years old), he literally burst into tears. I stooped down and bodily picked him up and right away, the one thing I sought to try and suppress made its distinct debut. With tears flowing from my own eyes, I carried the youngster over to the nearest pew, took a seat upon it and tried to console him. I encouraged the kid to go on and cry, assuring him that there would be better days on the near horizon.

However, as Benny wept loudly and proceeded to wrap his tiny arms around my neck, I wasn't at all sure who was actually comforting who. I never could stand human suffering, even if it was just being depicted on a movie screen. So, coping with it in real life, with a lamenting little boy in my arms, was almost impossible for me to endure. I felt helpless and impotent and that has to be the worst feeling in the whole world.

In a real sense, the tender moments I spent with little Benjamin Cain at Turner's Mortuary on my second day in Chicago, Illinois was a prelude to my relationship with his entire immediate family. By the time the funeral took place (that was within four days of my arrival in town), I was practically a cherished family member. When I spent time at the Cain house, young Benny rarely let me out of his sight, Jennifer Cain treated me like a biological son and Frankie acted like I was the reincarnation of his deceased brother.

In fact, Frankie behaved in a manner that worried and befuddled his mother. On the night before the wake and funeral, Mrs. Cain "tactfully" shared her concerns with me. It took place when Frankie decided to make a run to the grocery store and elected to take his baby brother along with him. At first, Benny balked at the idea but the lure of a candy bar soon changed his mind.

"You know, Lonnie, this has no reflection on you," Jenny began, "so please don't think badly of me. You have been a Godsend, a real blessing to this family and I mean it. I am truly grateful to you, so are the boys."

"I hear a 'but' coming on," I suspiciously injected. "Have I done something wrong, Jenny? Whatever it was, I assure you it wasn't on purpose."

"I told you it's not you, Lonnie. Well - it's really my son, Frank. He thinks the world of you. I - I'm not so sure about how he felt about Donald, that's all. They had their share of differences, but I never thought it was anything serious, just brother rivalry. But he never even talks about Donnie, he hasn't cried about his brother, nothing. He acts like he didn't care about him. And I can't quite understand it. You even seem to miss Donald more than Frankie does. Maybe he didn't love his brother and that's hard for me to deal with."

As I observed the anguish in Jenny Cain's face, my heart went out to her. "Individuals grieve in their own way, Jenny, sometimes alone and in private," I offered up. "Frankie loved his older brother, still does, and very, very deeply. I can almost assure you of that. And who's to say he's not bawling as we speak, he and little Benny? Hell, Jenny, look at the Kennedy family - just last year. Talkin' about 'The Kennedys don't cry.' Did you honestly believe, in dealing with that gruesome assassination last November, that they didn't spend a great amount of time crying their hearts out? I didn't buy into their . . . stalwart behavior, no way. The Kennedy family just didn't cry in public. Why? I really don't know the answer to that question."

Mrs. Cain sat in a state of frozen silence, then nodded her head. "I hope and pray you're right, Lonnie. Maybe Frankie has cried in private, with no one around. But, still, I can't help worrying about him."

I smiled in thorough understanding. "You are a typical mother, Jennifer Cain, and one who dearly loves her children. But take it from me, mark my words, Frankie's gonna be alright. He's a good guy, and he has a loving way about him. And he'll make you proud someday, and my little buddy will too."

CHAPTER FOUR
CLEARING THE AIR

Obviously, I didn't need a fortune teller or a crystal ball to warn me that the impending funeral of PFC Donald M. Cain would be exceptionally grievous and stressful. After being almost continuously bombarded with virtuous stories of the dead soldier (seldom do people demean recently deceased individuals, especially someone so young), even I had grown truly fond of him. That was inevitable on my part. Of course, my personal lament took a backseat to people who actually knew the young man. And that, of course, especially applied to Jennifer Cain and little Benjamin. In their case, during the traditional "viewing" segment of the ceremony on that sad day, the mortuary attendants had to physically hold them up erect. With their eyes fixed on the glass-encased remains, both Jenny and Benny wailed in immeasurable grief.

In observing that heartbreaking scene, I yearned to urge Frankie to step forth and take a hold of his shattered mother or, at least, his baby brother. At the time, Frankie stayed almost eerily silent, sitting on the front pew and looking downward in his lament. I was within five feet of him and was already weeping heavily. Then, suddenly, Frankie rose to his feet, slowly made his way to the coffin, and that's when things turned frantic. In a state of unrestrainable crying, Frankie leaned over the casket's glass-covering and seemed determined to embrace the body of his dead brother!

I, of course, was momentarily mortified and in a state of panic. So were many of the onlooking mourners. I feared Frankie was on the verge of shattering that glass, and regardless of how strong it was reported to be! Therefore, I quickly reacted and proceeded to grab Frankie. And I soon found myself trying to pry his outstretched hands from the coffin.

"Frankie, don't do this, kiddo," I pleaded with him. "Donnie knew you loved him and he loved you back! He really did, guy!"

Frank Cain's entire face seemed to be consumed by grief at the precise moment. He pitifully focused on me and, then, almost violently slung his arms around me. He was physically trembling when I opted to hold him back and his voice practically boomed in my ear.

"It's not fucking, right, Lonnie!" he yelled. "My big brother shouldn't be dead! It's not fair, goddamnit! Please, he shouldn't be dead, not Donnie! He doesn't deserve that, not Donnie! I loved him, all my life I loved him, Lonnie! What am I gonna do, what?"

"Just be thankful he was in your life, Frankie, even for a short while?" I spoke. "And honor his precious memory by always making him proud of you. And, Frankie, always remember that he dearly loved you, kiddo - you and Benny too. He used to tell me so."

"He did, Lonnie? Donnie really told you that?" Frankie responded. "We argued sometimes but I did love him. That is so good to know, Lonnie - that my brother really loved me. And I'm gonna miss the hell out of him, I already do."

At that juncture, as the sound of collective grief practically permeated the entire funeral parlor, Jenny Cain walked over and stood near me and her distraught teenager. Despite her personal mournful state, as I continued to console her son, she still emitted a smile. Remaining silent, Jenny reached over and gently caressed Frankie's shoulder. The mere calmness and serenity in Mrs. Cain's eyes rendered me likewise. I, soon, relinquished my hold on her teenager and she took my place, with little Ben standing beside her.

～

In the short aftermath of that tender and very poignant scene at Turner's Mortuary, the remains of PFC Donald Cain were carried out to the hearse and, then, driven to a somewhat distant cemetery. A lengthy procession of vehicles, which included the limousine I was riding in, trailed closely behind the hearse. And, finally, upon reaching our destination, the casket was unloaded. Then, after proper military honors were rendered to him, Donald M. Cain was solemnly interred. It was the last leg of a military mission that I would always remember and, in a very precious degree, forever cherish.

～

Although I spent a couple of hours at the repast that followed PFC Cain's burial, I was resigned to honoring a request my father had made earlier. With my spending so much time with the Cain family (although I had no regrets), he wanted me to spend the rest of my time in Chicago with him and his family, but essentially with him. And since I was scheduled to take the train to St. Louis on Saturday morning (only two days later), there wasn't a lot of time left.

We had already established that we were dually partial to drinking beer (although Dad didn't shy away from the hard stuff either) so, much of the time, alcohol was a third party in our interactions. Although I disliked it, my father was fond of puffing on cigarettes too. And so was his wife, Reba, and his brother-in-law, Alvin.

The tone of the conversations I had with the old man ranged from lighthearted to downright volatile. We weren't subject to coming to fisticuffs but since I wasn't afraid of him even as a young child, I surely wasn't scared of him as an adult. Our talks though, especially for me, were sometimes therapeutical.

At one point, I casually mentioned to Dad that I had dated a girl who happened to have epilepsy, but quickly added that the disorder was controlled by medicine. However, to say the very least, none of it set well with my father. The man got all out of sorts. I mean, he was visually peeved!

"I absolutely forbid you, Duke!" he yelled, slamming his fist on the kitchen table. "Do not see that young lady again! I forbid you to marry such a girl and bring lepsy into the Harris bloodline! Duke, do not do that to our family!"

My jaw dropped and, for a moment, I couldn't summon a single word. Then, I grinned, uttering, "Lepsy - lepsy? Dad, there's nothing in the Harris bloodline that hasn't been cured by alcohol by now. Lepsy? I didn't say 'leprosy,' Dad. Or do you suggest that I stone her, just the same?"

"You may think it's a laughing matter, Duke, but we are a "pure" and "proud" people," the old man argued. "I will not have a son of mine contaminating us. Never see that girl again, not ever!"

You know there are some things worth arguing about and some things that aren't. While I was somewhat amused by my father's ranting, I was a mite resentful also. It's difficult to take advice from a parent who had been absent from your life for over ten years. Plus, I never regarded the Harris clan as 'royalty,' like Dad apparently did.

However, in spite of the levity of some of our ongoing dialogue (in one sense, time was a non-issue because the old man was jobless and Reba was working), there were a number of serious moments too. For example, I asked Dad if he ever concerned himself with the well-being of me and my four brothers after he left Saint Louis. He looked at me with eyes of absurdity when he answered me.

"I have never stopped loving my babies, Duke!" he angrily insisted. "Not a single, solitary day passes by that I don't think of you boys! My arms, they ache to hold you boys and I am not kidding you."

"I'm reasonably certain you missed us, Dad," I inserted, "but - but did you wonder how we were getting along? How we were actually surviving?"

The old man frowned. "Aw, what kind of cold-hearted monster do you think I am, Duke? Why that's - that's a foregone conclusion! Believe me, there was a time when I wanted things to work out between me and your mother . . . but our love, it just wasn't there anymore. Ruby comes from good stock, and I've always given that to her. But we just . . . grew apart, that's all. I know the break-up hurt my babies, and especially you, Duke . . . but it just wasn't working! I know you counted on me and Ruby staying together, but . . ."

As I opted to interrupt my father, I tried to display a smile. "Dad, I had no illusions that you guys weren't headed for a divorce. I don't know how my brothers felt, but I didn't hold out much hope. And I truly loved you, but to be very honest - if I had the money back in those days, I would have personally bought you some Samsonite luggage. The way you were beating up on mom, on Gary, and, sometimes, on me, you really should have left a few years before. You know, Dad, kids don't stay dumb and naive forever."

The old man nodded, inserting, "But let me ask you this, Duke."

"Let me finish, Dad," I injected. "I'm saying that over the years, children grow to understand stuff. Naw, my gripe, or complaint, with you wasn't your decision to run off, it has everything to do with your not looking back. We went through some hard-ass times, Dad, some very trying and sad times too."

My father's facade was terribly morose when he asked, "Is that why I'm so hated by you boys? Well - all except, maybe, you, Duke?"

"I don't think the little guys hate you, Dad - not Taran, Vonnie or even Lovell. They barely even remember you and, maybe, that's a good thing. Who knows? Only time will tell. But Gary - now he's another story. I'm afraid I can't speak for him."

"I guess I was pretty rough on him, and I've lived to regret it," the old man solemnly replied. "I can't begin to explain it and I don't have a good excuse, not a legitimate one. He just wasn't like you, Duke."

I shook my head in thought-laden despair. "I think you failed to see the whole picture, Dad, a lot of parents do," I offered. "Every child is different, just like grown-ups are. Do you remember how you absolutely loved sports, back in the day, when we lived on Sullivan Street? And how I hated it? I didn't like boxing, playing any sports, or even watching it, as a matter of fact. Basically, I still don't."

"But you were a whiz when it came to books, Duke, and a damn good student as well," Dad grinningly stated.

"That's exactly what I'm getting at, Dad. I was good with reading, writing and arithmetic and Gary - he excelled in sports. So, if you would have stuck around, remained in our lives for another eight or nine years, you would have been bursting in pride when it came to Gary. I truly believe that. He was a superior athlete; a great wrestler, a good football player, baseball player, the whole smear. Meanwhile, I would have been an oddity, an anomaly to you, and, maybe, a disappointment too. Because what I care about sports competition ain't worth what the bird left on the proverbial limb. And I'll clue you in on something you may not know about me. And this is God's truth, Dad. I don't give a care what people think of me or how odd they might think I am. I'm my own man and I don't worry about what other folks think of me."

    I couldn't precisely say what my father thought of me during that particular time. In all honesty, it wasn't my intent to scold or chastise him, or to make him feel guilty or sad. I sincerely wanted to know his yesteryear mind-set and I wanted him to know my heartfelt take on the matter. Although Dad never paid child-support, my mother, Ruby, would occasionally tell my brothers and me that, "If your father doesn't come to see you boys, then it's all on him. I won't say much to Melvin - if he does show up, but he's free to visit you boys anytime."

    Personally speaking, I couldn't bring myself to understand how a father (any father), and especially one who lived less than three hundred and fifty miles away, could persuade himself not to visit his five sons (or his <u>babies</u>, as he called us). That naggingly baffled me as a little boy and a grown man as well. Admittedly, it still does.

CHAPTER FIVE

A FAREWELL TO CHI-TOWN

As I said before, the discussions I had with my father during the waning days of my military mission to Chicago were diverse, thought-provoking and, sometimes, comical. We even shared some laughs about a rather bizarre incident that involved Dad's only brother, Samuel, and my uncle's eldest son, Samuel Jr., also called 'Junie.' The old man vividly recalled the happening because he, too, was an active participant in it. In fact, he seemed proud of his supporting role in the episode. According to Dad, Sam. Jr. was a teenager when the incident took place.

The old man recounted that he and Uncle Samuel were leisurely driving around Saint Louis city in his brother's vehicle one day, when they happened to spot Junie on the street. And, in Dad's words, they were instantly "pissed-off" when they observed what they saw.

"There walked Junie," Dad replied, "pulling a large wagon up the street and busily selling, of all things, newspapers!" Then, he added, "We couldn't believe our eyes and Samuel was stewing at that point!"

Although I was in a subdued state of awe at that moment, I forced myself to ask, "And then what happened?"

"Well, Samuel pulled the car over to the curb, slammed on the brakes and almost flew out of the car. I followed suit. And my brother was all over Junie like - like white on rice. Samuel yelled, 'Harris's don't be selling no fucking newspapers and, especially, no son of mine!'

"At that point," my father continued, "Samuel grabbed up the wagon, papers and all; and tossed it into the backseat of the car. Then, we climbed back inside, seating Junie right between us, and headed straight up to the newspaper shack. Junie was scared and frozen solid cause he knew his dad was as mad as a wet hen!"

Although my father was totally unaware of it, I was thoroughly astounded. "And what happened when you guys got there?" I questioned.

"Samuel took the wagon, along with my nephew, and read the owner the riot act," Dad marvelled. "He was an old, red-faced peckerwood. Samuel told him, 'This boy is my oldest son, Sam Jr., and he's a goddamn Harris - and Harris's weren't born to pedal no goddamn newspapers for white folks! So, git this, fella, if you ever give my son another paper to sell out on the street, I'm gonna come back up here, burn this fucking barn down and blow your damn head off! If you don't believe me, just try my ass!"

As I sat still, trying to absorb my father's incredible account, I could only imagine how the owner of the newspaper facility felt during my Uncle Sammy's verbal tirade. I suppose the proprietor felt somewhat like I was feeling at that precise moment, shocked and practically speechless. However, my Dad seemed to be okay with it all, every facet of it. Even though I was inclined to, I never told him what I was really thinking or feeling in the aftermath of his astounding tale. I guess I didn't have the heart to rain on my father's smug parade.

To be honest, my thoughts at that precise time were focused on 'Yours truly - me. When I was but eight years old, I sold newspapers virtually every Sunday morning myself! And I wasn't aware, until that very moment, that my father (in spite of still living with us at that time) did not know I was doing it. Fact was, pulling and, sometimes, pushing a wagon of my own, I was selling, both, the St. Louis Post-Dispatch and the St. Louis Globe-Democrat papers on Sundays and I was very good at it. My customers often marvelled that, in spite of my young age, I was adept at counting money and giving them the correct change also. Sitting in momentary silence and looking at my Dad in the aftermath of his weird story, I could not help wondering, "Where did he think I got my money from during those yesteryear days, from robbing banks?"

Apparently, my old man was concerned about my stupor like state. "Duke - hey, are you alright?" he quizzed. "You was looking like you were a thousand miles away from here."

Seemingly, I had grown use to impromptu falsehoods, because my substitute reply practically rolled off my tongue. "Aw, I was thinking of what could have happened when Uncle Sammy got up into the owner's face," I spoke. "Luckily, the man didn't pull a gun on you guys. He might have blown Uncle Sammy and you away, and he could have shot Junie too for good measures. Ever think of that, Dad?"

Although a part of my response was tongue-in-cheek, my father came across as serious. "Shit - that damn red-neck was shakin' in his pants," he snapped. "He was the one who was lucky that day, lucky we didn't tear his shack down. He didn't know who the hell he was messing with. The Harris men don't be playing around." Then, a second later, he asked, "You ready for another beer, Duke?"

I answered affirmatively to the beer offer but when my dad went to the fridge to retrieve it and, then, to the outlying restroom,

I returned to my previous train of thought. Since the old man was apparently clueless as to what I did on Sunday during my childhood, I now wondered if he had any idea of what I did on Saturdays.

Occasionally, I took in a movie on that day, but most Saturdays saw me continually transporting groceries from nine a.m. until almost eight o'clock at night. I would camp out in front of the grocery store on Newstead Avenue, frequently sitting atop my red wagon, and repeatedly offering my transporting services to the grocery-shopping public. And since automobiles were quite scarce in the black community during the nineteen fifties, I made much more money on Saturdays than I made on Sunday mornings. And I had no problem whatsoever sharing my profits with my mother or my brothers.

Presently, though I hosted no regrets regarding those bygone days, I was somewhat resentful and hurt to surmise that my father was completely oblivious of my boyhood work history. Although I elected to keep my feelings to myself, sitting in the confines of my Dad's home, I could not help wondering where the old man's mind was in those long-ago days!

Even as my father and I engaged in in-depth conversations on, both, Thursday evening and throughout the following day, which was Friday, I made it my business to also interact with Reba, my father's wife, Alvin, my old man's brother-in-law and especially little Keith, my kid-brother. After all, the three of them were intricate parts of my Dad's ongoing life and since I had come to the consensus to let 'bygones be bygones' (bury the hatchet, sort of speak), I realized that our collective futures were preordained. In essence, upon restarting my stalled relationship with my father, it was right and proper to embrace his intimate loved ones also.

Now, while I couldn't speak for the aforementioned trio, it presented no problem whatsoever to me. I've always had an insatiable love for people in general and since Reba, Alvin and Keith were so congenial and accommodating to me, they were more than welcome to enter my love tent and I didn't mind telling them so, and especially my little brother. In fact, by the time I parted company with that kid, I felt I had loved him all his life.

Inevitably though, the fated Saturday morning was upon me and I soon found myself standing face-to-face with a lifelong nemesis of mine. I was never good at leaving people I loved and since I was unusually liberal with my affection in the first place, I had already endured a lot of heartrending partings in my lifetime. However, I hoped that future goodbye episodes, unlike the impending one, would incorporate a more minimal amount of people. Otherwise, I couldn't imagine myself dealing with such a heart-tugging scene.

It had been predetermined that young Frankie Cain would give me a ride to Union Station when Saturday morning came around (unfortunately, my father didn't have a car) and, exactly like last Tuesday, Frank was right on time. And to my utter delight, little Benny Cain was with him.

Alternately, I said farewell to my tearful dad, embraced him firmly and did likewise to Reba, Alvin and my kid brother, Keith. I fought back my own tears as I faithfully promised Keith that I would soon write to him. Then, I hugged the little guy once again and hurriedly grabbed my nearby duffel bag, even while vowing to call them when I arrive in Saint Louis. Secretly, I knew if I didn't get out of there, and at that precise minute, I'd become an emotional disaster.

Significantly, the individual I hated leaving the most was young Keith. (Though I kept it to myself, I could not help wondering if Keith, too (like my elder brother, Gary, and I), was sometimes mentally and physically abused by our father). And as I took in a parting glimpse of the youngster, I came to a heartfelt consensus, and right then and there, that I would always love and cherish him.

Minutes later, after I had left the vicinity of my dad's apartment on Prairie Avenue, I honestly thought I had gotten my emotions well-in-check. I even mentally pre-planned my forthcoming behavior. At Union Station, I saw myself giving little Benny a final hug, and then Frankie, and eventually climbing aboard the St. Louis-bound train, with no frills and no sobbing.

Well, I did embrace the pint-sized little boy and even kissed his cheek (although he laughingly wiped at his jaw) but when I turned to Frankie, he stopped me instantly.

"Lonnie, my mother asked me to say something to you," he informed me, staring directly into my eyes. "I'm surprised she didn't make me write it down - but here goes: First of all, she loves the hell out of you, man. She said to tell you that she thanked God for you, so do I. We don't know if you know it or not, but we couldn't have gotten through . . . our tragedy if you weren't in the picture. I know I couldn't have, Lonnie, and I thank the hell out of you. Thanks, man . . . and you keep in touch with us. You hear, my brother?"

At that particular juncture, all three of us, me, Frankie and young Benny were crying. Of course, it was par for the course on my behalf but, despite his unforeseen breakdown at his brother's funeral, Frankie didn't strike me as an easy crier. "I will never forget you guys, your wonderful family, Frankie," I vowed, placing my hand on the teenager's shoulder. "And I'll call you guys from time to time, I will - rest assured of that. And, kiddo, tell your mom . . . that I'll forever thank God for the Cain family too, Donald included."

With that said, I proceeded to reach out and embrace Frankie tightly, and for a prolonged time. Then, I turned, stroked Benny's little face and once again grabbed my duffel bag. I then said a final farewell to the brother-pair and stepped onto the adjacent train.

While I was deeply appreciative and humbled by Frank Cain's heartfelt goodbye speech, I could not help looking forward to a more peace-laden and carefree stay in my native environment, St. Louis. But, for certain, I would always remember that fateful journey to Chicago, Illinois. For during the course of my military mission I had learned a poignant and sobering truism about my own character. I had an innate gift for touching the hearts of others, and that, in turn, seemed to be key to my personal well-being. As simple as it sounded, authentic joy and serenity for me was in seeing other individuals happy. And that exhilarating premise, in my estimation, was a "long and winding road" worth embarking on.

That was my soothing and lingering thought as my train pulled out of Chi-town's Union Station on that Saturday morning, which was the final leg of my somber trip to Illinois. I had come a long, long way, but not distance-wise. It had little to do with the numerous miles that laid between San Antonio, Texas and Chicago, Illinois but, expressly, my emotional journey. My entire young life was plagued with a series of spiraling and exhaustive roads, some of them; almost too steep to climb, and I was blessed to have scaled them all. I knew, if not for the grace of God and a handful of helpmates He graciously installed in my life, I would have fallen by the proverbial wayside. Without any degree of doubt in my mind, I always believed that. As my train rolled towards my native hometown (which, again was Saint Louis, Missouri), I soon fell asleep and virtually slept the entire rail trek. And in a deep, serene and dream-like state, I vividly recalled just how far the good Lord had taken me.

THE LONG AND WINDING ROAD

"I shall be telling this with a sigh
Somewhere ages and ages hence:
Two roads diverged in a wood, and I . . .
I took the one less traveled by,
And that made all the difference."

<u>THE ROAD NOT TAKEN</u>
By Robert Frost

THE LONG AND WINDING ROAD

CHAPTER SIX

A HOUSE MADE OF TIN

For many years, over a decade, I derived a measure of pride from believing that I resided in a prestigious area called 'The Ville.' Situated in the middle of urban St. Louis, Missouri and teeming with benevolent history, it was renown, beloved and touted by the entire black populace of greater Saint Louis. Being a site of affluence and prominence, in addition to housing numerous commercial installations, it showcased such facilities as the Homer G. Phillips Hospital, Annie Malone's Poro Building, Tandy Park and the Charles Sumner High School. Without a doubt, it was a virtual Negroid mecca.

However, to my utter disappointment, and when my age caught up with my mind, I learned I was flatly wrong. Since the Ville's north boundary was a street called St. Louis Avenue and my residence was three blocks beyond that point (north of it, in fact), I and my family were sort of 'on the outside looking in.' As I stated though, I was totally ignorant of that miscalculation when I was a child. Therefore, I felt just as special as any native Ville resider felt. And that rather elitist feeling, coinciding with my father's all too-frequent claim that we were "upper crust" due to our mere heritage, made me think I was on top of the world.

Never mind that our community sparred with roach infestations, mice and rats as well, I felt far removed from living in a so-called 'ghetto.'

Fact was, we did live in the ghetto! But, later, when I began to mature and came to my senses (especially after I became aware of the struggles of Negroes in general), I was neither ashamed or sorry that I didn't live elsewhere. After all, we had nice neighbors, some of who had multiple kids; we were in walking distance of a black elementary school (which was also in The Ville), a sizable grocery store, a Baptist church and even a Woolworth's five and dime facility. In addition, there was the Jewish-owned 'Harry's Delicatessen' (only a block from our house), 'Ivory's Fish Shack' (just up the street from Harry's) and we certainly had access to The Ville itself.

Once there, we could enjoy Tandy Park (along with playgrounds, it offered ball fields and swimming pools), we could catch a picture show or get a haircut, etc. Plus, if we had a mind to, we could go to the not too distant 'Fairgrounds Park' which housed a popular and gigantic swimming pool of its own. However, instead of being located in The Ville area, Fairgrounds was located on a street called Natural Bridge and it was many blocks north of Sullivan street.

Although our home address was listed as 4281 Sullivan street, we did not live in a traditional residential area. Actually, I perceived it as a rather strange set-up, even as a kid. Sullivan street, similar to, both, St. Louis Avenue and Natural Bridge, ran east and west while Lambdin street marked our south and north boundary. That, of course, rendered Lambdin and Sullivan an intersection. Then, on the south side of the street (that being Sullivan itself) was an elongated, brick-constructed apartment building and at the western end, part of the building itself, was the aforementioned Harry's Delicatessen.

However, none of the foregoing struck me as particularly 'strange.' Apartments sitting side-by-side one another was something I had frequently seen. Plus, I knew quite a few kids who lived in those apartments and I had been inside one or two of them. They were traditional. Although I was a child and, therefore, looking through a child's eyes, I realized that there were thousands of things I had yet to see and a vast amount of experiences I hadn't had also.

Still, however, other than my neighbors on Sullivan street, I never knew anyone who lived in a 'tin' house and I never, ever saw any structures like them before. (Later on in life, however, I did see some tin Quonset huts but they differed from the houses on Sullivan street).

So, there they stood, bright tin and glistening like newly-minted silver dimes, and especially in the sunlight. And, of course, our dwelling wasn't by itself and nor was it built for a single, traditional family. Instead, it accommodated two individual families who were separated by a single wall in the structure's middle. Each family had a front door, a short set of front steps and three adjacent windows. In actuality, since it had the standard triangular shaped roof atop it, it looked very much like a regular house, but a house that was strangely made of tin!

As I mentioned, our house, while rather quaint and weird in appearance, was certainly not one of a kind. In reality, there were nine other homes that looked exactly like ours. All of the dwellings showcased a small front lawn and they were all methodically spaced apart. Our house, while facing westward, was approximately fifteen yards from Sullivan street's curve and, therefore, stood directly across from the elongated apartment complex I previously spoke of. Then, upon looking northward, there set a second two-family structure and, finally, a third one next to it.

A sizable gangway separated each building. However, in spite of the overall uniqueness of the residential area, there was one distinct commonality linked to my family's house and the other two houses that were aligned with it. Located across a paved walkway and displaying the standard front lawns, was three houses directly facing the trio of homes I initially described. Then, in addition, two identical structures paralleled Lambdin street (with Lambdin entrances) and two other domiciles were located behind our house, with their backs facing our home's rear. Notably, we would see our across-the-walk neighbors almost on a daily basis and although I never knew what my other family members felt about that factor, I liked it very, very much.

In reality, there was nothing special or unique about the interior of the house on Sullivan street. Like I mentioned, we had our share of bugs and rodents and they were frequent but tolerable vexations. (In all probability, the majority of our surrounding neighbors were privy to similar infestations).

Of course, I couldn't speak for all the 'renters' in the housing project, but the physical set-up of our particular home was rather simplistic and unremarkable. Upon stepping over the front door's threshold, an individual would already be well inside our living room. A small opened closet, facing you, was three feet on the right while the kitchen and dining area was viewable on the rear, left extreme of the dwelling. An observer could also see the northernmost dividing wall, which conspicuously separated our clan from the co-occupying family right next door. (And, on occasion, we could hear them stirring and them, us).

Conveniently, we had a wringer-type washing machine. We also had a gas-stove, which kept our family reasonably warm during the winter months. That stove set on the far side of the living room and gave residers (such as us) access to a small washroom (which contained a sink and a commode only) and, then, there were two outlying bedrooms.

While my mother and father shared one bedroom, the other one (only slightly larger), amazingly, accommodated me, my quartet of brothers and our maternal grandmother. However, since none of us boys knew any better (after all, we were all under ten years old), the arrangement seemed perfectly normal to us. At any event, we had to 'make do' with what we had.

Now, I would like to be able to say that, when it came to our rather large, extended family, we, at least, "Had each other." But that would be a bit of a stretch, if not an out-and-out prevarication. What we did have, owing almost exclusively to a man my brothers and I called "Daddy" was an existence that was often filled with strife and frequent outbreaks of physical and mental violence. Although love flowed between me, my siblings and our mom, and was further amplified by our grandmother's affection, it often took a backseat to the continuous turmoil and anxiety that was practically owned by the so-called 'man of the house.' For reasons I never remotely understood, my father seemed to be obsessed (if not, <u>possessed</u>) with causing familial conflict and confusion. Also, for reasons I could never quite comprehend either, I actually wanted to love him.

However, I came to realize at an early age that there is a vast difference from 'loving someone' and 'liking someone.' And whenever I reflect upon my dad, that precept comes acutely into play. My disdain for my father's rather evil and despicable behavior (as suppressed as it was during my childhood) rivalled my burning desire to, in some way, define the man. And to my utter sorrow, to a certain degree, that desire still burns.

CHAPTER SEVEN
A VOLATILE STORM

According to yesteryear standards (and, maybe, contemporary ones as well), my father, Melvin V. Harris, was an extremely handsome, virile and charismatic black man. He was light-complected with keen facial features (accented by a thin and neatly-trimmed mustache), he sported a head of ebony, straight hair, displayed a compact, muscular frame and managed to father six sons before reaching the age of thirty. In addition, my dad was well-spoken, well-read and highly opinionated.

Of course, the latter trait, "highly opinionated" can irritate the hell out of a lot of folks; an individual's knack for being blunt about any and every subject matter, but that, by far, wasn't my dad's worst personality trait, and especially in the assessment of an awestruck and wide-eyed six-year-old boy. And that's how I viewed myself when in the autumn of 1950, I was playing in the house (just outside my parent's bedroom) and happened to hear what my daddy was saying to my mother.

As he looked admiringly at his self in the dresser's mirror and proceeded to cock his hat acey-deucy (as usual, his head wear complemented his suit and tie), he conceitedly said, "Ruby, you oughta thank your lucky stars for marrying a pretty man like me."

Oddly though, my mom seemed completely unphased by what Dad said (I was soon to learn that he was repetitious with his verbal haughtiness), but, moreover, Mom knew how to get his goat too. Because when she responded, "Melvin, you ain't no prettier than I am. So, put that in your pipe and smoke it," he became angry. And I mean - really ticked off!

However, my father didn't miss a beat and alternately seized the moment. Even in my embryonic state, I knew he had a whole arsenal of reasons for staying out late at night and pretending he was "pissed-off" (a term he favored) was just one of them. It was bad enough he would return home most evenings pissy-drunk but, oftentimes, he would be violent and abusive. Meaning, he was subject to beat up on Mom and any one of his sons, but, all too frequently, my oldest brother, Gary, and, sometimes, me.

As strange as it may sound, I wasn't concerned with my fate in those days. I knew I'd endure, no matter what. But I hated the physical mistreatment of my mother and elder brother and the mental abuse that was regularly inflicted on Mom. I could almost reach out and touch her paradox. In loving Dad and being aware of his temperament, she also concerned herself with his safety while running the streets of St. Louis but was, oftentimes, sorry when he did return home. And I, as the second son in ranking, found myself sharing her worriment.

Our mother, Ruby (and, for some unknown reason, her three oldest boys called her 'Ruby'), wasn't at all exaggerating when she refused to take second place in Daddy's self-concocted beauty contest. She was quite attractive in her own right, and especially by white folk's standards. And don't let anyone tell you differently! Those were the unofficial standards way back when (and I'm not so sure those racist standards have entirely dissipated today). But, certainly, in the nineteen fifties and the decades prior to them, a black woman's beauty was judged by light-colored skin, silky-textured hair and Caucasian-like facial features.

For instances, call to mind 'colored' beauties such as Lena Horne, Josephine Baker and Dorothy Dandridge. So, since Ruby was of that elite type: light-skinned, long, brownish hair and petite in stature, she more than held her own in the attractive venue. However, to my mother's credit, I never spied her admiring herself in a mirror or heard her boasting about her good looks.

Although the vanity issue was a nagging drag on my parent's relationship, it was Dad's frequent drunkenness and abusive nature that gradually corroded their marriage. Of course, my father's philandering nature didn't help either. He seemed to have an insatiable craving for outside women and, sorrowfully, I personally came to that conclusion when I was around seven years old.

Now, if that gives you momentary pause, a rather mature assessment by a mere child, you may be further taken aback by what comes next. You see, I came to acutely 'know' my dad. I was aware of his gall, his cavalier behavior and, quite relevant, I was well aware of most of his early evening dallying hangouts. To be precise, I was knowledgeable of the various taverns he would go to and hook up with several different women.

Since my family was void of an automobile at that particular time (similar to most black families in those days) and I had a small bicycle, Dad was frequently less than a mile from our residence on Sullivan. If he wasn't cuddled up with a 'very-receptive' female at the 'Tandy Bar' on St. Louis Avenue, more than likely he was caressing and/or dancing with one at 'Duck's Lounge,' located on Newstead Avenue.

Upon sighting my dad at either club, I would promptly enter it, flash my very best smile, give him a quick hug and, then, ask him for a nickel or a dime - knowing all the while that I would be awarded a quarter and, sometimes, an even greater amount. And although my actions could be perceived as somewhat shady (maybe, extortion or even petty blackmail), I never saw it that way. Because regardless of what my dad was thinking during those episodes, I would never, with a capital 'N,' have told my mom about his indiscretions anyhow.

However, it was not due to my loyalty to my father, but, more so, because of my love and devotion to my mother. Fact was, despite my youthfulness, I was always concerned with my mom's overall well-being. And, especially, since her husband appeared to be totally apathetic of her feelings.

Now, in retrospect, I can't say that my dad restricted his mistreatment to my mother; his persistent habit to mentally hurt her. Within our household, with our live-in maternal grandmother in the mix, Melvin V. Harris made sure that his immediate family was amongst his victims also. Although I cannot recall him physically striking 'V.I.' (which is what her grandchildren called her), he was rather relentless when it came to knocking around our mother, me or any of my brothers. However, despite his reluctance to physically assault V.I., he had no qualms when it came to verbally berating her.

If our dad wasn't protesting grandma's mere presence in our house, he was griping about everything from her slight obesity and body odor to what he often labelled her "loser" sons. And since one of our uncles was in a mental facility (due to a disease called syphilis) and a couple of them was addicted to alcohol, his cold-hearted remarks severely wounded V.I.

Alternately though, our grandmother was able to tolerate Dad's mean-spirited put-downs, and especially the ones aimed at her three boys (maybe, it was because V.I. had given birth to ten other children), but Grandma never got used to him brutally attacking her baby daughter, who was, in fact, Ruby. Nor did V.I.

get used to her cruel son-in-law beating up on his five stair step sons. Oftentimes, she would shed tears.

As far back as I can remember, the rotund little woman, whom my brothers and I dearly loved, would thrust herself into our parent's all-too frequent squabbles and, sometimes, manage to deescalate them. Then, during other such episodes, depending upon how much alcohol Dad had consumed during the day, V.I. was a non-factor.

Even in the presence of us children (we would be collectively upset and crying), Ruby would emerge with a black eye, a busted lip or worse. Although Mom would often try and stand her ground and, sometimes, fiercely fight our father back (especially when his primary abuse was aimed at one of her kids), her efforts were to no avail. Her husband, after all, was stronger, more determined and, certainly, much meaner!

I could very-well attribute my father's fighting prowess to plain-old male dominance, especially since he considered himself to be a formidable and fitful athlete. Not only do I recollect seeing him pole-vault and play baseball at Tandy Park, he was practically hell-bent upon transforming me, my four brothers and many of the surrounding neighborhood boys into proficient prizefighters. Hell, our front yard was a virtual boxing ring! Honestly, instead of displaying a normal green grass lawn in front of our house, we contended with a makeshift, roped-off boxing area! Dad absolutely took pride in it.

However, in the wake of two distinct happenings, I can't rightly cite male testosterone or surging masculinity as a driving force behind Melvin Harris's rather crazed knack for physical violence. Fact is, when I hone in on the two episodes I'm about to refer to (and they are as vivid to me today as they were when they took place), it irks the devil out of me that while the old man emerged victorious and shameless when it came to battling females and slapping around small children (especially, with my mother at the forefront), it wasn't the same scenario when it came to confronting men.

The first happening occurred on a warm spring evening in the year 1952; a Friday, I think. My father arrived home, clearly reeking of whiskey and cigarette odor (he smoked over a pack a day), but instead of taking to his bed (which would have suited his drunken state), he was obsessed with going outside and playing 'catch.' And since I was more partial to hurling rocks and had no love for sports of any kind, he instantly demanded the indulgence of his first born son, my brother, Gary.

However, after grabbing his league ball and his own broken-in baseball glove, he told Gary to get his personal glove. And, sorrowfully, that's when the trouble began.

My older brother, who would ordinarily be receptive to the proposed venture, informed Dad that he did not have his glove and followed up with a quick explanation as to why. He had loaned his baseball glove to a boy we knew as "Bones" Flanagan, an older kid who lived right down the street from us (on Lambdin Street), but he had not, yet, gotten it back from Bones. Not surprisingly, Gary's excuse did not set well with our father. To be more blunt, it infuriated him! But after ranting and raving and threatening to do bodily harm to Gary, he loudly demanded that my brother go and quickly retrieve his "goddamn glove."

Standing offside and watching the proceedings was very painful for me. As always, I felt sorry for my oldest brother but I took some degree of solace in Dad's restraint of physical violence - well, up until that particular point.

Unfortunately though, my feeling of relief was short-lived. When my brother returned from his trek down the street, somber-faced and clearly without his baseball glove, the old man went ballistic! Even as Gary offered a feasible excuse, Dad commenced to hitting him and calling him a bunch of profane names. Then, only seconds afterwards, looking absolutely insane and furious, the old man was briskly headed down Sullivan Street and hell-bent upon making the same foot journey his eldest son had just made.

So, with Gary in tow (and, me, trailing closely behind), Dad was soon crossing Lambdin Street and converging on the Flanagan two-story flat. A moment later, I crossed the street too, but paused by the home's picket fence to observe the forthcoming proceedings. I shook my head in awe as Dad pounded on the front door as if he was a cop or somebody. Then, when the door swung open, I saw Bones, his younger brother, "Boogay," and, more, significantly, the two boy's father, Mr. Flanagan.

Of course, Mr. Flanagan knew our father and immediately addressed him. (Actually, the Harris and Flanagan families were staples in the neighborhood). "Hey, Melvin, what's going on, buddy?" he asked. "Is there somethin' wrong, something I can help you with?"

"Damn straight," my dad snapped. "Your boy got my son's baseball glove and refuses to return it. We here to pick it up. Just git the damn thing!"

Now, I had no idea what my father or Gary thought of Mr. Flanagan. But to me, since the man was muscular and stockily-built, he was a rather imposing figure and since rumor was that the man had served a stretch in prison to boot (of course, I wasn't sure if that was true or not), I secretly felt he was a scary man to reckon with. To Mr. Flanagan's credit though, he came across as soft-spoken and showed patience with our old man.

"Melvin, you need to calm down," he suggested, "and it ain't no need to be cussin' in front of these kids. Which one of you got the glove?" he asked his sons.

Standing next to his father, Bones was visibly flustered. "Pop, I told Gary just while ago, that I left his glove in my desk at school," he explained. "Can't get it 'til after spring break or . . . at least, not until Monday - if the custodian is there."

"Well, then, that's it, Melvin," reasoned Mr. Flanagan. "What the Sam-hell you expect Bones to do, huh?"

"I want that fuckin' glove!" Dad slurringly yelled. "And I want it right now, goddamnit!"

As suppressed anger marred Mr. Flanagan's face, he stepped out the house, trying to pull the door closed behind him and leave his two sons inside. But his effort failed. Both, Bones and Boo-gay emerged from the house and heard their dad say, "Melvin, I asked you nicely to stop your dirty talk. Now, I'm telling you to stop your stupid, drunken foolishness and git the hell back up the street! Go home - and sober up, Melvin!"

"I ain't drunk, goddamnit, far from it," the old man insisted. "And I ain't going a fuckin' place without my son's glove. You so damn tough, Flanagan, try and make me go!"

At that juncture, my father's challenge was complete. Showcasing a boxing stance (one that was familiar to every male child in the neighborhood) and brandishing bare knuckled fists, he was intent upon brawling with Mr. Flanagan. But unlike his chosen opponent, apparently Dad had no qualms about fighting in front of his kids or anyone else's kids.

The "fight," however (if it could be called that), was short-lived at best. Because when Dad swung at Mr. Flanagan and missed the man entirely, his opponent countered with a punch to our father's left jaw and sent him plunging backwards to the ground. Then, in the passing of but a few seconds, Mr. Flanagan was on his knees, straddling his downed challenger and practically raining blows on the old man's face. And even as Dad stubbornly refused to yield, threatening retaliation "if" he was let up, Mr. Flanagan's aggression continued.

"If I let you up, Melvin, you gonna git your act together?" he asked as he struck the old man one more time. "Because I can do this all day, ya' know? You need to carry your butt on home and get some sleep, man. Sober up, like I said. And stop making a plum fool of yo'self, especially in front of these boys."

"Just let me up, goddamn you," my father insisted, displaying a puffy face and a bloody nose. "I ain't done yet, not by a fuckin' long shot."

Unfortunately though, our father was done at that juncture. He had been thoroughly trounced and humiliated by Mr. Flanagan and he well knew it, his opponent knew it and the four onlooking boys knew it too. And, subsequently, after struggling to his feet and attempting to dust himself off, he turned and embarked on the return trip home.

And quietly strolling behind him and watching his unsteady strides, was my brother, Gary, and me. But words were not necessary when it came to me and my brother at that point. Our thoughts, however, coincided, I believed. Despite our joint silence, we actually relished what we had recently witnessed. The old man had gotten exactly what he deserved, a decisive and firm ass-whipping, and we secretly enjoyed it.

Honestly, I wish I could report that Melvin Harris was a changed and forthright man in the aftermath of his thrashing at the hands of our neighbor down on Lambdin Street, but, regretfully, I cannot. Our dad, though somewhat subdued for a spell in the aftermath of his springtime beat-down, was relentless and true to form during the subsequent summer and autumn months. Resurrecting his aggression on familiar turf, he was back to being his old, erratic self.

For instance, on one fall afternoon, due to underlying motives only Dad and the devil himself knew, he started smacking around his favorite victim (Gary, of course) and, eventually, commenced to beat up on Ruby also. Why? Because Mom, just like any loving mother (such as V.I.), was trying to prevent a crazed brute from injuring or, maybe, killing her child!

Traditionally, though very much contrary to my father's deep-seated disregard for others, the man was almost skillful at keeping his familial abuse under wraps. Although Ruby and my brothers and I displayed occasional facial bruises, he pretended that he never laid a hand on any of us. Oh, surrounding folks really knew differently, and that certainly applied to our immediate next door neighbors, "the Browns." (The wall erected betwixt our households was certainly not soundproof). In addition, many Sullivan residents had heard about the spring confrontation that took place on Lambdin street.

Nevertheless though, my father insisted upon playing the role of innocence and perfection; a man who was the ideal dad and a loving husband. And the old man seemed well-entrenched in his deceit, adamant, in fact - that is, up until the autumn afternoon I am about to vividly relive.

Wearing a face of pure evil and totally consumed by his ongoing and brutal tirade, my father seemed to be altogether oblivious of the fact that we had a visitor on that particular afternoon. It was a long-time neighbor named "Milton Jones," a man who was 20 years senior to our dad, and he could hardly fathom what he was seeing. In a state of momentary disbelief and shock, he witnessed Dad delivering a vicious blow to Ruby's face.

Personally, even as a child I would have liked to have killed my old man at that juncture, and I would have tried to - if I were bigger and had had the means at close hand. However, being the child that I was, similar to my on-looking brothers, all I could do was to grimace, fret and cry. But, owing to Milton Jones, the insidious horror was minimized to a degree. Mr. Jones instantly placed himself between our two parents and proceeded to bodily hold the old man at bay.

"Don't be hitting that girl like that, Melvin!" he pleaded, visually awestruck. "How could you do that, man? Ruby's a good girl, and a good wife. And just look, look whatchu doing to your babies! Shame on you! Are you plum crazy, sick in the head or what? That was awful, Melvin!"

"Um gonna show you how crazy I am, nigga!" our father yelled, trying to break away from Milton's grasp. Moments later, our neighbor did sever his hold on Dad, but instead of trying to strike Mom again, our father retreated to the adjacent kitchen area, vowing, "I'm gonna teach your black ass not to fuck around in my affairs! This is my goddamn family - and my goddamn house, not yours!"

Shortly, when the old man grabbed a large butcher knife from our silverware drawer, it was Mr. Joneses cue to exit the premises. And he made his retreat without hesitation. And less than a minute later, with Dad in hot pursuit and brandishing the knife, Milton Jones was outdoors and running for dear life.

"Luckily," and I felt that way throughout the ensuing spectacle, my father, the youthful athlete, could not catch up to our middle-aged neighbor! No matter how fast Dad ran, Milton managed to run a tad faster. Then, what seemed like a stressful eternity, after the two men had circled our residential complex numerous times (at least, five times), the chase was finally over. Both men, panting from sheer exhaustion, and Milton Jones, making sure he was a safe distance from his knife-wielding pursuer, the episode had finally fizzled out.

Only minutes later, my volatile old man, who was perspiring profusely and coughing too, slowly made his way back to our house, walked inside and closed the screened-door behind him. Meanwhile, similar to a bunch of onlooking and somewhat amused neighbors, I, along with a couple of my brothers, remained outside in a state of lingering awe. Even if my dad wasn't embarrassed by his bizarre and ridiculous conduct, I was certainly embarrassed for him. And I felt my mother and brothers felt likewise. I was thankful, however, that Milton Jones was safe and sound.

CHAPTER EIGHT

IN DEFIANCE OF A TYRANT

It might seem strange to some people, but the feeling of shame I incurred in the aftermath of my father's confrontations with, both, Mr. Flanangan and Mr. Jones, dissolved within two days of their singular happenings. Even as a young child, I was adept at putting events into a certain perspective. Whatever compassion and sympathy I felt in regards to those harrowing episodes was directed at my mother, Ruby, my brother, Gary and Milton Jones respectively; and surely not towards my abusive and mean-spirited dad.

As far as I was concerned, and regardless of the man being my biological father, Melvin Virgil Harris was deserving of all the humiliation and punishment that came his way. For I believed as a child as I believe today: people really do reap what they sow. However, in spite of wholeheartedly buying into that biblical precept, I still found myself clinging to affection for the man. Unfortunately, I didn't extract much joy from it, because I couldn't figure out why!

Now, maybe the average kid, just by saying that Melvin Harris was, in fact, my father would sufficiently explain why I continued to love him. However, I didn't deem myself 'the average kid' and I was much too rational and analytical (and selfless as well) to ascribe to that rather superficial explanation. Even if the old man had never laid a glove on me (and I'm not speaking literally) or had traditionally treated me like a crown prince, which was certainly not the case, I would still have hated his violent and evil conduct.

Sure, my dad was instrumental in giving me and my brothers a 'birthday' (and some fathers I knew audaciously bragged about that factor), but, we, as Dad's biological offsprings, knew him best for the frequent 'hell-days' he subjected us to. And he certainly didn't deserve any praise for those terrible days.

Well, thanks to a kind and merciful God, the other parent who was responsible for the birth of us Harris boys was totally opposite our masculine benefactor. Our mother, Ruby, was a genuinely nice and peace-loving person; gentle, caring and soft-spoken. Though it took Dad numerous years to eventually announce that Ruby was "an upstanding woman, coming from good stock" (notably, it was well-after their marital break-up), he continually dogged her out when they were still wedded. And that fact was undeniable.

Now, whether my father based his latter-year assessment on subsequent life experiences, some kind of epiphany or just elected to divulge his long-suppressed thoughts, I was very shocked when he first said it. Although I came to believe him in-time, my childhood memories tended to get in my way. And why not? When I recalled the awful names he hurled at my mother, the various beatings; the mental mistreatment he afforded V.I. and his cold-hearted criticism of a trio of Grandma's sons, it didn't add up! If Ruby came from 'good stock,' it stood to reason that

Mom's twelve siblings did also. And that placed V.I. under the same benevolent umbrella.

Frankly though, Dad wasn't critical of all of V.I.'s children. In fact, he seemed genuinely fond of my aunts, Blanche and Hannah (the latter aunt and her husband, Uncle Bill, would visit us quite often), and he appeared to have a favorable opinion of Ruby's brothers, Landy and Leo, as well.

Actually, you could attribute Dad's goodwill towards Uncle Leo to a single thing - something called a 'television.' In the middle of the ongoing 'Korean Conflict,' it was the summer of 1952, I believe, our soldier uncle, Leo, mustered out of the United States army. And when he came home to Saint Louis and rejoiced in seeing his five nephews (us, of course), he brought a brand new, black and white, Philco television set along with him. And that TV not only pleased and dazzled the entire Harris family (especially us kids), it instantly elevated our house to a newfound status.

As I mentioned previously, our front yard was already a makeshift boxing ring. But with the existence of a television set, our house was deemed as the most popular residence in the entire neighborhood. From the very moment it was turned on (and the news travelled fast), 4281 Sullivan Street soon became 'the place to be' in the immediate vicinity and our family came to enjoy a weekly and, sometimes, daily upsurge of visitors. Simply because a television was a costly luxury in those days (especially when it came to black folks), the Harris household reached an almost celebrity status.

In keenly looking back in time, Melvin Harris was right on target when he finally came to appreciate the woman Ruby actually was. While our television had a superficial and external allure, our mother was a portrait of quiet virtue. As I fore stated, she was compassionate, sympathetic and authentically nice to all the people she interacted with, and that included the parade of visitors who came to check out our television. I could not avoid wondering, however, when I observed all of those people, since the majority of them knew my father, were they surprised that he was married to such a friendly and gracious woman?

Although I was forever in a quandary regarding the old man's many flaws and faults (he had some good qualities but they were far and in between), I could almost reach out and touch my mom's overall benevolence. While Ruby's virtue was anchored and fortified by a strong belief in God, Dad was practically faithless. He always seemed to be mad and begrudging towards the Supreme Being and he wasn't fearful of saying so. He would, sometimes, say horrendous things like "Screw God!"

Thankfully, my father's disdain and negativity towards God did not weaken or tarnish Mom's faith, however. In fact, I believe it managed to magnify it. How else, I asked myself, could she have withstood the old man's mess for all the years she did?

Owing to Ruby's additional credit, she did not allow our old man's anti-God stance to contaminate her five sons either. On the contrary, she regularly endorsed faith and Jesus to us and encouraged us to attend Sunday school as well (there was a Baptist church less than two blocks from our house). Plus, Mom would frequently read the Holy Bible, counsel us to do likewise and, above all else, insist that "her boys" be fair-minded, kind and helpful to all people, even to individuals we only casually knew.

To a certain degree, our mother's philosophy was borrowed from a gospel song by famed black soloist, Mahalia Jackson (an inspiring tune that my brothers and I were quite familiar with), and I still reflect upon some of its lyrics on an almost daily basis. It simply says, "The good you do will come on back to you - and it don't cost very much." And, personally speaking, later on in my life, after I elected to mesh those words with a well-known

Shakespearean quote, which is, "The evil that men do - lives after them," I have never found fault with that wise mixture of premises.

While the foregoing may render me a mite gullible and somewhat simplistic too, I, along with my quartet of brothers, swallowed Mom's philosophy hook, line and sinker. In spite of being exposed to the adverse actions of Melvin Harris, all of my brothers (with myself added to the mix) were regarded as "good boys." I, for one, always rejoiced in light of that frequently stated analogy. Seemingly, none of us boys patterned ourselves after our dad.

Now, I'm not so naive (or harsh either) to suggest that my mother passed down benevolent genes while our father passed along only adverse ones. For in sharp contrast, the old man was capable of being almost excessively affectionate, to a certain degree, downright 'mushy.' He was even subject to kissing some of us boys in the mouth, if we allowed him to.

Our mom, on the other hand, might hug us (or pet us up in times of anguish), but very seldom did she kiss us.

That was just our "Mom's way," my brothers and I collectively came to believe. And while none of us doubted she dearly loved us, seemingly, not a one of us felt slighted by her anti-kissing stance either. Sometimes, however, our old man was on a diverse, opposing plane. Occasionally, he had no qualms about giving one of us a robust, sloppy kiss, or firmly embracing us or even verbally mouthing, "Daddy loves you very much."

However, and, of course, Dad's sincerity was, oftentimes, questionable, especially since we well-knew he was quite capable of turning right around and proceed to call us a nasty name or, even worse, beat one of us to a virtual pulp. And, unfortunately, a frantic and painful memory comes to mind when I think of my father in that particular respect and, specifically, because I was an active player in it.

On one very warm and sunny day (my brothers and I were on summer break at the time), my dad began his morning with a strong desire to just park himself in front of the TV set and try and keep as cool as he possibly could. (During that time, V.I. was no longer living with us, Ruby, who was working as a nurse, was on the day-shift at the Homer G. Phillips Hospital and the old man seemed happy to have a rare week day off from his job).

Therefore, Dad camped out in the living room and focused his attention on the adjacent television set. And with the aid of a soothing electric fan, a pack and a half of Camel cigarettes and a liberal supply of beer in the refrigerator to boot, he was the picture perfect of a man who was in his serene comfort zone. Problem was, with school not being in session, his five sons were right outside the house and busily playing as kids traditionally did.

Significantly though, an even greater problem was developing as the morning turned into afternoon and, then, midday began to creep towards early evening. It all evolved as my four brothers and I, both, individual and in pairs, 'disturbed' our father and informed him we were hungry. Collectively, we hadn't eaten anything the entire day and we, naturally, looked to Dad to accommodate us.

"Ya'll ain't that damn hungry," was one of the insensitive responses he spoke to me. "Grab a piece of light bread or something. And wait till your mother gits home."

Well, my brothers might have been stifled by the old man's weird reply (after all, he was practically absorbed in his beer-drinking mode as time progressed), but I wasn't. I kept pestering him about eating. But, callously, Dad just kept offering up Ruby's name and acting as if Mom was solely responsible for feeding us.

Therefore, after four o'clock that afternoon, from the very moment my brothers and I sighted our mother walking toward us, we rushed to her and almost 'unitedly' informed her that we were about to starve to death. Naturally, she asked us why hadn't we approached our father about eating and we quickly indicated we had. It was easy to tell that Ruby was, both, tired and highly upset as I entered the house directly behind her. Notably though, my brothers elected not to come into the house.

"Melvin, why haven't you fed the kids?" my mother asked. "You oughta be ashamed of yourself, just sitting around and sucking up quarts of beer."

My dad's reply momentarily surprised me. "They ain't even told me they were hungry!" he insisted. "I ain't no goddamn mind-reader!"

As I stood aside, practically stewing in sheer disbelief, I didn't even think about the words that came out of my mouth. "Yes, we did, Daddy," I stated. "I asked you myself, and about five or six times."

The old man glared at me in harsh condemnation, acting as if I was the one who was lying. "And what the hell does that make me, Duke?" he loudly posed. "You callin' me a liar, ya' little nigger?"

I was absolutely certain my father was trying to intimidate me, but I wasn't going to allow him to, not that day. "We did ask you, Daddy!" I yelled. "I know I did, and lots of times too!"

In that instant, my dad, seemingly infuriated, reached out and grabbed my shirt and punched me solidly in the face. Then, even as my mother frantically protested, he reissued his former query. "And what the fuck does that make me, little boy?"

Tears were streaming down my face at that point, but I wasn't about to yield to the man. "It makes you a liar, that's what!" I defiantly shouted. "And you know that's true!"

As his anger increased, it was obvious my dad felt he had to upgrade his assault. So, he punched me again and allowed me to fall to the floor. Then, he strugglingly knelt down beside me and, again, asked, "And what did you say it makes me, Duke?"

"A lie! It makes you a lie!" I shouted through my tears.

At that juncture, my father was in a total rage. Even as Ruby pleaded my case and insisted I was telling the truth, he hit me a couple of more times in my facial area. But I had made up my mind. Even if he killed me, I wasn't about to knuckle under to him.

"Now, am I still a damn lie, little boy?" he questioned. "Huh - am I?"

I was bawling heavily now, but I still insisted, "Yeah, you're still lying, Daddy! And you know, you know it!"

At that moment, my mother tried to physically stave off her crazed husband, determined to end his attack. However, I can't recall the extent of her efforts. Apparently, I passed out.

But, evidently, the old man wasn't quite through. As I laid on the floor, bleeding at the nose, he doused water in my face and posed, yet, another query to me. "Am I still a liar, Duke?" he asked, seemingly satisfied with his self.

I could not help shaking my head from side to side and nor could I stop from weeping anew. However, I still was not prepared to yield to my father's brutality. And he realized it for certain when I dared to say, "Yeah, Daddy, you're still telling a lie . . . and you know it."

Even as Ruby knelt beside me and placed my head in her lap (thereby getting blood on her uniform), I was poised to be struck again by my nearby dad. But he just stood erect, glaring down at me. Then, as my distraught mom proceeded to help me to my feet, my attacker elected to turn around and walk away. He even seemed somewhat dejected and indecisive as Mom opted to speak to him.

"What on earth is the matter with you, Melvin?" she asked, not really expecting a response. Then, as the old man halted and, alternately, looked back, she added, "How could you do him like this? This boy actually loves you! WHY - I haven't the faintest idea. But one day, Melvin, you will rue the day. Mark my words."

Surprisingly, the old man didn't utter a single, solitary reply. Instead, as me and Ruby kept our eyes trained on him, he slowly pivoted and proceeded to the outlying restroom. Although it didn't make an ounce of sense to me, as my mom and I stood in that living room, and jointly trying to stifle our tears, I found myself actually feeling sorry for the man. And I could not, for the life of me, imagine what was wrong with me!

CHAPTER NINE

AN UNEQUAL PUNISHMENT

My dear mother often told me I was a "hard nut to crack." And even at the tender age of seven, I could not rightly dispute her analogy. When it came to dealing with a man named Melvin V. Harris, my biological father, she came to invoke that assessment on a regular basis. And such was the case in regards to a long string of repetitious Friday evenings. Upon looking back at my childhood, I am obliged to admit that I was not only the proverbial "nut" that my mom frequently cited, I could, sometimes, be described as a "slow-learner" also. (In most cases, however, I deemed that totally uncharacteristic of me).

To my utter joy, I have always been a movie fanatic. Even today, if I go two weeks without attending a theatre, I feel almost melancholic, like I've been deprived of a close friendship or something similar. In spite of an excellence in modern television programming, I still relish leaving the confines of my home and attending an indoor movie facility. And for bad or good, I hosted the very same feelings when I was little boy.

Of course, like everyone around me when I was that young boy, my dad was well aware of my obsession with going to a picture show also. He knew, too, that on every other Saturday afternoon (weather permitting), I, along with my brother, Gary, would walk to one of the three theatres that were located in The Ville area. And once there, we'd check out an adventure flick, or a couple of westerns (such as the Durango Kid, Gene Autry or Lash LaRue) and, certainly, the ever-popular chapter or serial plays. And regardless of which movie house we chose, whether it was the Amytis, the Douglas or the Comet, Gary and I enjoyed it immensely.

To me, my adoration for movie-going was an innocent pastime. Even though it rendered me 'different' from my quartet of brothers (sometimes, I had to 'bribe' Gary with refreshments, coercing him to join me), it was a diversion that fostered no ill or adverse effects. I thoroughly enjoyed having Gary with me.

However, leave it to Melvin V. Harris to conceive and, then, exploit a downside element in it. Whenever Gary and I managed to "piss him off" or get on his bad side (which wasn't difficult to do), he would take his leather strap to our backsides and, then, proceed to tack on an additional penalty. And in almost every case, he demanded that we shelve our plans to attend a movie on the ensuing Saturday.

Well, since I traditionally financed the flick venture anyhow (not only the purchasing of snacks, but the admission fee too), it wasn't any skin off my oldest brother's nose. Therefore, when the slated Saturday did roll around, I was the lone kid who sat silently on our front stoop, fuming and grieving my heart out.

Meanwhile, Gary, who seemed to be content and as happy as a lark, passed the afternoon by continuously tossing a baseball or football around and was clearly unphased in the wake of our old man's secondary punishment mechanism. As the saying goes, my brother couldn't care less.

While I did not harbor any ill feelings towards my elder brother, I held plenty of them regarding my father. I could not help but wonder if he even remotely thought about how unfair and lopsided his punishment measure was. Of course, I well-knew the answer to that query. He didn't give it a second thought. In fact, on occasion he would go right outside our house and proceed to play catch with Gary his own self! But, to me, a second butt-beating would have been more acceptable, more humane and fair and much less tortuous.

Significantly, when my mother initially labelled me "a hard nut to crack," it, too, involved my insatiable appetite for movie-going. And not at all surprising, it, too, was associated with, if not, prompted by the adverse and erratic actions of my biological father.

Actually, it took my mother several months to come up with her patent assessment of me. I never perceived her as a person who made hasty judgments. Therefore, when she finally verbalized her opinion, I sensed it was quite painful for her. Nevertheless though, on the specific Friday night I'm recalling, as I sat, alone, on the front stoop of our Sullivan street residence, Mom's sincerity was unmistakable. Instead of criticizing me, she divulged her analogy with my personal well-being at the forefront.

It was approaching nine P.M. at the time and since the summer season was practically over, there was a sporadic chill in the night air. And in the wake of that coldness, and because I had been perched on that step for a couple of hours, Ruby came out onto the porch, bringing my cardigan jacket along with her. She, then, took a moment to gently position the jacket around my shoulders and soon seated herself next to me.

"Thanks," I told her, "I was just about to come in and grab my coat or a blanket myself. As V.I. used to say, it is getting a mite nippy out here."

"I just don't want you to catch a cold, kiddo," my mom remarked. Then, she asked, "Duke, why do you keep doing this to yourself? Ya' know - you are one hard nut to crack. Your brothers - they don't even bother to get dressed anymore. They darn well-know your daddy is lying whenever he claims he's gonna take you boys to the show on Friday evenings. But, week after week, you still try to keep faith in him. Why you do, I don't rightly know. Don't you realize by now, Duke, he lied again?"

"But - but he. promised this time!" I disgustedly offered. "Why does he keep doing it, Ruby? Don't he care, even a little bit! I mean - doesn't he care about his own sons? I'm beginning to . . . to hate him!"

My mother smiled, gently rubbing my back. "You don't hardly hate your daddy, Duke, and that's almost a miracle in itself," she stated. "You want to love him, you know. Well at any event, even if he showed up right now, it would be too late to still catch a movie anyhow. Why doncha come on into the house? And I'll even fix you a cup of hot cocoa, if you like."

As my mom climbed to her feet, I forced a smile on her behalf. "I'll be in - in just a little while," I promised. "Thanks again for my jacket. And I'll be alright. I just don't understand my daddy, that's all."

Ruby laughed out loud. "Well, Duke, when you finally figure him out, do me a big favor - would you?" she spoke. "Run and explain him to me. Who knows? You might be another Charlie Chan or a Sherlock Holmes. But try and perk up, kiddo. In the words of Scarlett O'Hara - Tomorrow is another day."

When I seriously reflect back upon Melvin V. Harris, I inevitably size him up as somewhat predictable and a creature of habit, mostly bad habits. He habitually drank too much alcohol, habitually smoked way too many cigarettes, habitually fooled around with women outside his marriage, habitually gave way to sudden rage and was very comfortable with telling lies. However, that was basically my latter-day opinion of the man and not the assessment I originally had of him.

I once knew a different father; a man who was affectionate, sentimental and caring, but, somehow, he gradually vanished. And I guess, as his doting son, I longed for his eventual return. Little did I realize when I was five or six years old that I would never see that man again.

I regarded myself as a typical kid in those days. I, like most young boys I knew, longed to have a dad of prominence; a father of great reverence and high regards. So, it wasn't difficult for a hero-worshipping son, such as I was, to elevate Melvin Harris to an elite status without a rational validation. And, from time to time, I was guilty of doing just that.

For example: Way back in 1949, when I was that five-year-old boy I alluded to, my mother (who was pregnant at the time) would periodically load up me and my brothers in the family car (yes, my parents briefly owned an automobile) and drive us down to the Mississippi River embankment. And once there, she would find a suitable parking space near the levee and wait for the docking of an enormous and luxurious riverboat called the 'Admiral.'

Although it could very well have been a sight-seeing outing, especially for us kids, it wasn't. Instead, it was a matter of accommodation and fond anticipation. For within fifteen or twenty minutes of our arrival at the riverfront, our grinning and waving father was standing on the deck of that ship and anxiously waiting to disembark it. However, the old man was not only happy to see his rather large brood, he was thankful his work shift had ended too.

In all honesty, I had no idea what my three brothers thought when we tagged along with Ruby on those various car treks to downtown Saint Louis (our fourth brother was still in Mom's womb), but, personally, I was in seventh heaven. Admittedly, I was a child of fantasy, and even naiveté. Without ever posing the question to either my mother or dad, I secretly awarded the rank of 'captain' to Melvin Harris.

And, furthermore, since Daddy was always deckside when the ship was coming in, I also fantasized that my father was extremely competent upon appointing a second-in-command to bring the boat safely in. A couple of years later, as I became much wiser and rational too, I learned that my father was, in fact, a riverboat 'waiter,' which, of course, was a far cry from being the person at the helm of a gigantic ship.

Admittedly, I was very disappointed and heartbroken when I came to realize that my dad was just another working stiff, an average black man who was struggling day-to-day to make ends meet and provide for his family. But, still, as a child, I managed to place him upon a pedestal. It might have had something to do with his prowess as an athlete, but not solely. It might have stemmed from the way he carried himself; his proud and almost exaggerated strut, but not a great deal. And it might have derived from his knack for overly praising me, but I thought not. In actuality, I eventually came to believe that the true source of my admiration for my father had little to do with the man himself.

Instead, it had everything to do with my personal perceptions of fatherhood in general. In spite of all of dad's imperfections and weird behavior, I viewed him as a fortunate and especially blessed man. Plainly stated, I envied him to the very maximum!

I must emphasize, however, my dad was quite memorable in his own right, but sadly not in a virtuous way. Though some of his actions were downright disgraceful, there were other things he did (while not so traumatic) that were, both, bizarre and blatantly deceitful. Being exposed to Melvin Harris on daily basis was like riding a super-fast roller-coaster. The dips and upsurges were almost breathtaking.

For instance, in the 1950's it was common for a debt collector to converge on a residential home, hoping to secure a semblance of payment and our house on Sullivan was not an exception. Some Caucasian man would appear at our front door, periodically in search of money.

Well, one day a Jewish gentleman showed up at our doorstep and my father went to the door, displaying a pleasant smile. However, before our visitor uttered a single word (I stood, watching from the adjacent kitchen area), Dad said something that instantly surprised me. You see, this same collector had come to our house just a week prior. And I knew that for sure because I not only observed him then, just so happened it was Ruby's birthday also. And similar to that particular day, my father had practically waylaid him then too.

"Vic, what happened to you 'last' week?" my old man asked. "I expected you last week, buddy, when I got paid. And here you come this week instead. I ain't got no money today. "

Our visitor, the man named Vic, was even more taken aback than I was and it was evident in his voice when he replied, "Naw, Melvin, I was by here last week, last Monday! Remember? You told me then to come back this week! Said this is your pay week."

"Aw - no way, you're all mixed up, Vic," Dad countered. "Tell you what though - you come back next week, Thursday, and I'll pay you double. But put me down on your calendar this time. Cause we don't want this to happen no more, never again. And I'm sorry you got mixed up. Happens to the best of us though."

As I remained in the kitchen, silently shaking my head, I could not help feeling sorry for the befuddled collector. However, upon hearing his response to my father's fabrication, I was jaw-dropping amazed.

"Well, maybe I did get the dates screwed up, Melvin," Vic relented, actually scratching at his white hair. "I have been burning the midnight oil lately, working too hard. But I'll put you guys down in my book, and come back next Thursday afternoon. But I'm gonna hold you to your promise, collect double, Melvin. Try not to disappoint me now."

"My word's my bond, Vic," my dad boldly stated. "And you try and get some rest, my man. We don't want you gitting sick or nothing. Remember - money's not everything."

"You sure right about that, Melvin," Vic smiled. "I'll see you next week then. Say hello to the misses for me. She's a sweet lady."

At that juncture, my old man slowly closed the door behind the departing collector but couldn't restrain himself from displaying a rather sheepish grin. Apparently, he felt no shame regarding his lying or his successful efforts in confusing the old collector. If anything, he looked quite proud of himself. That was, until he glanced over at me and became instantly miffed.

"Why aren't you outside somewhere, playing with your brothers or something?" he frowned. "You're always hanging around, always under foot."

Although I was inwardly tickled, I didn't dare resort to laughter. To my surprise, however, my father did when I softly remarked, "Oh, I'm sorry, Daddy, sometimes I get all mixed up and think I really live here. Sorry about that."

To what I personally regarded as a great honor, Melvin V. Harris was hired as one of Saint Louis city's first black (or Negroid) 'public service' bus drivers. And whether it was by coincidence or was pre-selected by my father himself, he was assigned a transportation route that was very near our home on

Sullivan street. Driving the 'Cass Avenue' bus meant that he was also required to travel a substantial distance on St. Louis Avenue which, alternately, was only three short blocks south of Sullivan.

Significantly, the Simmons Elementary School (where my brothers and I attended) was located on that very same St. Louis Avenue and it, too, was quite close to our Sullivan street residence. Actually, it was less than five blocks from our house. However, despite the proximity of the old man's bus route to our residence, I doubt that anyone expected (or even imagined) that Melvin Harris was capable of doing what he eventually did. And Dad didn't do it just once, he did it several times.

Although it may sound completely farfetched and definitely crazy, the man that I called "Daddy" (namely, Melvin V, Harris) had the outright gall to clearly veer from his stipulated bus route. In fact, around eight in the morning, while driving west on St. Louis Avenue, he'd turn right at Lambdin St., come down three blocks and, then, execute another right turn at Sullivan. And at that point, he would pick up four of his five sons (the youngest boy, Taran, was not school age at the time) and, then, drive us to the nearby school building.

However, if that venture wasn't nervy enough in itself, it was further hyphenated by Dad's almost manic behavior during those occasions. He seemed totally oblivious of the on- looking and greatly flustered passengers aboard his bus. And even when many of the riders opted to voice their concerns (a good mixture of them feared being late for their jobs), my father calmly tried to appease them by vowing to 'speed up' his driving time. But before tending to his promise, even in the middle of glancing at his wristwatch, he insisted upon performing a particular ritual. Exhibiting a very proud and cocky expression, he singularly introduced each of his sons to the antsy passengers. And oddly enough, they collectively looked truly pleased to meet us! Even as a young child, I was amazed in the wake of it all.

CHAPTER TEN

BROTHERLY LOVE

Upon recollecting my father's audacious actions when he drove the 'Cass Avenue' bus, I am clueless if he suffered any adverse consequences because of his rule-breaking behavior. Whether he was reprimanded, penalized or even fired, I wasn't mindful of it. Since he and my mother separated around that time, my mind was obviously elsewhere. However, if I had any skill whatsoever in reading people's feelings in those days (Ruby suggested that I had that 'gift'), I would guess that Dad emerged unscathed. When I recall the pleasant and smiling faces of the onlooking passengers during those episodes, the patrons appeared to be strangely reconciled to my old man's weird stunt.

But even more than that, the riders seemed to collectively like him. And I must admit, as one of his sons (and, maybe, the only one in the bunch), I was glad they did. My feelings, though, weren't so much a high tribute to my father as they were to my own inbred sentimentality.

Therefore, when I seriously analyze my regards for my dad, I find it's virtually impossible to distinguish genuine love from sentiment and an over-indulgence in sympathy. I truly felt somewhat sorry for him because, even in his outward arrogance and his facade of self-assurance, he rarely seemed happy. And that to me, paired with the knowledge that his biological mother had passed away when he was a ten-year-old child, rendered me much more tolerant of his shortcomings (or antics) than my four brothers were. Even as a little boy, I had a burning desire to uplift his spirits.

In some instances, I felt I was successful in making Dad a happier camper, and especially after he and Ruby separated. You see, I happened to have a pretty good singing voice in those days, and so did my brothers. However, I had zero inhibitions regarding it. Meaning, I felt I sang very well and I had no fear of singing in front of anyone and at any time. If I wasn't going around the house and singing Frankie Laine's 'Jezebel' or Nat King Cole's 'Mona Lisa,' I was vocalizing a tune I had heard on television. And it was the latter source, a certain song I borrowed from Eddie Fisher's TV show that made my dad virtually ecstatic. And as time passed by, along with making him joyous, it made him cry as well.

Right in the presence of my brothers (Dad would, oftentimes, have our baby brother on his knee), I would fondly belt out, "Oh, my Papa - to me he was so wonderful. Oh my Papa - I miss him so today." And before I could follow up with the second verse, tears were forming in the old man's eyes. And, then, by the time I concluded my song, he was noticeably weeping.

And I don't mind saying, completely unashamed in the company of my four brothers, that I, too, was crying at that instant. But it wasn't solely because our father was bawling, it was also due to my innermost thoughts.

It was then that I knew for certain that Melvin Harris, too, was a creature of deep sentiment and, maybe, subdued regret also. But it wasn't exclusively on behalf of what he had done in days gone by (although he had made numerous blunders), I surmised it was probably because of what he was <u>about</u> to do. Although he didn't opt to verbalize it, I personally believed he was reflecting on a time when he would no longer hear my song, and an even more grievous period when he'd no longer see or interact with his five sons. And that was heartbreaking for my dad and myself as well, because I couldn't avoid from feeling his pain.

Frankly speaking, the singing episode wasn't the only time I recalled feeling sorry for my father, nor the only time I observed him crying. One particular occasion made an indelible imprint on my young mind and mainly because it was, yet, another happening that directly involved me. And I must confess, until this very day, I recall it with marked amazement and a residual sense of stupefying anger. When I was but two days into the first grade at Simmons Elementary School, I was approached by a very light-complexioned black boy, who was actually a fellow classmate. He was soft-spoken, polite and soon informed me that his name was 'George Sneed.' I smiled, reached out and shook his hand and told him that I was Lionel Harris. Then, I quickly added, "But my nickname is 'Duke,' everybody calls me Duke - and you can too, George." Well, the boy smiled pleasantly and I went home that afternoon, feeling glad that I had made a new friend. And since I've always cherished nice people (adults and fellow kids), that was a stellar day for me.

Unfortunately though, my feeling of gladness was short-lived, to say the least. In fact, it didn't last throughout the rest of that particular week. And, moreover, owing to the rather warped thinking of so-called 'grown-ups,' it was abruptly turned into an insidious happening that completely boggles the mind - and, especially my young mind.

On the day after George Sneed and I had officially kicked off relationship, my newfound buddy came up to me again and was quite excited to tell me something I wasn't aware of. He apprised me that his dad was a 'Dr. George Sneed,' a dentist, and, more significant, his mom was 'Leola Harris Sneed,' a lady who happened to be one of my father's older sisters. Therefore, George Jr. and I were not only fellow classmates, we were also first-cousins! of course, was delighted and rejoiced in the news. And the same feelings seemed to apply to George also.

Now, initially, Daddy was well-pleased with the development. He even took the initiative to inform Ruby and me that George Jr. came home from school that week, marvelling about a little boy in his first grade class named Lionel Harris. According to my father, who was all smiles at the time, George Jr. said, "The kid has a head-full of black curls and he looked a lot like an Indian!" I, in time, laughed in light of that description - mainly because (although my skin color was a bit reddish looking) instead of focusing on any other image of an American Indian, I instantly thought about the image of the one showcased on a nickel coin. After all, most of the Native Americans I had seen were on a movie screen and they were almost always portrayed by Caucasians. And I certainly didn't look like them.

The joy surrounding the subject episode deteriorated rapidly. Within two days of listening to the old man's amusing story, I had to cope with, both, sadness and anxiety. By the end of the week, George Sneed Jr. and I were no longer classmates. Although I wasn't privy to the explanation, I was moved to a different first grade classroom. Though I was disappointed (I was also being separated from many of my former kindergarten pals), and a little vexed, I didn't resort to crying about it, but my father, alternately, wept enough for the both of us. Speaking to mom's personal disgust and outrage, he angrily divulged the gist of the happening.

"Just because her butt is married to a goddamn dentist," Dad reasoned (he habitually used profanity), "Leola thinks Duke's not good enough to be in the same class with her fuckin' son, the bitch! What kinda shit is that? Well, screw her ass! And to think - she's my own damn sister! How could she even feel that way, huh? That is sick, and it's damn stupid too! I mean - my own flesh and blood sister!"

Though Ruby wasn't one to cuss, in being the loving mother she was, she was visually upset also. Alternately, she posed a relevant question that even I, as a six-year-old at the time, kind of wondered about. "And why didn't they move George Jr. to another classroom, Melvin?" she asked. "George sure couldn't be a nicer boy than Duke. All those teachers at Simmons loves Duke. And what's the matter with that principal they got up there?"

Apparently, my father didn't have a sensible answer to Mom's questions. Instead, he just sat on the living room sofa, sulking in dejection and still quite tearful. Seemed he could not come to grips with what his sister had done and, although I kept my silence, neither could I. However, I was more sorrowful for my father than I was for myself. That prompted me to walk over to him and hug his neck and, soon, he returned my embrace.

As things panned out during my childhood, I never really got to know or interact with my cousin, George Jr., or any of his four brothers either. (Yes, there were five Harris boys and five Sneed brothers as well). Whether it was intentionally engineered or pure happenstance, our paths never crossed again and, apparently, our individual parents were content with the estrangement.

It might have had something to do with Dad's fractured relationship with his sister, Leola, but I can't be positive. But I do know, during my remaining years at Simmons Elementary, that I never again shared a classroom with George Jr. And that, to me (since we were at the same grade level), was somewhat odd.

Basically, children are resilient, so I didn't lose any sleep over that first grade happening. However, some years later, when I took out time to put it all into perspective, I found myself leaning towards my father's yesteryear reasoning. Though I didn't completely subscribe to it initially, it was rather stupid and asinine.

Since my Aunt Leola was married to a professional dentist (Dr. Sneed), she felt it catapulted her into a position of prominence. So, she did not feel that the son of a common working man (especially a lowly waiter on the Admiral Excursion Ship) should be in the same classroom with her 'elitist' son. And the fact that that 'common working man' happened to be her youngest biological brother, apparently, made no difference at all. Therefore, in the mind of my auntie (and, maybe, her spouse was in agreement), it was simply a question of social status.

Now, if I was right on the money about my aunt's reasoning, then I came to deem her feelings entirely illogical. Because if she considered her youngest brother and his immediate family as 'lowly commoners,' then what about the other black kids in that first grade classroom. Were they all offsprings of professional and prominent parents? Even at six years old, I imagined not. So, maybe my father, and myself also, was plainly in error. Maybe, in reality, dad's sister had an underlying begrudgment for her baby brother. In that case, only the two siblings knew for sure.

***

Despite my confusion in regards to that yesteryear happening at Simmons Elementary, there was one factor that plagued me throughout my lifetime; as a child and as an adult. For no apparent or plausible claim to fame, my father, his only brother and the majority of his six sisters, honestly believed they were elitist and special, several notches above so-called average Negroes. Although Aunt Leola was married to a dentist, during my childhood, none of them were professionally-trained; not a doctor, a lawyer, a teacher or even a dentist with the Harris name amongst them, but, still, they regarded themselves as upper crust, prominent and almost regal. And, seemingly (if they even came close to emulating Melvin V. Harris), they weren't beyond indoctrinating their children with the same pompous feeling of superiority.

Truthfully, if I were given a dollar for every time Dad told me, "You're a Harris" or "Remember you're a Harris," I would be wealthy. Furthermore, with my old man saying it so often, I gradually began to take him at face value. Inwardly, I really didn't believe I was actually more special than the average fellow (I was always blessed with self-esteem', but, after a while, I did come to think that there was some degree of validity to his lofty claim. Maybe, I was on the threshold of being brainwashed.

However, upon assuming there was real fire beneath my dad's braggadocious smoke, I never asked him "why" the Harris family towered above normal, everyday black people. Being quite young, I even tried to connect our name to the well-known 'Harris Taxicab Company' which operated in Saint Louis, Missouri, but eventually I learned that they were unrelated to our Harris branch.

Actually, I was well-grown when I finally discovered the driving factor behind the Harris family's claim to fame and prominence. And while many of those family members were greatly impressed and prideful in the wake of the underlying reason (especially, 'pure-blood' Harris's), I cannot say I was. Personally, I came to regard the rationale as pretentious, superficial and somewhat farfetched and even if it was absolutely valid, I could not extract a feeling of elitism from it. Regardless of an individual's heritage or social status, even as a child, I greatly admired kind, compassionate and good-hearted people. That rendered my love for people indiscriminate.

<hr>

Naturally, I am in no way suggesting that my father's side of the family was all bad, phony, snobbish or people of ill-repute. If I even remotely felt that way, I'd be the most gullible fool in the Harris clan and a semi-masochist to boot. Because throughout all the years that followed (even after my parents had divorced), I, contrary to most of my brothers, took it upon myself to still interact with most of the Saint Louis-based Harris's. But more than that, I grew to love quite a few of them. Therefore, the Harris's, too, had their share of good-hearted and benevolent individuals.

As I stated though, most of my siblings did not seem to have much interest in mingling with the Harris portion of our family heritage (every now and then Gary would join me in my visiting efforts). But not branding the other three right or wrong, for a prolonged time they seemed indifferent when it came to that side of the family and I could not fairly fault them for it. In reality, it was a by-product of our parent's break-up.

<hr>

When my mother and my brothers and I eventually moved away from Sullivan Street (that was in 1954), that transition, in itself, proceeded to only heighten the estrangement between my brothers and our uncle and aunts and their respective families. Precisely, when we resided on Sullivan, we were less than a mile from a number of Harris's.

Specifically, there was Uncle Samuel and his four kids, Aunt Peggy (or Ardelia) and her two daughters, and even Aunt Leola and her five boys; all of them, well within walking distance from our house. Therefore, when we relocated out on Burd Avenue (which my brothers and I considered as 'out west'), that practically sounded the death knell on the co-mingling of our different families. While my brothers seemed content in keeping their distance from dad's siblings (and, after a while, Gary felt likewise), my father's brother and his sisters appeared to mutually share their sentiments. However, I, on the other hand, viewed the situation quite differently. While my parent's divorce had pulled the curtain down on the first act in my young life, it didn't conclude the entire performance. In addition, I was very fond of my aunts and uncle and most of my cousins too.

CHAPTER ELEVEN
WOUNDS THAT WON'T HEAL

As far back as I can remember, though I was much too young to identify what it was, I habitually self-analyzed myself, along with the majority of my actions. Whether it's a nagging flaw or an inborn virtue in my character, I have, yet, to make up my mind about it. Therefore, when I focus on my enduring and long-time relationship with my father's side of the family (especially after his departure), I always emerged uncertain as to why I, almost singularly, elected to stay in touch with the Harris's when my brothers did not.

Of course, my father, meshed with the memory of his former deeds and misdeeds, was a major player in the mystery. After all, my brothers under me barely remembered him (let alone his M.I.A. siblings) and Gary, being the senior son, knew the man all too-well. Sorrowfully, the bulk of Gary's personal recollections of Dad were filled with acts of unkindness and brutality. And, in all probability, that had an adverse effect on my elder brother's estrangement feelings also.

Though I'm in no way qualified to accurately gauge the yesteryear feelings of any of my four brothers (Gary, included), I can candidly reflect upon mine. I wish I could report that I came to understand Melvin V. Harris, but I cannot. In being a troubled and tortured soul, the old man was a walking anomaly to me; an individual who really warranted study and scrutiny. But, admittedly, after withstanding literally tons and tons of water under the proverbial bridge, I still remain somewhat shell shocked and awed by him. And, therefore, along with my tendency to critically analyze my individual life-actions, I, sometimes, find myself devoting similar energy to the long-ago conduct of my father as well. But seldom do I come away feeling good in light of those reflections.

Frankly speaking, if early, unpleasant memories were the only remnants of an anxiety-filled childhood, it might be subsequently regarded as par for the course; just another sad and, all-too-frequent, tale of a ghetto-based and so-called 'dysfunctional' Negroid family. Society, in general, advocated that in most cases, the emotional trauma from such childhood circumstances would gradually dissolve with the passing of time. (They were dead-wrong and, in reality, didn't much care).

However, when it came to my immediate family, owing specifically to Melvin V. Harris, there emerged a serious side-effect that, tragically, had tremendous staying-power and lasted an excess of fifteen years. Specifically, it affected me and my oldest brother, Gary.

Although I stated it before, even as a little kid, I had zero interest in playing any sports activity. More than that, until I reached adulthood, I had little interest in even watching organized sports events, either amateur or professional. And if that made me some kind of oddball, then that was fine with me. Instead, I took pride in being scholarly; a good student who traditionally received 'excellent' grades. I was proficient in math, English, history and practically everything in a school's curriculum. Plus, I was an avid reader. Therefore, both, Ruby and Dad were proud of my efforts and I, like most youngsters, absolutely relished their joy and resultant praise.

However, leave it to a man like my father to transform a 'feel-good' thing into something detrimental and downright divisive. To my utter distress and to Gary's silent, but smoldering anguish, our old man made a conscious decision to proclaim me as "the little smart boy" and, turning right around, and brand his eldest son "the little dumb boy." And, to no one's surprise (especially, mine), even prior to Dad's permanent departure from our Sullivan street domicile, it was an action that severely damaged and all but severed the brotherly relationship between Gary and me.

As for my personal read on the matter, Gary could not physically lash out at our father in regards to the cruel, repetitious insult, so he elected to focus on me instead. For I was more accessible and more vulnerable too. From the very onset of our dad's mean-spirited put-down, I, too, felt victimized. While I continued to love my older brother (just as I did all my brothers), Gary, on the contrary, seemed contemptuous and hostile towards me. In fact, Gary emerged so entrenched in his distaste for me that he later insisted upon attending a different high school than I. And due to the fact that Gary and I graduated from grammar school on the very same day, it wasn't just mere happenstance. (At least, I felt that way).

However, well before our father made his inevitable exit from the home scene (and certainly well before me and Gary graduated from grade school), I could not brand his meanness one-sided. While he managed to go out of his way to mistreat and abuse his first-born son, Dad continued to rain havoc on the rest of the family as well. In spite of being a little lax and humane towards Lovell, Vaughn and little Taran, it was still open season on me and Ruby.

Therefore, in accordance to how the wind blew, he was still subject to knock our mom around and to also conjure up a reason to physically pound on me as well. So, co-existing with his habit of praising me lived an inner desire to harm me too. In a way of speaking, his inner 'Mr. Hyde' still ran roughshod over his surface 'Dr. Jekyll.'

Now, if it sounds as if I'm suggesting that Melvin Harris was two different personalities, maybe I am. I saw him as a man who could halt on a dime and, then, go in an entirely different direction. For example, when I was eight years old, my father decided to try and capitalize on my prowess as a 'bright' student. Without so much as discussing it with me, he took the liberty of entering me in a question and answer radio competition, replete with a live, in-studio audience.

Of course, the object of the contest was to establish which kid (boys and girls ranging from age eight to ten) was the smartest in the bunch and, in spite of my being the youngest in the group, Dad was quite confident I'd emerge victorious. However, the age factor did not remotely matter to my father, and neither did my ongoing nervousness upon standing on stage in front of thirty or forty glaring spectators. Seemingly dazzled by the top prize (which was two hundred dollars in cash), the old man was the picture of pompous certainty of my success and no one could have told him differently, absolutely no one!

However, to my heartfelt sorrow, I did not deliver for my father. When the competition drew to a final close (and after eight fellow participants had fallen to the wayside), I had garnered only second place and a nine-year-old little girl had snared the coveted top prize. But I did perk up somewhat when I learned the runner-up award was seventy-five dollars-worth of groceries. For I knew my mother would be very pleased by it.

Of course, my dad was an entirely different story. Even as six bags of groceries were loaded into the trunk of a summoned taxicab, I felt bad vibes from him. In addition, when he smiled and claimed he was proud of my efforts in the contest, speaking to the competition's host minutes earlier, I sensed he was lying.

However, not until we arrived home (Dad had said very little during the taxi trek), did I actually become aware of the old man's true feelings. As Dad paid the fare and watched the cabbie drive off, thereby leaving the two of us and the sacks of groceries sitting on the adjacent curb, he finally divulged his suppressed feelings.

"You ain't that goddamn smart after all, lettin' that damn girl beat you like that!" he complained. "<u>That</u> was a waste of goddamn time!"

Oddly enough, I didn't respond and nor did I cry. Maybe, I was growing immune to my father's bizarre harshness and he could no longer surprise me. Plus, I was pretty tired at that juncture.

As time progressed, I soon wished I had resorted to crying or had displayed some type of emotion that 'might' have aroused my father's sympathy. Who knows? Maybe, it would have persuaded him to put a cap on his usual craziness. As it was though, he made it his business to go and find my favorite bamboo fishing pole, angrily break it into four pieces and, then, pitch the remnants in the trash can out front of our house.

I, like my onlooking mother, Ruby, shook my head in subdued disgust, but, still, I refused to show my inner hurt. I was hellbent on not giving the old man self-satisfaction. Instead, I bade goodnight to my mom and headed to the outlying bedroom where, of course, my four brothers were sleeping. My spirits weren't totally crushed, however. For inside, I was quite proud of my performance during the foregoing contest and so was my mom. Actually, that was good enough for me.

Although I came to regard myself as a student of logic and an individual who is basically sane also (albeit, truly demented people come to admit they are crazy anyhow), I cannot staunchly denounce the premise that children who are prolongedly exposed to a parent such as Melvin V. Harris does not, sometimes, seem a little nuts themselves.

Of course, that premise is not ironclad and I don't attribute it to me personally. But I would be telling a boldface lie if I claimed I wasn't, both, adversely and benevolently affected by my dad's bizarre, erratic and, oftentimes, outlandish behavior. However, I thank God that I, seemingly like each of my brothers, came to the consensus that just by being the exact opposite (or counterparts) of our old man would automatically render us respectable, productive and upstanding men. I always viewed that as a shining plus and a genuine saving grace in the matter.

Conversely though, just by being in the presence of a man like Melvin Harris (and I prayed they were far and in between) was an impactful downer in itself. Moreover, the residual fallout from such an interaction was (and still is) all but impossible to completely shake off. Even currently, and throughout my entire foregoing life, I have sparred back and forth with it.

For example, although I have never regarded it as an ultra-serious problem, it has, sometimes, been quite difficult for me to be dogmatic and stalwart when dealing with a number of issues, and especially when children are involved. It's not that I'm indecisive by nature (I previously declared that I'm self-analytical and a student of logic), it's just that I almost habitually take out a minute or two to consider another person's viewpoint. And despite their small statures, I recognize children as 'persons' also.

In all fairness, my father was similar to a lot of young dads I've observed over the years; headstrong men who absolutely demand prompt and unswerving obedience from their offsprings. However, the dad whom I lived with upped it to an even higher level. Behaving more like a staunch army sergeant, he seemed to subscribe to the rather asinine command, "If I say jump, you are only permitted to ask - 'How high?' or even, "Yours is not the reason why, yours is to do or die." Now, maybe those two precepts are appropriate in a military setting, and essentially when spewing from the mouth of a noncom or an officer, but my dad was neither. Still, he operated from the forestated premises and he relished the power. Therefore, when the following incident took place, it showcased a vintage Melvin Virgil Harris.

Quite relevant to the happening I'm about to relive, my brother, Melvin Gary, happened to be nineteen months my senior. In respect to myself and our succeeding siblings, it was the lengthiest age gap between all of our respective births. (I'm pretty certain that the pronounced time lapse had everything to do with Dad's absence due to military service). Nevertheless, for the most part, Gary and I were close-knit in our early days together and, notably, I adored my oldest brother.

Prior to having a television set, I vividly recall Gary and me laying on our bedroom floor and listening to our favorite radio shows. We'd enjoy such programs as 'The Lone Ranger,' 'Gunsmoke,' 'The Shadow,' 'Fibber McGee and Molly,' the 'Jack Benny Show' and even 'Amos and Andy.' But when the TV appeared on the scene, we, of course, switched our attention over to it.

Subsequently, both, Gary and I came to marvel over a weekly television series called 'The Cisco Kid.' It was a western and Gary and I were virtually spellbound in light of the frequent derring-do and comical antics of the feature's staple protagonists, who was the Cisco Kid and his loyal sidekick, Poncho. Though I couldn't speak for my eldest brother during that select period in our lives, I especially loved seeing the duo come forth on our relatively small TV screen (swiftly riding their steeds) and, simultaneously, hearing the background announcer delivering his weekly introduction. He would say something like, "Here's that famous Robin Hood of the Old West - the Cisco Kid!" and I, like Gary, would be grinning from ear to ear. Personally, I could not have been much happier!

Now, I realized that television was in its early stages in 1950 or so but, even as a six-year-old child, something seemed out of whack to me. For some undisclosed reason, The Cisco Kid telecast was given a nine P.M. air-slot, and, yet, on a Monday evening. And from the word say-go I thought that was a strange choice. After all, the story plots were quite juvenile and simple, the action scenes were not overly violent (no player was mortally wounded on screen) and they seemed to pose no mental damage or trauma to onlooking, impressionable children. And, moreover, even as a little boy, I relished seeing 'good' triumph over 'evil.' That was the overall themes of the teleplays and hit home with me.

To my total sorrow (but not surprise), however, my father did not share any of my forestated feelings or enthusiasm. Instead, he concerned himself with the show's slated time-slot and, specifically, in regards to my chronological age. Although it may have been entirely innocent on my dad's part, I always thought otherwise. Even in those days, I secretly believed the word 'innocent' was incompatible with my father. And even more disturbing to me, I came to believe he actually craved confusion and turmoil, practically any little thing to overturn the fabled apple-cart.

However, regarding the 'Cisco Kid' issue, the old man took the initiative to step out of character momentarily. Out of everything he did, all of his cruel and strange acts of evilness, it was the first time I recalled him showing any semblance of favor towards my brother, Gary. In the case I'm citing, since Gary was the eldest son, and the Cisco Kid aired on a weekday night (and a school night, to boot), Gary was permitted to stay up until nine-thirty P.M. while my bedtime was set at nine, a half an hour earlier.

Not surprisingly, in Melvin Harris's rigid, regimented and unyielding mind, "set at nine" meant precisely that; not one minute after nine or two minutes after nine, but exactly nine o'clock on the spot - or, sometime, prior to it. Therefore, when eight fifty-eight rolled around (and my dad was adept in watching the clock on the adjacent living room wall), it was high time for me to head to my bedroom.

Furthermore, if I wasn't near the hallway and making my way to that bedroom within minutes of the 'set time,' the old man would start yelling at me like a maniacal banshee. It way crazy! The man was absolutely hell-bent on my not seeing any part of the Cisco Kid feature! And it may sound as if I'm exaggerating or being over-critical of my father's behavior, but I'm not. Even if I resorted to begging, asking him to please let me see Cisco and Poncho, at least, "ride over the hill" (which was, as I indicated, the series visual prologue), my dad would practically go berserk! Not only would he respond with a boisterous, "Hell naw!," he would pepper his reply with threats and harsh profanity. "Take your goddamn ass to bed," he'd add, "and don't give me no more of your lip, damnit! Go-to - bed, Duke!"

And that, as usual, settled the matter. I knew that further resistance on my part would be pointless. Despite my pleading and bawling too, my father wasn't about to change his mind. So, almost traditionally, I would purposely pause in the washroom (just long enough to dry my eyes, and 'hear' the Cisco Kid's opening dialogue) and, then, proceed to the outlying bedroom. Once there, I would always try my best not to wake up my slumbering brothers and, most of the time, I was successful. However, how they managed to sleep through our old man's loud ranting was a real mystery to me.

Incidentally, as vexing and annoying as the foregoing account was to me, every time I reflect upon it, I eventually find myself somewhat tickled. Not about the episodes themselves, however, but due mostly to their immediate aftermaths. Notably though, the mirthful aspect has little to do with the senior Melvin Harris, but everything to do with his namesake, Melvin Gary.

As I formerly mentioned, Gary's official bedtime was nine-thirty. Therefore, he was free to stay put in the living room and enjoy the Cisco Kid telecast to the very hilt. And, apparently, he enjoyed it every time. Then again, maybe he did not. But I really wouldn't know for certain. Because, as time went by, and as Dad and I replayed the same scene practically every Monday evening, Gary appeared to relish my repetitious anguish.

Oh, he wouldn't say something silly or childish like "na-na-na-na" or "goody-goody for you," but he would resort to something that was just as aggravating. When the Cisco Kid finally concluded (as I laid in bed, still pouting, it seemed like an entire hour had passed instead of just thirty minutes), Gary could barely wait to join me in our bedroom. And once there, he would tease and taunt me with a whole series of whispered remarks.

With unmistakable enthusiasm in his voice, he would say something like, "Duke, you should have seen Cisco tonight! Boy, he leaped over four horses, just to git to his own horse!" or "Man, Cisco beat the living stuffin' out of three of the crooks! And Poncho could only handle one! That Cisco, he's a bad motor scooter!"

In a virtual nutshell, my eldest brother got a real kick out of his yesteryear embellishment and playful teasing, all of it fashioned to make me envious and jealous of his unprecedented 'special' status. In actuality, I wasn't really bothered by it. I just couldn't figure out my old man. But, funny thing. Years afterwards, long after Dad's eventual departure from our lives and I was able to watch the Cisco Kid serials without any restrictions, I never, ever saw Cisco leap over _two_ horses, let alone four of them!

CHAPTER TWELVE
TWENTY-ONE DOLLARS AND CHANGE

In retrospect, I never regarded the 'Cisco Kid' episodes as traumatic or overly-serious, reoccurring memories that especially stick to my craw. When I do reflect back on them, it's mostly from the humorous aspect I alluded to. However, I must admit that I do still wrestle with one childhood reminiscence that, to me, runs parallel to a well-known remark that President Franklin D. Roosevelt made immediately after Pearl Harbor was attacked in 1941.

Although no one perished or was injured on my adopted date that "lives in infamy," I believe my individual psyche was critically wounded on the day I'm on the verge of reliving. But even if my homespun diagnosis is too extreme (or is deemed melodramatic), the scars from the happening remains open and unhealed.

It it's possible for a child to be born with a genuine work ethic, then I feel I fit the build. I can hardly remember not having some semblance of a job, and no matter how menial or low in pay status it was. Whether it was emptying trash cans for select Sullivan street neighbors (four households at fifteen cents a week), or selling the Post-Dispatch and Globe-Democrat newspapers on Sunday mornings (sometimes, making almost two bucks per day), or using my wagon to haul groceries all day on Saturdays (a good day netted me about three and a half dollars), I was 'Johnny-on-the-spot.' Unless it was extreme inclement weather or I was ailing, I was always out pursuing money.

Now, if being free-hearted is also an inbred quality, then I plead "guilty as charged" to that analogy too. As I stated earlier, I had no problem in frequently treating my brother, Gary (or any of my brothers, in fact). to a weekend movie and complimentary refreshments also. Notably though, I wouldn't break myself with my benefactor acts and I believed in saving funds for special occasions.

One such occasion was a holiday that me and all of my brothers (along with literally millions of kids across America and beyond) absolutely delighted in celebrating and that, of course, was Christmas. And since our father had already verbally destroyed the myth of 'Santa Claus,' I was determined to have a bunch of store-bought gifts under our artificial tree when the traditional time came.

In mid-September of 1952, that was a foremost and driving factor for me. According to my well-kept log (Yes, I maintained a paper record of my savings), I had a whopping $21.39 cents to my credit and I was more than confident that I'd have forty or fifty dollars to spend when December finally rolled around. Not too bad for a hard-working eight-year-old kid.

Alternately though, my youthfulness, paired with my tendency to trust others (adults, especially), led to my grievous undoing. Perhaps, I should have deposited my money in a commercial bank, and not a child's piggy-bank made of plaster. Or, perhaps,

I should have hid my savings in my own, top-secret place around the house, and not in plain-sight on the top shelf in the living room closet. Then again, perhaps I should have had an honest and upstanding biological daddy, and definitely not a man like Melvin V. Harris.

However, since none of those three hindsight suppositions came into play, I was up that well-known creek without a single paddle. On the fateful September afternoon I'm recalling, upon returning home from Simmons Elementary like I regularly did, I was taught an object lesson in cold-hearted, human deception. Conspicuously laying on the living room linoleum, in full view, were two, distinct items. One was a familiar looking claw-hammer and the other, the powder debris of my smashed piggy-bank.

Most certainly, my money was gone, every red cent of it, and although there was no one around to point the finger of blame at, I instantly deduced who the true culprit was. Of course, it didn't call for a genius. In reality, no window in the house had been left unlatched or was broken (I quickly checked them all), the front door was not forced open (in fact, I unlocked it with my door key), my four brothers were all accounted for, and Ruby was working the day shift at Homer G. Phillips Hospital. (Besides, wouldn't a burglar have grabbed the TV?). So, who was left? Plus, what kind of person could bring themselves to commit such an audacious and despicable act? None other than Melvin V. Harris!

Now, if one was inclined to think that my father 'fessed-up' to his crime, they would be grossly in error. Later that very evening, Dad faulted some phantom thief, claiming a bedroom window had a defected lock. And although I knew I was playing with fire (the old man's retaliatory rage), I could not refrain from speaking up.

"And the thief came right into our house and, then, headed straight for my piggy-bank, huh?" I asked. "And didn't take nothing else, huh?"

My father displayed his innocent face. "What are you trying to say, Duke?" he calmly, but intimidatingly queried. "We just have to be more careful in the future, that's all. Just chalk it up as a learning experience. Duke, life is full of disappointments, remember that. I feel for you."

Of course, it was ludicrous to chalk the piggy-bank episode up to mere experience. Instead, I chose to chalk it up to, yet, another monstrous deed that came directly from the Melvin V. Harris playbook; just one more unforgettable example of the old man's callous and demented behavior.

Although I pretended to take the theft issue all in stride (later, Ruby, too, dared to assail my dad for his blatant thievery), it was a heartrending sham on my part. Till this very day, I still suffer certain repercussions from it. Recognizing it as a residual flaw in my character, I find it almost impossible to save or hold on to money.

This may strike many people as bizarre and, somewhat, nutty too, but, essentially, unless my monetary funds are in a commercial bank, money seems to almost magically trickle away from me. It may require a psychiatrist to verify it for certain, but I honestly believe my idiosyncrasy is an underlying outgrowth from the piggy-bank incident during my long-ago childhood. However, I never lost sleep over it.

Now, this may sound strange and somewhat unbelievable to the average person also, but I have always tried to be above-board and honest. Even as a little boy, and before my father impacted and, occasionally, stifled me with opposing and, oftentimes, devilish conduct, I was virtually obsessed with doing 'the right thing.' Not only that, but if someone happened to wrong me, I wasn't begrudging and I had no burning desire to get even or seek revenge.

Instead, I would seriously weigh every situation, try to assess my fault in the matter, and then make a determination. And in most cases, I chose "getting away" over "getting even." Meaning, whenever I found myself dealing with a mean-spirited or caustic person, I would make a firm decision to stay the hell away from such an individual, and regardless of their gender. In her quiet wisdom, Ruby always told all of her sons to surround themselves with benevolent and nice people and I, as one of those sons, was always appreciative of her advice.

Unfortunately though, I couldn't adhere to those guidelines when it came to the senior Melvin Harris. I was much to young to flee the home scene and, besides, there were five vulnerable obstacles standing in my way; my mother and my quartet of brothers. In actuality, the five of them were the focal point of most of my feelings.

Outside of the piggy-bank issue, I never felt permanently traumatized or prolongedly harmed by the things my father did to me (the verbal threats, the physical lambasting, the numerous broken promises and lies, none of it), because, although I cannot begin to explain it, I always knew I would emerge alright. However, I wasn't at all sure about my mother and my siblings. I constantly worried about their well-being and, as Ruby liked to say, that was "a tough row for a little boy to hoe." Sorrowfully, when I look back on my childhood (and especially when my dad was still around), I cannot recall a time when I wasn't seriously concerned about them.

Additionally, when I reflect specifically on my brother, Gary, I can't remember a time when I was not acutely aware of Dad's overly harsh mistreatment of him either. Though Gary, surface-wise, seemed oblivious to it, I absolutely hated the 'smart boy/dumb boy' comparison. It was grossly evil, exceedingly unfair and unjust and, worst of all, it gradually eroded the close-knit relationship that Gary and I once enjoyed.

Despite stating it previously, I cannot emphasize enough that that childhood erosion was stubbornly enduring. Well after our old man had flew the familial coup (that was in the year 1954), it lasted throughout our pre-teen and high school years as well. And it was a prime example of a William Shakespeare quote I came to frequently ascribe to, which was, "The evil that men do - lives after them."

However, in spite of the joyous fact that Gary and I, eventually, overcame Dad's very cruel and divisive actions (which pitted two brothers against each other), from time to time I still wonder about it. Upon granting the old man undeserved leniency regarding the issue (giving him the benefit of the doubt), I could never bring myself to believe he intentionally opted to drive a begrudgment wedge between his two eldest sons. To be perfectly frank, I didn't think our dad 'even' or 'ever' gave it a second thought. At least, I hoped he didn't.

But, admittedly, if I had to rate the old man's vast array of wrongdoings on a numbers scale, with the digit number one being the most severe, I'd be compelled to assign the 'brother-estrangement' issue the number two slot. Whether it intentionally orchestrated or not, it was monstrous and almost unforgivable. I awarded it the secondary ranking solely due to its longevity and impact, but, still, it fell well-short of the top spot. Before long, as time marched on, the old man managed to outdo himself. After all, the marriage between him and our mother may have been on life-support, but the infamous Melvin Virgil Harris was still alive and kicking!

CHAPTER THIRTEEN
GRIEF IN BLACK AND WHITE

Long before a barrage of events finally convinced me that it was inevitable, and for the best, that my parents would legally dissolve their volatile marital union, I honestly believed that my dad actually relished a particular aspect of 'fatherhood.' Not in a commendable or benevolent sense (that of being regarded as an admirable and ideal patriarch), but solely because he was adept at churning out offsprings with the precision of a factory assembly-line.

Never mind that our mother, Ruby, had a 'little' something to do with the finished product, but Melvin Harris was especially braggadocious and proud (of himself) when he spawned one son after another. I recall him ragging on the topic with his only brother, Samuel, boasting that he (singling out his self, of course) was virtually teeming with "strong, masculine genes." (Essentially, it was because his brother had sired, both, boys and girls and my old man was claiming a degree of superiority in regards to the 'male' issue).

Over a period of time, I was never quite sure if Dad was 'kiddingly' yanking Uncle Samuel's chain, or if he truly meant what he was suggesting. From a man who self-described himself as "pretty," who could get him accurate read on him?

However, I was quite aware that my father had issued his boast of masculinity to someone other than his elder brother. And one of those others happened to be a fellow black father named 'Jacob Carson,' who was a friend and long-time neighbor of Ruby's older sister, Zeora 'Hannah' Strickland. In fact, our family was visiting Aunt Hannah, Uncle Bill and their five offsprings in downtown Saint Louis's Carr Square Village when I overheard my dad grinningly resurrect his boast.

Apparently, Mr. Carson, who, up to the specific time I'm citing, had fathered, at least, six daughters, was somewhat envious of Dad's knack for producing sons. And that was rather evident in Jacob Carson's voice when he asked my father to share his "secret." As young as I was, I knew a peculiar response was forthcoming when I noticed the pronounced smirk on the old man's face.

"Well, Carson, I'll tell you, old buddy. It's all in the way you move your hips," Dad spoke. "You know, when you're doing it. To get a boy, man, you gotta rely more on your left hip."

Now, whether my dad thought he was talking over my head or plain-old didn't care if I heard him or not, I wasn't quite sure. (Even by then, I had been exposed to so-called French comics). All I know is that I instantly resorted to laughter and so did Jacob Carson.

"Harris, you are so full of it - it's a crying shame," Mr. Carson grinningly replied. "But I had it coming. Ask a crazy question and you get a crazy answer back. 'Rely on your left hip.' But, ya' know, I'm gonna give it a try. It couldn't hurt."

Although I still get tickled whenever I relive that long-ago verbal exchange between my father and Mr. Carson (I feel likewise when I recall the related dialogue between Dad and Uncle Samuel too), I find myself turning somewhat somber shortly afterwards. In spite of my father's crowing and harmless teasing, I never once believed Dad felt remotely blessed in having healthy children, and regardless of their gender. Even after affirming that 'his boys' had all of their fingers and toes at birth (according to my mother, the old man was fanatical about that procedure), he didn't seem thankful. And his lack of appreciation was always puzzling and grievous to me.

As I divulged earlier, I was always envious of my dad's fortune and couldn't comprehend why he didn't share my sentiments. To me, when a child is born into the world with no apparent physical or mental defects, it's something to celebrate. But, unfortunately, that was a feeling that was attributed to one of Melvin Harris's little boys, but not him.

There was one thing I was very certain of, however, and it was in regards to my mother. Seemingly, she and I was on the same wavelength. Whether she gave birth to a boy or a girl, she said she always thanked God for having a healthy child because, after all, there was no guarantee attached to the process. Therefore, she took nothing for granted and felt extremely fortunate.

After a while, it became clear to me (even as a little boy) that Melvin V. Harris was entirely incapable of altering his standard mind-set or his everyday lifestyle. Even after he learned that Ruby was pregnant for a sixth time, he still drank excessively, still stayed out till the wee hours of the night and still engaged in his usual philandering. To some degree, he curtailed his physical abuse, but, other than that, he stayed true to form.

Notably and unfortunately too, I can personally attest to the old man's habitual penchant for fooling around with outside women. However, it had nothing to do with my 'gainful' spying mechanism and, in addition, didn't require my having to leave the vicinity of our house on Sullivan street either.

There came a time when I lost interest in my father's dallying and blatant indiscretions. Little did I realize, however, that some acts of deception have a mind of its own. Moreover, it is, sometimes, capable of seeking others out.

Superseding the happening that I'm about to recount is an unusual, personal admission. That is, if it's a crime to be a 'mamma's boy,' then I'm happy to plead guilty to it. To be absolutely truthful, my four brothers could, probably, be convicted to the same offense.

Traditionally, I was always trying to make life easier for my brothers and our mother, especially Mom. Oftentimes, when Ruby was still trying to work (even when she was expecting), I would do something to try to lighten her daily burdens. And whether it was trying to cook something for dinner (which I wasn't very good at), washing and ironing our clothes (thanks to our in-house washing machine) or making up the beds, I did it without being asked.

On one fateful, workday morning, Ruby wasn't feeling very well. She not only verbally announced it, she looked the part and went on to haphazardly make up her bed. That was entirely out of character for our mother because she was a real stickler at leaving the master bedroom tidy. So, since I was home from school and nothing that interested me was showing on TV, I decided to try and make things right. All I desired was to see my mother smile when she returned home from work. My good intentions, though, soon rendered me shocked and depressed as well.

When I removed the spread from my parent's bed, I decided to add an extra touch to my sprucing up chore. Instead of neatly affixing the bed sheets, I elected to change the bedding altogether. (Actually, I had ironed up a bunch of sheets the day before). However, when I proceeded to remove the bottom sheet, something fell to the floor.

And since it came from my mom's side of the bed, I figured right away that it belonged to her. In addition, due to the fact that my father never made it his business to straighten up any bed, I quickly surmised, too, that my mother was almost positive that her husband would never stumble upon it either.

To be sure, my father would not have been 'totally' surprised if he had found the item in question though. In reality, it wasn't something that he wasn't acutely aware of. Instead, his individual surprise would come directly from learning that his long-time wife was in possession of the subject item. Of course, those were my after-the-fact thoughts.

When I knelt down to retrieve the item and took a moment to scrutinize it, I soon shook my head in amazement and seething anger. And, then, as I slowly took a seat upon the still-unmade bed, I focused on my mother and that's when my tears began to fall.

In my hand was a black and white photograph, an amateurish one, at best. But depicted on it was two people I instantly recognized. The first person was my father and the second one, owing to my former visits to Duck's Bar on Newstead Avenue, was a light-skinned woman I had seen and met several times before. Both, my dad and his female companion were topless (although the lady was wearing a brassiere and a slip), but that, in itself, wasn't especially shocking to me. As both adults looked as proud as a couple of peacocks, my father was holding an arm-baby, a newborn who could not have been over a month or two old. That, of course, was the source of my personal anxiety and heartbreak. But, less than a minute later, my deepest sorrow shifted over to my mother.

Frankly, I don't know what other kids might have done in the face of discovering such a revealing and damning photo, and neither did I know what any of my brothers would have done either, but I almost immediately decided what I would do. Nothing!

Since Ruby already had the photo in her possession, I figured the damage was already done. And I wasn't about to heap anguish on top anguish, or even make Ruby feel even worse by letting her know that I found concrete proof of the old man's ultimate-infidelity.

Therefore, I chose to pretend complete ignorance. So, instead of changing the bed sheets, I carefully placed the picture back under the mattress, straightened the old sheets out and made up the bed. Many years went by the boards before I spoke of the matter with my mom or anyone else.

Now, I'm not positive but I imagine that my actions, or inactions, rang somewhat strange to the ears of a lot of people. I imprisoned the memory of that photo in my mind for a long, long time. But I admit to being a strange little kid. I've never been able to fathom hurting people I dearly love and cherish. That also explains why, though I was positive Ruby was carrying a sixth child when the photo issue transpired, I never took it upon myself to ask her why she did not have the baby. I didn't have the heart.

Again, I was well-grown before my curiosity was sated in regards to that yesteryear mystery. According to my mother, she 'discovered' that incriminating photograph in the midst of her sixth pregnancy (finding it inside one of Dad's suit coat pockets) and, to add insult to injury, it was just a couple of days after the old man had boisterously declared, "I don't want no more damn kids!" Therefore, rather than carry the child to term, Mom stayed completely silent when it came to the photo and, reluctantly, submitted herself to an abortion instead. She added, she never forgave herself for that decision.

As for me, in spite of my own decision to stay mum regarding that revealing photograph, whatever love I had for my father was seriously damaged. I could not bring myself to hate the man, but my affection and respect for him was gradually slipping away. Over and over again, I would pose a series of questions to myself. What kind of cruel, insensitive monster did me and my brothers have as a dad? How could he do what he does? And, in God's name, what drives a man like Melvin V. Harris?

As a matter of reference, I have, yet, to come across any rational answers to those queries. For a short while I even faulted the living God for installing the old man into my life in the first place. Then, I reasoned, perhaps I would do well, upon being just and fair about it, if I left God's name out of the equation altogether. Subsequently, I became reconciled to the belief that my father was operating on a different plane and level, and one that was expressly controlled by a very sinister being. For if God is real (and I truly believe He Is), then Satan is also.

Upon looking back, however, out of everything my dad did during his toxic years with his maiden family; the physical and mental devastation, the frequent deceptions and out-and-out lies, and his recklessness in pitting one brother against another brother - I consider the photograph episode (along with its residual fallout) to be the grand topper, my personal perceived number one.

Though it might seem weird to others, I compare it to the infamous slaying of Shakespeare's 'Julius Caesar.' When Brutus, a fellow Roman whom Caesar regarded as a 'true' friend, plunged his dagger into Caesar's blood-soaked body, it was labelled as, "the most unkindest cut of all." And as far as I was concerned, that damning photograph, paired with Ruby's grievous and long-time regretful abortion determination, was the epitome of my father's wrongdoing and vices. In essence, it was the most unkindest act of them all!

CHAPTER FOURTEEN
AN AUDACIOUS BEHAVIOR

In the same time-frame of my discovering that my Dad had fathered a child outside of his marriage (at the time, I was not aware of the sex of the baby), I learned that Ruby's older sister, Hannah, and her family were no longer residing in Carr Square Village, located in downtown St. Louis. I, along with a couple of my brothers were somewhat saddened because we had grown fond of frequently visiting our cousins in their long time home setting and, in addition, it would, subsequently, disrupt our access to the neighboring Carson girls as well. They were the daughters of Jacob Carson, the man my father kidded with about the 'left hip' premise.

However, in spite of the sentimentality of the visiting Harris boys, the relocating Strickland family appeared to be collectively glad about the transition. Instead of living in a rather cramped apartment dwelling (as I mentioned, my aunt and uncle also had five children), they had paid down on a three-story house which was located in the western portion of Saint Louis city. Seemingly, it was a virtual blessing to all of them, and especially for my Uncle

Bill and cousin Pauline, who was the eldest of two daughters. To be precise, Pauline, who was a registered nurse, and Uncle Bill were the major contributors behind the undertaking.

While Aunt Hannah filled the role of a stay-at-home 'housewife' and mother, Uncle Bill held two, separate jobs. He worked almost seven hours on a moving van during the day, came home for about an hour, ate a hardy supper and, then, pulled an eight-hour evening shift as a laborer at a facility called 'Scullin's Steel.' Both of those jobs epitomized manual labor and sheer grit and, even as a little boy, I was in complete awe of the man. And so was my mom, Ruby, and she didn't mind telling him so.

Fortunately, my mother's admiration for her hard working brother-in-law was reciprocal. There was a considerable age difference between the pair and my uncle appeared to regard Ruby as a cherished younger sister who, as a little girl, was on the scene when he was courting Aunt Hannah in Fredericktown, Missouri (during a time that Bill Strickland called "way back when").

However, not only did my uncle like my mother for sentimental value, he esteemed her for her gentle sincerity and her ever-present sense of humor. Unlike his long time spouse, Hannah, who could come across as belligerent and somewhat crude from time to time (and especially when it came to her own husband), my mom had a real knack for making him smile and, sometimes, laugh out loud. And for a man who seemed to be forever on the 'go' and working, I delighted in seeing Uncle Bill happy and content.

Meanwhile, even as the Strickland clan settled in at 1372 Burd Avenue (that was their new address), my personal well-being was steadily on the decline. Even as I became more proficient in singing "Oh - My Papa." my papa, himself, was seldomly seen by me or any of my brothers. After coming across that telling photograph, I made it a point to never visit his tavern haunts again and I made a conscience decision to devote the bulk of my attention to Ruby and my quartet of brothers.

In a manner of speaking, however, and especially during 1953 and early 1954, Melvin V. Harris was more of an occasional visitor at our Sullivan home than an actual resider. And even when he was physically present, his mind and heart seemed to be elsewhere. Observing him, I would silently ask myself, "If he doesn't want to be here, why doesn't he just go?" And, finally, after a slew of episodes of going out at night, and not coming back home for days on end, he was gone. In a way, I was sad, but in another way, I was relieved and glad. Even if the old man no longer loved my mom, Ruby did not deserve his unpredictable conduct. Again, my heart went out to our mother. After all, she couldn't disappear at-will or abandon ship like our errant father did. Thankfully, she was in it for the long haul.

Now, if a strong degree of coldness is evident in my foregoing observations, then I make no apologies for it. I'm certain it's because (over the years) I've known too many men who walked away from a broken marriage and acted like the children were solely a part of their former wife's community property. Of course, I've known some men who did not fit that mold but, regretfully, our old man wasn't one of them.

Incidentally, before my father made his final exit, he apparently deemed it appropriate and necessary to add a 'small' postlude to his departure. Within the same week of withstanding another degrading visit from our assigned welfare worker (who was a snobbish-acting racist white woman), Melvin Harris obviously thought it was high-time for his other five sons to become aware and acquainted with his toddler son.

While I was immediately resentful (a behavior that I was later ashamed of), my quartet of brothers were initially in denial. Since they had not seen the aforementioned photo, they were taken aback by dad's bold 'surprise.' I, on the other hand, could and should have been nicer to the kid. To be fair (which was an afterthought), the little boy was an innocent bystander and he hadn't done anything wrong. Hell, he was barely two years old!

Of course, I wasn't actually upset with the youngster. But it was another matter with my dad. While Ruby was in our nearby house, busily cooking dinner, here was my proud and audacious father at his insensitive best. He was standing offside our front yard, boldly parading around his outside child and acting like it was 'highly appropriate.' Well, I didn't think it was and I'm sure he was aware of my feelings. He arrogantly dismissed them, however, and proceeded to compound my anger by becoming dictatorial.

While my brothers elected to keep their distance from our old man, Dad concentrated on me, demanding, "This is your baby brother, Keith, and I want you to love him!" "Well, I don't," I quickly countered. "I don't know him and I don't much like him!"

Apparently, the little boy somehow deduced he was being insulted. (Maybe it was due to my incensed tone). Because even before 'our' daddy could respond to my gruff words, the kid opted to 'spit' on me! I couldn't believe it and, obviously, neither could Dad. I wanted to laugh, but I chose not to.

"What the hell's wrong with you, Keith?" the old man remarked, looking down and smacking the back of the kid's head. "Tell your brother you're sorry, and right now!"

I was still somewhat upset. "He don't have to, and I don't even care," I insisted. "And he ain't my brother, he ain't!"

Little Keith apologized, even though he was bawling profusely. And although I was too stubborn and anguished to admit to it, I felt sorry for him. Even as a child myself, I could never bare to see another kid crying. I actually wanted to stoop down and hug him! However, before I resorted to tears myself, I turned away and, then, rushed into the adjacent house. And despite my dad calling out to me several times, I refused to yield. Sorrowfully, over ten years would pass by before I was to lay my eyes on little Keith again.

CHAPTER FIFTEEN
FEAR OF THE UNKNOWN

From time to time, my mother would say, "When God closes one door, He would soon open up another." Although I never knew who actually authored that quote, I was sure it was Mom's way of being ever so hopeful and optimistic, no matter what problem or setback arose. Like the time when she quoted Scarlet O'Hara to me, stating, "Tomorrow is another day." Ruby wasn't an individual who allowed life to get her down and leave her languishing there. To my mother's great credit, her glass was always half full.

Regretfully, I, as Ruby's second son, found it difficult to share her optimism. I wanted to, but the actions and inactions of a fellow named Melvin Harris kept me in a state of worriment. The marriage between my parents was essentially over and there was nothing I or anyone else could do about it. Though I had no hope or burning desire that reconciliation was possible, I greatly feared the immediate future.

Not at all surprisingly, my Dad was the focal point of my fret. Since our father was deficient and substandard even as a in-home dad, I wondered what kind of father would he be if he were no longer in our immediate midst. It didn't take long, however, to realize some aspects of my wonder.

When that snooty welfare worker initially invaded our lives on Sullivan street (verbally lambasting us for the audacity for having a television), I knew exactly what type of dad the old man would be; not only an absentee one but one who would eventually be 'missing in action.' I wish I could claim I was disappointed or even disenchanted but I cannot. When it came to my father, it was par for the course.

For a good while, the living status of my family remained about the same. We continued to eat sufficiently (a lot of bread puddings and suppers consisting of northern beans, ham hocks or neck bones and corn bread) and thanks to our in-house washing machine and an iron, we continued to wear clean and well-pressed clothing. In addition, (when we weren't hiding it from that white welfare agent), we were able to turn to the TV for light entertainment. In fact, I could finally watch 'The Cisco Kid.'

Meanwhile, I continued to haul groceries on Saturdays, sell newspapers on Sunday mornings and, when time permitted, interact with my brothers in various ways. Sometimes, on Sunday afternoons, we'd pair-up and go to the movies together, we'd collectively go swimming or fishing at the not too distant Fairgrounds Park and, on occasion, engage in what my brothers and I called 'junking.'

Essentially, that meant we'd come together (mostly during the summer) and, with a couple of wagons in tow, would embark upon a long and, oftentimes, fruitful journey. Strolling down alleys and side streets, and searching through ash pits and trash cans, we would find one treasure after another. And although most people might regard the discarded items as 'junk,' my four brothers and I relished their potential. We were all confident that our brother, Gary, could convert that so-called junk into functional treasures, and mainly 'toys' that we came to regard as 'good as new.' No matter how far our search and find journey took us from Sullivan street, we enjoyed it to the very hilt.

Little did we know during those particular days, as our mother struggled to make ends meet and my brothers and I, to our overall embetterment, found ourselves in a more humane and civil environment, that circumstances were on a course of rapid change, but a change that was exceedingly drastic and rather somber as well.

Even though Ruby continued to work at Homer G. Phillips Hospital and was actively receiving public assistance, her efforts to continually come up with the monthly rent fee for our Sullivan street domicile was becoming more and more challenging. However, although the change factor would eventually help lighten her financial load, the unexpected catalyst that launched that sudden alteration was one of a heart-crushing magnitude. In the summer of 1954, Ruby's older sister, Hannah, suffered a massive stroke and passed away. Tragically, the Strickland family was not in their new home a good four months before Aunt Hannah died.

To say I was sorry in regards to my aunt's sudden death, is putting it mildly. My emotions overtook me and I cried profusely and prolongingly. Up until that time, I had never incurred that kind of loss and I had never attended a funeral either. However, my personal lament had an underlying component to it. I found myself wrestling with what I felt was the sheer injustice of it all. My heart went out to all of my cousins and especially to Carol and Lloyd, who were the youngest of the Strickland clan.

And I was deeply sorry for Uncle Bill, a 'good' man who I admired as hard-working and uncommonly decent and virtuous. And I was positive he dearly loved his wife and five children. So why, I silently asked God, would such a man be subjected to such a heartbreaking and awful fate? It just wasn't fair, I believed, and I couldn't begin to understand it. Although my mom maintained that one should not question God's motives, and at any time, I admit to harboring questions. Even in my state of anguish though, I just prayed that I wasn't becoming anti-God like Melvin Harris. That, to me, would epitomize the entire tragedy.

However, before I became totally entrenched in my lingering anxiety, which was directly in line with my tendency to critically analyze things, another development sprang forth. Shortly after Aunt Hannah had been laid to rest, Ruby called my brothers and me together as a family and informed us that we would no longer reside at 4281 Sullivan. Instead, owing to the compassion and generosity of our Uncle Bill, we would alternately be moving to 1372 Burd Avenue. It was, of course, the three-storied home he had purchased earlier in the year.

Although I was unsure how my mother and brothers felt in regards to our impending move to Burd Avenue (very much like me, I suppose), but I had mixed emotions. I was never any good at leaving people and I was genuinely fond of most of the people who lived on Sullivan and in the immediate area. After all, my brothers and I had long interacted with kids like Curtis Carr, Donald Carey, 'Baby James,' 'Baby Johnny,' and even a boy called 'Baby Junior.' Through the years, we played with those kids and, sometimes, fought with them too.

Then, there were long time neighbors; like the Browns, the Colemans, the Sykes family, the Moores, the Flanagans and even Milton Jones and his wife, Marie. All of them, I greatly cared about and hated saying farewell to them. In addition, it wasn't just the people I regretted leaving. It was the surrounding area itself, together with its array of amenities. I would certainly miss the fifteen cents fish sandwiches from Ivory's Fish Shack, the occasional chicken dinners from a restaurant known as 'Sara Lous' and the tasty hamburgers from the well-known 'Billie Burke's Place.'

And, most definitely, I'd dearly miss, if not, grieve for all of the nearby movie houses, theaters like the Amytis, the Douglas and the Comet, all of them, my personal retreats from a tumultuous and trying childhood. What awaited me, I aimlessly asked myself, when we move to our new residence on Burd Avenue?

For sure, however, in spite of my fear of the unknown (if that's what it boiled down to), I could also see the good aspects of our transition, and especially when it came to Ruby. I knew it would help her financially and I hoped it would help her well-being also. Even at the age of ten, I was cognizant of the fact that trying to raise five children alone was no leisurely picnic.

In fact, I deemed it darn hard, frustrating and hectic as hell! Trying to work her job at the hospital and adequately take care of five sons under the age of twelve was an uphill battle for my mom - and for any mom, for that matter. And although I never heard her complain or gripe, not once, I deeply felt for her. She was a remarkable woman and a dedicated mother and I admired her completely.

I am delighted to report that my feeling of admiration, or exaltation, did not perish singularly at my mother's feet. As I stated priorly, well before I even fathomed the possibility of the Harris family ever living under the same roof with the Strickland clan, I held the utmost esteem for my Uncle Bill. He was everything I aspired to be as an adult. He was a good husband, a good father, a good provider, and a man of simple virtue. And more impressive to me, although he shared a smoking habit with Melvin Harris, the similarity between the two men ended there. And I joyously celebrated that fact!

To be even more precise, William 'Bill' Strickland and my father, Melvin V. Harris, were at opposing poles. While my dad was considered to be extremely handsome (and not only by his self), Uncle Bill was not. Although my uncle sported a muscular frame (and he was as strong as an ox), he also had a rather elongated head and was noticeably cockeyed. Seemingly, he could be squarely facing a person and actually looking elsewhere.

But it may sound funny or somewhat peculiar, but people appeared to have no problem whatsoever adjusting to his unusual glance. However, in spite of his sometimes squinting eyes, his common sense approach and soft-spoken manner catapulted him above most men I ever knew. That, too, along with his refusal to say profane words distanced him even farther from the man I grew up calling "Daddy."

The latter quality, my uncle's insistence upon not cussing (or cursing), was quite fascinating to me. Almost everyone I knew cussed, even kids. Notably, my father spewed out profanity like a drunken sailor. But other than saying that something was "blame" (such as 'blame-fool' or 'blame stupid'), or calling nonsense "boogey-joogey" or a "bunch of malarkey," Uncle Bill hardly ever said anything mean-spirited or intentionally unkind. Plus, a person always knew where he or she stood with him. In Bill Strickland's world you were either <u>right</u> or you were <u>wrong</u>, and nothing in between. Either <u>black</u> or <u>white</u>, and no visible gray. And, believe me, whenever a person interacted with my uncle, they longed to be on his 'right side.' Occasionally, they would be privy to a staunch lecture from him, sometimes, come away feeling like they had been through holy hell!

Now, I would like to say that Uncle Bill's offsprings were carbon copies of their father (all of them, save Carol, who was

Gary's age, were older than us Harris boys), but I'd be lying in my teeth. They inherited 'some' of their dad's commendable virtues but, with the exception of Lloyd (who was the youngest of his three sons), they were the loudest, most argumentative and the 'cussingest' individuals I ever came to know. However, unlike their Uncle Melvin, who regularly resorted to profanity in times of anger, the older Strickland siblings seemed to cuss for the mere sake of it. Whether they were talking to strangers, friends or even each other, profanity rolled off of their tongues like saliva. Borrowing Ruby's words, my cousins "cussed without provocation."

Although I could claim that the elder Stricklands were oddities or try and credit their vulgar language to the raw streets of Saint Louis, I'd be fantasizing and fooling myself. Fact was, with no disrespect on my part, their mother (and our Aunt Hannah) could cuss to a fare-the-well herself. And unfortunately (and always to my onlooking awe), when it came to her long time husband, Bill Strickland, she had no qualms about spewing her profanity in his direction either.

Though Uncle Bill remained unresponsive during those episodes and appeared to take his wife's insults in stride, Aunt Hannah was subject to call him some God-awful names and seemingly without reservations! I mean she would call him things like "long-headed motherfucker" or "cockeyed son-of-a-bitch" and appear to think nothing of it. And then, only minutes afterwards, she would smilingly rebound with terms of endearment. She would refer to him as "Honey," "Baby" and, sometimes, "Sweetheart" and then proceed to set a piping-hot plate of food in front of him. And while it was a bit bizarre and almost outrageous to others, it came across as 'normal' and 'lackluster' to the Strickland siblings.

During those instances (and they were frequent), I, as an observer, would always tense-up, somewhat fearful that Uncle Bill would angrily and violently retaliate (of course, Melvin V. Harris was still afoot during those times), but he never did. Meanwhile, my cousins, in spite of being right in the vicinity in the wake of those episodes too, showed no reactions whatsoever. I guess they were used to it.

I know it sounds as if I'm criticizing my deceased aunt, but I beg to differ. When I grieved over her sudden death, I genuinely loved her, still do. Basically, she was a nice person and was very fun-loving. She loved to laugh, loved to cook, like to kid-around (as did Ruby) and she thoroughly enjoyed having outside company. I always looked forward to our frequent visits to their downtown home and the same applied to my mom and brothers.

However, regardless of my personal affection for Aunt Hannah, I could not suppress my puzzlement when it came to how she treated Uncle Bill. Contrarily, she was exceptionally nice to everyone else, including her five offsprings. I couldn't understand it, none of it, but I sincerely wanted to. Because, in reality, I adored them both.

Although I was tempted to tell my mother about my heartfelt feelings about the matter, I never pressed her on it. I figured she would only say something like, "Just keep on living, Son" (she often cited those words when she couldn't come up with a definitive answer), and I would emerge even more confused and frustrated than ever. But the time came, without me uttering a single word about the 'controversy' within the Strickland household, when my mother elected to casually weigh in on it.

"Duke, I know your Aunt Hannah sounds a little harsh and mean-spirited when she, sometimes, talks to your Uncle Bill," she commented, "but her bark is really bigger than her bite. It's just her way and . . . she just be talking. Bill don't pay her no never-mind, thank God. But, do you know what? Let somebody else call theirselves talking about her husband and she will bite their head off, chew 'em out soundly. My sister's funny that way, always has been."

If Ruby had invoked her "Just keep living" adage when speaking of her brother-in-law and older sister, it would have, eventually, proved appropriate. By continuing to live and, alternately, move in with the Strickland clan, I grew to not 'fully' understand certain things, but to, somehow, put matters into a different perspective. As simple as it might sound, I came to believe that sporadic crudeness and vulgarity was just the Strickland's 'way.' Right up there with their collective cigarette smoking habit (initially, they all, save Carol, smoked almost profusely), it was a standard way of life for them. And they appeared to relish that life. By contrast, however, the Harris family was altogether different from them; not better or more decent and, certainly, not more likable or lovable, but surface-wise different.

Owing mostly to the long-time wrath and naked rage of our biological father (although he was no longer physically relevant), we knew first-hand just how harmful and devastating profane names could be and we conditionally cringed and practically shrieked whenever we were within earshot of them. Therefore, in our former environment (inside that tin house on Sullivan street), boisterous vulgarity traditionally coincided with acts of physical violence. Unfortunately, the Strickland clan was not aware "from whence the Harris's had come."

CHAPTER SIXTEEN
THE HOUSE THAT JACK BUILT

Making the move from Sullivan street to Burd Avenue was almost like culture shock. When we resided on Sullivan, especially when Melvin Harris was not around, it was an atmosphere of quietude and calm. Except for neighboring kids getting into occasional scrapes and fisticuffs, it was traditionally peaceful and void of the usual city fanfare. With the absence of the old man (specifically the last two years of life on Sullivan), even the makeshift boxing ring had disappeared. Small patches of grass could be spotted in our front yard.

However, Burd Avenue, thanks to our rather free-spirited cousins, was often a place of bustling activity and, sometimes, loud merriment. In addition to having a parade of visitors coming in and out of our house (friends, neighbors, well-wishers, etc.), we garnered a certain notoriety. If a person was within a block of our 1372 address, that individual would know we were present.

Our eldest male cousin, Billy (often called 'Buddy'), was an avid jazz lover and he, obviously, felt that the outside world shared his sentiments. Everyone in the neighborhood (and, probably, in surrounding neighborhoods too), was aware that Billy had a very loud and powerful high-fidelity phonograph. And even when a jazz record was not on its turntable, the sound emitted by it was practically deafening. So, needless to say, the entire Strickland family was fond of loud music.

Naturally, my family did not rock the proverbial boat. After a short while, we not only adjusted to the Strickland 'way,' we embraced it. At least, I did. I got used to walking 'down' or 'up' the street and hearing blaring music, I became somewhat immune to the frequent profanity that flowed from the mouths of my animated older cousins and I was adept at quickly removing myself from areas inside the house that contained excessive cigarette or cigar smoke. For the most part, I relished our new environment.

Living with the Strickland clan was hardly a leisurely walk in the park though. For one thing, our cousin, Pauline, was a notorious 'hollower.' She habitually yelled at us kids, spicing her rant with a profane name or two, and since she weighed nearly 300 pounds, we weren't inclined to challenge her. I, along with three of my brothers, were able to withstand her hostile words but, sadly, she scared our baby 'bro,' Taran, to death. Recalling Ruby's assessment of Aunt Hannah, I came to believe that Pauline's bark was bigger than her bite too. But, of course, little Ty didn't see it that way. He was only five years old and was somewhat fragile. Plus, he was still brooding over our long gone father.

In one respect, our baby brother had something very much in common with the youngest Strickland boy. Lloyd, who was often called 'Lloyd Henry,' was severely struggling with the death of his mother. Even as a ten-year-old, I could almost reach out and touch his weighty grief. From the moment we took up residence at 1372 Burd Avenue, my heart ached for him. Furthermore, from the get-go, I felt he was a taste resentful or begrudging towards my family.

Whether it was true or a figment of my imagination, I perceived him to have major misgivings regarding us. I imagined him questioning, "If my mom had not passed away, would the Harris family even had been invited to share their home in the first place?" However, if I was totally off the mark regarding my feelings (admittedly, I'm capable of being too sensitive), I still felt somewhat uneasy around Lloyd. But I was hopeful and optimistic that the passing of time would eventually remedy my discomfort.

In contrast, when it came to both, Billy and Gerald (the older Strickland brothers), my siblings and I liked them a great deal. Billy, or Buddy, epitomized the description 'cool, calm and collect' and impressed us with his impeccable dress attire. He seemed to fancy himself as a lady's man, so I, sometimes, compared him to Melvin V. Harris. Of course, Billy was not nearly as conceited as my dad (that was an understatement), but he was cocky enough. Plus, unlike his brother, Gerald, he was median built and looked very snazzy in his clothes. He occasionally walked around the house wearing an athletic undershirt, boxer shorts, and shoes and socks with garters. And I viewed that as odd because, after all, he would eventually have to put his trousers on. And I deemed that a difficult task since he was already wearing laced-up dress shoes. But I was just a busybody young kid, so what did I know?

Although cousin Gerald was as large as his oldest sister, Pauline (Gerald also looked like he tipped the weight scale at 300 pounds), he was, surprisingly, agile and, more commendable, was pleasant and fun to be around. Obviously, he liked kids and my brothers and I knew it. He also liked to tell jokes (some of them, off color), teach us various card games and scare children out of their wits.

He often would assemble me and my brothers in the downstairs living room, render the immediate area pitch-black and proceed to tell us some of the most macabre and horrendous stories he could possibly concoct. And he could come up with some whoppers, replete with his own simulated sound effects, and manage to frighten some of us silly, and especially the little Harris's. Gerald was a born and gifted storyteller and we loved being in his presence.

Unfortunately though, even as small children, my cousin, Carol, and I could not get along. Well before we came to live under the same roof, she and I had numerous squabbles. We'd even resort to fistfights from time to time and since she had some advantages, she was mostly victorious. Not only was she older and bigger than I was, I could not bring myself to be fiercely aggressive with her. Although Carol marvelled over her Uncle Melvin's good looks, she was completely unaware of his volatile and brutal nature. To me, hitting any female was inexcusable and cowardly also. And I was adamant (if not, dogmatic) about not being like my father.

However, Carol 'Ann' (which was her given name) and I did have a few things in common, things that helped us to co-exist. We both enjoyed movies at the theater and the ones shown on television as well, we were both fascinated with film stars in general (mention any movie and we both could recall the leading actors in it), we frequently watched TV and, most apparent, we were two beings with very deep emotions. To be even more exact, we were both deeply sentimental and empathetic.

As a matter of point, Carol and I were well-aware of every movie that aired on network television and whether it was of the horror genre (and some of them would greatly frighten cousin Carol), or a comedy, or otherwise, we would meet up in the first floor living room (which was the site of the TV) and give the slated feature our undivided attention. And, occasionally, we'd have popcorn or some other snack item.

During the majority of times, Carol and I liked having other people join us in our television watching and whether they were my brothers, Carol's siblings or anyone else, it made little difference to us. But there was one particular movie that neither Carol nor I felt comfortable or at ease when viewing it with others. We certainly couldn't bar others from the living room whenever the film was televised, but we silently wished we could. The name of that film was 'The Fighting Sullivans," and, not that it would have made a great difference to Carol or me, it was essentially a true story.

The Fighting Sullivans was a movie that focused on the lives of five, close-knit brothers, a single sister and a loving mother and father. It depicted most of the boy's childhood misadventures, their everyday familial lives and proceeded to go on and capture their young adult period as well. For the most part, it was a feel-good and inspiring tale, a story that touched one's emotions and induced some viewers to virtually fall in love with the entire Sullivan family. That, in itself, precisely explained the adoration shared by myself and my cousin Carol.

As I mentioned though, The Fighting Sullivans was nonfictional, so there was no fairy tale ending in the mix. When World War 2 was underway, essentially in the aftermath of the Pearl Harbor attack, the Sullivan brothers were feeling patriotic and dutiful. Therefore, they soon came together and decided to enlist in the United States Navy. Not just some of them, but all of them - even the youngest brother who happened to be married and the father of a small child.

The Sullivan brothers went down to the local induction office together, signed up one after the other, and insisted upon a single, ironclad stipulation: No matter where they would alternately serve, they would all have to remain physically together. And although the navy officials were somewhat leery of the Sullivan boy's unusual condition, they eventually gave in to it.

Well, I would like to be able to say that there was a sweet and fulfilling ending to the movie; some soothing and uplifting salvation to it, but I didn't feel that way. Obviously, neither did Carol Ann. The five Sullivan boys were killed-in-action together, serving aboard a ship that was torpedoed. That factor was grievous and pitiful enough, but when a naval officer (played by actor, Ward Bond) went to the Sullivan home, bearing that horrendous news, it was excruciatingly heartbreaking to, both, Carol and myself.

Furthermore, when the officer broke the news to the parents that all five brothers had died, we were both heavily weeping. An onlooker would have surmised that my cousin, Carol, and I personally knew the Sullivan boys. Personally, I have seen a whole slew of sad films during my lifetime (movies like 'Stella Dallas,' 'Leave Her to Heaven' and 'Imitation of Life') and I even overcame my yesteryear inclination to shed tears over them, but, admittedly, I still cry profusely whenever I see The Fighting Sullivans. And, certainly, it has everything to do with my having four brothers and my deep love for them. However, over the years I also came to see and appreciate the silver lining in regards to that heart-tugging, yesteryear film. Due solely to the awful plight of the Sullivan brothers, the entire United States military apparatus decided against allowing all the members of an individual American family to serve in a war zone. I never discussed it with Carol, but I derived a certain solace from that determination.

As time marched forward, the Strickland and Harris families came to pleasantly coexist and co-mingle in the three-storied house located on Burd Avenue. In the beginning, my family was afforded the entire second floor; we ate, slept and lounged there as well. Then, as the months rolled by, we were almost given the run of the entire house. As kids we'd explore the third floor (which was all bedrooms), watch television in the first floor living room (although we still had our small Philco TV), play in the basement and enjoy a lot of activities in the large backyard.

Oftentimes, my brother, Gary, who was always skillful with his hands, could be found in that backyard and busily working on some kind of contraption or another. Seemingly, Gary could build everything from a slingshot to a skate-truck and he took great pride in his diligence and workmanship.

Significantly, and quite vital to a rather haunting memory, one of the contraptions erected by Gary was a pair of very tall stilts. I wasn't any good at building things, but I felt that even I could have made them. Apparently, all it required was two sturdy and elongated planks of wood (similar to what was considered two-by-fours), a couple of small pieces of wood to stand on, and a hammer and nails. Although it might have taken me a day or two to assemble those stilts, Gary finished them up in about an hour. Incidentally, the stilts were so tall they could only be mounted from the top of the back porch.

Unfortunately, the pair of stilts I'm referring to did not last very long. But it wasn't due to shoddy workmanship or because they were fragile either. Instead, it was solely due to a measure of bullying and, in my viewpoint, an act of human meanness.

Our cousin, Buddy, was basically a nice guy, but he didn't have much patience with kids or, maybe, he had forgotten when he was one. I surmised that because he frequently fussed at us Harris boys for leaving toys and stuff around in 'inappropriate' or 'unacceptable' places. Of course, that was in accordance to Buddy's discretion. In general, he accused us kids of 'cluttering up' the backyard.

Well, on one fateful afternoon, shortly after Buddy (or Billy) had singled out Gary and had read the riot act to him for leaving the stilts lying around in the yard, he had, apparently, gotten fed up with verbally assailing my oldest brother about the same oversight. (I guess he thought Gary was disrespecting him).

At any event, Buddy became so furious he grabbed a hatchet from the basement and headed directly to the adjacent backyard. And once there, behaving like a raving maniac, he began hacking away at Gary's stilts. Then, as Gary, Carol and I stood in the yard, observing his angry actions, Buddy rose to his feet and strutted back towards the basement. And via his facial expression, he seemed to be highly satisfied in the wake of his deed.

Now, I had no idea how Carol felt about her eldest brother's actions, but I was pissed off at him. I deemed it wrong and evil. However, Gary was visually livid! In fact, Gary was so upset and so angry, I instantly foresaw his ensuing behavior. Thinking nothing of it, Buddy had left the hatchet lying next to the chopped up stilts. And with a face of genuine rage, Gary ran over and retrieved it just as Buddy began to descend the basement steps. And I shouted at my unsuspecting cousin, and just a split second before Gary violently hurled that axe at him.

"Buddy, look out!" I frantically yelled. Fortunately, and thanks to an onlooking God, Buddy not only heeded my warning and 'looked out,' he instantly ducked his head. Had he not, I shudder to think what could have really happened. And that distinctly describes how Carol and the would-be victim, Buddy himself, felt in the immediate aftermath of the hatchet event. Buddy was physically trembling and he had cause to. When he stood back erect and then affixed his eyes to the basement's wooden entrance door, there rested the recently hurled axe. It was solidly embedded in the door frame.

For a brief moment, I was fearful Buddy would try to physically respond to Gary's actions, but I was wrong. He looked directly at Gary, who still displayed an incensed face, and then slowly opened the basement door (the hatchet, still in place) and walked inside. Apparently in a state of shock, Buddy did not utter a single, solitary word.

In the very short, and serene, aftermath of that harrowing stilt and hatchet incident, I could not refrain from thoroughly analyzing it. "Suppose Buddy had not ducked in time, what would have happened?" was the primary question I posed to myself. "If Gary had killed or had seriously injured our cousin, how would Uncle Bill have reacted?" was yet another query I entertained. After all, it was Buddy's father who had invited my family to reside on Burd Avenue. "If the worse scenario had transpired, how would my uncle be able to cope with such a devastating tragedy?" Once again, I thanked the living God for His presence.

However, I intently focused on my brother, Gary, on that particular day also. By nature, he wasn't unduly violent and he wasn't mean-spirited either. He was just frustrated that day, I reasoned; entirely fed up with people messing over him. And I deduced in that aftermath, and I still believe it till this very day, that it was actually 'Melvin Virgil Harris' he was slinging that axe at, and not Billy Strickland. I truly reasoned, that after all the physical abuse and browbeating Gary endured from our crazed father, he was really striking back at the old man. Upon initiating his destructive actions, Buddy was representative of our estranged dad and he had come chillingly close to paying for an embedded debt he really did not owe.

Although the passing of time, mercifully, allowed that backyard incident to all but fade away, personally I will never, ever forget it. It was an indelible learning experience for me (and could be for others as well). To be precise, it taught me to never tease or taunt people, and no matter how docile or harmless I perceive them to be. Because, in reality (and I'm talking generally now), you don't know what a person has endured or suffered through prior to you interacting with them. I figure that everyone has a breaking point, but no one can predict when it will come into play. As Ruby would aptly put it, "Enough is enough and too much stinks." In other words, an individual can take just so much.

When it came to my Uncle Bill, I suppose some people regarded him as an imposing figure. Although those people would be grossly in error, I could almost understand their misconception. William 'Bill' Strickland was big and brawny (in no way, fat) and in light of his squint-like, indirect gaze, one could feel a little intimidated. However, to me, owing mostly to his gracious act of providing lodging to me and my family, he was a man to admire. Right away I deemed him a role model, and especially since I never had one in real life. To be perfectly frank, up until that particular juncture in my life, all of my heroes were on celluloid (the silver screen) and, sadly, the majority of them were white men.

Basically, Uncle Bill was that serious, no nonsense man I alluded to earlier. Although he liked to laugh, he was in no way a jokester like his son, Gerald. However, in certain ways, mostly unbeknownst to my uncle, he often tickled my funny bone. For example, one time he became very upset with his daughter, Carol. It was mid-afternoon at the time and Carol was walking around in the house, wearing a gown and looking somewhat disheveled.

Apparently flustered, Uncle Bill called himself scolding her when he asked, "Carol Ann, are you sick or something? Here it is pernt ne'er evening time, and here you are, prancing around in your blame nightclothes! Least, by now, you could have washed yo' hair and combed yo' face! I mean - I mean. Girl, you know what I'm trying to say."

Cousin Carol was set to respond and, maybe, offer up a reasonable excuse, but she was momentarily distracted. Admittedly, it was because I was standing nearby and actively laughing in regards to her dad's "comb your face" foul up. However, I wasn't at hand to hear Carol's response because Uncle Bill turned to me at that juncture.

"Boy, you git outta here," he insisted. "Go on outside and play somewheres."

Without any argument or delay, I was gone within mere minutes and I learned that that was wise when it came to my Uncle Bill. Not that he would become abrasive or volatile, but I never wanted to get on his bad side. Still, he made me chuckle from time to time. And a few of those 'times,' oddly enough, evolved around one of Uncle Bill's favorite pastimes, which was none other than smoking a cigarette. For the life of me, I couldn't understand it, but he seemed to thoroughly enjoy it.

Looking back, Bill Strickland seemed to be extremely tired and in working as a furniture mover (I actually observed him singularly carrying a refrigerator up two flights of stairs on his back) and, then, as a steel foundry laborer, he earned the right to be. When he had a rare day off from his night job, he would come home, light up a cigarette and plop down in his favorite easy chair inside the first floor's living room. That's when I and some of my brothers came in. Behaving like kids (and, of course, that's what we were), we would quietly camp out in the adjacent corridor, near the main stairwell, and anxiously anticipate what would come next.

Although our uncle had all the intentions of watching the evening newscast on TV, it was, oftentimes, an exercise in futility. And the Harris boys well-knew it, counted on it, in fact. We also knew that Uncle Bill would soon give way to sleep (due to his weariness) and would likely fail to put out his cigarette first.

Therefore, we, as the nutty and mischievous kids we were, sat silent and listened to our uncle's very loud snoring and waiting for the inevitable. We knew the burning cigarette would abruptly arouse him and (to our shame) that was our primary desire. (Later on in life, I branded our collective behavior cruel and unkind but, at the time, I, along with my brothers, thought it was hilarious).

"Hot-ta-mighty!" Uncle Bill would yell, simultaneously dropping the lit cigarette and slapping at his burned fingers. Then, upon spotting us snickering kids, he'd say something like, "Whatchu little boots lookin' at? Go outside and play somewhere - dad-blamit!" And, naturally, we quickly scattered. But as awful as it was, we found ourselves looking forward to the next time it would occur. In spite of it being a painful experience for our uncle, it seemed funny to us stupid kids.

However, there was another moderately amusing incident that involved our beloved uncle. And, coincidentally, it took place in the same site where the cigarette happening transpired. However, when I seriously thought about it in the ensuing aftermath of it, I did regret I had yielded to laughter.

Sitting in his living room chair and occasionally viewing the TV, Uncle Bill was busy, filling his cigarette lighter with fluid. But since I had seen him performing that task before, I didn't pay much attention to him. That was, not initially. Then, I heard him cry out, "Whoa-hot-ta-mighty!" And when I turned around and alarmingly looked his way, I saw that his entire left hand was aflame! Again, shame on me, but I could not help myself. Upon seeing my uncle as he frantically tried to extinguish the fire by continually smacking at it with his right hand, I was suddenly reduced to laughter. Thankfully, he was successful. Moments later, after the flare up was totally subdued, Uncle Bill was shaking his head and, grinningly, looking in my direction. Apparently, he was chuckling at his self.

Even as my laughter subsided, I still had sense enough to be concerned. "Are you alright, Uncle Bill?" I asked.

"Cain't fault nobody but my blame self, boy" was my uncle's response. "When you ain't payin' attention to whatchu doing, that's what happens. So let that be a lesson to you."

"Yes, Sir, I sure will."

It was quite obvious that William 'Bill' Strickland and I were on the same page regarding the lighter fluid mishap. He had been devoting more attention to the adjacent television set than to the process at-hand. He readily confessed his carelessness and distracted thinking on that particular day. And just as he proposed, it was a learning experience to me.

However, when it came to 'right' and 'spur of the moment' thinking, my uncle later proved to be, both, proficient and decisive in those areas. In fact, in my viewpoint, he proved to be a living and breathing Johnny-on-the-spot.

The foregoing accolade was not a figment of my boyhood imagination either. Instead, it was a direct outgrowth from a life-and-death incident I observed. And when it took place, I emerged completely in awe of my uncle.

Preluding the happening I'm referring to was the fact that we had a foot of standing water in the basement of the house on Burd Avenue. The sewer had backed up and Uncle Bill, instead of hiring a professional plumber, decided to handle the problem himself. (My uncle thought of himself as a 'jack-of-all-trades' and, for the most part, he was pretty adept at fixing various things). On the day I'm recollecting, as I sat on the basement steps watching and staying out of the water, he happened to have his youngest son, Lloyd Henry, assisting him.

Well, I had no idea what cousin Lloyd was thinking about (or, if he was thinking at all), but there was a light bulb dangling right above his head. It wasn't illuminated, however, because it had to be further screwed into the socket to yield light. As it transpired, without uttering a single word to his father (who was nearby and looking downward at that precise moment), Lloyd reached up and proceeded to twist the bulb in. I was instantly shocked speechless while poor Lloyd was in the throes of being literally shocked, if not being purely electrocuted! With my mouth hanging open, I never seen anything like it before. Lloyd was physically vibrating and gyrating!

Thank God though, totally unlike me, my Uncle Bill had obviously seen such an alarming sight before. However, even more than that, he knew exactly what to do. As cousin Lloyd shook violently, with his hand still actively affixed to the light bulb, his father reared back and delivered a thudding blow to Lloyd's chest. And that, fortunately, knocked Lloyd loose, therefore sending him reeling backwards to the water-filled floor.

Alternately, Lloyd Henry went on to be fine and, seemingly, emerged with no lingering ill effects. But to say the least, he was one blessed young man. He was blessed and fortunate to have had a wise and quick-thinking father on hand to save his life. And although I pre-surmised the forthcoming answer, I later asked my uncle why he elected to physically punch Lloyd with his fist rather than try to yank him loose. And just as I presumed, Uncle Bill reasoned that if he had grabbed Lloyd, that he, too, would have been zapped with that electric current. So, that incredible happening, too, was a learning lesson for me and, certainly, my cousin Lloyd Henry as well.

In grateful retrospect, out of all the lessons that I learned from Bill Strickland, not only when we lived on Burd Avenue but years afterwards, his penchant for human compassion and uncommon selflessness had the greatest and most enduring impact on me. Obviously, he cared deeply for others; their plight and trials and overall well-being.

And in my mind (as young as it was), my uncle was the first and foremost Christian man I came to know. Even today, after rubbing elbows with numerous men who deemed themselves 'Christians' (clergymen, included), he still tops my list.

Notably, when I sing praises to my uncle, it has little to do with the words he spoke. In fact, he wasn't that big a talker. Neither does it have anything to do with his refusal to spew out profane and spiteful words (though I truly admired that in him). In essence, my admiration and aspirations, had everything to do with his frequent actions; the benevolent and repeat decisions he made to assist and accommodate a diverse group of relatives.

During my family's almost six-year stay in the three-story house on Burd Avenue (from 1954 through 1959), we shared lodging with mom's oldest sister, Blanche (sadly, Aunt Blanche, similar to her sister, Hannah, suffered a fatal stroke there), our teenaged cousin, Doris Nevels, Uncle Bill's bedridden dad (my brothers and I called him "Papa Strickland") and, last, but in no way, least, Uncle Bill's fraternal twin sister, Willie Lou Buckner.

If ever there was a character, it had to be "Aunt Willie" (which she insisted that me and my brothers call her). She was a caretaker to her and Uncle Bill's invalid father and since we Harris's were obliged to share the second floor with Papa Strickland and her, we all became well-acquainted. To me and my family's utter dismay, we also became very familiar with Aunt Willie's rather nagging and aggravating way of communicating with her dad as well. Although a debilitating stroke had rendered the old man essentially speechless, his daughter almost constantly fussed at him.

Just by being in the immediate area during those times were, both, trying and somewhat tortuous. Willie Lou, with her high-pitched voice and a knack for spitting out words a mile-a-minute, managed to make any individual within earshot to suffer just as much as 'Reverend' Strickland did. That's correct, Papa Strickland was a former minister and it was somewhat evident in light of his responses of irritation to his nerve-wracking daughter. He would regularly cry out, "Lawd - Lawd, oh - alright."

Uncle Bill's sister wasn't a bad person though and, in reality, my family and I liked her. She just didn't have a lot of patience with the man she called "Papa." And I came to believe, just like I considered cousin Pauline a natural hollower, Willie Lou Buckner was a natural fusser. So, as time went by, the second floor became a sphere of co-existence.

Upon revisiting those long-ago days, there was one single thing about Aunt Willie that managed to freak me and most of the people in the house out. And up till this very day, I still marvel over it. Aunt Willie worked a daily job when she and her dad resided on Burd Avenue and she, therefore, rose very early in the mornings with the intent of getting to her job on time. That was a good thing because all of us on the second floor shared the bathroom situated on that floor.

In fact, for the most part, Aunt Willie was already in and out the washroom, and headed out the front door when my brothers and I got up to prepare ourselves for school. Prior to leaving, Willie Buckner would regularly take a shower.

Not merely happenstance, but the foregoing information was the focal point of the account I'm on the verge of disclosing. Within virtual minutes of Aunt Willie's morning shower, maybe fifteen minutes at tops, she was dressed, groomed and well-out the front door! Our aunt would be moving so speedily and so frantically, water would be visually dripping from her body upon her departure. In reality, Aunt Willie would barely dry herself and, then, would hurriedly face the outside elements.

To me, it was baffling and phenomenal! Whether it was ninety degrees in the summertime or two below zero in the winter time, it seemed to be immaterial to Aunt Willie. Sure, in the final analysis, it was our aunt's personal business and I don't think anyone spoke to her about her unorthodox and rather bizarre routine. But I must add this: During the many, many months that Willie Buckner and Papa Strickland lived with us at 1372 Burd Avenue, I never remembered her having the sniffles, and let alone a common cold.

CHAPTER SEVENTEEN
CIRCLE OF FRIENDS

Owing to "Brown vs. Board of Education," segregation in America's public schools was outlawed in May of 1954. Therefore, when my brothers and I set our sights on going back to school in September of that same year, we not only anticipated going to an entirely new school but one that would contain white kids as well. Up until that period in our lives, meaning us Harris boys, the only white folks we had interacted with were the Jewish ones who worked at Harry's Delicatessen, located down the street from our house on Sullivan. And that was a rather tepid relationship at best.

    Personally, I was not enthused or impressed with the desegregation premise per se. More than that, since I was always an avid and discerning reader, I knew a great deal about slavery, racism and the general mistreatment of people who looked like me. And I couldn't remotely understand the rationale behind it, not any of it. Therefore, I was not anxious to mingle with so-called 'Caucasians' and I cringed at the possibility of being called a "nigger" by one of them. Eventually though, I made up my mind to put my best foot forward. I resolved to do my level best, but with a mind void of optimism or joyous anticipation.

For to be honest, I would have been content to have remained at Simmons Elementary.

The 'Ralph Waldo Emerson School' was located on a street called Page Avenue. It was less than seven short blocks from our residence on Burd, so walking there every weekday morning was a cinch. Thankfully, there were no busy boulevards along the way, not even any traffic lights, so even the little Harris's (Vaughn and Taran) could walk safely there. Most of the time, however, either Gary, Lovell or myself would walk with them.

When I started at Emerson, I was ten years old and, therefore, at grade level 'five-low' (they had 'low' and 'high' in those days and half-year advancements as well). My first teacher was a white woman, a Mrs. Smithers, and I shortly concluded that she was not very fond of <u>colored</u> or <u>Negroid</u> people. Call me paranoid, but, maybe, if she had elected to identify black people by one of those foregoing racial terms, I would not have been so leery of her feelings. But when Mrs. Smithers deemed us "you people" and with a frequency that was downright aggravating, I was almost positive I was in the presence of my first flesh-and-blood 'bigot.' "Things were much better here before you people came," she'd remark. Or, "I don't know what you people are used to, but we don't do things that way at Emerson."

Well, as things turned out, whether I was right or wrong regarding my first impression of Mrs. Smithers, when January of 1955 came, Mrs. Smithers was no longer teaching at Emerson Elementary. And it certainly was not because she was fired. So, at the tender age of ten, I tasted my first dose of 'white flight.'

Apparently, white flight had a contagious element to it. Additional Caucasian teachers made their exits from Emerson during the next year or so. But the racial exodus was not restricted to just individuals. It also worked its voodoo on institutions. For instance, there was a large, private school just down the street from our Burd Avenue residence and it was less than a hundred yards from our door, in fact. It was called 'Principia' and it had been a prominent staple in the area for numerous years.

Seemingly though, with the dawning of the desegregation era, it - eventually tightly folded up (lock, stock and barrel) and then moved to a distant and affluent location in Saint Louis county. If one wasn't cognizant of the authentic truth, they could have concluded that that learning facility was fleeing leprosy or the bubonic plague or something. Ironically, I was pretty sure that 'Principia' associated itself with something called 'CHRISTIANITY.'

In direct contrast to the departed Mrs. Smithers, my 'five-high' teacher at Emerson Elementary became an endearing favorite of mine. Her name was Brenda Jensen, she was married, had two little girls of her own and she was a Negro. Seemingly, she loved to teach, loved to talk and laugh and, to my delight, came to truly love me.

I almost immediately took to Mrs. Jensen and I instantly felt her feelings were reciprocal. With my curly head of hair as a surface attraction, she kidded me on the first day I made her acquaintance. She smilingly detained me at the close of the school day and, after allowing the other students to vacate the classroom, opted to speak to me. Somehow, I surmised she was going to refer to my hair and I was right about my perception.

"Lionel Harris, where on earth did you get all those beautiful, adorable locks from?" she marvelled. "Your hair is the cat's pajamas, little fella! My little girls would give you a natural fit about 'em."

I don't know why, but I always felt uneasy when someone complimented me about anything. I tried to play off my discomfort by offering up a tease. "The 'cat's pajamas,' that's a new one on me," I smiled. "But you have girls, Mrs. Jensen? How many? I mean - what's their names?"

"Anna and Marsha - but they're a few years younger than you. They're seven and five. But they would fall head over heels in love with you. Those curls!"

Still, I was a mite jittery. All I could think of was, "No boys? Shoot - I've got four brothers, and they're real nice." Mrs. Jensen was still all smiles when she remarked, "Real nice. I guess that means you really like them, huh?"

"Aw, yes, ma'am," I replied. "They're some good guys. And, Ruby, our mother - she's nice too."

Naturally, at that juncture, my teacher inquired about my father. That's when the interaction went south. I didn't want to talk about my dad and, right away, Brenda Jensen deduced it. So, she reissued her smile, casually shook my hand and said she'd look forward to seeing me the next day. I was thankful she didn't press me about my absentee father because it was hurtful to talk about him. I guess, down deep, I still had feelings for him. Why that was, I wasn't exactly sure.

Someone said that, "Time heals all wounds," but I beg to differ with them. Time might heal some wounds, but not all of them. Time does, however, bring about change and when it came to the relationship that I pleasantly formed with Brenda Jensen, change practically snowballed by the minute. She soon regarded me as a stellar student, a born conversationalist and, to her utter joy, a budding humorous. I had a real talent for making her laugh.

The passing of time also proceeded to break down, if not, vanquish, inhibitions in our relationship also. Before long, as Mrs. Jensen found comfort in calling me "Lonnie," I was confiding in her regarding my missing dad and, alternately, I emerged all the better for it. My teacher would manage to ease my pain, assuring me that my old man was the "hands-down loser" in our ongoing estrangement.

"Lonnie, I don't know all of your brothers," she told me one day, speaking with genuine conviction, "but I've seen a couple of them, walking around the school. They're beautiful little boys, just like you. And I'm here to tell you - there's no way, not in a million years, that your father doesn't agonize over his sons. Just by getting to know you, Lonnie, that man is probably beside himself in grief. He misses you boys, more than you could possibly know. And I'd bet real money on that."

Subsequently, I withdrew quiet refuge from many of the analogies put forth by Brenda Jensen. I considered them as wise and basically true. For I, too, subscribed to the belief that Melvin Harris brooded over leaving his five sons behind and upon hearing an adult say it (especially an adult whom I dearly cherished), I felt almost serenely validated. Then, after a while, as I relished hearing Mrs. Jensen say, "I'd love to have a little boy - just like you" and I found comfort in referring to her as "My second mother," the mechanism of heartfelt confiding became reciprocal. In essence, Brenda Jensen shared a few personal things with me and one of them, although she was visually thrilled about it, rendered me somewhat alarmed.

"I'm gonna let you in on something, Lonnie?" she began, "but you have to keep it under your hat, or - in your case, under your curls. It'll be our little secret, alright?"

"You don't have to worry about that, Mrs. Jensen," I proudly replied. "I told you before, I am real good at keeping secrets. You'd be surprised. What is it?"

"Well, remember when I told you that my doctor had cautioned me not to chance having another child?" my teacher asked. "Well, my husband and I prayed on it, and we prayed in earnest to God about it. And guess what, Lonnie? I'm expecting a baby at year's end! Ain't that good news?" Instantly, I was scared and I'm sure I looked scared too. "But why, Mrs. Jensen?" I asked. "Why you gonna take a chance like that? Don't - please don't do it! I'll be your little boy, and you know I will!"

My teacher's smile widened at that point, and then she became misty-eyed. As she took a moment to stroke my head, she softly stated, "That's exactly why, Baby. Right there. What mother wouldn't wanna have a precious little son like you, Lonnie? A little boy who's caring, thoughtful, loving . . ."

"But it could turn out bad, Mrs. Jensen!" I yelled, cutting my teacher off. "I love you and I - I don't want nothing to happen to you!"

As my play mother took a moment to seek out my eyes (I was gradually tearing up by then), she sought to console me. "Honey, I'll be alright," she assured me. "I know you're young, and you're a little worry-wart too, but someday you'll grow to have great faith in God too - just like my hubby and I have. The Lord has the power to overrule any doctor who walks the earth, you know? God is at the helm of everyone's ship, Lonnie, even your little ship. I'll be fine, you'll see."

Ordinarily, I would have found real comfort from Brenda Jensen's words of reassurance but, for some reason that feeling was not forthcoming. Though it was pessimistic on my behalf, I dwelled on the very worst scenario. Although I had celebrated my eleventh birthday only a month prior to Mrs. Jensen's pregnancy revelation, I had already had my fill with death and sorrow.

In fact, I was virtually terrified by it. Less than fourteen months after my Aunt Hannah passed away, her sister Blanche suffered the same fate and right in the midst of my immediate family and the Strickland clan as well! Due to a massive stroke, we struggled with the demise of Aunt Blanche too. In addition, though there was no formal funeral services for him, my father seemed like a death casualty himself. So, with all of that swirling through my mind, I was still skeptical regarding my teacher's news.

"But - but suppose it's a girl?" I offered. "I know a man - he ain't got nothing but girls, and a bunch of them! It might not be a boy!"

Brenda Jensen took a moment to firmly hug me at that particular moment. "Now donchu go throwing no wet blanket on our plans, Lonnie," she said. "Don't be hexing us. It's gonna be a baby boy, and I feel it in my bones. So, do me a big favor. Just pray for us and wish us well. Will you do that for me, Lonnie? Promise?"

Admittedly, I did feel better after that. Maybe, I was over reacting, I thought. And a moment later, as my teacher's optimism managed to rub off on me, I couldn't sustain my dread. And since Mrs. Jensen was so happy about the development, I willed myself to feel similarly. So, I smiled, took a moment to return her embrace and verbally gave her my promise. With all my heart, I would steadfastly pray for her - and her boy baby.

To my great joy and good fortune, Brenda Jensen, my 'five-high' teacher, was not the only close friendship I forged at the Emerson Elementary School. She and another teacher (whom I met later on) were the only adult friends I made at the schoolhouse, but I rapidly became good buddies with a trio of boys around my age too. Their names, respectively, were Willie, Alonzo and Harold. All of them were black and just like me, they all lived within a half a mile radius of Emerson School.

However, although I was fond of each of them, for the most part, I interacted with them separately. Willie was an only child and he almost immediately adopted me as a surrogate brother (I learned later, however, that he had lost a biological brother to death). He was a avid talker, very mannerable and plain-old nice.

Willie, too, was a so-called product of a broken home but, unlike my brothers and me, he had a stepfather. Notably, while Willie didn't much care for his stepdad, I found the man to be a little strict but basically he was easy-going and cordial. Plus, he was especially kind and very respectful to Willie's birth mother. And being an individual who was on the outside looking in, and one of Melvin Harris's sons, I regarded those factors as admirable.

Although Willie seemed to take it for granted, he had a lot of things going for him that I didn't have. For example, he had his very own room (though we had bunk beds, my brothers and I still shared a single bedroom), he had a telephone, a record player and a refrigerator that had food in it. (It wasn't that the fridge on Burd was empty, but we, as kids, could not remove food items from it at-will). Not so with Willie. There were countless occasions when we trekked to his house and then feasted on lunch meat or a couple of boiled hot dogs. And for a boy like me, who hardly knew what breakfast meant, it was a welcomed treat.

My buddy, Willie, did know that he had a couple of advantages over me and he, sometimes, exploited them. Not maliciously, but subtly. Since Willie received a modest, weekly allowance and also worked a morning paper delivery route, he regularly had money in his pocket. And due to the fact that there was a large commercial area located within twelve blocks of my house on Burd, he frequently opted to walk there to purchase things. The name of that shopping area was 'Wellston' and it was replete with department stores (Woolworth's and J.C. Penneys, the mention a few), restaurants, grocery stores and, to my great joy, a couple of movie theatres.

Well, my pal, Willie, didn't relish walking to Wellston by his lonesome and because I was his "brother" (which he deemed me) and practically 'destitute' too, he often sought me out to join him. I was in no way resistant though (actually, I was downright glad), because he always enticed me with the promise of buying me a hot dog, french fries and a large soda pop. And for a kid such as I was, who, sometimes, couldn't afford a school lunch, I was a willing and anxious fish. I fondly recall those yesteryear hikes, and sometimes while licking my lips.

My second newfound friend, Alonzo, had several things in common with Willie. For one thing, they both lived on a street named 'Semple,' which placed them only a block and a half from each other. Secondly, neither of them had siblings and, thirdly, their biological parents were no longer together either. But when it came to Alonzo, the latter factor wasn't altogether a negative one. Actually, as an observing young outsider (me, again, of course), I was somewhat envious of him.

You see, at the house on Semple street, Alonzo lived with his biological father, his paternal grandmother and his stepmother as well. And, apparently, the divorce between Alonzo's birth parents was quite amicable because he spent most of his weekends with his biological mother and she, too, had remarried. Therefore, Alonzo had two sets of parents and a doting grandma, to boot.

Frankly speaking, my pal, Alonzo, was the first boy I ever met who reminded me of my father, so I sort of knew from the very beginning that he and I would have a rather rocky relationship. He was light-skinned, he had fine-textured hair (which he called 'good hair'), he wore an array of stylish and somewhat expensive clothing and he considered himself "cute" and "adorable." Even before we embraced our teen years, impressionable and infatuated young girls seemed to constantly admire and compliment him. And even if they failed to praise him for his good looks and fine looking 'threads,' Alonzo wasn't too modest to voice it himself. From where I stood, he and my estranged dad were fashioned from the very same cloth.

While I could never pinpoint the origin of my old man's arrogance and high opinion of himself, I came to understand where Alonzo was coming from. It appeared that his dual-set of parents were engaged in an ongoing popularity contest wherein the ultimate winner would garner Alonzo's supreme affection and favor. However, the parent's 'luring' mechanism wasn't a 'hot dog and soda' though, it was money and material things. As Alonzo made his weekend pilgrimages from his dad's house to his mom's place, and then returned to Semple street, he was often awarded a few tangible gifts. And while it wasn't his parent's ultimate goal (on the part of neither set of parents), they managed to pamper and spoil him. But, of course, that was my viewpoint, not that of Alonzo's parents.

In spite of the foregoing scenario, Alonzo and I maintained a relationship for nearly a decade. As kids and schoolmates, we attended movies together, we often came together and played a board game called 'Monopoly' and even attended the same high school after graduating from Emerson Elementary. Still, as I mentioned earlier, our friendship wasn't always cordial and smooth-sailing.

Although Willie and Alonzo resided a good four or five blocks from my residence on Burd, there was another boy, Harold, who lived right down the street from us. In fact, if I directly crossed the street and then headed south, I would converge on his "crib" (that's what Harold called a house) within a mere two minutes.

My buddy, Harold, was the youngest of four children. He had a sister (who, eventually, dated my cousin Lloyd), a middle brother named Emerson (who tagged along with my cousin Billy), and an elder brother called "Junie." And to my delight, not so much

Harold's, initially he was the only friend I made who had both biological parents still living together as a married couple. As I said, I was happy about that.

I liked my friend, Harold, a whole lot. Although he frequently expressed himself with an assortment of profane terms (that happened to be commonplace with numerous black boys I was acquainted with), he wasn't mean-spirited or deceitful and he didn't go for 'bad,' like far too many young Negroid boys did. Most of the time Harold and I would ride our bicycles together, embark on long walks together and take in a movie or two on the weekends.

Notably though, in regards to our movie-going, Harold exhibited a habit that was, both, weird and equally comical. He and I weren't very discriminating regarding the flicks we'd select. We enjoyed westerns, pirate pictures, 'Tarzan' adventures and what have you. However, Harold especially could not get enough of going to horror movies. Whether one was showing at the Union, the Wellston, the Victory or the Pageant theatre (all of them were less than a mile from us), Harold would excitedly insist that we go see it. But, once there, things would become whether bizarre.

When the featured horror movie finally got underway, the very exact film that Harold was so anxious to see, it was obvious that he could not bare to watch most of it! Actually, it would freak me out just observing him! Why? Because whenever the gruesome monster or ghoul would appear on the movie screen, Harold would instantly cower down behind the back of the seat in front of him. And while displaying stark and authentic fear, he would look up at me and timidly ask. "Duke, is it gone yet?"

Time and time again, I found myself shaking my head and surrendering to laughter during those occasions. However, it wasn't in response to Harold's repetitious queries (he continually posed the same question to me throughout the on-playing flicks), I just couldn't come to terms with my friend's strange behavior or his insistence upon viewing such features.

Initially, meaning the first time I observed Harold's rather bizarre conduct, I thought he was putting me on, especially when he asked me if the monster was on-screen. I jokingly gave way to fibbing, telling him the ghoul or monster was off-screen when it really wasn't. But when I saw Harold's face afterwards, I never did it again. He was truly terrified!

Oddly enough, Harold and I went on to see numerous films that featured monsters and gory creatures but never again did I opt to fool him or lie to him. When he informed me of his frequent nightmares, that sealed the deal for me. I could never derive comfort or amusement from seeing others mentally stressed-out.

CHAPTER EIGHTEEN
GOD'S BOOK OF LIFE

If it's a crime to love people too deeply and too intensely, then I would have to plead guilty on all counts. I am incapable of harnessing my affection. While some people perceive that as a weakness and, maybe, a flaw in my character, I am the same today as I was as a little boy. Therefore, in the late fall of 1955, when my six-low teacher somberly broke the news to our class that Brenda Jensen had died while giving birth to her child, I was instantly devastated. As tears literally gushed from my eyes, I rushed out of my classroom and sunk to my knees in the adjacent hallway.

Although I was ashamed of myself later on, I was, simultaneously, grief-stricken and decidedly angry as well. I had practically begged my 'second mother' not to chance having another child but she wouldn't hear of it, wouldn't even consider my plea! Momentarily, I was very mad at Brenda Jensen.

The bearer of that heartbreaking news, Miss Davenport (who looked to be in her mid-twenties), was somewhat in awe of my individual reaction. Quite a few of my classmates gave way to weeping (especially the ones who had been taught by Mrs. Jensen), but I was the only student who proceeded to flee her classroom. In addition, since Miss Davenport was in the midst of her maiden teaching assignment, she was relatively new to the Emerson School. Nevertheless, she was very sympathetic when she elected to trail me out to the corridor and proceeded to speak to me.

"I am so - so very sorry, Lionel," she stated. "I wasn't aware of how close you were to Brenda Jensen. Your buddy, Willie, just told me about it. And, if you want to, you can stay out here for a little while."

"You didn't even know Mrs. Jensen, did you?" I asked, not really expecting a response. "She was a very, very nice lady. But what - what about the baby? Do you know if it, if the baby died too?"

"By the grace of God - no," was Miss Davenport's rather upbeat reply. "And I was told that he's doing fine, under the circumstances. He weighed around seven pounds, they said. And she wanted a boy, I was also told."

"Guess that's the important thing," I begrudgingly remarked. "Her baby boy is alive and well - and she's gone, huh?"

"Lionel, I know you feel just awful and that's understandable," my teacher softly inserted. "But it'll be alright, eventually. And you'll be alright too. Because God - He will make it alright. Just watch, and you'll see."

Although I remained hunched down, nodding my head in agreement to Miss Davenport's words, I didn't feel consoled, not in the least. Brenda Jensen was also confident that God would "make things alright" too, and now she was dead, gone forever. And I would never see her again. So, moments later, when Miss Davenport left me to myself, my crying began anew. For I sincerely and dearly loved Brenda Jensen. In my lament, I could not help but wonder why people had to die, and especially the good ones.

My mother, Ruby, was very wise and quite philosophical and I was always appreciative of her viewpoints. Whenever the subject of death came up (which, to me, was far, far too often), she always tried to put it into a certain perspective. She consistently amazed me and not only when it came to the untimely demise of Brenda Jensen, but in regards to her familial loses as well. In the span of two short years, death had claimed the lives of two of her sisters and a couple of her brothers also.

Within a two-week period, our uncles, Major and Harvey, unexpectedly passed away. I am not insinuating that Ruby wasn't grievous, because she certainly was. Nor am I saying that she took it all in stride, or that she acted as if death was trivial. Instead, my mother sought a more sacred and higher ground. Regardless of 'who' passed away, Ruby was steadfast with her uplifting message. She never wavered, not one bit.

"It's never easy saying goodbye to someone you love, Duke," my mother told me, shortly after Brenda Jensen died. "And I'm sure not telling you not to cry from time to time, or not to be a little angry too. I know you think it's totally unfair, and I can't fault you for it. You're so, so very young. But one day you'll come to understand. Your little name, my name, everybody's name is written down in God's 'book of life.' God records the good we do, and the evil we do. And it does not matter how long we live, the important thing, and I always want you to keep this in mind - the important thing, the foremost thing, is how well we live our lives."

Pure serenity comprised my mother's facade as she spoke further, adding, "Duke, you could live to be a hundred or almost a thousand years old like Methuselah in the holy bible - but if you live a devil's life, and do mostly acts of malice and evil, you will be unworthy of God's mercy and be undeserving of His kingdom too. So, always try and do good works and try to fill your heart and mind with good and selfless thoughts too.

Because I'm looking forward to you and all of your brothers to be favorably in God's book of life also. And guess what, kiddo? I am very positive that Brenda Jensen's name was benevolently written in the Lord's sacred book too. And she now resides in God's beautiful kingdom."

While I could never sing enough praises to Ruby Harris for her wise and soothing counsel, I greatly admired her for her discernment quality. She seemed endowed with a gift to be able to read people and that, of course, pertained to people like her five sons, and especially me. So, when she tagged me a "hard nut to crack," she realized it was virtually impossible to sell me entirely on anything. So, when death frequently raised its somber head (in spite of her heartfelt words of encouragement), my mother was keenly cognizant of my innermost sorrow.

Although it seemed completely insignificant to others, my four brothers included, she always tried to uplift my spirits by treating me to the one thing I mostly craved, which was a movie being shown in a theater. On some of those occasions, I would meet up with her at her work place, Homer G. Phillips Hospital, and we would make our way to one of the pre-selected movie houses. Sometimes, little things are an awful big thing to a kid and Ruby knew precisely how to touch my heart. Of course, my mother never forgot the Friday evenings I sat on the front stoop on Sullivan street, waiting for my disingenuous father.

As it would come to pass though, my insatiable love for motion pictures would prove to be a virtue rather than a vice. Since I kept abreast of all the movies that were currently screening, as well as the specific theatres they were on display, I became a prized and popular resider at our house on Burd Avenue. In addition, with my ability to give a compact synopsis of any movie in question, along with my penchant for identifying the principal players in it also, I emerged practically invaluable. Therefore, to my personal feeling of joy, I became like the 'go-to' boy for movie information. To be quite honest, I loved the notoriety.

As it turned out, I was privy to an unexpected, but very appreciative benefit from my home-spun consultant service. Now and then, basically owing to my unique cinema prowess and comprehensive input, I was invited to tag along with some of my adult movie-going cousins and companions. And that, naturally, was right up my proverbial 'alley.'

Admittedly, my choice of using the term "tag along" is not at all happenstance. It was because my involvement in being treated to a flick was usually impromptu and, oftentimes, at the spur of the moment. Traditionally (and I didn't deem it as 'unconventional' until I got older), the primary people who would welcome my company were daters; couples who were romantically connected. And not so surprisingly, but more conducive to their amorous relationships, the movie venue was subject to change also. Instead of going to an indoor theatre, offtimes me and my benefactors would journey to a not-too-distant drive-in facility. I loved that too.

Basically, the people who indulged me were my cousin, Pauline, and her boyfriend, Frank (a fellow who was introduced to Pauline by my mother and who, later on, became Pauline's husband), a younger cousin named Doris and her steady beau, Albert (they, too, eventually wedded), and, on a few occasions, my mom and one of her suitors, and especially a guy named Otis. And although all of those folks had diverse personalities, they seemed pleased with my conduct while I was in their presence.

Essentially, and intentionally, once they afforded me the fare for the movie, whether it was an indoor or outdoor complex,

I never asked for anything else. I 'tagged along' solely to view the flick (or flicks) that was screening and my adult benefactors knew it beforehand. That single factor, that of being content and satisfied, I deemed key to being invited back again.

By sheer nature, I always worried about my mother; not sometimes, but all the time. Ruby was constantly trying to make life better for my four brothers and myself and, though I kept it to myself, I longed for her to meet and, eventually, marry a decent, respectful and caring man (someone who was exactly the opposite of Melvin V. Harris, and I did not view that as a pipe dream).

However, with five little crumb-crunchers on her resume, I realized the odds of finding such an individual was virtually nil and void. Still, though, I remained hopeful. After all, Ruby was still attractive, she had a congenial personality and she epitomized compassion.

In reality, my mother dated a select group of men and, all and all, they appeared to be pretty nice guys, but I, and my quartet of brothers, grew very fond of one of them. He was the man I previously cited, the one named 'Otis,' and, unlike the other men who courted Ruby, he was the only man who saw her five sons. Not that we were invisible to her other suitors or because they were wearing blindfolds either, but most of mom's pursuers acted like we didn't exist. I wasn't stupid or gullible, and neither were my brothers, so we all knew what actually motivated Mom's various daters.

Otis, on the other hand, may have been principally driven by the same desire but, seemingly, he honestly liked children and had a pretty good idea how to snare their affection. With little expense to Otis, he would come to our house on Burd street and delight us with gifts of candy and assorted toys. But instead of distributing his surprises outright, he would make it a traditional game. Upon encouraging me and my brothers to search his person (most of the time he was wearing a trench coat), digging through various pockets, we would soon locate our treasures, all five of us. And whether it turned out to be candy or something like matchbox cars, we would collectively emerge all smiles. Upon tucking that singular happening away in the regions of my mind, I have always marvelled over how easy kids are rendered happy.

Now, I would love to report that our mother and Otis became engaged, got married and went on to live happily ever after, but, unfortunately, that blissful scenario only occurs in fairy tales and fictionalized movies. Oddly enough, I would even like to disclose that Otis and Ruby, alternately, decided to go their separate ways (you see, I truly loved Otis as a person), but, sorrowfully, that was not the case either. While my mother and Otis was still at the dating stage, Otis was fatally shot on a St. Louis street. Although we later learned that Otis was mixed up in drug trafficking, it, in no way, diminished my heartfelt lament. Death may very well be a part of life, I concluded after the murder of Otis, but I wondered why it was so much a part of my life.

When a child finds himself, or herself, abandoned by a father and is almost continually revisited by the transition known as 'death,' I imagine it's natural for that particular child to almost constantly worry about losing the steadfast parent as well. At least, those were my feelings when it came to my mother. Despite knowing that she was committed to her children for the long haul, I was never free of fretfulness.

Although I actually revered the day that Uncle Bill took our family in, I was simply overwhelmed by the succeeding events that transpired. With the entity of death as a focal point, I besieged myself with a whole slew of soul-searching questions. Questions such as: "Why is death the ultimate scenario? Why didn't Brenda Jensen deliver her child void of complications? Why, when it came to mom's sisters, couldn't they have had 'slight strokes' instead of massive ones? Or, my two uncles. Why didn't they suffer 'serious' heart attacks and not fatal ones? Then, when it came to Otis, why couldn't he have been 'badly' wounded and not shot to death on a Saint Louis street? And, furthermore, why couldn't my father have been an 'credible' parent and not the sorry wash-out that he turned out to be?"

I was almost pre-occupied with the aforementioned queries and until times got better (and thank God they did), I found it virtually impossible to shake and co-exist with them. However, before times would get somewhat better, my family had to contend with, yet, another setback. In the fall of 1957 (notably, a week after the governor of Arkansas denied high school entry to nine black students), our mother slipped on spilt milk at her work site and severely fractured her hip. Therefore, for many weeks afterwards, instead of working at Homer Phillips Hospital, Ruby was a recovering patient there.

Alternately, our mother was kept on the payroll during her hospitalization (since she didn't consider suing, that was the least her employers could do) and when she got well, she resumed her work duties. Unfortunately though, almost from the onset of Ruby's hip injury, she began to struggle with the severe pain of rheumatoid arthritis. True to form though, my mother appeared to take it all in stride. However, although I kept it to myself, I was disheartened by the unfairness of it all. I felt Ruby was undeserving of such misery.

On the school front, even as our mom was recuperating from her hip surgery, my brother, Gary, and I were looking forward to graduating from Emerson Elementary in the spring of the coming year. At that juncture in our academic life, Gary and I were sharing the same classroom and, of course, the very same teacher. However, unless another student took the initiative to inform you, you would not have known we were related, let alone be biological brothers. We had the same last name and, maybe, resembled each other, but that's as far as it went. Gary spoke few word to me and, after a time, I learned to comply. It was a sad commentary, but our relationship had been badly damaged by Melvin V. Harris and it was, seemingly, beyond repair. Though I dearly loved my brother (always did), it was obvious that the affection was not mutual.

For the first time, in grade levels eight-low and eight-high, my oldest brother and I were subjected to classroom teachers who believed in the concept "spare the rod and you spoil the child." 'Corporal punishment' was still permissible in those days and our teachers (a man and a woman, both of them, black) resorted to it regularly.

Evidently, they attended disciplinary classes together in college (admittedly, I'm being facetious) because they both favored lining up students and paddling their posteriors (boys and girls alike) and they both wielded their 'rods' without inhibition. In essence, they both hit quite hard.

During those whipping episodes, Gary and I behaved similarly. It was not because we were related though. In my case, it was solely due to perspective. While Gary was just plain-old tough and stubborn (he never emitted a whimper during those 'collective' paddling episodes), I took my licks in subdued and silent anger. From the very moment I started grade school, I regarded a classroom as a place for learning and academic enhancement and I wholly resented being arbitrarily being lumped in with disruptive and unruly students. I didn't consider myself a goody-two-shoes but I wasn't a defiant knuckle head either. To me, recess was set aside for play activity, lunch time was when students ate a meal and classroom time was when youngsters were expected to learn and study. It was just that cut-and-dry to me.

Apparently, Alice Athens, my eight-high teacher, came to appreciate my serious, no-nonsense conduct too. After a mere three weeks in her classroom, a select group of fellow classmates were citing me as the 'teacher's pet,' which was a term I hadn't heard since being befriended by Brenda Jensen. However, I wasn't fazed by the kid's teasing and taunts because I was able to put their digs into a certain perspective also.

In actuality, when I was a pre-teen I believed then just as I believe today. Unless you are abrasive or mean-spirited, if an individual authentically likes you, they will continue to cherish you no matter what you do, but if they authentically dislike you, they are capable of making up bad and untrue things about you - to sustain their dislike or hatred for you. That's quite simple to me too.

While Mrs. Athens was not demonstrative with her affection for me (on occasion, Brenda Jensen would kiss my forehead or cheek), she was very supportive of me in a special way. Whenever our class took field trips (and they were quite frequent), if I wanted to participate, she made it affordable to me. Oh, she didn't out and out pay my way, but, instead, if the field trek venture cost around thirteen dollars (or whatever), she would hire me to perform some chore around her house - either after school or on a Saturday or Sunday afternoon. And whether it was cutting her grass, washing her car or cleaning out her garage, she would always award me the price of the upcoming field trip and a three or four-dollar overage.

Alice Athens was not only sympathetic and mindful of my meager financial status, she was also cognizant of my cravings outside of her classroom. Being that she and her husband did not have a child of their own, they treated me to a mobile carnival one evening and to a couple of drive-in theaters as well. And those ventures, of course, were pure ecstasy to me. Even as a kid, I could never get enough of 'selfless' and 'good people.'

Admittedly though, when I reflect back on the half year I spent with my eight-high teacher, it was not all joyful and easy-going. Mrs. Athens (who was about forty years old at the time) was a veteran teacher who was rather stern, always challenging and, sometimes, a taste insensitive too. Her classroom sessions focused on mathematics and English to personal hygiene and nutrition. Significantly, it was the latter area, nutritional values, that indirectly taught me a stark and sobering lesson, and one I shall never forget.

Innocent enough on her part, Alice Athens assigned our class the task of writing a composition regarding our daily food consumption or, more precisely, what we traditionally ate at our respective homes. To me, the assignment was no big deal and was plain and simple. My biggest concern with the piece was the length requirement. After all, when I finished writing about the northern beans, ham-hocks and cornbread aspect, along with how we, occasionally, concocted homemade syrup (sugar and water), there wasn't much left to tell. My brothers and I seldomly ate breakfast and lunch was practically nonexistent too, so I was restricted to the supper meal. And that was somewhat minuscule in itself.

Since my relationship with my brother, Gary, was still very much strained and distant, he and I did not compare notes on the nutrition composition. In fact, we never even thought about it. But when the assignment was finished and our teacher went to scrutinize our written offerings, she was instantly taken aback. In my personal viewpoint, Mrs. Athens was so surprised that she instantly lost her cool. Meaning, she did not take the time to think before she spoke.

"Lionel, do you and Melvin live under the same roof?" she asked, frowningly looking down at two sets of papers.

I was completely dumbfounded. "Yes, ma'am, we live together, in the same three-storied house," I slowly replied. "I mean - you know we're brothers, Mrs. Athens."

Our teacher appeared to be troubled and upset. "Then why does Melvin report here that you boys have a meat product for almost every meal?" she questioned. "Meats like chicken, beef, pork chops, steaks and the likes? I don't get it, Lionel. And you hardly mentioned meat at all in your composition."

I was momentarily exasperated as I cut my eyes to my nearby older brother. And similar to Alice Athens, I didn't take out the time to think rationally either. If I had done so, maybe I would not have said, "He's lying, Mrs. Athens. The only time we have meat is - well, sometimes on Sundays, when everybody in our whole house eats together. And then it's mostly chicken. We eat a whole lot of beans, just like I wrote down. But other than neck bones or ham hocks mixed in with the beans, we hardly ever eat meat. Shoot - I wish we did. No, ma'am, I don't know what Gary's talking about."

There were a few snickers from on listening classmates but other than that 'few,' the immediate atmosphere was - rather quiet and solemn. My brother was eerily silent and sedate. And pretty soon, Alice Athens seemed to sense my brother's resentment (or embarrassment). Therefore, instead of pursuing the issue any further, she decided to move on to other compositions. And, admittedly, I was very relieved and glad when she did.

Not too long after the nutritional controversy that took place inside of Alice Athen's classroom, I found myself entertaining an array of relevant thoughts and emerged somewhat wiser. Originally, although I kept it to myself, I could not refrain from being a little upset with my teacher. In spite of how nice and supportive she had been to me up to that point, I felt she should have taken me aside and talked to me in private about the differences in the compositions submitted by Gary and myself. I viewed her actions as subtly callous and an example of poor judgment on her part, and especially for an adult.

However, I learned a memorable and invaluable lesson from it also. In the wake of that happening, I made up my mind to never do anything like that to anyone. Deep in my heart, I believe there's a way to do things and way not to do things. Unfortunately, my eight-high teacher, without intentional malice, was guilty of doing the latter.

Even as I bore that subdued grudge against Mrs. Athens for her role in the composition affair (my anger lasted about three days), I seriously focused my attention on my brother, Gary, shortly afterwards too. Of course, we never took the time to discuss the matter, not once. But owing to my feeling of empathy for my older brother, I soon came to a rational revelation.

Although Gary and I were in the same classroom and was the same grade level, my brother was a year and a half older than me. Therefore, he was more mature than I was and, maybe, more concerning as well. To his credit, Gary knew what a standard nutritional (or nourishing) meal consisted of, and I didn't. Gary also realized we were 'poor,' and I didn't. And whether my eldest brother found shame in our family's meager straits, I wasn't sure, but he certainly had the right to have his individual feelings. And I was, at least, old enough and mature enough to know that much.

CHAPTER NINETEEN

LIFE WITH THE FELLOWS

In September of 1958, when I embarked upon my four-year high school journey, I was in the company of some very familiar faces. Since Willie, Alonzo and another running buddy, a boy named Walter, graduated from Emerson Elementary in June of that same year, they, too, decided to attend the nearest secondary school in the vicinity. That facility was called the 'Soldan-Blewett High School' and was located on Union Boulevard. Notably, it was less than eight blocks from Emerson and was approximately 15 short blocks from my house on Burd.

Not surprising to me, my brother, Gary, was not among the select group of Emersonites headed to Soldan. Instead, Gary pre-chose to attend a technical high school named 'O'Fallon' and it was situated adjacent to another large boulevard called Kingshighway. However, since the institution was several miles from Burd Avenue, it required public transportation or the initiative to walk.

Though I never told Gary or my mom, I was emotionally hurt by my brother's preference to attend O'Fallon Tech. In spite of the facility being skill-oriented and not academically-stringent, I took Gary's decision personal. To me (and I admit to being sensitive), Gary hated sharing a classroom with me at Emerson and I felt he was determined to distance himself from me at the secondary level. And upon revisiting the composition episode, I was quite certain I was right.

Throughout my childhood (not that it dissolved later), I was overly protective when it came to my brothers. I was remorseful later on in my life, but I once pulled my little brother, Vaughn, out of Harry's Delicatesson, telling him that, "Jews will cheat you," which were words borrowed from my old man. Then, I audaciously trailed a neighbor's bullying kid into his own house because the boy had deliberately pushed my brother, Lovell, to the ground. And, during another occasion, when I sighted Gary fist-fighting with a boy who happened to tower over him, I picked up a large stick and struck his opponent with it. However, true to form, my brother was instantly displeased by my aggressive action. He not only told me to "butt-out," he took out time to identify me and practically apologized to the guy for my interference. Go figure!

Now, it may appear that I'm regressing when I revisit my protective behavior when it came to my four brothers, but I have a specific reason for doing so. It may be perplexing and strange to the average person, but my feelings (and they were innate and heartfelt) transcended blood relatives. In essence, an individual did not have to be kin to me for me to champion their cause or "have their back."

That is specifically how I felt about the former Emersonites who accompanied me to Soldan High School in the autumn of 1958. However, by the time I was scheduled to commence my

Sophomore year, the 10th grade, my friendship circle had grown to encompass nine other boys and they, too, were like my surrogate brothers and I loved them all.

When it came to those additional nine boys (and, as I stated, Willie, Alonzo and Walter was not included in the count), there was two boys I knew prior to entering high school. They were a brother pair who not only lived four blocks from my residence on Burd street but, coincidentally, shared last names with me (Harris). I frequently played with Charles and Robert when we were kids and there was two things I always remembered about them. Firstly, their biological parents were still together (two of the nicest individuals I had ever met) and, secondly, the brothers played musical instruments and they both dreaded being called in the house for practice sessions. Charles, the elder of the two, played the piano and Robert, some kind of horn.

The other teen-aged boys who comprised our rather large social group were 'fellows' named (and we came to refer to ourselves as "the fellows") Larry, Henry (or Moose), Sherod, Jerry, John, James and Arthur (also called Woody). With the exception of Arthur, we were all average-looking black young men. Unfortunately though, due to a childhood malady, Arthur was made to contend with a humpback and a shortened leg as well. However, to the collective credit of the 'Fellows,' none of us, either kiddingly or otherwise, maligned or teased Woody in regards to his physical appearance. For we all dearly and truly loved the guy.

As time went forward, I was virtually at the helm of that camaraderie ship. Just as I loved and felt protective towards my biological brothers, I came to feel the same way about my surrogate brothers, the fellows. Yes, that included all twelve of them. Although the majority of them were bigger than I was (at best, I weighed about one hundred and thirty-five pounds), if I perceived that any of them were remotely threatened by anyone, I would instantly step forward in their defense. Admittedly, some of those times I'd emerge hasty, foolhardy and plain-old wrong as well.

Now, when I look back and allow myself to take a censuring view of my teenage-self and my numerous cohorts, I cannot rightly deny a certain premise. When we walked together down the street (and especially at night), I'm almost sure we looked foreboding and threatening, and especially when it came to Caucasians. Simply because we were all black boys, I'm sure we were pigeonholed as a 'gang' and, more so, a gang of troublemaking thugs. But in our collective case, that assumption was far removed from the truth.

In spite of not knowing the true origin of my brotherly affection for the fellows, I didn't love them indiscriminately. They were genuinely god-fearing and nice young men! By nature, they didn't look for trouble, they didn't desire to harm anyone, they weren't vandals or stick-up artists and they weren't into drugs, not any of it. In fact, if you put aside cigarette smoking (some of us), we were collectively void of bad or unwholesome habits. In essence, me and the fellows were not purveyors of mischief, wrongdoing or any semblance of evil.

In earnest, if we had one vice (and it was a vice because we were underage), it was because we all enjoyed drinking beer. And we would frequently find ways to procure it, and especially in the summertime when school was not in session.

However, even what we did during those occasions was quite innocent and benign. We would pool our money together, persuade some random adult to purchase a supply of beer for us and then converge on one of our residences that was, of course, void of any adults. And once there, with no girls involved, we would pair off and indulge in a popular card game known as 'bid whist.' And, oftentimes, and I'm certain it might sound rather odd (or gross) to a lot of people, but we would engage in making homemade ice cream during those times also. Owing to a churn-type wooden ice cream machine, the 'losers' of the ongoing card playing contest were obliged to continually hand-turn the machine's lever and, eventually, we would feast on the finished product. Sure, it may sound weird and distasteful to others, but the fellows and I thoroughly enjoyed that ice cream.

I imagine a percentage of people could jump to a conclusion upon reading my foregoing account, but they would be plainly in error. We all enjoyed female companionship and were not sexually attracted to each other. In fact, most of us had 'main squeezes' (or staple girlfriends) and when we were not playing bid whist, shooting pool or just 'hanging out,' we were on the hunt for girls. If we weren't searching out pay-at-the-door house parties or basement dances on the weekends (hooking up with various females in attendance), we would pursue girls in movie theatres, as well as in the school setting when it was still opened.

Therefore, like normal teenaged boys, our hormones, too, were raging and working overtime.

As I previously acknowledged, my close-knit group, in spite of it being thirteen of us, was not mean-spirited, was not thuggish in nature and was a far cry from being a so-called gang. Oh, there were traditional gangs around at the time. Factions like the 'Sarah and Finney Boys,' the 'Compton-Hills Boys' and the 'Track Boys' (which was short for the Hodiamont Track Boys) and the latter menacingly came to regard us as a rival gang - and merely because there was a number of us.

Although they were referred to as 'boys,' the majority of them were grown, violence-prone men who seemed to have nothing to do but to forcefully 'crash' (foregoing the door charge) basement or house parties and, then, brutally attack fellow black boys and, sometimes, the on-premise parents themselves. And every now and then, without any semblance of remorse or shame, they would even stoop to stealing the party-goers checked in coats or raps, and regardless of how cold it was outdoors.

Personally speaking, I absolutely despised the actions of those gang factions. In being a well-informed reader, I was acutely aware of Rosa Parks and the Montgomery bus boycott, I grieved over the bombings and murders down south (Emmett Till, included) and I had just read about the Supreme Court's ruling on the Little Rock, Arkansas school system, so I immediately considered the evil that was perpetrated by those black thugs as the epitome of what I deemed 'self-racial loathing.' And I still feel that exact way today. Unfortunately and tragically, only the century and the decade has changed. That's a sad and heartbreaking commentary.

Again, I reemphasize that my running buddies and I were not a so-called gang. Fact was, we morphed into a formal social club and named ourselves the 'Junior Bachelors.' Driven by an enterprising spirit, we initially hosted a bunch of pay-at-the-door dances ourselves and then went on to loan money out with a reasonable profit in the deal. The latter undertaking was orchestrated by a grown man named 'Perry' and his lending domain was a well-known Saint Louis-based facility called 'McDonnell Aircraft.'

Mr. Perry (and that's what we called him) worked at McDonnell's and it seemed ideal for our business venture there. We began our endeavor by turning a tidy profit but as time marched forward, owing to the greed and small-mindedness of our adult helpmate, we were eventually taken advantage of. Although Mr. Perry, who was sporting a brand new automobile at the time, secretly tried to bribe five club members with a mere fraction of the funds he actually owed us (including me), I felt compelled to expose him. He cautioned the five of us to keep silent regarding his proposed 'buyoff,' but I elected to inform all the others, every single one of them.

In my mind, it was plain and simple. We entered into the money-making venture together, so when it came to a monetary settlement, as meager as it was, we deserved to get equal shares. Although I hoped to never lay eyes on Mr. Perry again (and I told him so), I truly believed (then and now) that if the five of us guys had played along with Perry's deceitful proposition, it would have been the gradual unraveling of the Junior Bachelor Social Club, and the slow corroding of our close-knit relationship as well. And that, to me, would have been downright tragic.

During a couple of isolated happenings, I allowed my temper to get away from me and, in retrospect, I was plain-old stupid and foolish. In spite of my small-stature, I had no fear of anyone. And also due to my minute size, I could not understand a person confronting me with any kind of weapon either. (Of course, that was rather dumb in itself). So, when the following episode transpired, that was the feeling swirling around in my head.

Most of the fellows and I were attending a basement dance at the time, and the so-called Track Boys were on the scene too. In actuality, the latter group consisted of about ten fully-grown men and a number of high school dropouts also. Well, during the ongoing dance, the Track Boys circulated a verbal threat that they were going to jump on the "junior bastards" (seemingly, they enjoyed calling us that) before the evening ended. Therefore, upon getting wind of that rather intimidating threat or rumor, and then realizing we were outnumbered as well, we collectively decided to make a casual and gradual exit from the premises.

From the very second I was informed of the threat, I was pissed off. After hurriedly fleeing from the same bullying gang a month earlier, I had told the fellows then that I didn't know about them, but I wasn't going to run from those "thuggish-ass niggas again!" And although I initially complied with making an early departure on the night I'm recalling, I wasn't wholly sold on the idea. In my gut, I longed to stick to my guns.

Coincidentally, that's exactly what aroused my subdued fury that evening - a gun! As the Track Boys proceeded to trail me and my seven friends out onto the front lawn of the dance site, one of them yelled out, "Run, you goddamn, punk-ass junior bastards!" and then fired a round of bullets into the air.

Mad as hell, I immediately turned around to face the teenager who was perched on the adjacent lawn, holding the pistol. I didn't even consider running or even walking faster. And, notably, other than my long time buddy, Willie (who sprinted pass me as if the shooter had a starter pistol), my onlooking club cohorts didn't budge either. Instead, they stood their ground as I did something absolutely insane! I walked straight towards the boy who was brandishing the weapon.

Establishing eye contact, I yelled, "Nigga, who you gonna shoot? More than that, why you want to shoot us? You don't know us! And we don't know you! Ain't nobody running from your black ass!"

Even as tears were streaming down my cheeks, I was prepared to speak further. However, it was then that my friend, Woody, grabbed my left arm and proceeded to step in front of the gun-toting boy and softly spoke to me. "Come on, Duke, let's go," he said, tugging at my shoulder. "He's not worth it, none of them are worth it. Come on."

There was a lawn filled with onlookers at that juncture, but I found myself focusing on the sad face of Woody. I was trying to halt my tears, but I couldn't. I was walking alongside my sympathetic comrade, shaking my head. I kept saying, "I can't understand it. I can't . . . understand it."

Much later, when I had the time to regain my composure, I found myself thinking of the teenager, holding that gun. Throughout that ordeal, despite keeping the gun barrel trained on me, he remained silent and looked somewhat fearful his own self. Right away, I could tell he didn't really want to shoot me, or anyone else. I surmised he was just trying to impress his bullying, evil-inspired comrades and that, alternately, made me feel sorry for him. I found myself wishing for him what I always wished for myself: That God would graciously grant him friends and allies who truly loved and cared about him and not disingenuous and self-centered thugs who comprise a street gang. I wished the same thing for all fellow black teenagers.

Later also, when I took the time to really reflect back on that pistol episode, it dawned on me how stupid, foolhardy and reckless I behaved that particular night also. I didn't know what I was thinking about or if I was thinking at all, but it happened and I couldn't explain why it did. My mom always maintained that "God takes care of fools and babies" and, maybe, there lied the answer. I wasn't a baby. In fact, in body and mind, I was a teenager. Therefore, I was teenaged fool.

Now, I do not want to keep hiding behind my mother's yesteryear assessment of my being a "hard nut to crack," but one would think I had learned some degree of sense from the previous disclosed gun incident. Not at all so. In light of, yet, another serious happening, I began to wonder if I had an underlying death wish. Maybe I needed a psychiatrist! Although I was 'tight' (extremely close) with all the fellows, I had my favorites (Willie, Walter, Arthur and Larry, for example), but I enjoyed a special bond with Robert, the youngest Harris brother who ran with us. I know my affection had a great deal to do with his immediate family.

Specifically, I not only cared about Charles, the older brother, but I also came to cherish the Harris parents, the younger sister, Betty, and the youngest brother, 'Little John.' I spent a lot of memorable and happy days with the entire Harris family at their home. Therefore, when an angry and muscular black boy approached me inside the Soldan High School and boldly told me, "I'm gonna kick Robert Harris's black ass for him," the fight was soon on.

Upon defiantly telling the boy, "Well, you can start with me," I delivered a left cross to his right jaw. He, naturally, retaliated with some punches of his own, but before the battle escalated into a full-scale brawl between the two of us, my opponent looked in the immediate distance and sighted Robert and some of the other fellows converging on us. Therefore, he instantly hurried away in the opposite direction, probably in fear of a collective beat-down.

When an alarmed Robert and the others finally stood affront me, I took a moment to rapidly explain the situation to them. I repeated the boy's threat and, momentarily, Robert and I were headed in the direction of the fleeing assailant. Walking side by side, we hastened down the corridor as a few of our comrades trailed closely behind us.

As a prelude to what was about to occur, it is necessary to note that, other than Woody (Arthur), none of the fellows, including me, carried any type of weapon. Personally, I always withdrew comfort from that single fact and although Woody was well-known for carrying a switchblade knife, I also disliked him having it. I didn't want to see him seriously hurt anyone and I dreaded him getting injured also.

Just so happened though, Woody was one of the guys who was following me and Robert on the morning of the fisticuffs confrontation. So, when we finally caught up to my retreating adversary on the school's first floor (actually, the boy was defiantly waiting on us) and, then, noticed he was brandishing a jagged-edged hunting knife, Woody quickly pulled out his switchblade, snapped it opened and offered it to me. I waved it off, flatly refusing to take it, and although Robert had the good sense to halt his advance, I did not. Sporting two balled up fists, I opted to reengage my former opponent head-on, relentlessly throwing a flurry of punches.

Well, as blind luck actually had it, prior to the beginning of the initial battle, I had just entered the school building. (That's why I was still on the basement floor). Therefore, I had, yet, to go to my locker and was still wearing my winter coat. That coat was made of synthetic leather (plastic), it was white in color, and it had a thick, cloth lining. I was glad I was wearing that coat that day. Because when the knife-wielding boy tried to stab me in the chest area and I, simultaneously, delivered a hard blow to his face, the knife's blade momentarily got tangled up in my coat's lining.

Not only was I not injured at that precise point, it allowed me time enough to punch my attacker several times again. And, then, as my assailant wildly attempted to stab me anew, I inadvertently met the weapon with my opened right hand and proceeded to render a solid and impactuous left hook to the boy's nose.

Apparently, that particular blow, both, hurt and stunned my attacker. Because, right then and there, he opted to flee the immediate vicinity. He left me standing in the middle of the hallway, and to my complete surprise, the boy's hunting knife was deeply embedded in my right hand.

Strange though, and certainly to my further surprise, it didn't remotely hurt! As the array of onlookers displayed expressions of pure dread, I felt no pain whatsoever. Even when I decided to remove the blade from my hand in the presence of the school's nurse, I felt nothing. In fact, as the nurse scrambled to halt the bleeding (she did her level best), she was much more upset and alarmed than I was. And for the school nurses' sake mostly, I was relieved when a summoned ambulance eventually arrived outside the school.

Personally, I was virtually awestruck in regards to my wounded hand. It was throbbing somewhat and was seeping blood, but it wasn't at all hurting like I expected it to be. Just minutes later though, I was in a state of dreadful anticipation. Instead of focusing on my hand itself, I was more so concerned about where the screaming ambulance was headed. Naturally it was en route to a hospital, but not to just any old hospital. The designated medical facility was Homer G. Phillips and since I knew my mother was working the day-shift, I figured she would be there, awaiting my arrival. Therefore, I braced myself for an angry tongue-lashing.

Well, just like I imagined, my dear mother was inside of Homer Phillip's emergency room when I arrived there and, exactly like I dreaded, as the saying goes, "she jumped on me with both feet." And, in addition, she soon mouthed the words I imagined she would.

"Who were you fighting for this time, Duke?" she angrily asked. "Boy, you will never, ever learn, with your stubborn and bull-headed self! Those so-called friends of yours are gonna get you killed one day! Then, I guess they'll be satisfied. Who was it? Who were you fighting for, huh?"

As I rather sheepishly responded to Ruby, for the first time I grimaced in sheer pain. That was because a long needle was being stuck into my opened wound. "Robert," I frowningly admitted. "I was fighting for my best friend - Robert."

"I knew it, I just knew it," my mother responded as she noticed the distorted grimace on my face. "Oh, I hope it hurts, hurts like the devil!" she then added. "I pray it hurts so darn much that it'll knock some degree of common sense into that thick, bone-head skull of yours!"

Now, I may have been mistaken or grossly in error, but I found myself believing that the doctor attending to my injured hand was in direct cahoots with my onlooking mother. Because in the midst of Ruby 'hoping' I was sustaining horrific pain, I actually was. Even as the deadening fluid was being shot into my raw-looking hand, it felt like holy hell! It was the worst pain I had ever endured in my young life.

However, only time would tell if the ordeal would, somehow, quell my recklessness and continuous stupidity. Admittedly, at that particular juncture in my life, I wasn't at all sure myself.

CHAPTER TWENTY
ENVY AND JEALOUSY

Out of all the individuals who was included in my immediate social circle, Alonzo was the most flamboyant and controversial. I admitted earlier that he and I had a stormy, love-hate relationship from the word say-go. In fact, over the years, we had a series of somewhat moderate fist fights. He and I would square-off over a bunch of asinine and dumb things; things like 'renigging' during a bid-whist card game (which was playing the wrong suit) or embarrassing remarks that were made in the presence of young ladies.

Sometimes Alonzo would emerge victorious during those juvenile fisticuffs; giving me a bloody mouth, and other times I'd win; impacting him with a bleeding nose. As weird as it might sound, it partially defined our ongoing comradeship.

Somewhat strange also, our occasional physical conflicts did not, in any way, deter me from being protective of Alonzo also. And, ironically, if I had to point out the single member of our group (or club) who caused the most gang-like skirmishes, I would have to cite Alonzo.

However, it was not because 'Lonnie' was an out-and-out troublemaker (we often called him Lonnie), it was more so due to his state of being. Individuals in rival factions (especially gang members) almost traditionally disliked him and whether it was due to his good looks or his light skin color, paired with his material assets, or because teenaged girls were infatuated with him (rendering onlooking boys simply jealous), they frequently wanted to "kick his ass." And despite the fact that Alonzo occasionally brought it upon his self, the fellows and I were strongly opposed to such a thing transpiring. Similar to the well-known motto of the 'Three Musketeers,' we collectively ascribed to, "One for all and all for one."

Personally speaking, I always identified Alonzo as "well-to-do." Even when we were in the eighth grade at Emerson, he wore a variety of three-piece suits and had an array of expensive and attractive jerseys, or sweaters, in his wardrobe. He wore leather jackets and coats, brand named shoes like 'Bannisters' and 'Stacy Adams,' and sported popular headwear such as 'Knox Jaguar' hats. In addition, when he turned sixteen, he was driving around his very own automobile. So, all and all, Lonnie was more fortunate than the vast majority of black teenagers attending Soldan High and many of the white boys as well. In a certain sense, affluence was occasionally a nemesis to him.

However, as I mentioned, Alonzo was, sometimes, the blame for his own problems. If he was attracted to a young lady at a party or somewhere, he thought nothing of 'hitting on' her (meaning, trying to seduce her) and exhibited little or no regard for the targeted girl's on-site date or boyfriend. Although, in later years, it would be called 'dist' (meaning, disrespect) when it came to the young lady's male escort, it was a prime igniter of a lot of disputes between black young men. Sometimes, the resentful escort would have his so-called 'boys' (or raps) with him, and the free-for-all brawl was soon underway. And that's what compelled Lonnie's 'boys' into the fray.

Due to a latter day self-examination, I am obliged to own up to a flaw in my own character when it came to my comrade, Alonzo. Although I never again felt it in regards to anyone else during my lifetime (at least, thus far), I, too, was simply jealous of the guy. I wanted what he had, silently begrudged him for having it, and I felt he was blessed and I was not. Nothing that was overly complicated.

To be candid, there was a remarkable aspect to my long-ago connection with Alonzo too; not good remarkable but bizarrely remarkable. You see, Lonnie and I happened to be the same size and almost the same build. Therefore, when Alonzo grew tired of wearing some of his clothes (like suits and jerseys), he would pass them on (or down) to me - and I would eagerly and graciously accept them. Sure, in my pride, I could have turned them down but I was jealous and envious, but not remotely stupid. Having four brothers and a mother who was struggling financially, my wardrobe was sparse and shabby too.

To his initial credit, Alonzo wasn't overly magnanimous when he gave me his hand-me-downs. He would even discreetly drop clothes off at my house from time to time. But like a cow who would yield a pail of milk and, then, turn right around and kick it over, he could make a conspicuous mockery of his generosity. Sometimes, when I decided to wear the clothing items he gave me, he would single me out and say things such as, "Don't Duke look stylish in that suit I gave him?" or "How do you think Duke looks in that sweater I gave him?" And he would pose those queries, mostly addressing girls on the scene. Like I stated previously, that was one of the causative reasons behind some of our arguments and fist fights. Still, however, I continued to welcome Lonnie's gifts.

It may appear that I went to extremes upon trying to convey the distinct flavor of my yesteryear affiliation with the fellows;

from my endearing friendship with Robert and, then, recounting my unorthodox relationship with Alonzo, but the entire group of guys were special to me. I felt extremely fortunate to have them in my life and I sincerely hoped they felt likewise towards me.

While there were no clear-cut leaders amongst the fellows, I was, arguably, the most persuasive individual in the pack. And due to a relatively unusual personality trait I maintained, I garnered a certain degree of respect from them also. Because I was adamant about not using profanity, not uttering a single curse word (I credited that to my mother and Uncle Bill), my running buddies seemed impressed by it.

Notably though, they were not so much in awe of my self-restraint efforts to forego cussing that they came to emulate it though (on the contrary, a few of them even tried to entice me to abandon my resolve by baiting me with profane jargon), but, after a while, they deemed it admirable.

And perhaps it was that quality, mingled with my ever-present compassion and sincerity, that yielded me an extra measure of influence on the fellows. Even as a teenager, I lived by a certain code and I was quite vocal with it. I was forever expounding on what was right, what was wrong, what was just and unfair and most of my intimate comrades were very much in sync with my philosophy. And when I took the initiative to shed light on Mr. Perry's divisive and underhanded scheme, they eventually applauded me for it.

However, I cannot claim that the policy I advocated was always fruitful or successful. On the contrary, in certain, isolated cases, it brought about disastrous results. It wasn't mere happenstance that the episodes I am about to cite involved the St. Louis Police Department or that they were driven by classic white racism. Each incident was typical of what black teenaged boys had to endure in the late fifties and early sixties (not that it was any different prior to that period or even nowadays).

For four consecutive weekends, the fellows and I (sometimes, all of us, sometimes nine and, maybe, less than seven of us) attended a pay-at-the-door basement dance or house party in Saint Louis city's central west end. We would come together to leave the affair (just as we came together to converge on it hours before) and, subsequently, embark on the collective stroll that would lead us back to our respective and outlying places of residence. Other than occasional laughter and various discussions that focused mostly on foregoing issues that transpired at the party, we were relatively quiet and orderly in our retreat. We weren't foreboding, rowdy or threatening in the midst of our foot-journey, so I felt we were exempt from any kind of fanfare or controversy.

Of course, as it would turn out, I was dead wrong! Although I considered myself to be well-read, scholastically astute and blessed with a measure of discernment as well, I was guilty of, sometimes, overlooking a subtle little difference that actually made all the difference in the world. Despite my idealism and high regard for the tenets of righteousness, I forgot that me and my cohorts were collectively black and, ever so often, we were made to deal with white racism. But four weekends in a row? And, essentially, in the same neighborhood? Now, come on!

Our maiden encounter with the so-called 'boys-in-blue' (all of them Caucasian, incidentally) was relatively peaceful and non-confrontational. When we sighted a couple of police paddy wagons headed towards us (sirens blasting away), I took the initiative to remind the fellows that we hadn't done anything unlawful or illegal and cautioned them to stay calm. In addition, I whisperingly told Woody to toss his switchblade as well. So, I figured, all and all, we would emerge from the episode unmolested.

Of course, I was totally wrong on that count too. After the squad of cops falsely accused us of "shooting up" a nearby party and 'gleefully' lining us up and roughly frisking us (not a single weapon was found), they then informed us that we were under arrest. However, even as they split us up and began to load us in the patrol vehicles, I posed a series of questions to them.

"Why are we being arrested?" I asked. "I mean - what are we being charged with?"

"Peace disturbance - smart-ass," snapped one of the officers. "And we can add resisting arrest to it, if you wish."

"Well, tell me this, officer," I defiantly replied. "Just whose peace did we disturb, huh? The ants and bugs on the ground? I betcha don't do this to white boys in Ladue!"

The red-faced officer was on the verge of grasping his billy club when a cooler head prevailed. My buddy, Woody, addressed me, saying, "Duke, don't argue with him. It won't do no damn good. Be cool."

"Yeah, you better 'be cool,' like your crippled friend said, ya' little nigga," my cop adversary spoke. "Don't make me crack yo' goddamn skull for you."

Although I was still boiling inside, I forced myself to heed Woody's advice at that point. He was clearly right, continuing to argue with that bigoted law officer was absolutely pointless. Therefore, in a state of subdued silence, I sat inside that paddy wagon as it soon set course for the nearest police station. And since it was located at the corner of Page Avenue and Union Boulevard, which was less than a mile away from where we were abruptly 'waylaid,' we were there in less than ten minute's time.

There, we were all quickly booked, charged with 'peace disturbance' (we were never told whose peace we were disturbing) and were informed that we wouldn't be released until a parent or a legal guardian came to the station to pick us up. In actuality, since we were walking over a hundred yards from the nearest home residence, it was ludicrous to maintain that we were disturbing anyone's peace. So, as far as the fellows and I was concerned, we were plainly jailed for W.W.B., which was walking while black.

When I relive the four weekends when my running buddies and I were racially profiled and, alternately, incarcerated overnight, I smile at one juncture and become sorrowful at, yet, another juncture. Racial animus and harassment was never amusing to me and the mere injustice of those yesteryear episodes have remained forever angrily etched into my brain.

Nevertheless, there was a comical aspect associated with one of those weekend incidents and I was principal to its occurrence. Obviously, my long-time pal, Willie, was not impressed with my leadership abilities. That was evident when the gun-brandishing happening transpired as well as when the four arrest episodes took place. In spite of my verbal counsel to our group, encouraging them to be fixed and resolute in the midst of all of those episodes, Willie would speedily distance himself from the rest of us. Similar to his reaction when that black teenager fired a pistol into the air, from the very moment Willie heard the sound of sirens in the distance, he would swiftly make an about-face and head in the opposite direction. He was hell-bent on not being locked up, regardless of the innocence component.

However, during the course of our fourth (and final) trek to the Page-Union police station, Willie did something he had never did previously. Instead, of going home to his not-too-distant house on Semple Avenue, he elected to come to the jail facility we were taken to. In fact, he entered the station while the rest of the guys and I were still being processed.

Almost instantly, I looked at him with censuring eyes (holding my pants up because my belt had been taken away) and so did the onlooking fellows. However, Willie elected not to even look in our direction, let alone to speak to any of us. Instead, he pretended he was there for the sole purpose of quenching his thirst from the nearby water fountain. And he was actively doing just that when I decided to speak up.

"Hey, officers, that dude was with us too," I spoke, smiling all the while. "In fact, he's really our leader."

Before Willie could react or utter a single word (he was visually shocked), an adjacent white cop grabbed him in the collar. Then, as Larry, Woody and the other fellows began to laugh, Willie angrily attempted to scold me.

"Lionel, you shor' is wrong, man!" he cried. "I would never do you like this! How could you do this?"

Actually, I have no idea what Willie said next because at that particular moment, one of the police officers was busily escorting me to the outlying cell area. I know I should have been ashamed of myself, but I wasn't. Furthermore, I should have felt bad when I, later, looked out and saw Willie being placed in a cell of his own, but I didn't. As it turned out, my buddy, Willie, did not speak to me for several weeks afterwards (I was regretful of that), but, eventually, he forgave me. I realized it was a lousy thing to have done and if I had the chance to undo it, to be perfectly frank, I wouldn't. Criticize me if you wish, but I rather enjoyed it. Can you imagine going through life and interacting with a lifelong friend who occasionally brags, "I'm the only one of us who never saw the insides of a jail cell?" I couldn't!

THE LONG AND WINDING ROAD

Not that there was a virtuous or uplifting aspect to our series of racist-driven jail incarcerations, but there was a highly regretful and totally unexpected downside that further marred my fourth run-in with local police officials. And, specifically, it had a great deal to do with my Uncle Bill, a man I regarded as my role model and surrogate father.

When it came to the first three times that the fellows and I were locked up at the Page-Union precinct, my mother made her way to the station (via taxicab) and got me released into her custody. (Posting bail was not a part of the detaining process, and neither were we given official police records). Naturally, mom would be initially upset but when she gave me the chance to explain the entire situation (she was acutely familiar with white biasness and racism herself), she emerged sympathetic and somewhat forgiving as well. Although she frequently reminded me that I couldn't change a racist and sick world, she never emphatically told me to stop trying.

Now, I knew beforehand that Ruby would not be the person coming to my rescue in the wake of our fourth arrest episode. In fact, when I called home to my Burd Avenue residence and spoke to my cousin, Carol Ann, telling her about my in-progress dilemma (she was too young to come to my aid), I wasn't sure if anyone was coming to get me. Hoping they'd eventually release me on my own recognizance, I was in a state of limbo.

As I said, I knew for sure that my mother was not going to show up at the police station to secure my release. To be precise, it was because she was in Indianapolis, Indiana, visiting her niece, Norma (who was her late sister, Blanche's, grown daughter), and she was not scheduled to come back to St. Louis until three days later.

As it turned out, I stayed put in my jail cell for a very long time; so long, in fact, that I, alternately, saw all of my comrades (including Willie) being taken from their cells one-by-one and, subsequently, gaining their release. I felt very sad and very alone, but, in reality, I wasn't alone. Situated three cells down the corridor, catty-cornered to my cell, were two hard-looking, black male prisoners. And I could clearly read their rather devious minds even before the on-duty turnkey (who was also black) showed up.

"Hey, my man," one of the men addressed the turnkey, "why doncha put junior flip over there in our cell with us? He looks real lonely now that all of his homeboys done flew the coop."

Instantly, the turnkey glared at the prisoner spokesman with eyes of absurdity. "I ain't about to put that youngster in a cell with you two sick-ass motherfuckers," he responded. "Tell ya' what though, I'll turn my back and you two niggas can screw each other. What about that?"

"Fuck you!" the second man shouted. "Ya' Uncle Tom sonofabitch!"

Goes without saying, I was grateful to the turnkey official. He completely ignored the angry name recently hurled at him and decided, instead, to talk to me. He wanted to know if anyone was coming to "sign me out" and when I informed him that I didn't know, he, then, asked me if I wanted something to eat. I quickly accepted his offer and he, soon, brought me a rather dry bologna sandwich and a hot cup of black coffee. And although he opted to apologize for not having any cream or sugar, I was so hungry at that point, it tasted as good as a steak dinner to me.

Within an hour of eating my jailhouse meal (it was approaching 4:00 a.m. by then), my turnkey ally came back to the cell area to retrieve me. He was smiling in pleasure, truly happy I was finally being released, but when he announced, "Your uncle's here to pick you up, Lionel," I found myself momentarily wondering just how bad would it have been if I had been molested by those two prisoners. Just for a fleeting moment, however.

To be perfectly honest, I absolutely dreaded facing my Uncle Bill! Thoroughly aware that he only saw things in 'black or white' and, then, further capsulized them to either 'right or wrong,' I anticipated a tongue-lashing that I would never forget. Then, to make matters even worse, I flashed a smile when I first sighted him. Stupid, stupid me - that certainly didn't sit well with him!

"Boy, you need to wipe that gall-darn grin off yo' face," my uncle angrily spoke. "Ain't nothing funny here - dang-blasted! You just a blame fool, that's all!"

Although I dropped my smile, and right quick (I did not wish to raise my uncle's anger level), I wasn't grinning willy-nilly. Actually, I was thinking of Ruby, and a remark she would make when she, sometimes, dealt with a distasteful matter. She would say, "I would rather be bitten in the butt by a "snaggled-toothed mule" than to contend with such and such - and as I glanced into the miffed, crossed-eyes of my Uncle Bill, I then knew exactly what she meant.

Momentarily, in trying to be as sincere and humble as I could be, I said, "I'm sorry for making you go through all of this, Uncle Bill, but I . . ."

"Boy, I don't wanna hear it!" my uncle snapped. Then, as he opted to check his wristwatch, he added, "Here it is, five o'clock in the morning and . . ."

"Four - four o'clock, Uncle Bill," I inserted, apparently not thinking at all and heaping more coal on the fire.

My uncle was practically livid! "What?" he cried out, thinking I was making light of him. "Look, boy, if you say one more word, I'm gonna ram my fist down your throat! Now, come on outta here." Then, as he calmed himself and shifted his attention to the white law officer behind the desk, he said, "Oh - and thank you, officer."

"You are very welcome, Mr. Strickland," was the lawman's rather disingenuous response as he, simultaneously, passed me my belt. Then, he sought out me, teasing, "See ya' next weekend, Lionel - ol' buddy."

I, of course, didn't flash any semblance of a smile in the wake of the cop's dig. I glanced over to the onlooking turnkey and made it a point to shake his hand when I fondly said, "Thanks for everything, Mr. Todd, I appreciate you."

"But I don't wanna see you here no more, Lionel Harris," the turnkey replied. "You take it slow."

I hurried to catch up to my uncle at that point. I didn't wish to piss him off any further. And even as I climbed into the passenger side of his pick-up truck, I had no intentions of saying anything else, not one syllable. If there was any dialogue exchanged between us, Uncle Bill would have to initiate it. I was adamant about my feelings.

Moments later, as he started up the truck, my uncle did speak first. "What's your story this time, Duke?" he asked.

"Well, me and my friends . . ."

"Boy, you ain't got no boogey-joogey friends!" Uncle Bill shouted, cutting me off. "You may have one or two friends your whole lifetime, but not a blame tribe full of 'em. Those boots you run around with, they ain't yo' friends!"

Upon still seeing the merit in remaining subdued and silent, I longed to tell my uncle about the racist aspect of the arrest affair and assure him that the fellows and I were unjustly thrown in jail, but he was not in the mood to listen and I knew it. To him, my comrades were a bunch of black hooligans and they were always up to no earthly good. In reality, that was exactly how those racist cops regarded us, as well as the majority of the people who looked like them. However, it greatly grieved me to know that people who looked like me, oftentimes, bought into that biased mind-set also.

~

Incidentally, the next time I saw the inside of a traditional police station, I was a grown man and was employed by the St. Louis Police Department. But, you know, when I later took time to seriously analyze my jailhouse swan song, I squarely believe that when I was made to endure those four or five hours in that small cell, paired with the deviant sexual desires of those two older black men and, then, proceeded to cap it off with Bill Strickland's irate (but understandable) conduct, I was of a mind-set to never again be arrested and incarcerated.

CHAPTER TWENTY-ONE

LOVE IS IN THE AIR

Prior to arriving home on the fateful morning that my Uncle Bill rescued me from the Page-Union police station, he threatened to "mash my mouth" (that was because I slipped and referred to the fellows as my 'friends' again), but that was the final leg to his disenchantment with me. He never again brought the issue up and neither did I. It was as if the incident never occurred.

In spite of hitting a few bumps along the way, I loved and admired my uncle and I always strived to be in his good graces. And I felt his love for me too. Oh, he wasn't the type of guy to verbally tell you that he loved you, especially when it came to another male, whether you be an adult or child. Sometimes, words are not necessary.

However, I could tell by the way Uncle Bill looked at me - say, like when he and my mother would go grocery shopping at the nearby 'Kroger's Supermarket,' that he dearly cared about me. When I was a little over eleven years old, and the three of us would procure groceries for the entire large household, I would traditionally keep a mathematical account of the monies being spent. And during those times when my grand total would be just one or two pennies off (taxes included), Uncle Bill would grin widely and playfully muss my curls. In addition, he would say something like, "Duke, you are a real whiz with those figures! You're pretty good, boy!" And to his further credit, I entertained little doubt that he cherished Ruby and my four brothers just as much as he did me.

I esteemed my uncle as a good, Christian man and a real credit to his biological father, Rev. Strickland. And when it came to my mom, in addition to providing lodging to her and her large brood, he emotionally supported her as well. Like a devoted hereditary brother, he stood by her when Ruby's second sister passed away and her two brothers also. And even when Ruby fell and fractured her hip at Homer G. Phillips Hospital, Bill Strickland, along with cousin Pauline, kept us kids nourished and in-check. And, seemingly, it was no big deal to our uncle or his eldest daughter, Pauline.

In retrospect, I had just turned ten years old when my family moved from Sullivan street to the house on Burd Avenue. So, except from what I viewed in various movies, I knew absolutely nothing about what some folks deemed "matters of the heart," the thing aptly called 'romantic love." (It surely wasn't remotely on display inside the Harris residence at 4281 Sullivan). However, as the years gradually crept towards my teenaged status, the older residents in the three-story complex on Burd were practically smitten by it. Requited love seemed to be cropping up all over.

I previously mentioned that my cousins, Pauline and Doris, met and married their future 'financies' (Ruby's comical substitute for 'fiancee') while we were still living on Burd. In fact, Pauline and Frank joyously recited their matrimonial vows right in the backyard there.

But the love bug did not stop with those two couples, and it went on to bite others. Specifically, the other individuals who were bitten (or smitten) were cousins, Lloyd Henry, Gerald and Carol

Ann, and even Ruby. Apparently, love is in some ways contagious. At least, it seemed like that to me in those days.

When it came to the three youngest Strickland siblings, the courting process was, both, convenient and somewhat economical too. I was almost positive that each of them (the males and the females) were poised to walk a hundred miles to rendezvous with their respective sweethearts, but they didn't have to. When it came to the Strickland siblings, each of their love-mates lived within a half a block from our house on Burd Avenue.

Lloyd's girlfriend, Marilyn, stayed right up the street (she was my friend, Harold's older sister), Gerald's young lady, Fern, resided almost directly across the street from our place and Carol's boyfriend, Donald, was a member of a rather large family that lived less than seventy-five yards down the street. Without a semblance of intent on their part (I didn't think), when it came to their love connections, the three youngest Stricklands were not needful of public transportation or filling stations when it came to courtship dallying.

To my youthful assessment, the love liaisons between Gerald and Fern and, later, Carol and Donald were pretty traditional (at least, in public). Meaning, they interacted like most boyfriends and girlfriends I happened to have observed. But when it came to cousin Lloyd and his staple girl, Marilyn, the term 'demonstrative' practically leaped out at me and, I'm quite certain, to anyone else who might have observed them. I had seen the movie entitled 'From Here to Eternity,' but I'm here to tell you that Burt Lancaster and Deborah Kerr had nothing on Lloyd and Marilyn! Even to a wide-eyed novice like me, they appeared to be in love with a capital "L."

As a point of reference, Lloyd Henry was working at a commercial fowl facility during the onset of my remembrance. It was a facility where the public could buy live chickens and the likes. Therefore, as an unsavory aspect to his job itself, Lloyd would return home daily, practically reeking of smelly fowl secretions and feces too. Like that familiar saying, "It was a dirty job, but someone had to do it."

Naturally, lots of soap and water was the order of the day from the very moment Lloyd left his work site. And, eventually, my cousin would retreat to one of the bathrooms in the house and, then, reappear, looking clean, refreshed and odor free.

Unfortunately though, that wasn't always the scenario. Sometimes Marilyn would come over to our house (and, virtually, just minutes after her beau arrived home) and before long, as the couple withdrew to the back porch, they would be tightly locked in each other's arms and passionately kissing. Even in the middle of a heavy rainfall (thunder and lightning and all), their intense petting and smooching would continue. Now, I realized I was a child when I was witness to Marilyn and Lloyd's love scenes, and I also knew that I was looking through a young boy's rather judgmental eyes too, but I was totally awestruck by the episodes. Even in knowing I could be branded as 'nosey' or a 'snooper' (sneakily watching something that was not my business), I still remained bewildered by it all. In fact, as I feared being scolded for my spying, I was so affected by the issue that I forced myself to speak to my mother about it. And I could tell she was subduing her laughter as I spoke.

"I know one thing for sure," I vowed, frowningly recalling what I had seen. "I am never gonna be in love like that! Just thinking of it makes me wanna puke. If that's love or true romance, I don't want no parts of it!"

Ruby did laugh at that point. "Just keep on living, Duke," she told me, "and I'm gonna tell you something, something I want you to always remember: Never, and I mean never, say what you won't do in this life. As God is my witness, things have a way of coming back and biting you right on your behind. And it seems to happen every time a person says he's <u>never</u> gonna do something or the likes. And that's just a word to the wise, kiddo."

"Well - have you ever loved like that?" I questioned. "And I mean - ever?"

My mother smiled, almost with absurdity. "I probably felt that way about Melvin, your ol' daddy?" she admitted. "Once upon a time. He was my first real love. But to borrow from you though, I don't wanna be in love like that ever again. Duke, when a woman has five babies with a man, it's hard not to be a little daffy about him."

I don't know why, but I was momentarily on the verge of saying, "Almost six babies" (thinking of the aborted child), but I didn't want to hurt my mother. Instead, I asked, "Do you still love him, just a tiny bit?"

"I don't think so, too much bad water has gone under the bridge, too many hurtful memories. But, Duke, it's okay for you to still love your daddy. It really is."

"Well, I don't still love him," I quickly insisted. "He doesn't deserve anyone's love, no ones."

Ruby grinned gently. "Yes, you do, Duke," she insisted. "And like I said - it's perfectly alright. He's still your father."

As I previously mentioned, my mother, too, had a periodic love life when we resided at 1372 Burd Avenue. Before and after the ill-fated Otis arrived on the scene, she had her share of suitors. Notably though, one of them was head and shoulders above Ruby's other dates and boyfriends. Unfortunately though, it wasn't because the alluded to man was noteworthy, remarkable or even because he was exceptionally kind or nice. It was solely because he stood around six-foot-four, a size which physically dwarfed a small-statured guy like my personal favorite, Otis. Otis was five-eight, at best.

The man I'm speaking of was named William and he was several years younger than our mom. Not that that made a significant difference, it didn't, but when I had time to really get to know him, I sorrowfully concluded that he wasn't even as old as I was - at least, not in a mature way. In reality, he was only thirty-five years old when he came into the picture, but he behaved more like a teenager, and the type of teenager I didn't much like. He seemed woman-crazy and since he constantly smoked cigarettes and excessively drank an array of hard liquor like Melvin V. Harris did, I could not help but be turned off by him. Although I truly realized that having five sons was a great liability to Ruby, I knew (not thought) she deserved a better man than William. Was I guilty of being judgmental? Hell yes, I was!

Although I secretly regarded William as somewhat of a dinosaur (meaning, due to his size, I felt he had outgrown his brain), I never told my mother about how I truly perceived him. Since he wasn't mentally or physically abusive when interacting with Ruby, I deemed that an exemplary feather in his cap. Additionally, he had a job and, maybe, he wasn't influenced by our welfare monies. Yes, those kind of male predators were very much afoot in the fifties and sixties too.

However, there did come a time when I personally opted to talk to my mom about William. It wasn't because I greatly disliked the man though. Admittedly, it was plainly due to my homegrown, self-derived moral code. Even as a small child, I felt mothers were grossly wrong to have 'live-in' boyfriends, and especially in the presence of onlooking, impressionable children. Therefore, when William began to spend some nights inside Ruby's bedroom (which was something other suitors had not done), as audacious as it sounds, I took the initiative to say something about it to my mother. In one aspect, I regretted my action, but only <u>one</u> aspect. I spoke to Ruby in strict privacy, and with only her and me in the immediate area.

"Can I say something to you, Ruby?" I nervously started off. "Talk to you about something that's really bothering me, and not have you get real mad at me?"

"Well - I don't rightly know, Duke. I don't think I'll get upset with you. Is it something I did wrong or something you did wrong? What's on your mind?"

"It's like this," I began. "You know how you always encourage us to do the right thing, me and my brothers? You know - to try to always walk the straight and narrow, no matter what?"

"Yeah, I still believe that's the best way to go," my mother responded. "But, do me a favor, stop beating around the bush. Come out with it, Duke."

"I - I know I'm only fifteen," I stated, "and I still have a lot to learn. But it's about William."

"And you don't like him, right?" my mom guessed.

"Naw, that's not it. He's okay. It's just that - one day you're gonna want to tell me, or one of the boys, about morals. You know, what's morally right and what's morally wrong? You - you already do it, all the time."

Ruby was noticeably somber when she asked, "And you don't like William spending the night at our house. And especially because we're not married? Is that what's bothering you?"

Almost ashamedly, I nodded my head affirmatively. "I . . . I really can't help myself," I confessed. "Yeah, that's how I feel about it. And I know I've got more nerve than a brass monkey. I don't know. Maybe, there's something seriously wrong with me."

"Aw, naw, Duke there's nothing wrong with you. And I sure ain't upset with you, not even a little taste. And I'll think about how you feel, I honestly will."

As time pressed on, my mom did devote serious thought to the concerns I raised during our frank discussion about her male companion, William. Apparently, she mulled it over so intently and so decisively, that she eventually decided to marry the guy. And that happened to be the <u>one</u> aspect I alluded to earlier, and the one I would, alternately, live to regret.

While abusive behavior was a non-issue (actually, since me and my brothers were no longer little when the marriage took place, we would have disassembled William if he had even thought about it) our stepfather proved to be almost a carbon copy of our biological father, Melvin Harris. William also drank too much alcohol, smoked way too much and turned out to be similar to far too many men I had come to know (single ones and married ones). Putting it rather crudely, he was another skirt-chasing black man who frequently allowed his little head to overrule his big head.

In retrospect, when I made the decision to speak to Ruby about her man-friend, William, spending the night in her bedroom, I neither expected her nor hoped she would issue William his walking papers, or break it off with him. After all, I didn't hate the guy and I certainly knew there were men who were even worse than him in the world. My dad, for instance.

However, to be honest, the marriage factor didn't even enter my mind! Actually, since William was in his mid-thirties and had never been married before, I surmised that even if Ruby mentioned the word 'marriage' to him, he would promptly head for the hills or, at least, to East Outer Mongolia. And since five sons were intricate parts of the deal too, I figured it was no way he'd agree to marriage. Obviously, I was grossly in error! I only wished I had been mistaken about his character and maturity.

CHAPTER TWENTY-TWO

FOR LOVE OF FAMILY

During my early high school years, although I was, sometimes, verbally criticized for my choice of running buddies (not only by Ruby and my Uncle Bill), I, nevertheless, loved the fellows dearly. I suspected that due to the fact that they were so numerous, that most onlooking adults regarded them as mere 'associates' or, worse, young black ruffians who were up to no earthly good. But they were way, way off the mark with their superficial assessments.

In reality, my friends were nice and mannerable teenaged boys who were not out to harm anyone and were the sons of decent, caring and hard-working parents. And in spite of my having a quartet of biological brothers of my own, I cherished them as my brethren also.

Occasionally (like the majority of ongoing relationships), our close-knit alliance incurred turmoil and a few nagging vexations as well. And, unfortunately, quite a few of those unpleasant happenings transpired right at my front doorstep on Burd Avenue. Specifically, they would involve and evolve around my eldest cousin, Pauline, and would play out practically every time some of my buddies would stop by my house to gather me for some impending outing.

Since the Harris family essentially resided on the second floor, whenever the fellows came by to retrieve me, they would traditionally ring the doorbell and fully expect they would soon be greeted by one of my Strickland cousins. However, after a while, they came to almost unitedly hope it would not be my rather large-framed cousin, Pauline. Although they weren't remotely offended by her size, they absolutely hated her gruff manner and social skills. For they were abrasive, insensitive and, ofttimes, downright crude.

Immediately after opening the door and sighting the fellows standing in front of her, she almost spontaneously said something crude like, "Whatchu little ignert motherfuckers want?" And, then, even before the guys could come up with any semblance of a rebuttal or a return reply, she would turn to the nearby stairwell and yell up to me. "Duke, you gotta bunch of little niggas down here, wantin' to see your ass!" she'd add. "Get on down here!"

In reality, I would be in the vicinity of the stairway area when I heard the doorbell ring, therefore I was aware of the nasty way my cousin had greeted my friends. Sometimes I'd make a feeble attempt to lighten the moment by uttering something like, "Well, I'd rather have a bunch of little niggas wantin' to see me - than a bunch of white folks, holdin' a shotgun and a noose!"

Of course, my joviality fell way short of alleviating any of my comrade's hurt feelings. Even as I descended the stairs, their soured expressions told it all. They were collectively pissed off!

My mother, Ruby, would occasionally say that, "Even iron tends to wear after a long period of time," and when I take out time to reminisce those yesteryear retrieval episodes that took place at the house on Burd Avenue, I can truly appreciate that adage's merit. Eventually, the fellows, with the exception of Willie, unitedly decided to cease stopping by my house altogether. They had had enough and I couldn't justifiably fault them for their decision.

The proverbial 'straw that broke the camel's back' involved my pals Larry, Woody (or Arthur), Jerry and Willie. In essence, they comprised the group that came to 1372 Burd on the afternoon I'm about to recall. But although my cousin, Pauline, was the supreme catalyst in the matter, it didn't transpire in her presence. Instead, it played out shortly after I hooked up with my four cohorts and the five of us were actively walking northbound on Burd.

My buddy, Jerry, took the initiative to lead off the verbal protest. "Duke, I know she's your goddamn cousin," he angrily began, "but I am fuckin' tired of hearing her damn mouth! Every time - the same shit! 'Whatchu ignorant motherfuckers want?' We wanna see Duke, not your big humongous ass!"

"Yeah, man," Larry quickly chimed in, "I be so close to speaking up and calling her a fat, funky-ass motherfucka!"

Now, maybe, I should have stayed silent and allow my friends to just vent and express their anger, but I didn't. Odd as it was, I was somewhat amused. "Well, I'm glad you didn't," I addressed Larry. "She would have grabbed hold of you and then sat on your butt. And that would have been the end of you."

Seemingly, the protest on-hand had been pre-discussed, when I wasn't around. That was because Larry actually singled out Woody, stating, "See - he thinks it's damn funny. See what I mean?"

Coming up with an instant reply, Woody was quite serious when he told me, "It's nothing funny about it, Duke. She's your damn cousin, like Jerry said, and we know you can't pick out your relatives, but you should tell her not to talk to us like she does. Get on her case about it."

"I have talked to her about it!" I lied, trying my best not to laugh. "I mean - I tried to tell her."

Larry, then, glared at me, but with doubtful eyes. "Yeah? And what did she say?" he asked.

Admittedly, I could barely get my reply out without yielding to mirth. "She didn't <u>say</u> nothing," I, again, joked. "She just grabbed me and sat on me. But she didn't put her full weight on me - because I'm her cousin. And that's why I know it would be the end of you, Larry - cause you're not her cousin."

Willie and the other guys were bugging up, laughing aloud, and, soon, I, too, surrendered to chuckling. Everyone else was laughing, save Larry, and I momentarily felt bad for him. That's why I reached over and placed a comforting hand on his shoulder.

"Boy, git your damn hand off of me!" Larry smilingly reacted. "Get away from me!"

"Aw - it's like that, huh?" I kiddingly asked as Larry knocked my hand away. "Tryin' to play hard to get, huh? Well - I'll get you alone later on, just you and me, and we'll kiss and make up. Cause I loves you dearly."

The entire group gave way to contagious laughter in the brief aftermath of that memorable episode. But, notably, within the passing of but ten minutes, the initial anguish and aura of hurt feelings had, seemingly, vanished entirely and we went on to enjoy the rest of that day together.

In my heartfelt estimation, absolutely no one, neither my abrasive cousin or anyone else, could dampen our spirits or sever our unique friendship bond. In spite of everything, all joking aside, the fellows knew I truly treasured them and I felt they loved me also.

～

Although my long-time friend, Willie, continued to come to my house on Burd Avenue in spite of my cousin Pauline's continued verbal abuse (no matter what, he steadfastly called her 'Miss Pauline' and afforded her respect), the rest of the fellows proceeded to boycott it altogether. However, in no way did that deter me from visiting their respective homes. In fact, there were a couple of them that I virtually loved going to.

In having four siblings, I had never slept anywhere other than on Sullivan street or on Burd Avenue but, thanks to my buddy, Larry, and his accommodating parents, I spent several nights under their roof on Wells Avenue. And as an additional amenity, when the subsequent morning came (although I never mentioned it), I was treated to something I had seldom had - a delicious, hot breakfast! And I thoroughly relished interacting with Larry, his parents and Larry's two younger brothers, Conway and Clarence.

Now, in trying to convey my heartfelt feelings when I reflect upon visiting, yet, another friend's residence, I find it somewhat difficult to come up with the appropriate words. For if I merely 'loved' spending time with Larry and his family, then I positively adored being in the company of Charles and Robert's household. Although, initially, I was hard pressed to explain it all (in essence, my overt affection for my two running buddies, their mother and father and sister and kid-brother as well), I gradually came to understand it fully.

It was quite simple, really. Due to the fact that the Harris couple were still together, still raising their biological children and, most commendably, appeared to be still in love with each other, I was bubbling over with serene admiration. In my eyesight, they appeared to epitomize the word family.

In stark reality, I have never been a person who tried to suppress his true feelings. Therefore, from the word say - go the entire Harris family knew I thoroughly cherished them, and especially the youngest boy, known as 'Little John.' I was born a perennial 'hugger' and every time I laid eyes on the youngster, I would embrace him. And he seemed to enjoy it as much as I did. And, on various occasions, I had no qualms when it came to embracing his three siblings and parents as well. So, all in all, I came to relish being treated as an intricate part of the Harris clan. By contrast, I never experienced spending the night in the

Harris home (as I did with Larry), but I dined countless times at the Harris's dinner table. And those were some of the happiest times in my young life.

I imagine it could be chalked up to human nature, but I have never ceased being in awe of certain, seemingly, universal questions. Firstly, "Why is it, when you have something to your virtuous credit - do you take it for granted?" And, secondly, "When you are essentially barren of something you greatly desire - you secretly covet it?" Frankly, that was my personal mind-set when I interacted with my friends, Larry, Charles and Robert. They almost constantly surprised me.

For instance, when I think of Larry, I often reflect on our mutual pal, Alonzo, too. Not that their personalities were similar (they were not), but solely due to a thing called an <u>automobile</u>. Since Lonnie was the only young man in our group who had his own car, we had to contend with a recurring problem. Eleven or more fellows could not lawfully ride in a single vehicle, so, oftentimes, half of us were left high and dry when we engaged in ventures that required transportation. However, on weekends mostly, we had a saving grace. Thanks to Larry's dad, Larry was permitted to drive the family car.

In a very tangible sense, my good buddy, Larry, was my personal saving grace. Whenever Alonzo chose to stop by my house (at that time, my family had moved to 5574 Page Avenue), with the intent of picking me up, he would insist that I pay him fifty cents for the purchase of gasoline and, quite frequently, I couldn't accommodate him. In the words of a well-known adage, I was 'broke, busted and disgusted.' And when Lonnie elected to drive away, I felt abandoned and stranded too.

Fortunately though, my morose wouldn't last long. Because approximately 15 minutes after Alonzo's departure, Larry would pull up in front of my house, wheeling his old man's car and soon we were off, en route to join up with the rest of the fellows. And, to Larry's merit and my sincere gratitude, he never demanded money for fuel and seemed insulted whenever I confessed I was broke.

From time to time, I happened to be at Larry's house when he approached his father and requested borrowing the family vehicle. Sometimes, his dad would be a little high or 'tipsy' (frequently, it was on a Friday evening and, obviously, his pop had consumed a few after-work drinks), and before he honored his eldest son's request, he would subject Larry to an almost incoherent sermon. In addition to cautioning Larry not to speed or drive recklessly, he also warned him against drinking alcohol as well. And although I, respectfully, kept my mirth at bay, thinking of the absurdity aspect, Larry, on the other hand, was totally ticked off. Although he elected to remain silent, anger practically consumed his face.

Finally, in the short aftermath of his makeshift lecture, Larry's dad tossed him the car keys, presented him with three or four bucks for gas and told him to, "Be careful out there." And although Larry forced himself to say he would, it was more than obvious that he could hardly wait to vacate his house.

"I git so damn sick of that drunk motherfucka preachin' to me," Larry complained as we strolled towards the nearby automobile. "There he is - drunk as a skunk and he got the nerve to tell me not to drink! Stupid-ass nigga - always giving me advice! Always yappin' at the mouth!"

"Maybe it's because he cares about you, man," I calmly inserted. "After all - he is your father."

Larry's anger surged a notch further at that point. "Well - I wish the hell he was <u>your</u> goddamn father!" he shouted. "You can have his black, ignorant ass, Duke!"

With a slight grin on my face, I almost suggested that we draw up the legal papers, but I changed my mind as I seated myself inside the car. I felt it was best to let my friend cool off. But in my silence, I dwelled on the underlying paradox. In his state of anguish and fury, Larry was willing to callously discard his old man while I, in my ongoing quietude, felt discarded by my dad. I could not help wondering if anyone is ever truly satisfied with their lot in this world.

***

When my esteemed comrade, Larry, offered up his biological father to me, saying "You can have his black ass," I later thought of Charles and Robert's dad. In my fantasies, I would welcome the senior Mr. Harris with opened arms. He seemed to dearly love his wife and children and he was forever talking about what was "right, just and proper" and what was "plainly wrong." Therefore, I not only revered him for his familial devotion, he and I appeared to be on the same page morally and ethically-wise as well. And, in addition, and to my soothing and sincere appreciation, he genuinely cared about me and opted to display his feelings for me in ways I had never known before. Commendably, he treated me like I was one of his very own, cherished offsprings.

Now, if you even remotely feel that Robert and Charles shared my sentiments about their hereditary dad, it was certainly not overtly evident. Down deep, I was sure they loved and esteemed him, but (similar to Larry and his pop), they tended to resent him. Apparently (totally different from me), they resented his authoritarian nature and common sense advice, and even when he was clearly correct and rational.

Prime example: There was a period when Charles, Robert and I were interested in a group of young ladies who were known to pal around with each other. In fact, a couple of the girls lived in a two-family flat located on a street called Wabada and my two brother-friends were actively dating them. (Actually, their young ladies were first cousins). And I was in the social mix, just tagging along and hoping to make a romantic link with the best friend of the elder cousin. Quite often, the girl I'm alluding to would be hanging out with the cousin pair too.

As quite usual, I was visiting the Harris brothers on the specific afternoon I'm on the verge of recalling, so I was present when Charles informed his father of our impending plans. Notably, it was a weekday and school was still in session, so after Charles indicated that we were headed to Wabada street, intent upon hanging out with the trio of girls, Mr. Harris posed a certain query - but not singularly to Charles; but to Robert and me as well.

"What about homework, fellows?" he asked. "Should I be concerned about it? Robert? Duke? All three of you."

Although the brother duo was momentarily silent, I almost proudly spoke up. "I finished mine up in study-hall this afternoon," I said. "I didn't have that much in the first place."

"I didn't have any," chimed in Robert. "Me neither," Charles tossed in.

The senior Mr. Harris seemed somewhat leery, but soon replied, "Okay, guys, but still it's a weekday, and school's in session tomorrow. Charles and Robert - I expect to see you two back here before ten o'clock. And, Duke, my curfew applies to you too. I've got you phone number and don't think I won't check on you."

"Yes, Sir, I hear you loud and clear," I happily responded.

Although, both, Robert and Charles verbally berated their dad throughout our ensuing foot journey over to Wabada street (it was about a mile and a half trek), I wasn't remotely upset or disenchanted. In fact, although the brothers highly disliked their father treating them like a couple of "snot-nosed kids" (Charles's disgruntled words), I felt good inside. Preferring not to share my innermost feelings with my two comrades, I stayed silent and allowed them to vent. Completely unbeknownst to either of them, I was on cloud nine!

You see - during that particular time period in my life, my mother was working the evening shift at Homer G. Phillips Hospital and my Uncle Bill was laboring at the Scullins Steel facility. Therefore, no one was overly concerned about me getting home prior to ten o'clock in the evening (or eleven P.M., for that matter), no one except John Harris. And that endeared him to me even more.

All in all, the subsequent rendezvous with the three young ladies on Wabada street went quite well. As the six of us sat, perched on an elongated front porch, I found myself talking and joking with the 'spare' girl (her name was Patricia), while Charles and Robert periodically kissed and caressed their very-receptive girlfriends. Respectively, Charles's steady girl was named Georgia and Robert's young lady was named Joyce, who were the cousin pair I previously mentioned.

In retrospect, we were behaving like typical, teenaged young folks; nothing risqué or terribly inappropriate. And although Charles was somewhat senior to, both, me and Robert, he was relatively new to the dating game also. However, that did not prevent him from 'falling head over heels in love' and, more significantly, it did not dissuade him from 'floor-showing' in the presence of his newfound love interest either. And his younger brother and I witnessed that first-hand when it came time for us to bid good night to the female trio.

Rather casually, Robert informed his older brother that it was 9:15 P.M., but when he added, "Remember what Daddy said," Charles became totally unhinged.

"Fuck Daddy!" Charles shouted. "I don't have to jump 'cause Daddy said so! Hell - I'm almost seventeen years old, and I'm a man! Daddy don't run me!"

Not becoming upset himself, Robert seemed to take it all in stride. He looked over at me, stating, "Let's go, Duke, we better make it on in." Then, as he glanced back at his brother, he added, "Okay, Charles Thomas, you gonna be on punishment again."

Obviously, Charles was still intent upon performing. "Fuck Daddy and his damn punishment too!" he yelled. "I ain't no little boy no more. I git sick of all his shit!"

At that precise juncture, Robert almost exhaustedly gave up. He kissed Joyce goodbye as I waved farewell to everyone and, minutes later, Robert and I rounded the adjacent corner and was, then, strolling southbound on Belt Avenue. We didn't say anything to each other for a while but, in all probability, our thoughts were jointly focused on Charles, our boisterous and dissenting companion.

However, it wasn't because Robert and I was worried or overly concerned about the penalty our defiant comrade would incur for disobeying the senior Mr. Harris. Instead, we both knew Charles to a tee and we fully anticipated what Charles would likely do next. That led us to almost, simultaneously, halt our advance when we were approximately two and a half blocks from Wabada street and look back into the far distance.

And owing to the overhead street light, which was located at the Wabada-Belt intersection, we could actually observe Charles slowly rounding the same corner we had rounded minutes later and, then, break out running like holy hell! Man, you would have thought the police was chasing him! And as me and Robert stayed put, patiently waiting for Charles to catch up with us, we could barely contain our laughter. Of course, I can't speak for Robert, but that episode has always been one of my fondest memories.

CHAPTER TWENTY-THREE
UNFORGETTABLE CHARACTERS

There were a whole range of people I associated with during my teenage years who were undeniably memorable to me for a variety of reasons. And, then, there were certain individuals whom I met who I could not forget, even if I wished to. Personally, I always called those select people characters; a male or female who could, sometimes, render me speechless and, on occasion, awestruck. Whether driven by some idiosyncrasy or some bizarre viewpoint or lifestyle, they continually amaze me, as well as the average on-hand observer.

One such individual was a young man named 'Jerry' and, as I indicated earlier, he was one of the 'fellows' I ran around with. However, before I explain why I deemed Jerry a character, I feel it's necessary that I divulge something that was rather unusual about me in my youth. It may be a glitch in my personality, but people could randomly lie to me and, no matter how unbelievable or fantastic the lie sounded, I seldomly challenged the validity of the falsehood.

For example, in those days if someone came up to me, claiming they had walked on the moon (even prior to Neil Armstrong's lunar stroll in 1969), I would pretend to believe them. Furthermore, giving way to my sense of humor, I might even ask him or her, "Is the moon really made of cheese?" Admittedly, it was quite weird on my part but after all is said and done, the fabrication (or lie) is usually harmless and (most important to me) there looms no hurt or ill feelings in the wake of it.

Unfortunately, my running buddy, Jerry, happened to be a habitual liar. Without provocation or coaxing on anyone's part, Jerry could look into your face (not only my face) and spin a tall tale that would completely stun a person. He would expound on everything from "inheriting thousands and thousands of dollars" to "visiting Hawaii when school shuts down for the upcoming summer." And when talking to a guy like me (who seemed to hang on to every word), he would even apprise me of relevant details.

For instance, I recall Jerry telling me that his 'Uncle James' had given him one hundred dollars. Then, the very next week he said (again) that his Uncle James gave him one hundred bucks. But, somewhat uncharacteristic of me, I didn't remain silent on that particular occasion.

"I thought you told me your uncle gave you a hundred last week," I injected. "He gave you another hundred dollars this week too? He must be wealthy or something."

Jerry wasn't the least bit irritated or befuddled. "Naw, that was my 'Uncle Jimmy' last week," he offered. "Him and Uncle James are brothers."

I nodded my head in feigned understanding. "Aw, okay - I guess I'm all mixed up," I congenially responded. "I stand corrected."

Now, whether it was true or not, I was probably Jerry's favorite sounding board. However, he certainly did not confine his fabrications solely to my two ears. Instead, he was an equal opportunity liar, meaning he lied rather indiscriminately, and especially when it came to the other fellows.

In fact, in regards to our close-knit social circle, Jerry engaged in falsehoods so frequently and so blatantly that, subsequently, his first name became practically synonymous with the word lie itself. To be more specific, when Jerry was not physically in our presence (none of us wished to hurt his feelings), we would kiddingly say things like, "Man, you know you're telling a damn Jerry" or "Boy, you sure can Jerry" or even "You know damn-well you're Jerrying." Then, later on, when Jerry did arrive on the scene and the fun-making ceased altogether, he was still treated as a prized family member. Even in our youthful states, we collectively realized that not a one of us was flawless or perfect.

There are some people who you meet along the path of life who you are naturally drawn to and, seemingly, they to you. It is difficult to explain unless there's real credence to individuals having similar spirits. But from the very moment I met my cousin Pauline's boyfriend, Frank (who went on to become her husband), I liked him very much and he appeared to like me back.

Frank Poe was a country boy from Arkansas and he surely dressed the part. He came on the scene, 'flooding' (meaning, the cuffs of his pants were noticeably above his ankles) and was wearing a shirt that was too small for him, but in spite of his attire, he was friendly and all smiles. And in priorly knowing that my mother had taken the initiative to introduce him to Pauline, I instantly welcomed him also. Admittedly though, I secretly hoped that my older cousin would not verbally disparage him and, alternately, run him away!

Well (as I previously revealed), to my utter delight and great surprise, I was grossly wrong in my suppressed concern regarding Pauline. Not only did the two of them hit it off well, they fell in love and soon married. Then, to my personal joy, as time proceeded to march forward, I became a frequent companion in their marital union.

The very same woman (my cousin Pauline), who was previously regarded as an abrasive, mean-spirited ogre by the majority of my running buddies, came to treat me like a cherished younger brother or surrogate son. Along with, occasionally, accompanying the couple to a number of drive-in theatres in the Saint Louis area, I was also treated to weekend trips to distant locales like Decatur, Ill., Fredericktown, Mo., Springfield, Mo., Kansas City, Mo. and Chicago, Ill. And I'm glad to report, that during none of those out-of-town treks, did I see the crude and loathed demon who had once ruffled the feathers of my assortment of friends. In my opinion, Frank Poe (who was sometimes called 'Poe-baby'), brought the best out in my cousin, Pauline.

By and by, thanks greatly to Frank, the majority of the fellows downgraded their long-time distaste for my cousin, Pauline. At least they ceased berating her. That was because Frank, being my cousin's husband, became key to enhancing our group's rather sparse finances. Acting as a go-between (and I'm certain some monies came his way), Frank would load us up in his pick-up truck, transport us to a car wash that was located in St. Louis county and leave us there to put in a day's work. Then (just like clockwork), later in the evening after we were paid for our car washing labor, Frank would return to retrieve us. And since Frank performed his services weekend after weekend, the fellows collectively grew to like him a great deal. That, in itself, made me happy.

In reality, Frank Poe was somewhat of a hustler, but not in an adverse or shady sense. He was constantly trying to make money. Although he was gainfully employed at a construction company, he was forever doing odd jobs on the side. And from the time I was twelve years old until I reached the age of seventeen, I went from being his 'helper' to being his 'partner.' We worked together, doing everything from cutting and grooming lawns, to detailing newly-built homes, to whitewashing basements, and essentially for wealthy or well-to-do Caucasian people.

Just so happened, I was working with Frank when I was casually called a <u>nigger</u> by a little white boy. Although the kid was only five years old, he voiced that racial slur as if it was my surname. While I was simply mowing the front lawn, the youngster (whom I had never laid eyes on before) walked up and said, "Hi, nigger." Then, as I immediately looked his way, I frowningly replied, "Hi, you little peckerwood!"

Unbeknownst to me (not that I would have minced my response), both, Frank and the little boy's mother were within earshot of my retaliatory remark and they reacted differently. The mother appeared to be highly upset while Frank looked somewhat shocked and subdued.

As the kid's mother rapidly approached my position, she scoldingly stated, "You didn't have to say that to him! He's just a five-year-old little boy and he doesn't know any better."

I was visually pissed. "Well, I'm just a twelve-year-old little boy," I loudly countered, "and I don't know any better either! And I just wonder who taught him the 'nigger' word!"

The woman turned as red as a beet. "Aw, you're one of those smart . . ." she blurted out, but then caught herself.

"A smart what - what?" I defiantly asked. Then, I turned to the bystanding Frank, informing him that, "I'm ready to go, and I'll be in the truck. I don't need her money!"

Seemingly, at a loss for a proper reaction, Frank stood silent as I pivoted and walked away. However, he didn't follow after me or even attempt to get me to change my mind and, therefore, I ended up sitting patiently inside the truck, waiting for at least 45 minutes. Then, when Frank finally showed up, apparently after completing the yard job alone, he was ready to talk about what had recently happened.

In actuality, since Frank was a native of Little Rock, Arkansas (the southern city where the state's governor defiantly opposed school desegregation), I was well-prepared for what he might say. Sorrowfully, he did not disappoint me.

"Duke, you've gotta git that chip off your shoulder," he started off."White folks are born prejudiced, and they cain't help it."

"Aw, Frank, that's not true," I responded. "If that little boy's momma hadn't taught him the 'nigger' word, he wouldn't know nothing about it. She oughta be ashamed of herself! That woman is teaching her little boy to hate Negroes, and probably his old daddy too."

Frank wasn't really upset with me and I could tell. "Maybe so, Duke," he relented, "but it's how this world is. Peckerwoods on the top, and colored folks on the bottom, the very bottom."

"Well, it ain't right, Frank, and I don't understand it, none of that crap," I replied. "How can you look at a person, see his skin color - and hate a man's guts because of it? We, black people, were the ones in slavery, not their racist, white asses! I - I'm sorry for my language, Frank. I'm just mad. And guess what? I was actually smiling - just before that kid called me out of my name."

Coincidentally, Frank was smiling as he opted to pass me two twenty dollar bills. "Here's your cut," he softly stated. "Try and forget about it, Duke. That young heifer ain't worth worrying about, none of them are."

Momentarily, I tried to give one of the twenties back to Frank. "Here - I didn't help you finish up, so I don't deserve both of these."

"Keep it, Duke, you're my little assistant, right?" Frank spoke, starting up the truck. "Because when you do work, you do a damn good job. Jest keep it."

Cousin Pauline's husband, Frank, was a genuinely nice guy. However, as time would prove, he wasn't always so fair-minded when it came to our work relationship. In fact, in a few cases he tried to be what I called a "downright slickster." But because I cared about him so much and no serious or long-lasting harm was ever done, I could never bring myself to begrudge him. For the most part, I took it all in stride and in good spirits also.

As a point of reference, when Frank and I would engage in the process of white-washing basements (and I mean relatively large basements), we would be paid substantially for our labor and that's when things would, sometimes, go awry.

In the midst of such occasions, Frank traditionally referred to our wages as 'good money' and he made sure that I knew exactly how much money we'd earn prior to each job. He would say something like, "We're gonna get four hundred bucks for this job and we'll split it right down the middle, two hundred a piece. Do that sound 'bout right, Duke?" And, of course, I was well-pleased. For that was 'good money' to me also.

Sometimes (and essentially when school was not in session), we'd work ten or twelve hour days, trying to complete our white-washing projects. And due to those long hours, we took a lunch break. However, instead of both of us leaving the work site and going out to dine together, Frank preferred to go to some fast-food restaurant and pick us up some food. And with me being a youngster, he often allowed me to select the eating facility. Then, after I would choose a place like 'Kentucky Fried Chicken' or maybe 'White Castles,' Frank would soon be on his way. But each time he would specifically suggest that I, "keep on working."

Well, I fell for the okey-doke (or scheme) the first and the second time as well. Thinking nothing of it, I continued, nonstop, to apply white paint to the wall's surface. However, on the third occasion, after an entire hour had passed by and my coworker, or partner, had not returned, it became clear to me that I was being duped.

I figured, unless the selected restaurant was located on the Illinois side of the Mississippi River or Frank was involved in some kind of automobile accident, there was no valid reason for the lengthy delay. Therefore, upon Frank's eventual return, I was poised to hear a big Jerry. And, when he finally did return, armed with burgers, fries and drinks from White Castles, my ears were not disappointed. Frank claimed he had ran out of gas en route to the fast-food facility and apologized for taking so long.

Since Frank was successful in his first three trickery endeavors (I even pretended to believe his 'out of gas' excuse), I knew it was just a matter of time before he would try it again. When the fourth time came about, he and I played out the same scenario. After I chose Kentucky Fried Chicken as the fast-food venue, Frank left the basement area to procure our dinner. And, like always, he encouraged me to continue working.

Admittedly, after my coworker ascended the basement steps, I purposely did not resume my painting task. Instead, I decided to take a seat and was fully intent upon taking a breather until Frank returned. But prior to his eventual reappearance, something occurred that put an entirely new slant on our continuing work alliance. Just by casually dialoguing with the home's owner, and our soon-to-be benefactor, I learned that we were actually being paid more than the amount Frank had previously told me. In regards to the project we were presently doing, we were slated to be awarded five hundred dollars. News to me! Frank told me we were being paid four hundred dollars!

Strange as it might seem, I didn't so much as flinch in the wake of the home owner's disclosure. I behaved as if I was well-aware of the authentic payment. Furthermore, I did not emerge upset with my rather deceptive partner either. However, I did elect to go back to white-washing the walls as I decided how I would handle the new development. And then, about twenty minutes later, when Frank returned with our chicken dinners in tow (he had been gone a good hour at that juncture), he was somewhat surprised that I had not made more progress on my painting endeavor. Actually, Frank descended the stairs just as Mr. Farley, the man who I had spoken to, was walking up them. In fact, they cordially greeted each other.

"Duke, whatchu been doing?" Frank asked, focusing on the wall area. "Seems like you were at that same spot when I left outta here."

My behavior was rather nonchalant. "Aw, I got to jaw-jacking with Mr. Farley," I smilingly replied. "I couldn't get a word in edge-wise. That man can talk! But guess what, Frank? We are doing such a good job, he's gonna throw us out an extra one hundred dollars! Yeah, instead of giving us $400, he's upping it to a whopping $500 dollars! Ain't that something? He's a real nice guy."

My returning coworker appeared to be frozen in silence, clearly taken aback for a prolonged moment. Then, finally, he casually said, "Well - that is good news. I guess, maybe, we hit the jackpot of this one. Yeah, that is something other-else. Good news."

As I mentioned earlier, in spite of Frank Poe's penchant for being, sometimes, slick and deceptive, he was basically good-natured and a real joy to be around. On the many pleasure treks I took with him and his wife, he was a congenial and generous travelling companion. And as a twelve-year-old kid and, later on, a teenager, I felt truly blessed and fortunate to have such an individual in my life. And I felt likewise when it came to my cousin.

However, there was a single characteristic that, while purely unique to Frank, rendered him, both, comical and somewhat confounding. It was why I deemed him as a genuine 'character.' In all honesty, neither prior to, or in the long aftermath of interacting with Frank, did I ever meet any person who could frequently misuse or alter simple words or phrases like Frank could. Hands-down, he was a virtual master at mangling and abusing the English language.

To Frank Poe's personal merit, and in spite of not being an educated man (most of his life, Frank was illiterate), he always worked jobs that paid more than a decent salary. Whether he was doing construction work or laboring in a lumber yard, he earned 'good money' and, commendably, took his wages home to his wife. But, due to only a few years in grammar school, his vocabulary was limited, to say the least. Notably though, it was not because Frank was resigned to keeping it that way. Apparently, he seemed hell-bent on being rather creative and improvisational as well.

Oftentimes, when I conversed with Frank (which was quite regularly), I would sit, slowly shaking my head in silence, but on the very brink of laughter. However, it wasn't because he was a jokester or was frequently anecdotal, it was solely due to his verbiage. In all fairness, the words he spoke were not altogether absurd or stupid and they were so similar to the term he should have used, the on-hand listener could guess what he really meant to say. At least, that was true of me.

For example: One time, when Frank was somewhat venting, telling me about a heated dispute he had had with a fellow white worker on his day-job, he accused the man of trying to deputize his job. And although I immediately knew he intended to say 'jeopardize,' I didn't say otherwise. And then, on, yet, another occasion, when he tried to apprise me of how infuriated he was with a certain individual, he claimed he almost went dessert on the man. Again, I surmised right away that he meant to say 'berserk,' but, still, I failed to correct him.

Admittedly, sometimes my innate sense of humor would come into play when I interacted with my esteemed comrade, Frank Poe. Case in point: One afternoon, while I was socially visiting Frank at his home, he smilingly handed me an official check which was made out to him, and since the amount on it was over three thousand dollars, he proudly provided me with an explanation.

"Do you know why they're paying me so much money?" he asked me. "It's because it's <u>radioactive,</u> going all the way back to the early parts of last year."

Well, I was acting quite silly, and I was certain Frank was meaning to say 'retroactive,' but I dropped the check like it was a hot potato. Of course, my onlooking partner did not remotely catch my joke and, instead, retrieved the check from the floor and opted to try and teach me a thing or two.

"That means they're paying me for a whole bunch of weeks way-back-when, weeks going all the way back to the first part of last year," Frank informed me. "You know, Duke, like back-pay or something."

In further regards to Frank, I didn't quite relish poking fun of him. For I cherished and cared about him much too much. But I must acknowledge that some things were genuinely mirthful when it came to him. For, yet, another example: Although Frank smoked cigarettes, just like his wife and all of his Strickland in-laws, he also enjoyed smoking cigars on occasion. Seemingly, however, not just any old cigar would do. Every now and then, and especially in the aftermath of me and Frank completing a basement white-washing project, Frank had a craving for a special cigar. Therefore, we were practically compelled to stop at a store or confectionery to procure it. And since I always had a sweet tooth when I had money in my pocket, I would be right by his side.

And that's when Frank, immediately sought out the on-duty clerk and proceeded to ask, "Hey, fella, do ya'll carry Elmer Duck cigars in this here store?"

Now, although I wasn't being my usual self, I momentarily observed the look of puzzlement on the faces of the various clerks during such occasions and I could not hold my tongue. Acting like an on-scene interpreter, I'd say, "He's wondering if you guys sell 'El Producto' cigars. That's what he really means."

In the short aftermath of those particular times, Frank didn't seem remotely offended by my translating efforts. He would buy his requested cigar (if the facility carried it) or would, sometimes, settle for an alternate brand if they did not. But, strangely, no matter how many times I opted to divulge the actual brand name, Frank would still ask for Elmer Duck cigars the next time and the time after that.

In spite of my steadfast work-partner and benefactor, Frank, consistently saying <u>remire</u> instead of 'admire,' rememory instead of 'memory,' retermine instead 'determine' and hope me out instead of 'help me out,' I, sometimes, felt he was pulling my leg; just pretending that he was unaware of his verbal blunders. And till this very day, I still wonder about it.

In essence, I cite the following: Frank was employed by a prominent lumber facility for many years. The name of the place was the 'Southern Cross Lumber Company' and, yet, when Frank referred to it, he proceeded to call it the Santa Claus Lumber Company. I couldn't buy into it way-back-when and I still don't at present. I cannot fathom Frank working at the same business site year-in and year-out, putting in a standard forty-hour week, and not knowing the true name of the company that employed and paid him. That premise, to me, was and is beyond comprehension!

However, upon casting off all of my underlying suspicions, regardless of Frank's amusing quirks and deceptive behavior, he was a virtual God-send to me - he and my cousin, Pauline. And I wish with all my heart that every young kid could have comparable individuals in their lives. It would make for a much better world.

CHAPTER TWENTY-FOUR

AMERICA'S UNSUNG HEROES

As I alluded to earlier, when I was a little boy living on Sullivan street, a slightly larger boy residing on Burd avenue, and throughout my ensuing teenage years, I was almost forever working or, at least, was actively looking for a job. When I was eight years old, I was emptying trash for assorted neighbors, selling weekend newspapers and hauling groceries procured from the local supermarket. At the age of ten and eight years beyond it, I still sold newspapers, cut an abundance of suburban lawns, served as a porter and shoe shine boy at a barbershop, washed cars, detailed newly-built houses, whitewashed basements, worked as a stock boy at a popular men's clothing store and even tutored my younger cousin, Barbara Ann, in arithmetic.

However, while some of those jobs were taxing and garnered rather meager wages as well, there was one money-making endeavor I engaged in that I regretted but, eventually, came to appreciate and savor. When I was fifteen (and school was out for the summer), my oldest brother, Gary, and I traveled to a town named 'Benton Harbor, Michigan' to engage in the task of strawberry picking.

I'm not sure "when" or "how" my mother met them, but there was a married couple who lived within two short blocks of our Burd residence. Their last name was 'Surrett' and Ruby saw fit to introduce them to me and my four brothers. The Surretts seemed to be nice people, they had a couple of kids of their own, and they pitched an idea to our mom, and with me and Gary as the focal points. The couple talked excitedly about their connection to the fruit-picking circuit, divulging that they were slated to journey to Michigan and proposed that Gary and I accompany them there.

I was initially skeptical, so was Gary, but when Mr. Surrett went on and on about how lucrative the venture would be, he managed to sell us on the idea. He specifically talked about the 'smallness' of the strawberry containers and claimed we would 'easily' make fifty to sixty dollars a day, the both of us.

As you might surmise, none of the enticing rhetoric proved to be true. The strawberry containers were not at all small, 'pickers' labored from sunrise to sunset (constantly bending over or stooping) and me and Gary couldn't earn a paltry forty dollars per day, even if we opted to pool our wages together!

Naturally, my brother and I were not the only ones out in the blazing hot sun, dealing with the abundant, elongated strawberry patches. And neither were the Surretts and their children our only co-workers. There were loads of Mexican-American farm laborers on-hand; assorted minorities who picked fruit year-round and they were serious, intense and quite dogmatic about it. In reality, it was a staple and sustaining way of life to them.

To put it lightly and politely too, the whole strawberry picking endeavor was a tremendous letdown to Gary and me both; a virtual wash out in the first degree. And due to my own foolhardiness, there emerged a very dangerous component to it also. On one memorable afternoon, Gary stepped forward and prevented a razor-wielding Mexican teenager from cutting my throat.

After I noticed that the strawberries were relatively larger than the ones in my assigned row, I proceeded to cross over to the adjacent row and that's when the weapon-brandishing boy took exception to my actions. My intent was not remotely malicious and, right away, it became crystal-clear to me that I had committed a <u>no-no</u>. I, therefore, resolved to never do it again and was awfully glad Gary was nearby to disarm my angry, would-be assailant. No telling what might have transpired if my brother wasn't around. And later I thought - maybe Gary liked me after all.

In reality, I learned an invaluable lesson in the wake of that 'razor' episode in Benton Harbor, Michigan. Like most endeavors, there's a code of ethics that apply to fruit-harvesting as well and novice 'pickers' should try to familiarize themselves with them and, then, adhere to them.

However, there was another impression I withdrew from the entirety of that Michigan misadventure as well. Upon resolving to listen to adults with a more discriminate ear in the future, I emerged with a genuine appreciation of all migrant workers, and especially hard-working parents who were raising children. To labor day in and day out and travel around the country for the sake of feeding and supporting their families was something I truly admired, respected and greatly appreciated. In my estimation, they were <u>then</u>, and they are <u>now</u>, the unsung heroes of American agriculture.

As my life-journey continued to march forward, the insight and wisdom I amassed from my disappointing trek to the state of

Michigan was acutely instrumental to a happening that transpired during the succeeding year, which was 1960. I was made aware that my Aunt Blanche (who was one of my father's older sister) and her husband, Van, happened to be in the migrant farming business themselves. And whether it was merely coincidence or I had previously shared my strawberry picking venture with the couple (they were the parents of my tutoring student), they opted to recruit me for one of their upcoming summer endeavors. But instead of strawberries, the luring fruit was cherries, and instead of Michigan, the specified destination was place called Sturgeon Bay, Wisconsin.

Notably, my aunt and uncle not only invited me to tag along with them there, they also asked me to try and get some of my friends to sign up for the venture also. To be frank, my initial instinct was to flatly turn thumbs-down on the issue (I was still brooding over the Benton Harbor fiasco), but after I deliberated at length, I found myself leaning towards saying a "yes." However, I had a major stipulation on my mind and I would participate in the venture only if it was strictly adhered to. Although I was only sixteen years old, I wanted to sign on as a 'straw boss' (which was a field supervisor) and be paid eighty-five dollars per week, along with free meals. And although I was pleasantly but secretly surprised, my terms were quickly accepted. Alternately, I shook hands with my Uncle Van to seal the deal and left his house with my mind set on recruiting others. To be earnest, I wasn't very optimistic in regards to my success in that particular area.

As a matter of courtesy, I forthrightly asked my brother, Gary, if he'd be interested in going with us. Actually, I anticipated him nixing the proposal and I hoped he wouldn't choose to scold or punch me when I asked him.

Well, without a semblance of thought, and no coinciding violence either, Gary said "no." But, to my surprise, my younger brother, Lovell, did wish to go. However, he chose to sign on as a dishwasher in the mess hall and not a regular cherry picker. Although Lovell never expressed it in words, I surmised that when Gary and I told him about our misadventure in Benton Harbor, he wanted no parts of the fruit-picking procedure.

And there was a related fallout also. Since I had shared my complaints about the Michigan fiasco with the majority of the fellows as well, there was a slim chance that I'd sell them on the upcoming venture too. And, admittedly, I neither had the nerve nor the firm conviction to try to talk them into it.

However, to my utter joy, my elementary school comrade and longtime running buddy, Walter, as well as a high school classmate named James 'Ironhead' Mathews did wish to go. And, then, when my best friend, Robert, expressed his desire to join the undertaking also, I was momentarily ecstatic.

At that juncture though, when I seriously took the time to think about it, I was almost positive that Robert's dad would veto the notion. After all, his son, Robert, had never been out of town on his own and, as I mentioned earlier, he was very protective of all of his children. And, to be honest, I thoroughly admired him for being that way.

In retrospect, when my buddy, Robert, went to pitch the cherry-picking idea to, both, his mother and father, I was basically in the mix for moral support. Candidly speaking, I was nervous and rather uneasy. Quiet as kept, I was fearful I'd be blamed for coming up with a 'hair-brained scheme' and was poised to be scolded for it. Fortunately, that did not happen. In fact, it was a far cry from it. The senior Mr. Harris thought intently about the venture and, alternately, looked at me.

"Duke, tell you what, I'm gonna allow Robert to go," he announced. "But you have to promise me you'll take good care of him. In fact, you two must look out for one another, take special care of each other. Will you agree to that, Duke?"

In addition to being quite relieved, I immediately flashed a smile. Not only because I was well-pleased but because, in reality, I was only six months older than Robert. "All of that goes without saying, Mr. Harris," I replied. "Robert and I will always look out for each other, we always do. And you've got my solemn word on it."

In actuality, when I insisted upon being a straw boss prior to our Sturgeon Bay trip, I just assumed I would be dealing with teenagers or high school youngsters who were around my age (after all, Uncle Van had encouraged me to recruit some of my close-knit friends as workers), but I was plainly in error. Within mere days of our impending departure for Wisconsin, I was informed that the greater majority of our assembled work crew would be grown men. Notably though, not just ordinary grown men, but adult men who happened to have criminal records. And to be more precise, we would be dealing with a group of male felons and ex-convicts! And that was when I learned, too, we would be picking them up at the Employment Office which was located in downtown Saint Louis.

Reflecting back, there were three vehicles that comprised our convoy to Sturgeon Bay, Wisconsin; two automobiles and a very large truck that was originally a commercial moving van. The truck, essentially, accommodated the majority of the recruited work crew and was precisionly altered or modified to render the rather long road journey much more comfortable and tolerable for the workers. Specifically, the rear doors were cut down to halves and a number of drilled holes (with screens) were situated above and around the front cab area. Of course, that was done to yield a semblance of ventilation to the riders inside the van.

However, since it was indeed the summertime (and despite traveling mostly at night), I was certain that it was still relatively hot and stuffy inside the back of that truck and I felt very bad about it. Although I was fortunate enough to ride up front in the cab of the truck, sitting adjacent to the vehicle's driver (who was my Uncle Van), unfortunately, my brother, Lovell, and my friends, namely Robert, Walter and James, were among those enclosed passengers and I truly felt sorry for them, and similarly when it came to their fellow riders.

In addition, although I kept it entirely to myself, I wasn't at all comfortable when it came to the men we had retrieved from that employment facility. Admittedly, I was guilty of being somewhat judgmental and I hated being that way, but, after all, our laboring entourage were not exactly 'stellar' and 'upstanding' citizens. So, I was quite leery of them, each and every one of them.

As I indicated, the large converted moving van was not the sole vehicle involved in our cross-country trek to Sturgeon Bay. There were a couple of cars and their passengers were strictly support personnel; individuals such as a field supervisor, two foremen and two veteran cooks; one of them, a woman. In reality, they were all long-time associates of, both, my uncle and my aunt and they seemed to be ready and quite able to tackle their job roles. So, apparently, they, too (like Uncle Van) were familiar and adept when it came to the fruit-picking circuit and, with the passing of time, I came to appreciate and enjoy each of them immensely.

As it turned out, when our three-vehicle convoy finally arrived at our designated compound in Sturgeon Bay, Wisconsin, I learned almost immediately that I was absolutely correct for being suspicious of the group of men we picked up at the Employment

Office in St. Louis. Right in the middle of disembarking our respective vehicles (it was almost two-thirty in the morning) and with our individual minds focused on gaining access to one of the numerous cabins that stood before us, two official state automobiles entered the complex and pulled up directly behind our position.

Although the entire area was well-illuminated by a series of overhead lampposts, I was quite sure that, even without those lights, every single person in our traveling party was acutely aware of what the swirling blue lights meant. Meaning, we collectively knew we were about to deal with the so-called 'long arm of the law.'

Without a doubt, the two oncoming men were state troopers (both of them, white) and since their vehicle lights were still flashing, none of us assumed the uniformed duo was a part of a cordial welcoming committee. Moreover, the grim-faced pair had no intentions of being polite or civil.

After boisterously calling for the "boss" of our group (Uncle Van hurriedly stepped forward), the ranking officer wasted no time addressing the problem at hand. And, soon, to the utter shock of Van, myself and every person who had ridden in the two automobiles, we were accused of 'allegedly' harboring criminals! Not ex-criminals, but apparently some who were still active.

According to the outraged and senior trooper, every time we stopped to make a pit stop during our long journey, the selected service station was, subsequently, held-up! And only because the victimized attendants were reluctant (or too afraid) to identify the guilty 'Negras,' there were no official arrest orders being issued. "But," asserted the trooper spokesman, "we know damn well it was youse people. And I'm warning yo' asses - if a one of youse break a single gardamn law in this here county, we gonna come rat back out here, and in full force, and haul your roguish asses in. So, take my advice, boys, stay the hell put in this here compound - cause we sho gonna be on the look-out for youse!"

As an undercurrent of grumbling emerged from some of the men in our group (maybe, the select perpetrators), Uncle Van seemed momentarily dumbfounded and almost stricken. Finally, he asked, "Are you sure you got the right group, Officer? What you're saying is kinda hard to believe."

"Are you shittin' me?" the younger trooper spoke. "People gave us the description of yall's moving van and said it was a gang of ugly-ass niggers hangin' out the back of it! You're the ones alright, and we gonna git you sooner or later too. And I, for one, can hardly wait."

Only minutes later, as the police officials proceeded to make their departure, I looked directly into the face of my uncle, mostly in admiration. He had played the accusation off well and calmly, although he knew, nine out of ten times, that the guilty culprits were amongst us. (Hell, in my estimation, we could have had men who were on the F.B.I.'s most wanted list in our party).

However, Uncle Van didn't see fit to discuss or dwell on the matter. (I admired him for that also). Instead, he elected to engage in a comprehensive orientation, apprising our very attentive group of what was ahead of us and what our daily work routine would consist of. He touched on everything from our scheduled wake-up time and our ensuing breakfast hour, to how we should function and conduct ourselves in the outlying cherry fields. Then, after verbally familiarizing us with the general layout of the entire compound (although it was still quite dark), he gained access to an adjacent cabin which housed our hygienic and bedding supplies (such as soap, towels, washcloths, pillows and blankets), and proceeded to orderly distribute those bundles to each and every individual. And, finally, after we were assigned our respective cabins, we collectively called it a night, fully aware that four-thirty a.m. was right around the corner.

Though I could not speak for anyone else, I, for one, did not sleep a wink during my maiden night in Sturgeon Bay. However, it wasn't because the beds were uncomfortable (although the mattresses were straw-filled) or even because the accommodations weren't exactly the best. It was solely due to how I felt about the majority of our work crew. There I was, just 16 years old, and I was supposed to play 'boss' to grown men whom I now perceived as a bunch of incorrigible criminals. I figured I could very well be physically assaulted or even shot or something. I willed myself to close my eyes, asking, "What the hell have I gotten myself into?"

Now, it is difficult to explain why, but when the rousting hour rolled around, I rose from my bed feeling refreshed and somewhat optimistic too. I imagined it had a great deal to do with outward aesthetics. After rising before everyone else assigned to my cabin (Lovell and Robert included), I had washed up, dressed myself and was soon outdoors, standing in front of our domicile. Looking in the distance, I not only felt exhilarated and soothed upon watching the sun's steady ascension (it was purely spectacular, in my viewpoint), I was emboldened even further by a song that was, simultaneously, playing on nearby phonograph. It was a tune entitled 'On The Horizon,' which was sung by a man named Ben E. King, and it was, both, symbolic and appropriate for the occasion at hand. What I saw and how I felt at that precise moment in time was something poets dreamed and wrote about. To me, it was no less than magnificent and awesome!

As it would come to pass, I was delightfully surprised and totally wrong about my presumptions regarding our recruited work crew, who, essentially, were the male felons we had picked up at the Employment Office back in Saint Louis. They seldomly balked at obeying my instructions or demands and when they did mildly resist my orders, I found I had a couple of influential allies on my side. Owing to two close-knit buddies (their names were Marvin Troupe and Simpson Wayne), every time the other men gave me any static or negative feedback, they would immediately intercede. They would speak up, saying something like, "Don't give the boy a hard time. He's just doing his damn job.", and soon their co-working comrades would comply to my wishes. And since I frequently found it necessary to send the cherry-pickers back to attend to 'half-done' trees (in spite of having elongated ladders to aid them, they, sometimes, skipped over large clusters of cherries), I greatly appreciated 'Simp' and 'Marvin's' support.

Well, everything went exceedingly fine for a period of time. While wearing a rather large Mexican sombrero (or hat), I became quite adept and comfortable in my straw boss position, my brother, Lovell, seemed resigned to his dishwashing job, all of the workers (including my three teenaged buddies) were earning money and eating three 'squares' a day (meaning, liberal and nourishing meals) and the entire assemblage was getting along almost like one big, happy family.

On Sundays, which was our only off-day, my fellow workers would even form a softball team in their ranks and challenge other migrant workers (mostly Mexican-Americans or Hispanics) to a competitive game. And I, of course, having no desire whatsoever to participate as a player, would sit on the sideline and root our team on. Every now and then, however, I'd latch on to a few bottles of beer and that would make my day.

On some Sundays when a ballgame was not on the agenda, we would come together as a group, then climb aboard our truck and spend the entire day at the not-too-distant beach area of Lake Michigan. And it was on one of those particular outings, after undergoing a life-death experience, I learned an invaluable lesson. In the wake of it, I emerged thoroughly convinced that a man's time on earth is preordained.

To be honest, I never regarded myself as a strong or skillful swimmer. And not only that, I never particularly liked swimming. I hardly ever accompanied the fellows when they chose to go up to a site called 'Sherman Park' or the YMCA for a day of frolicking in a gigantic pool of water. So, why I decided to try and swim out to the raft, located almost a hundred years out from the shore area and then turn right around and swim back to dry land, is still beyond sane comprehension to me. (Maybe, I had seen too many Tarzan movies).

Actually, I had made it to the raft and I should have stayed there for a period of time. But I didn't and I soon paid dearly for my bad judgment. In the middle of my return trek to the shore area, as my strength abated and my arms became virtually impossible to lift (I knew nothing about treading water), I clearly panicked and, moments later, I was in the throes of drowning!

Almost instantaneously, however, I was keenly cognizant of something that was truly remarkable; but a rather bizarre assertion that numerous drowning victims reportedly ascribed to. As I was literally bobbing up and down in those waters, ingesting part of that nasty lake, I plainly relived my young life in vivid flashbacks.

Among other things, I reviewed my first day in kindergarten, a select time when I had seen my father on the Admiral boat, the day I grieved heavily over Brenda Jenson's untimely death, the night I confronted the gun-wielding Track Boy, and even when I walked into that knife at Soldan High School. And then, suddenly, I could visualize my mother standing on the Lake Michigan shore and frantically (but quite helplessly) watching me drown. And that was precisely when a trained lifeguard grabbed a hold of me.

Minutes later, I was pulled from the lake and was lying face-down on the ground and practically vomiting gushes of water from my mouth. And as Lovell, Robert, Walter and other familiar faces stood around, worriedly looking down at me, the lifeguard actively revived me. Naturally, I was extremely thankful to the guard and considered myself a most fortunate young man.

Oddly though, in but a moment's passing, instead of being fixated on my foregoing fate, I found myself concentrating almost exclusively on my mother Ruby. I surmised, since she had the faith in me to permit me to embark on the ongoing trip, and even allowed Lovell to accompany me on it, it would have been a downright affront to her if I had, somehow, perished during the venture. My rescuer (the lifeguard) told me shortly after the ordeal, that upon seeing me go under so many times, he had never seen a drowning victim surface and then attempt to resume swimming afterwards. Though I kept it to myself, I credited my survival efforts to the single vision I had had of my mom.

While I'm not sure if the drowning episode was a prelude to things that were slated to go awry, it seemed to at least parallel it. Around that same period of time, my Aunt Blanche (along with my cousin, Barbara) showed up at the complex and within just a few days of her arrival, due to a certain change she implemented, there was heavy dissension in the air. Up until that period, the fruit-picking crew and everyone else were being charged seventy-five cents per meal. That, of course, added up to the sum of two dollars and a quarter each day. However, since the food portions were quite liberal and very appetizing as well, everyone seemed to be okay with the assessed cost. Although the cherry-pickers, on the average, earned a mere $30.00 per day, they still appeared to be satisfied with their ongoing lot.

However, after my aunt arrived at the work camp, the three daily meals still cost the standard seventy-five cents each, but the serving portions were noticeably altered. In fact, they were literally cut in half and that arbitrary decision certainly didn't set well with the majority of the work crew. Then, to add insult of injury, they were also informed that a second serving of food would require additional monies.

Notably, within mere days of the abrupt and rather unreasonable change, some of the men were so upset and so disenchanted about it, that, in the wee hours of a select morning, they broke into the mess facility and proceeded to drastically trash and vandalize the place. Assorted furniture was destroyed and various food supplies (such as fruit, vegetables, soda, juices, milk and eggs) was strewn throughout the entire facility. Call it a play on words, but the mess hall was a total mess!

Of course, the happening was not remotely amusing to my Uncle Van or my recently-arrived aunt either. They were taken aback and livid! And it wasn't funny to my brother, Lovell, especially. In fact, he staunchly balked at cleaning up the place and insisted upon being paid a substantial amount of money if he signed on to the task of doing it.

To be sure, I had never 'heard' of a fourteen-year-old kid going on strike before, but that's exactly what my younger brother did. I do not actually recall him making up an official protest sign or even seeing him marching around the mess hall, hoisting it into the air, but he was hell-bent upon sticking to his guns just the same. And, apparently, he wasn't prepared to budge!

Ordinarily, I would have found myself in the throes of a dilemma: Lovell was on strike and Uncle Van wasn't willing to meet his monetary demands. But whether it could be chalked up to coincidence, mere happenstance or a stroke of fate, I was almost instantaneously exempted from wrestling with that particular quandary. In the short aftermath of the mess hall break-in (the ensuing afternoon, in fact), my best friend, Robert, informed me that he was seriously ill, and confessed he had been feeling that way for several days. To be precise, he was suffering from nausea, headaches, frequent diarrhea and was dealing with a high fever.

Naturally, I was alarmed and visually worried as well. And since there wasn't a physician in our party, and no one who was medically astute either, I immediately made a judgment. Since I had solemnly promised Robert's dad that I'd look out for Robert throughout our ongoing trip, I felt it was wise and sensible to bow out of the venture and return to our hometown. And, of course, my decision included my younger brother, Lovell.

Therefore, since I had saved up ample monies (after all, there was no place to spend my weekly earnings), I soon resigned from my straw boss position, took the initiative to facilitate our traveling plans and graciously asked Uncle Van to transport the three of us to the not-too-distant Greyhound bus station. And, to my uncle's congenial credit (he said he hated losing my services), he honored my decision and adhered to my request.

As it came to pass, my friend, Robert, was afforded adequate medical treatment back in St. Louis (he was diagnosed with 'severe dysentery'), his mom and dad were well-pleased I had brought him back home and, of course, he was eventually alright and rendered healthy. Personally, other than regretting that I left my comrades, Walter and James, behind in Sturgeon Bay, I was quite alright too. And all I could say about that yesteryear cherry-picking experience was that it was "one helluva ride!"

CHAPTER TWENTY-FIVE
HOME - SWEET HOME

My four years at Soldan High School were somewhat strange, to say the very least. I was a consistent 'B' student; not solely because it was the very best I could do, but, basically, because it was all I wanted to do. Although I seldomly carried a textbook home, I developed a technique that rendered me an above average student. Since we were permitted to select our own class schedules (from the sophomore year and beyond), I always chose my classes back-to-back, from early morning to mid-afternoon, and would have consecutive study halls at the end of the school day. However, unlike a lot of fellow classmates, study hall was not a leisurely social outlet for me. It was exactly what it was fashioned to be, an express period (or periods) that was set aside for studying and preliminary homework. And since surrounding students were well aware of my routine, they seldomly disturbed me.

Another odd thing about my time at Soldan High dealt expressly with my home address. During the four years I was enrolled there, my family and I lived in four different residences. We started off at 1372 Burd Street, then moved to 5574 Page Avenue, then to 5534 Palm Street and, finally, to 1400 North 9th Street, which was located in downtown St. Louis. Some of the fellows 'kiddingly' accused us of moving every time the rent was due, but that wasn't remotely true. I would tell them that my family was just picky and very hard to please. Sure, I was somewhat of a kidder myself.

When it came to those four diverse addresses, and my firm determination to graduate from Soldan-Blewett, only one of them required the use of public transportation. Fourteen hundred north 9th street, which was part of the Cochran Housing Projects, was so far away from Soldan that I had to catch the 'Hodiamont' streetcar or ride a service car (sometimes called a 'jitney'). In regards to the other three residences, I had to rely on my legs and two feet and some of those daily journeys was quite long.

When we moved to the 5500 block of Page Avenue, my brother, Gary, and I were in our sophomore year. It was shortly after my mother had married William and since it was the entire second floor of a two-family flat, it gave us a little more space than we had on Burd. And, actually, it was located less than a mile from our Burd residence. In fact, if the 'Principia School' was still in the neighborhood (that private white institution that yielded to white flight), we would have been living cater-cornered across the street from it.

Notably, we happened to be living at our Page address when I engaged in that 'knifing' episode at Soldan High. Due to that harrowing incident (I was fortunate I didn't lose the use of my right hand), I was made to wear a sling for a while. And every school morning, acting in the role of an endearing best friend, Robert Harris would stop by my house and assist me in the simple task of slipping on my shoes and tying them. Then, he and I would embark upon the trek to school.

The house located on Page Avenue was also the site where Alonzo would bring me his hand-me-down clothing, where he would offer me his fifty cents auto rides and where, afterwards

THE LONG AND WINDING ROAD

(when Lonnie would leave me behind), Larry would show up and afford me free transportation.

Sorrowfully though, 5574 Page Avenue was also where my eldest brother, Melvin Gary, angrily and verbally challenged our resurfacing and long, lost father, namely Melvin Virgil Harris. Upon recalling the mistreatment and abuse he had endured at the hands of our old man, Gary virtually double-dared our dad to, "Try and bounce me around again - like you did when I was a kid."

And I also remember my hostile behavior on the very same evening, when I took exception with my substandard stepfather. As I bore witness to William gloating over his being a "better dad" to us boys, pouring more salt into Dad's wounded ego, I opted to take the floor. Not pulling my punches, I angrily informed them, "As fathers, neither one of you niggas are worth two dead flies!" And at that particular time (and afterwards), I truly meant it.

When I reflect back on my teenage years, I especially liked living on Page Avenue because it wasn't far from Robert and Charles's residence on a street called Hodiamont. In fact, the foot journey was a straight shot, just five blocks west of my house. So, when we upped and moved to Palm street, I regretted not being near the Harris family and was doubly sorry I'd no longer be walking to school with Robert anymore. At that period, I was just going into my Junior year (the 11th grade) and, therefore, it was still a long way from graduation day.

Speaking of a 'long way,' that aptly described my weekday hike from Palm street to Soldan High School. Our new residence was less than fifty yards from a street called 'Belt,' a street that ran north and south, and over seventy percent of my foot trek to school occurred on that stretch. In fact, it took me all the way to Page Avenue, which was within three blocks of my former residence.

And once there, upon reaching that Page junction, I would pivot eastward and, in less than ten minute's time, would veer south on Union Boulevard, which was where Soldan High was situated.

However, to my personal joy, when it came to that daily, rather lengthy walk, I was never lonely. That was because I was never, ever alone. In reality, by the time I converged on my school, I had a regular and familiar crowd with me. Specifically, after walking but two blocks from the intersection of Palm and Belt (adjacent to my home residence), I met up with my running buddy, Jerry, at Ashland street, and then, one block later, a young lady named Eileen joined up with us at Greer street. Then, as the three of us resumed our stroll, another long-time friend, Henry (or Moose) soon appeared on the scene, then Larry, then Willie, then James and, occasionally Woody (who would actually go out of his way to join up with us), and by the time we all converged on our common destination, which was Soldan High School, of course, our group could have been viewed as a rather boisterous and spirited crowd; which was predicated by our light-hearted rhetoric and residual merriment.

The foregoing was a real game-changer to me. Within a relatively short while, as our daily pilgrimage became routine and commonplace, a foot-journey that I originally regarded as exceedingly lengthy and tedious as well, seemed to be almost magically shortened, interesting and, oftentimes, fun. In essence, I grew to love and savor those morning hikes.

However, my memory of living at 5534 Palm street had a few downsides to it also. Although I was able to extract a somewhat moderate refuge from the adage, "All's well that ends well," I never quite came to terms with the relocation process itself. Being a person of deep sentiment, I secretly grieved over moving so far away from my endeared friend, Robert, and his beloved family too. And, incidentally, I also happened to be residing on Palm when I signed on to that Sturgeon Bay cherry-harvesting trip, wherein I was later compelled to make emergency provisions to bring my seriously-ill best friend, Robert, as well as my younger brother, Lovell, back to our hometown.

Although I never regretted making that decision, I had mixed emotions about the trip itself. Similar to life itself, that particular venture was froth with peaks and valleys (mostly valleys), and it's a long-ago happening that remains vividly present in my mind. However, when I, subsequently, paired it with the Michigan fiasco that took place during the previous year, I emerged adamant about never participating in an endeavor that even remotely resembled them. Still, it was an experience I relished.

Now, other than viewing a ton of exaggerated and demonstrative romances depicted on the silver screen (although I vividly recalled the real-life love scenes played out by my cousin, Lloyd Henry, and his young lady, Marilyn, on Burd street), I knew hardly nothing about so-called 'matters of the heart.' Since me and my four brothers lived under a roof with two parents who seemed to be constantly at odds with each other, authentic and normal love was practically non-existent in our household. And, personally, because I was all-too privy to my father's ongoing womanizing, I never pointed the finger of blame at my long-suffering mother. Therefore, both, the birds and the bees had flown by me.

However, in spite of my inexperience and naiveté (but rather high regard for womankind in general), I was not above being suddenly smitten with a charming and attractive young lady. In my case, it was the girl named Eileen, who was the aforementioned walking companion who daily awaited me and my running-buddy, Jerry, at the intersection of Belt and Greer street. But to my utter regret, time would reveal that Eileen didn't feel likewise towards me. Notably though, when it came to matters of the heart, I was also living on Palm street when my heart was first broken.

But before I was made to contend with that sorrowful reckoning, I confess to behaving somewhat daffy, bizarre and rather stupid as well. Just so happened, Eileen and I had 'Biology 1' together and as it turned out, we both became somewhat detrimental to each other. Of course, it wasn't health wise or in any way dangerous or hazardous, but was purely school-related and grade-wise. "Leeny" and I (which I came to call her) almost constantly talked to each other, wrote and passed a lot of silly notes and jokingly kept each other in mirthful stitches and, rather insensibly, while the class was being conducted.

Not surprisingly, our ongoing behavior ticked off our teacher (a middle-aged white man named 'Mr. Lennie') and he displayed his anger several times by ousting us from his classroom, the both of us. We would absorb his criticisms laughingly and take his contempt in stride also. But to our mutual sorrow, our teacher, alternately, had the last laugh. At the end of the final semester period, he elected to fail us both.

While a distraught and vulnerable Eileen burst into a flood of tears in the wake of her 'F,' I was completely livid! I had never in my life been given an 'F' (and a 'D', only once) and because I had received 'C's during the first two semesters in that biology class, I didn't feel that my final grade was fair. More than that, I deemed Mr. Lennie's actions vindictive and unreasonable and I was guilty of allowing my temper to override my common sense.

To be precise, I threatened my biology teacher with violence! Though it was entirely out of character for me, I verbally vowed to "kick his stupid ass!" (Apparently, my budding love rendered me foolhardy and volatile). As it turned out though, my threat managed to harden Mr. Lennie's heart and, further down the road, sealed my romantic fate with Eileen as well. Owing to Leeny's pronounced bawling, the teacher reconsidered her grade and awarded her a 'D' instead. Naturally, he still failed me.

Being stuck with my very first 'F', in my viewpoint, was punishment enough. However, the wheels of fate were still rapidly spinning. When school started up again, I was subjected to the very same disgruntled instructor for Biology 1 (meaning, Mr. Lennie), Eileen had moved on to Biology 2 and, most aggrieves to me, Eileen became acquainted with her 'soul-mate' in that very class, a young man whom she would eventually marry. I, in the final analysis, would earn an 'A' for my scholarly performance in the Biology 1 classroom. Actually, it was without fanfare and quite easy. As the saying goes, "It was Deja vu all over again."

Since my oldest brother and I attended different high schools and I was frequently working most evenings, Gary and I seldomly interacted with each other. Of course, that was true when we were at Emerson Elementary also. Actually, the last time we spent more than an hour together was when we were in Benton Harbor, Michigan during the strawberry-picking fiasco. We never ran in the same social circle, so we were still, in some ways, estranged.

While I continued to be dismissive of sports in general (all forms of it), Gary always loved it and seemed to excel whenever he participated in them. At O'Fallon Tech, he was on the wrestling team and also played varsity football. Therefore, when we entered our first fall season on Palm street and I was informed that Soldan's kick-off football game would pit our school against O'Fallon High, I was moderately interested in it.

However, since Gary didn't so much as mention it to me, I had no intentions of going to see the contest. But when some of the 'fellows' sought me out and practically browbeaten me to go see it, I soon changed my mind. They, too, were aware that my brother was a starting player for the opposing school and they twisted my arm even further by reminding me that Henry (Moose) would be playing for Soldan. So, upon bowing to their coaxing (or nagging), I accompanied my friends to the 'Saint Louis Public Schools Stadium' on the specified afternoon. That was the name of the site on Kingshighway Boulevard where the competition took place.

To say the very least, the football contest between O'Fallon and Soldan drew a packed house. Not only were there students from the two rival high schools in the stands, it seemed like every secondary school in the region had sent their teenagers there also. People were milling all about, scrambling to secure select seats and behaving like they were at the Mardi gras or somewhere similar. And for a prolonged period, until the game itself commenced, a spectator could barely hear him or herself talk. It was just that darn rousing and noisy!

Now, since I was not into sports, and especially football, I knew very little about the game's rules and even less about the various positions that made up a traditional football team. Oh, I could identify the so-called 'quarterback,' but that was about it. So, when I heard someone say that a young man named 'Frank Pickens' was Soldan's "star halfback," I jokingly admitted that I didn't know a star halfback from a star half-wit.

My fun-making and jovial mood did not persist, however. Just a matter of fifteen minutes later, in the wake of a serious development out on the football field, I was compelled to deal with instantaneous alarm and anxiety. However, I certainly wasn't alone in my onsetting dread. Fact was, the entire stadium erupted into a boisterous and almost ear-piercing furor.

With collective eyes trained on the adjacent field, and essentially focusing on Soldan's football team, it was apparent that one of Soldan's players had been severely injured. Notably, it wasn't an average player, and nor was it our school's quarterback.

It happened to be Soldan's prized halfback, the boy I identified as Frank Pickens! As Frank was carrying the football and was trying to gain substantial yardage, he was abruptly stopped by a slew of O'Fallon High defenders. And wouldn't you know it? The primary defender, who had actually dinged tightly to one of Frank's legs, was Melvin 'Gary' Harris, my oldest brother. And, shortly, he was almost singularly blamed for breaking our star player's ankle.

Now, although my brother was essentially fulfilling his role as an opposing player (doing the job he was trained to do), his name was immediately mud when it came to pissed-offed and vindictive Soldanites. And by the time the game was concluded, similar to an unruly lynch mob in a western flick, there was a boiling consensus aimed at confronting the 'culprit' named Melvin Harris and "kicking his black ass!"

Of course, I was made aware of what was brewing and since I wasn't pressed for time (in reality, after Frank was carried off the field on a stretcher, there was plenty of game-time remaining), I thought intently about what actions needed to be taken. I assembled the on-hand fellows and some of our Soldan allies (other group of boys who collectively hung out together), informed them all that Gary was, indeed, my brother and assured them that I was not about to stand by idle and watch my brother being physically brutalized, and especially since he was doing what was expected of him as a football player.

Therefore, as the ongoing game edged towards the inevitable completion and I had priorly encouraged my supporters to rendezvous with me outside the opposing team's official dressing facility when it did conclude, I headed that way. For it was at that site where competing athletes showered, dressed and, then, made their departure for home or elsewhere.

The rather large group assembled there (mostly black boys and a few grown men) were already bragging about what they were going to do to Gary when my allies and I arrived on the scene. One would have thought that my brother had murdered an innocent little child, listening to the incensed rhetoric and threats that was being spewed out! They seemed poised to kill my brother if they possibly could. However, as I proceeded to stand in the middle of them, as I became fixated on the fact that Gary was simply doing his job, I emerged just as angry as many of them were. And that made me even more adamant about my resolve.

When my brother finally exited the dressing area, looking like a classic jock and toting his shoulder pads on his back, I stepped out in front of the mob before anyone else had the chance to speak to him. And as Gary frowningly halted, purely surprised to see me, I took the initiative to address the gathering.

"I know everyone's pissed-off and furious," I loudly spoke, "but before you pounce on this here dude, you're gonna have to go through me and my partners! And that ain't gonna be so damn easy!"

Although there were a barrage of threats hurled directly at me (profane names and racial slurs were boisterous and plentiful), I was prepared to speak further and clearly apprise the crowd of my underlying motives. But before I could utter another word, a nearby spokesman came forth and instantly snared the floor. It was a fellow Soldanite whose name was 'Lamont' and I was not only well-acquainted with him, I was quite fond of him as well. In addition, he seemed to genuinely like me back and he and I had formerly attended, both, 'Sociology' and 'Psychology' classes together at Soldan High.

Specifically singling me out, Lamont grimacingly asked, "Who the hell is this nigga to you, Duke? One of your raps, your goddamn cousin or somebody? Who the fuck is the dude?"

"He happens to be my older brother, Lamont," I responded, "and it's really a shame what happened to Frank Pickens - but my brother was out on that football field, playing for O'Fallon Tech. and trying to win the darn game. He didn't go out there, trying to injure Frank on purpose."

Yet, another angry voice chimed in at that point. "Well, I don't give a flyin' fuck whose goddamn brother the nigga is!" was the substance of the yelled out remark. "The punk-ass motherfucka needs his black ass kicked!"

Lamont apparently knew the guy who issued the foregoing rebuttal and turned around to sternly address him. "Well, he's Duke's damn brother," he told the fellow, "and that seals the fucking deal to me." Then, he calmly switched his attention back to me, stating, "I didn't even know you had a brother, Duke. We're tight, you and me. So, ain't none of these lame-ass niggas gonna fuck with him, my man. You can count on it."

As I smiled and opted to shake hands with Lamont in appreciation, the gathering began to slowly disperse. In the middle of a lot of dissenting mumbling and profanity, the confrontation was averted and everything seemed fine and dandy. And that's when Gary stepped forward, still holding on to his football gear, and proceeded to speak to me.

Displaying a most sincere expression and no grin whatsoever on his face, he said, "You little thug!" Then, only seconds later, he side-stepped me and strutted away like a pompous John Wayne or a Robert Mitchum. He left me surprised, somewhat miffed and shaking my head in sheer amazement.

Later, during the evening of that same day, my brother claimed he could have "single-handedly" fought off all the "rabble-rousers" at the Public Schools Stadium and I, in turn, told him that his parting words (which were "You little thug") just warmed the cockles of my little heart. Of course, I was joking but I wasn't about to let Gary know he had gotten under my skin. But despite my brother's lack of appreciation, I was still glad I was on-hand to come to his rescue earlier during the day.

I always found it kind of funny how well people, over a certain time period, can adapt to certain unpleasantries in their respective lives. Not funny 'ha-ha' but funny 'ah-ha.' In the spring of 1961, when our family (our step-father, William, included) moved from Palm street to the Cochran Housing Projects, which was situated in downtown Saint Louis, I was silently depressed in regards to the specific location of our apartment building. (As usual, I kept my inner feelings to myself because I didn't want to hurt my mother's feelings).

Fourteen hundred north 9th street was located directly across the street from a facility named the 'Consolidated Trucking Company,' and among other things, that meant that big and small trucks (so-called 'rigs') would be continually pulling in and out of their lot throughout, both, day and night. And while I was confident that I could endure the noisy traffic sounds during daylight hours, I was positive I'd be deprived of sleep at night. However, in less than a week's passing, I was practically oblivious of the late-night truck sounds. I came to sleep like a baby.

While the Cochran Housing facility had its share of high-rise buildings (twelve stories, mostly), the complex my family lived in had but six floors. We had a large living room, three bedrooms, a kitchenette, a bathroom and a front balcony that overlooked 9th street itself. But, like most public projects I had seen, the place had its share of roaches also. No matter how much pesticides the average tenant used, or how often, the roaches would go on vacation briefly (suitcases and all) and soon return in full force.

Therefore, even if an individual was in bed by him or herself, they were seldomly alone.

But because I still attended Soldan High School and my closest friends (the fellows) resided in St. Louis city's western portion, I was hardly ever on the home front. I essentially regarded our downtown residence as just "a place to hang my hat." Plus, I wasn't too fond of my stepfather, William.

In all fairness, William wasn't a real bad sort of person. He wasn't mean-spirited, violent or vulgar but was, ofttimes, a bit silly, aggravating and extremely undependable. For example, although my stepdad worked five days a week at a place called the 'American Can Company' and was paid bi-weekly, he never (and I emphasize the word never) came home with his entire paycheck. Although Ruby got off from work before he did (Mom still worked at Homer Phillips Hospital) and came home to immediately begin cooking supper, William was always "too starved" to wait for the completed meal. Regularly, the man was so hungry that he frequently fried up ten or twelve eggs prior to the forthcoming supper time. Our mother was forever fussing at him regarding his impatience and his knack for getting in her way in the smallish kitchen.

Apparently though, being famished was not an issue on the select Fridays when William received his paycheck. If he came home at all, it would be early the next morning (which would be Saturday), he would be drunk and reeking of strong alcohol and more than half of his two-week pay would be gone. Notably, throughout my childhood and my ensuing teenaged years, I often shared whatever monies I earned with my mother and since William continued to be the man he was, I was obliged to be the boy I was also.

To my disenchantment, William's idea of being a 'stepfather' was to be a half-ass provider, an occasional whoremonger, an over-zealous jazz fan and a weekend drunkard as well. He never interacted with us boys; never thought of taking my younger brothers to a sporting event or a movie and was unbelievably immature and shallow. In my suppressed opinion, upon him being a man who stood around six foot-four, I could not refrain from viewing him as an age-old dinosaur who had outgrew his brain. In all fairness though, since he was somewhat docile and was not a physical threat to Ruby, he certainly had a leg up on a man named 'Melvin Virgil Harris' and that, to me and my four brothers, was a very good thing.

Although it seemed like I was forever catching buses, streetcars or service cars while we resided in the Cochran Projects, I was happy about a number of things. We were in walking distance of downtown Saint Louis's shopping district, we could visit the not-too-distant Mississippi riverfront if we had a mind to, and, something that was like 'hog heaven' to me, we were relatively close to five or six movie theaters. While the 'Loew's State' and 'Ambassador' movie houses were located downtown, there were four other theaters in the immediate vicinity.

If an individual strolled along a street called Franklin (which was only three blocks from our apartment building), you would converge on the 'Marquette,' the 'Criterion,' the 'Regal,' and after turning a corner, the 'Roosevelt' theatres. And when I could afford it (just as I had done most of my life), I would not only treat myself to a flick or two at one of the aforementioned movie houses, I would take one or two of my brothers along with me. It is said that, "Old habits die hard."

In addition to my disappointment with my stepfather, there was a very pronounced downside to our relocation to the Cochran Projects. It prevailed with the dawning of the winter season, and when it came about, I emerged feeling helpless, powerless and unbelievably depressed. It directly involved our mother, Ruby.

Without the slightest doubt in my young mind, I believed that the onset of my mother's rheumatoid arthritis was the very day she slipped on spilt milk and fell to the floor at the Homer G. Phillips Hospital. That was when she fractured her hip and, alternately, became an inpatient at her workplace. From that particular day forward, Ruby was almost constantly besieged with severe body aches and pain. Mom wasn't even forty years old and was made to contend daily with the frail and disfigured hands of a woman who was almost twice her biological age.

Personally, I regularly grieved and brooded over my mother's ongoing suffering. And I begrudgingly felt, that after all the sadness and anguish she was subjected to during her lifetime, she was clearly undeserving of a poor and debilitating health status too. Every so often, my mom would say that, "God never gives a person more than they can withstand." But when it came to her, however, I always wondered, "What the hell was God thinking?" Maybe, I should have been ashamed of myself but, at that particular time, I wasn't!

Now, there's a well-known Chinese proverb that says, "One picture is worth more than a thousand words" and I credit that adage with great merit. However, I maintain that nothing, absolutely nothing, is more heartbreaking and damaging to a child's psyche than to have to stand by idle, and be unequivocally helpless, while visualizing a cherished and endeared loved one who is in the throes of suffering.

On a snowy, wintry morning (it was two below zero outside), as I stood at our front window, looking down upon 9th street (we lived on the fifth floor), the foregoing was precisely how I felt. As Ruby waited for the arrival of the 'Cass Avenue' bus, there my mom stood, with both of her gnarled hands wrapped in cloth handkerchiefs, and trying to ward off the constant chill. And there I stood, her son, standing at a window and oblivious of the tears that were steadily streaming down my face. Those kind of memories never fully subside.

Of course, in reality, I knew there was absolutely nothing I could do, and regardless of the severity of my sympathy or empathy in light of Ruby's debilitating health. I was neither a physician or some kind of faith healer, just a woeful, teenaged son who was still attending high school. However, I made myself a solemn promise, and right then and there. As I watched Ruby climbing aboard that Cass bus, I vowed I'd be a real plus in her life, totally contrary to the two men she elected to marry, and be an upstanding son she would always be proud of. I was adamant in regards to that promise.

CHAPTER TWENTY-SIX
A GATHERING OF BROTHERS

I am not sure if I underwent some kind of epiphany, a sudden metamorphosis or if I just grew up overnight, but midway through my senior year in high school, I engaged in a great deal of soul-searching. I began to wonder about what drove or motivated me, what pained and anguished me, what rendered me happy or thankful, and exactly where my life was headed. But more than all of that, it suddenly became clear to me that my biological father had a lingering and rather caustic effect on my entire being.

Basically, all I did since the old man bowed out of my life; my lackadaisical attitude regarding school, my sporadic recklessness, my paternal-like affection for my quartet of brothers, as well as for the fellows, and even my pronounced distaste for my stepdad were all weaved into my underlying feeling of father-abandonment. Because of my own sentimentality, it all boiled down to a particular question that had plagued me throughout my life. Though I was completely reconciled to my parent's break-up and subsequent divorce, I still wondered, "How could a father, any father, walk away from five children and not even miss them?"

Entering into the year 1962, that foregoing query was almost irrelevant to me. It became acutely clear to me that all along I was trying to extract something from my dad that, seemingly, he did not possess, and something that, maybe, was unique in me. I had an insatiable love for people, my father had mostly contempt. I craved righteousness while my old man ran roughshod of it. Melvin V. Harris, while apparently teeming with carnal passion, appeared to be void of compassion. Though I esteemed women, and especially mothers, he behaved as though he disdained them. And, so dear to my heart, while I absolutely adored children, my father dismissed their worth.

In all candor, but regretfully, my dad represented practically everything I loathed in men, and I fully realized that by just being the exact opposite of him, that I, as well as my four brothers, and every young boy who was made aware of my dad's life, could develop into an upstanding man and an exemplary father too. Without the slightest doubt in my young mind, I came to believe that negative flaws can be, subsequently, transformed into positive attributes. In the spring of 1962, as I became firmly reconciled to the forestated premise, I took a bird's-eye view of my ongoing life and made a concise decision.

Throughout most of my teenage life, I was always fearful that I'd someday get one of my close-knit friends badly hurt or, maybe, even killed, and I certainly didn't want such a thing to happen. I desperately needed to get my temper in check, not only for the sake of the fellows, but for myself. However, since I had no illusion of changing overnight, and my fears continued, I took concrete steps to deal with my problem. Without mentioning it to any of my buddies, I prepared to join the armed services immediately after my high school graduation.

Admittedly, there was another reason I decided to remove myself from the home front directly after my June graduation though. It certainly wasn't in the name of love and affection. On the contrary, it might have been the exact opposite. To be frank, I was quite hard on my stepfather, William, and, probably unduly hard. I didn't think much of him as a man or as a father. But, maybe I was the blame. Perhaps, I expected way too much of him and held him to standards that were far too high for him, or even the average man.

Naturally, I desired a stepdad who was totally unlike my biological father. William surely did not fit the role. Unfortunately, both William and my old man were prototypes of the black men I had come to know. (That's not to say that men of other races were any different, but at that time I didn't know any of them).

Still, I wanted to be fair to William, and, more importantly, to my mom as well. So, in being fair-minded, my decision was affirmed. I hoped and prayed by taking myself out of the picture for a while, William might make an effort to step forward and try to be the husband and father he could and should have been. Just like the little old ant in that popular song, "I had high hopes."

―――

In April of 1962, just a couple of months' shy of my graduation ceremony, I took the enlistment examinations for the army and the navy and passed them both. Therefore, in spite of leaning towards the army (after the drowning episode, I wasn't very fond of water), there was one thing I knew at that particular time. Approximately two weeks after I'd officially graduate from Soldan High, I would be leaving Saint Louis, Missouri for a good while. And I would say my goodbyes to the fellows via the U.S. mail services in the aftermath.

When the first week of June of 1962 came on the scene, my mother had her hands full. And she had substantial out-of-pocket expenses as well. She purchased three different dress outfits, specifically suits. Not only did me and Gary graduate from high school on the very same day (one of us, during the day and the other, in the evening), but our younger brother, Vaughn, finished up elementary school several days prior to our commencement ceremonies. Vaughn bade farewell to grade school and looked forward to saying hello to high school in the fall. Ruby was delighted and proud of all three of us, but was quite tired too. After all, she attended all three events.

Upon dismissing my desire to join the navy, my army career officially kicked of on the 20th day of June. Leaving from our Cochran project apartment, I rose very early that morning, extended my goodbyes to my mother and brothers and then took the Cass bus to the recruitment office. It was located on the corners of St. Louis Avenue and Grand Boulevard. Although I was a little sad (after all, I loved my family), I was also upbeat about my decision to start a brand new life. It was an adventure to me and I was confident I would excel in it. Call me "cocky," but that was exactly how I felt on that maiden morning.

Owing to my personal life-experiences, I was never a great believer in coincidence. I attribute a lot of things to fate. Like when my Aunt Hannah passed away and my family subsequently moved to Burd street, or when my Uncle Bill was on hand to prevent Lloyd Henry from being electrocuted that day, or when I alerted Buddy to that viciously thrown hatchet, or even when Robert's dad charged me with "taking care" of his son while we were in Wisconsin. All of that and more, I credited directly to fate. Furthermore, I perceived God as the supreme architect of all fate.

The reason I alluded to the foregoing was because of what eventually came into fruition on the initial day of my army induction. It was in the works, however, from the very moment I climbed aboard the Cass bus that morning.

While I was waiting at that bus stop, there happened to be another young man standing in the area also. It was obvious that he, too, was intent on catching the bus but I assumed he was headed for school or work or somewhere. The fellow and I never made eye-contact and since I hardly knew anyone who lived in the Cochran apartments, I was almost certain I didn't know him. However, when I boarded the bus in front of him and glimpsed his profile as he paid his fare, he looked familiar. But I couldn't place him and it bothered the heck out of me throughout the ensuing bus ride.

Then, when the bus converged on Grand Blvd. and we, simultaneously, stood to disembark it, it suddenly came to me. Not only had I seen the guy before, we had even engaged in a rather lengthy conversation during the time. Back in April, when I was still undecided about going into the navy or the army, I conversed with the same young man and one of his friends.

We were all sitting in the 'examination' room at the main induction center during the time. As events progressed, upon proceeding to trail the boy off the bus at Grand, he soon paused and frowned at me. That's when he grinned and posed a question to me.

"Say, are you going into the service today too?" he asked.

Instantly, I offered my hand in friendship and smiled at the young man. "Yeah, that's why I'm here today," I replied. "But - do you remember meeting me? We were at the 'Mart Building,' just a couple of months back."

"Man, I knew you looked familiar!" the fellow exclaimed. "When I first saw you a while ago, I said - where the hell do I know him from? My name's Norris Mills, remember?"

"Well - now I do. I'm Lionel Harris, but people usually call me Duke."

As the guy and I vigorously shook hands, he asked, "Soldan, right? But you were talking about, maybe, enlisting in the navy. What made you change your mind?"

"As crazy as it sounds, Norris, I was still thinking about the navy two days ago. I flipped a coin, and guess what? The army won."

"Now, that's one for the books," Norris laughed. "But I'm glad you did, man, glad you chose the army instead."

At that point, as my new acquaintance and I stood affront the recruitment office, another thought struck me. "Do you remember the last words I said to you and your partner way back in April?" I asked him.

"Damn, man, I'm lucky to even remember yesterday," Norris smilingly responded. "What was it?"

"I said - who knows? Maybe we'll all end up in the same basic training unit. Where's your friend? Is he going in today too?"

Norris Mills took a moment to glance over at the nearby office building. "Yeah, Jerome's going in today too. He's probably already inside. Come on, Duke, he'll be surprised as hell to see you. Man, I know I am."

The young man named Jerome, indeed, was inside the recruitment facility and was casually talking with a group of other fellow black guys. In fact, he was smilingly looking at me and my newly-found comrade when we entered the place. However, before Jerome spoke, a couple of nearby fellows greeted Norris first. Then, when, yet, another boy appeared to know Norris as well, I was in a state of wonderment. Apparently, I was in the presence of a cluster of friends.

As it turned out, Norris, Jerome and two of the other young men who were amongst the conversing assemblage, were not merely cordial friends, they were all running buddies, all former classmates at the 'Hadley Technical High School,' and, more significantly, they had all enlisted in the army together on what was called the <u>Buddy</u>-<u>Buddy</u> <u>Plan</u>.

To be quite specific, it meant that Norris Mills, Jerome Smith and two other black young men named George Mondaine and William Crawford would essentially remain together throughout their tour of duty in the United States army. And they all seemed to be well-pleased with the premise.

Now, in spite of my being an 'outsider' when it came to the close-knit group, I didn't remotely feel like one. And after we got the formal introductions out of the way, I gradually began to feel like I was one of the fellows.

Less than an hour later, when a military bus pulled up in front of the recruitment office and our individual names were loudly called out, one-by-one we boarded the bus and the 'five' of us (me, and the aforementioned fellows) proceeded to sit around each other. Like magic, I bonded with those four Hadley High graduates just that quickly, and right in the midst of about twenty other boisterous inductees. But we all had one thing very much in common. We were all en route to Fort Leonard Wood, Missouri where we would soon start basic training. A new horizon and a brand new beginning awaited us all.

***

It is very difficult to explain (if it's even possible to explain it at all), but camaraderie amongst men in the armed services is something to actually savor and marvel at. Close-knit and endearing relationships rapidly form and render men more like lifelong brothers than just casual friends. Maybe, it's because soldiers have so much free time to converse with one another, or because they are completely separated from their biological families, or even because they're tackling uncharted territory together, but it seems to come into play time and time again. I perceive it as a heartfelt phenomenon.

Our first week in Leonard Wood was called 'zero week.' It was a period set aside for procuring military clothing, footwear and essential personal supplies, receiving a series of standard and, sometimes, painful shots and filling out a hodgepodge of standard forms. During that latter phase, I took the initiative to sign up for a $40 per month allotment. That simply meant that my mother would receive $80 each month (the army matched my monetary donation) and I would, alternately, earn a 'whopping' $38 on paydays. Therefore, since Uncle Sam provided new recruits with what we came to call "three hots and a cot" each and every day, our starting salary was a mere $78 per month.

When the initial week of 'basic training' got underway, it seemed like every individual who climbed aboard the bus when we left Saint Louis two weeks prior, was assigned to the very same training unit. We were all placed in Bravo Company, Second Battalion, Second Regiment (B-2-2) and were distributed alphabetically in two or three different barracks. Then, with all of that done, we collectively settled into wrestling with two months of rigorous and grueling training.

Personally speaking (although I kept it to myself), I was, in no way, looking forward to any facet of the traditional, militaristic training and viewed it as a vexing, but well-expected evil; which, more or less, was an initial hurdle that had to be leapt over. In reality (in lieu of college), I enlisted in the service with a firm assurance of being extensively schooled in 'business and administrative principles' and wasn't in the least macho or gung ho regarding any part of combat-readiness. Still, however, I knew I had to put my best foot forward and play what I, sometimes, would call the "silly game."

When I came up with my decision to join the army (or any armed forces branch, for that matter), I faithfully promised myself I would turn over a new leaf. I didn't want to be the same impulsive boy I was in high school. But it is said that, "Old habits die hard," or something like that. So, when a certain incident took place inside my barracks and I became entwined in it (less than three weeks after my arrival in Fort Leonard Wood), that was my sole excuse for allowing the old Duke to resurface.

There was a young soldier assigned to my billets named 'Darber.' He happened to be a Caucasian, he was basically a loner, and he acted a little timid, if not effeminate. Other than saying, maybe "Hey" to him occasionally, he and I never interacted with each other. Now, I had heard a few fellow barracks mates complaining about the Darber boy, loudly railing that he had an offensive body odor but I couldn't personally attest to that charge. Besides, in my viewpoint, that was Pvt. Darber's business.

Apparently though, there was a group of soldiers who didn't remotely share my feelings. More than that, they decided to take matters into their own hands. Behaving like an unruly lynch mob, about six or seven black soldiers (including a Hadley Tech. graduate named Gillespie) were struggling with the Darber kid and were dead-set on giving him what was known as a 'GI party.' In military context, that simply meant that they were intending to strip him naked, throw him into the latrine shower and proceed to roughly wash him up themselves. However, regular bar soap wasn't the group's only cleansing agent. I noticed that one of Darber's assailants was holding a wire brush and was poised and ready to use it. By the time I elected to intercede, the mob had rendered the boy, who was tearful, half-nude.

"Hey, you dudes are not gonna use that damn wire brush on that boy!" I shouted, walking towards them. "Have you guys lost your damn minds? Let him go!"

"Who the hell gonna stop us, your little punk ass?" one of the perpetrators responded. "Mind your fuckin' business, Harris!"

"Like hell - I will!" I barked back. "Just 'cause we outnumber the white boys down here, don't mean we gotta act like them. Turn him loose - or git busy trying to kick my ass first!"

"And my ass too!" chimed in one of my Saint Louis homeboys. "Harris is right! Ya'll don't have a right to fuck up that little fay boy!"

"Yeah, let the honkie alone!" one of the Hadley graduates inserted. "Give him the soap and let him wash his own ass! Unless you're some kind of pervert or something."

"What's wrong with you niggas?" protested one of Darber's attackers. "Why are ya'll sticking up for this funky peckerwood?"

"Because he's a flesh and blood human being," I argued. "He doesn't deserve having his skin scrubbed off. That's sick!" At that juncture, although he was a member of the original mob, the young man named Gillespie had a change of heart. He spoke to his cohorts as he relinquished his hold on the white soldier. "Yeah, fellas, we don't have to go through with this shit," he told them. "Don't make sense for us to get bent outta shape for some honkie. So, why don't we let him be. Okay, guys?"

Although Gillespie's fellow perpetrators seemed to be frustrated and somewhat pissed off as well, they gradually desisted restraining the Darber kid and, soon, went about going their separate ways. Then, as Darber himself proceeded to collect his cast away clothing (still in a state of tears and anguish), he, eventually, walked away and headed directly to the outlying latrine. Even as I thanked the individuals who came to my aid, I could not help feeling sorry for him. To be honest though, compassion was a part of the old Duke that I still very much savored.

Out of all the Hadley High graduates who befriended me, I grew to like and enjoy Jerome Smith the best. (Right away, after climbing aboard that military bus back in St. Louis it became quite clear to me that in addition to the four enlistees who were on the Buddy-Buddy Plan, there were five or six other Hadley alumnus amongst them). All of them were highly likable and cordial, but Jerome and I hit it off almost instantly.

Jerome was easy-going, virtually always smiling (his high school comrades even called him "Smiley" occasionally, and probably because he had deep dimples in both cheeks) and he frequently made me laugh. However, instead of telling jokes or reciting witty anecdotes, he often engaged in something we black folks traditionally called "selling wolf tickets."

To be precise, that meant that my newfound friend would almost constantly threaten to inflict bodily harm on select individuals in his social orbit. And, of course, Jerome was not remotely serious and no one took him seriously either. Everyone was well-aware that it was just a playful and amusing rouse on his part.

In spite of the emerging fondness I had for Jerome though, I sincerely enjoyed being in the presence of his former school classmates too, and especially his close-knit pals. In fact, if a bystanding observer didn't know any better, he or she would have assumed that I, too, was tied into the priorly drawn-up 'Buddy-Buddy' contract. After a very short while, however, I came to regret that I was not. By the time the 4th of July rolled around, me and the four young men who were pertinent to that pact were like five brothers rather than five friends.

However, within a few days of the Independence Day observance, my surging bubble was abruptly busted. Due to overcrowding in B-2-2 (which I branded "buzzard luck" on my part), I was suddenly reassigned to a neighboring training unit called Echo-2-2. Although it was located just down the street from Bravo-2-2, the move had an immediate downside to it. Despite the two companies being in the same numerical basic training week, their standard training activities did not always coincide. For instance, one day B-2-2 would be subjected to marching out to the distant rifle range while E-2-2, on the other hand, was scheduled to engage in the same training mechanism on the following day. At any event, it was a separation that greatly saddened me.

As it turned out, I was quite positive that Jerome Smith was keenly appreciative of my disenchantment as well. Because on the very day following my uprooting, he, too, was transferred over to E-2-2. And although we weren't assigned to the same barracks (that was because my surname started with an 'H' and Jerome's began with an 'S'), we made it our strict business to frequently visit each other and meet up during the ongoing and varied training procedures. In addition, we often ate chow together, spent our evenings together and, as time progressed, enjoyed the weekends together also. Although, we continued to mingle and interact with many of our St. Louis homeboys, especially the Hadley Tech. graduates, 'J' (which I came to call him) and I were virtually inseparable. Not only that, but in my opinion (who was an individual who traditionally exuded heartfelt sentiment), J was the best friend I could ever hope and pray for.

Now, I am almost positive that the forestated would strike numerous people as somewhat hasty, premature, weird and, maybe, a little gay. But I was born with a certain, ironclad philosophy. I've said it before and I'll say it again and again. I have no inhibitions when it comes to people I love and cherish. Furthermore, I don't mind telling people how I sincerely feel about them. "Give loved ones flowers while they are still alive to see and smell them," was my mantra. And I still ascribe to the premise that, "If people truly love you, they will love you no matter what. But if they dislike or hate you, they are capable of conjuring up lies or falsehoods to sustain their ingrained loathing for you." My hope for people (in general) is that they become discerning enough to identify the sheep from the wolves. And that's something I borrowed from my dear mother. And when she told me that, "Truly good people are at a real premium in this world," I aligned myself with that wisdom too.

My friend, Jerome (or 'J'), was a real positive in my young life and I felt I was likewise in his. In fact, when we were in our sixth week of basic training (just two weeks after qualifying with an M-1 rifle on the shooting range), I learned proof-positive how valuable a friend he really was.

On a Saturday afternoon as I sat on the sidelines at an indoor gym and watched J, Norris Mills, William Crawford, Goerge Mondaine and a group of other soldiers competing on the basketball court, I began to perspire profusely. Actually, I hadn't felt well for days on end and, maybe, for an entire two-week period. I had previously told Jerome how I was feeling (that was on the recent Friday morning) and he soundly encouraged me to go on sick-call, but I refused to do it. And, stupidly, though I feared it was something serious, I didn't want to be T.R.O. ed. In military terminology, that stood for "training recycled over."

On the way back from the gym, my stomach was practically searing in stark pain. It seemed like something very sharp and cutting was moving inside my lower abdomen and I was reeling in severe agony. I was acutely aware that Jerome was worried (his face told it all) and he virtually begged me to go to the hospital. But I flatly refused, still fixated on the T.R.O. factor. Then, when we finally converged on my assigned barracks, I immediately took to my bunk and tried my level best to withstand and stave off a harsh and unrelenting pain. Lying on my back and actively grasping my midsection, I was still heavily sweating, fretful and engulfed in sheer agony!

At that point, I momentarily focused on my concerned and very attentive friend. Looking extremely worried, J was rushing back and forth to the outlying latrine and frantically bringing me hot towels for my extended stomach. But even upon doing that, as he proceeded to gingerly apply those hot towels to my bare abdomen, he was crying profusely and behaving as if my ongoing pain was his pain also and, alternately, that rendered me tearful as well. Then, finally, and thanks to an interceding and merciful God, that select and poignant memory remains ever-present in my mind. That was because, after enduring a final surge of horrific gut pain, I passed out and my grieving best friend immediately summoned an ambulance.

The very next thing I recalled was my lying on my bed at the U.S. Army Hospital in Fort Leonard Wood, Missouri and becoming instantly aware that I had a seven-inch incision along my stomach area. In addition to that, there was an elongated tube that was penetrating, both, my nose and throat and was somewhat irritating. According to the attending physician, I was diagnosed with an "intestinal obstruction" and was rushed to the surgical unit upon my arrival at the hospital. "Without that emergency operation," he said, "you could have likely died." Then, he added, "Thankfully, you were brought here in the nick of time."

    I naturally extended my sincere gratitude to my doctor right then and there and, later on, I thanked the chief surgeon involved in my operation as well. Then, I proceeded to extend a prayerful appreciation to God Himself and, finally, I gave my heartfelt thanks to a special young soldier named Jerome Smith. Lying on my back in my hospital bed, I firmly embraced him, told him that I dearly loved and cherished him and swore I would feel that way about him throughout my remaining life. And even though I still maintain that fate was very much afoot during that unforgettable happening, I still feel the same way about J today.

CHAPTER TWENTY-SEVEN

THE HANDS-DOWN LOSER

The United States Army Hospital at Fort Leonard Wood, Missouri was a one-story, ramp-style and wood-based structure. I am certain it housed every facet of a traditional general hospital, but it was spread out over a large tract of land. To my suppressed displeasure, however, I learned firsthand how enormous that medical facility was. That was due to a particular phase of my so-called "rehabilitation."

According to my assigned physical therapist, I would actually strengthen my stomach muscles by frequently pushing another patient around in a standard wheelchair. Therefore, within seven days of my surgery, that was what I was instructed to do.

Apparently though, my therapist was intent on pumping up my arm strength as well. Instead of being assigned to an average-sized patient, I found myself accommodating what some folks described as a "tons-of-fun." He was a 30-year-old white Specialist five, he, seemingly, weighed over 250 pounds, but, to my sorrow, the man definitely was not fun. In fact, I deemed him a "racist redneck" and he behaved as though I was his personal slave or man-servant. On the first day we met, he started off calling me "boy."

"Hey - look, man, my name is Private Harris," I instantly informed him. "You can call me Harris or private, or just 'Hey - you' but I've got your boy hangin' low, if you get my drift. But don't call me boy."

The specialist sat before me, smiling. He was apparently amused by my response. "Aw - kinda touchy, huh?" he asked. "Private, I didn't mean no harm. Don't git your drawers all twisted up. But I was told you 'spose to transport me wherever I wants to go. If ya' don't like your damn assignment, tell the brass about it."

"No, my man, I'm telling you," I replied. "My name is Harris."

"Okay, Mr. Harris - Mister Private E-1 Harris," the specialist facetiously spoke. "Um about ready to chow-down now. Care to transport me over to the mess hall? Please, please, kind sir."

I silently gave in at that point. But even as I maneuvered the wheelchair, I was still slightly miffed. I soon smiled, however. It was quite clear to me that the guy would do well to miss a great deal of chow time. But my mirth did not linger long. When the soldier (his name was Pearson) mentioned to me that he had had a standard appendectomy, my disenchantment resurfaced. Hell, my lower abdomen incision was almost twice as long as his was! I reasoned that the fellow should have been pushing me, not the other way around. But, then again, he happened to be white.

Unfortunately, the maiden confrontation I experienced with Spec. Pearson was quite indicative of the remaining time he and I spent together. The soldier was one of the 'good ole boys' from Tuscaloosa, Alabama and he couldn't help playing the part. He and I locked horns daily in the wake of his authoritarian, racist jargon and when we finally parted company for good, I rejoiced. In my viewpoint, he was a die-hard, self-absorbed racist and he had nothing but contempt for people of color. Afterwards, I just hoped and prayed that the man was not a prime example of the majority of Caucasian people I would encounter throughout my military tour. To me, that would be downright tortuous and tragic!

Whether it was an act of fate once again, mere coincidence, happenstance or whatever, my discharge from the hospital occurred on the very same day that Jerome and his fellow Hadley-nites graduated from basic training. Furthermore, as that group prepared to catch the evening Greyhound bus to Saint Louis that day, I, too, was in their company. The distinct difference was that my fellow St. Louisans were being afforded a traditional two-week leave and I was being granted a 14-day home convalescence period. My newly-established friends, in time, would return to Fort Leonard Wood to receive their 'Advanced Individual Training' (A.I.T.) and I would return to Leonard Wood to face what I deemed 'the unknown.' I was casually told I would not have to finish up the last two weeks of basic training, hinting that I would be privy to my prescribed A.I.T. also, but nothing was written on official paper. Therefore, I was hopeful but a bit leery.

As the succeeding days came and went, my recuperation period in my hometown was spent with Jerome, my immediate family and an array of individuals who were still accessible from my high school years, and especially the residual fellows. However, owing to Uncle Sam and the hovering 'draft' premise, that latter group (my running buddies) had shrunk numerically. One boy, John, had actually joined the army before I did, the two brothers,

Charles and Robert, enlisted in the Marine Corps, so did Walter, and, both, Willie and Jerry were in the air force. Therefore, I was able to spend leisurely time with guys like Woody (or Arthur), Larry, Sherrod, James and Alonzo.

Notably, when I had the chance to hook up with Alonzo, there was something burning in my heart. It had been for months on end (even before high school graduation) and I seized the chance to get it off my chest. While sitting inside a rather noisy bar called 'Berneice's Place,' and in the company of, both, Larry and Woody, I specifically addressed Alonzo and asked him for an accommodation. Since it was almost impossible to hear yourself talk in that boisterous club, I implored Alonzo to accompany me outside for a short conversation.

Shortly though, when the two of us stood up to make our exit (I told Larry and Woody we'd be right back), we were both subjected to playful ridicule and signifying. The minds of our two comrades drifted back to the past.

"You two dudes ain't gonna fight, are you?" asked a smiling Larry. "If you are, gimme a chance to sell some tickets. I could sho' use the money."

Then, Woody tossed in his two cents, teasing Alonzo. "Remember he's been trained in judo and karate, Lonnie. He don't be playing no more."

I laughingly shook my head, saying, "We're just gonna talk, guys. We'll be back in a few minutes. Meanwhile, order a drink on me. And I did say a drink, not two or three. Be right back."

Minutes later, Alonzo and I were outside and standing offside the club's entrance. Via his frown, Alonzo had no inkling of what was on my mind.

"So, what's going on, Duke?" he questioned. "What's the big mystery?"

Upon looking my cohort straight in his eyes, I began, "Man, I know this is long overdue, but I wanted to say something to you - even before I decided to join the service. I just wanted to apologize, tell you I'm sorry, sorry for all those bad times we had together over the years. But I was just stupid - and jealous-hearted. I was jealous because . . . I thought you had everything going for you, and I had, well, very little."

Alonzo chuckled, but I had no clue as to why. "Shit, Duke, I was sometimes jealous of you," he stated.

"Of me?" I grimaced. "What the devil did I have going for me? The best clothes I had, you gave 'em to me. And I showed my gratitude . . . by wanting to fight you. Yeah, that made a lot of sense."

"But, Duke, people always liked you. The girls dug me, but the niggas, all the damn hard-legs, always wanted to jump on my ass, all the time. I didn't have to do nothing, or even say shit. Niggas automatically wanted to kick my ass."

"Hell, Lonnie, that was because they were jealous of you too," I countered. "I mean you had so much - money, nice threads, your own automobile, and girls galore. That's why lame dudes wanted to hurt you all those times."

"But people really liked you, Duke, and no matter what. Most of the niggas, a lot of the babes, every damn body. Even when we were at Emerson, people dug you. Old lady Athens, she was crazy about you, and so was Mr. Burnett. So, hell - I'm guilty myself, guilty of being jealous of you."

I thought quite seriously about Alonzo's rebuttal and was somewhat tickled. I was completely surprised by his jealousy admission. "But I'm the foul one, Lonnie," I insisted. "All those clothes you gave me; the suits, the jerseys. You could have just thrown them away, or could have given them to somebody else -

someone who had sense enough to appreciate them. So - will you accept my apology, man? I'm really sincere about it."

Showcasing a reflective grin, Alonzo opted to briskly shake my hand at that juncture. I was inclined to hug him but I was relatively sure he considered himself 'too cool' for that outward display of male affection. Therefore, after he casually remarked that my apology, "Wasn't even necessary," we soon returned to the tavern and rejoined Larry and Woody. Of course, I had no idea how Alonzo felt after our talk but, as for me, I felt good inside.

When my two-week convalescence leave was over, I returned to the U.S. Army Hospital in Leonard Wood, had the stiches removed from my stomach area and was, alternately, assigned to what was identified as a 'holding company.' At that site, upon being restricted to light duty, I spent an additional two weeks, all with the sole intent of rendering me physically fit to resume my military life.

Notably, my ongoing recuperation period did not mean that I would be permitted to just leisurely sit around and cool my heels. Instead, I was assigned to the facility's Headquarters Building and was charged with doing a whole gamut of clerical chores. Since my upcoming A.I.T. was to be 'business administration,' I was certain it had much to do with the slated work assignment.

Despite the fact that my advanced training had not yet began, I emerged a natural when it came to clerical skills. I voluntarily worked nine hours each day inside the facility's main office. There, I implemented a comprehensive filing system; replete with neatly labelled manila folders, and then placed them in alphabetical order. Working from a large stack of cardboard boxes,

I meticulously arranged military personnel folders in eight, side by side metal cabinets.

Alternately, I received high praise from my on-site superiors and fellow soldiers alike. The officer in-charge, a Caucasian captain named Hensley, seemed genuinely fond of me. He would often smile and pat me on my back, saying something like, "Damn good job, Pvt. Harris" or "Thanks for working overtime, Harris." So, when the captain informed me that I would definitely be going to my 'second eight' (referring to the A.I.T. component) when I finished up my rehab period at the Headquarters complex, I gleefully regarded his words as the gospel truth. I was certain, practically positive, that I'd begin my business training very, very soon.

As it came to pass, I was absolutely wrong, woefully disillusioned and totally pissed off. I have never been able to understand (and I never will) how a person could look another individual directly in the face, flash a big smile, and unashamedly voice a blatant, bold-face lie. However, Capt. Hensley did that precisely to me. On the morning I made my departure from the holding company, he was on hand to bid me farewell and grinningly said, "Good luck in A.I.T., Pvt. Harris. And I'm sure you'll do a top-notch job there too, just like you did for us here."

I was sitting on the passenger side of a jeep when the officer delivered his goodbye speech, but when I glimpsed the young driver's profile, he wasn't remotely smiling and seemed somewhat sedate. But I did not know why; that was, not until almost a half an hour later.

To my surging anger and grievous disappointment as well, my military chauffeur pulled up in front of an Orderly Room and stopped the vehicle. However, it wasn't a facility that was remotely connected to any kind of advanced instructions or academic schooling. It was, instead, a traditional basic training designation. Therefore, it instantly became clear to me why the jeep driver was so solemn and eerily quiet throughout our vehicle journey.

I felt like venting my disgust right then and there, but I elected to suppress it. After all, my young driver was just as white as the disingenuous and lying-ass Capt. Hensley and, although he seemed turned off by Hensley's foregoing behavior, I didn't expect him to understand or appreciate my inner feelings. Even upon grabbing my duffel bag from the back of the jeep and looking as mad as hell, I could not refrain from wondering if there were any 'authentically good' Caucasian people in the world. And if there were, I silently maintained, they seemed to be far and in between.

Less than fifteen minutes later, as I entered the Orderly Room and was officially informed that I had, indeed, been T.R.O.ed (again, Training Recycled Over), I was further disheartened when I learned what training week my new basic training unit was in. Specifically, they were about to go into their fifth week and right away I hated the significance of that news. In my case, it meant that after I had marched miles on top of miles out to the rifle range in the sweltering heat of August (essentially to become proficient with an M-1 rifle), I could now anticipate traveling the same terrain in the chill of the fall season. The only difference was that the army was changing over to the new M-14 rifle and I would be marching alongside a group of soldiers whom I had, yet, to meet.

I absolutely dreaded the impending foot-journey and wasn't sure I'd jell with the recruits in my new unit as well. At any event though, I was geared to put my best foot forward. (Of course, it wasn't like I had any other options).

As it turned out, the distance between my second basic training unit and Jerome's advanced training site was less than a mile. And unless I was out on night maneuvers, we saw each other almost daily, and especially on Sundays. On that day, we'd hook up, sometimes attend church services, proceed to eat lunch and supper together, and end up at one of the movie theatres on post. To my delight, J loved movies just like I did. Then, some of the times, we would hang out with Norris and some of the other Hadley Tech. graduates. Most of them were nearby and easily accessible because they were collectively studying 'telecommunications.'

Everything was going pretty well for a time, I stopped griping about my "buzzard luck" circumstances, even forged a congenial relationship with a couple of young guys in my new unit and then began to anticipate the day I would finally finish up basic training altogether. Then something, out of the blue, happened, an event that not only affected military personnel at Fort Leonard Wood, Missouri, but every service branch throughout America and elsewhere. Due to the ominous 'Cuban Missile Crisis' of October, we suddenly found ourselves on military alert. Just so happened, I was visiting Jerome and our other close-knit companions when it occurred and I was compelled to immediately return to my assigned unit. However, as I hurriedly made my departure, I was not only severely saddened, I was fretful regarding the fate of us all.

When the Cuban missile scare finally came to a dramatic end and war was averted between the United States and the Soviet Union, I, like most of the world, was relieved and truly thankful. I had far too many loved ones in the armed forces at that particular time and I wasn't prepared to lose or mourn any of them. It might be difficult for others to fully understand, but my affection for each and every one of them had never dissolved or waned. (I wasn't aware of it at the time, a time when I had not even celebrated my 19th birthday, but I would maintain those same sentiments throughout my life).

Only a few days after that frightening alert was called off, I officially (and finally) completed basic training. But while I had come to thoroughly believe that there was a profound lesson embedded in every life experience (although it may take years to surface), I still regarded my entire set-back as a vexing, ill-timed distraction. Recalling my emergency operation, my so-called physical therapy, the ensuing deception in that holding company and the complete T.R.O. premise, made me cringe in remorse and wonder. I was endeared to Jerome for the special part he played in the affair, but was oblivious of any other rationale.

Although I should have been overjoyed, I was still brooding over my harrowing set-back in the short aftermath of my graduation exercise. I tried to shake it off, but I could not. Then something transpired that eventually altered my outlook. It came in the form of a fellow black private named Lance Green and it caught me completely by surprise, but a very pleasant surprise. However, the 'it' I'm referring to was not some kind of act or deed Pvt. Green performed, it was simply in light of the sincere words he extended to me in the aftermath of our graduation ceremony. Lance was fondly recapturing a happening that took place almost two weeks prior. In reality, I, too, savored the subject episode.

In retrospect, Pvt. Green and his best buddy, Jacob Scott (both 17) were the only two soldiers I truly bonded with when I was thrust into my second basic training unit. Since I was assigned to the bunk next to Lance and his childhood friend, Jake, was a frequent visitor of his, the three of us interacted on a daily basis. We were constantly engaged in conversations, we ate chow together, sought out each other during field exercises and even polished our footwear on occasion while we were in the barracks. Since Jacob and Lance were both from Kansas City, Missouri and I was a native of Saint Louis, we all felt closely connected.

Although I certainly was not an authority in regards to Lance's overall personality, right away I perceived him as happy-go-lucky, warm-hearted and personable. He was the very first recruit to welcome me to my new environs and was markedly sincere. In fact, he helped me set up my lodging area. So, when I glimpsed him looking severely despondent one afternoon, sitting silently on his bunk and grasping a piece of mail, I immediately became concerned. I tried to mind my own business, but upon noticing tears in his eyes, I was too alarmed to keep quiet.

"What's the matter, Lance?" I asked. "Bad news from the home front?"

Even in the throes of his heavy despair, my young comrade tried to issue a smile. "Aw, Duke, I don't wanna spoil your day by complaining about my darn problems," he remarked. "I'll be alright, guy."

I had been laying back on my bed when I first spoke to Lance, but I chose to sit up when I said, "Look, Lance, you'll be spoiling the hell out of my day if you _don't_ tell me what's bugging you. I'll be so worried about you - I might even become a hopeless drunk. All kidding aside, Lance, we may not be the tightest friends, but we've got kindred spirits, I believe. So, I've grown to care a great deal about you. What's up?"

My newfound friend expressed himself as he sat, shaking his head in genuine disbelief. "My dad - he left us when I around six years old, ya' know? Naw, you don't really know, I guess. But, he walked off from me, my mom, and my little sister, Julie. I mean, Duke, he just up and left us 'high and dry.' No goodbyes, no farewell words, nothing! How the hell could a so-called father do that, how?"

Though it was entirely unbeknownst to my distraught young comrade at the time, I, of course, acutely understood his innermost feelings. "That letter you're holding, is it from your dad?" I questioned.

"Yeah, it's from him. Duke, I've been trying to find my father for years. You know, to try and reconnect with the man? To try and find some answers and ask him his - motives. I tried my damndest! Turns out, he lives in Kansas City, Kansas, and less than a hundred miles from where we live. He's been that damn close to us, all this frigin' time! But . . he still don't want no parts of me, his own fucking son! Julie too, I guess. Says he got married again and he's happy with his present life, a lousy-ass bastard! How could he feel like that, Duke? What did I ever do to him?"

In his weighty grief and anger, Lance Green wept freely at that point and I could not retain my own tears. "Do you know what, kiddo?" I softly asked him. "I know this is going to sound, maybe, a little weird to you. But it's your father, Lance, who's the hands-down loser in this matter, he definitely is. I feel pity, genuine sorrow for your dad. Because you know what? He is missing out in having a wonderful, caring and loving son like you. I kid you not. You and I, we have only known each other for a short while, but I swear I can see it. I saw it on the very first day that God chose to mesh our lives together. Nothing in this life is mere happenstance, Lance. Instantly, I saw an engrained goodness inside of you and I could almost reach out and touch it. So, bide my words, kiddo, in the final analysis, your missing old man is the greatest loser in the deal."

In spite of his continuous sobbing, Lance Green displayed a pronounced grin at that juncture. "Do you really think that's true, Duke?" he asked. "And you're not just saying all that, just hoping to make me feel better about things?"

"Oh - I am hoping and praying to make you feel better, Lance," I replied, swiping at my own tears and extending a fond smile, "but it's the gospel truth, nevertheless. And mark my words about this too. I predict that you will be a superior and top-notch dad yourself, one of these fine, old days. In being the kind, considerate and loving dude I see before me today, you are a shoe-in to be the super parent I'm referring to. I have no doubt in my military mind. I am a true believer in building on the deficiencies, Lance, meaning we should strive to profit and build on the various negatives and flaws we encounter during our lives, and especially when it comes to childhood. If we are subjected to fathers, or mothers, who set poor examples for us, we owe it to our children not to be the same way. And I know you won't be, when it comes to the children you sire. Because you're gonna love and cherish your kids like your parents should have done to you. And you'll adhere to that mind-set, Lance. I wholeheartedly believe in you."

When Lance Green smiled and took a moment to stifle his tears, it was apparent to me that he did feel somewhat better. "Where did you learn all of that stuff, Duke?" he fondly questioned. "From some book or something?"

I grinned, but quite reflectively. "Yeah, it's from a book alright, a book written by a fellow named Melvin V. Harris," I jokingly replied. "I imagine your dad and my old man were cut from the same damaged cloth. My father bowed out of my life when I was a kid too. In addition to me, he had four other sons at the time. I pity him too, Lance, because he's a bonafide loser as well. Lance, I thoroughly believe that a person can't go through life hurting innocent and vulnerable people, and especially children. And just like a man named William Shakespeare said: "The evil that men do lives after them." And that, my wonderful friend, is from a book."

Several weeks had gone by the boards since I engaged in that heartfelt dialogue with my barracks mate, Lance Green. I truly hoped I had lightened his despair during that occasion, but I wasn't positively sure. However, when he sought me out on graduation day, I came to believe that I had made a lasting impact on him. He cited our former heartfelt conversation as a prelude to his feelings.

"Jake's parents drove down for the ceremony," he informed me right after the exercise. "They're gonna drive us back to K.C. and we'll start our 14-day leave. Then, we'll end up in Fort Campbell, Kentucky - so we won't be coming back this way."

"I know," I smilingly said, "and I'm gonna miss the hell out of you two dudes. Couldn't have gotten through my ordeal without you two cats being around."

Lance casually shrugged off my words of gratitude. "You're the main man, Duke," he spoke. "What you said to me the day we talked and cried together . . . man, it's something I'll never forget, not ever. You turned my sadness into happiness. And when I wrote my mom about you, and told her what you said to me, I kinda burnt some bread on you. I told her you're gonna be a minister one day, and a great one. And I really believe that, guy."

I responded with an outburst of laughter. I shook my head, saying, "Well, as John Wayne said in the movie 'The Searchers,' 'That'll be the day."

Even as he became somewhat misty-eyed, my young comrade momentarily laughed along with me. But his merriment vanished altogether when he stated, "I really appreciate and care about you,

Duke, and I will never forget you. And . . I wish only the very best for you, from now on out."

I, just like I expected I would, became somber and a bit choked up at that point. "I meant every single word I said to you on that day, kiddo. You're a nice, pleasant and good-hearted guy and you'll always live in my heart. Please, stay that way, Lance. And I'll always cherish the time I spent with you and Jake. And, kiddo, will you do me a big favor?"

"Just say it, Duke, and you got it."

"Promise me you'll take good care of yourself and Jake too," I requested. "He thinks the world of you and dearly loves you, just like I do. True friends don't come along everyday. And never take it for granted, never."

As Lance Green nodded in compliance to my foregoing plea, he, then, stepped forward and firmly slung his arms around me. I instantly followed suit. "And I'd appreciate it if you'll do likewise for me," Lance stated. "Take great care of yourself too. And don't forget, I've got a lot of faith in you."

"Yeah, and that's ditto when it comes to me, Lance."

Within 15 minutes of our poignant and heartfelt farewell, Pvt. Lance Green and I took time to seek out our missing friend and fellow basic training graduate, Jacob Scott. We found him standing outside our home barracks and busily talking to his father and mother. Therefore, after I was formally introduced to the visiting couple, the three of us engaged in a cordial and light-hearted conversation. Soon, however, Jake and Lance excused themselves. They entered our former living quarters, grabbed up their respective duffel bags and soon came back out.

Finally, after my two comrades tossed their duffels into the trunk of the Scott's nearby automobile, it was time to face the inevitable, which to me was a phase in life that I always dreaded. Nevertheless, I had to go through the motions. I, alternately, shook the hands of Mr. and Mrs. Scott, rendered a farewell handshake and embrace to my departing comrades and, then, stood in the adjacent road, smiling and continually waving goodbye. I kept my eyes trained on that moving vehicle until it was completely out of sight. Although Lance Green and Jacob Scott were in my life relatively briefly, I grew to love and dearly esteem them and I thanked God He elected to cross our paths. Way back then and even presently, I considered myself very fortunate.

CHAPTER TWENTY-EIGHT
BIRDS OF A FEATHER

Playwright William Shakespeare wrote, "Parting is such sweet sorrow," but I always took issue with the term sweet. I greatly dreaded goodbyes, so for a young man like me who lovely people so deeply, the sorrow aspect was pure agony to me. It seemed like every time I bade farewell to a loved one, a piece of my heart went along with them.

It was depressing and emotionally painful to me when I bade adieu to Lance and Jake after basic, but when November of 1962 came to the forefront and I was obliged to say farewell to my best friend, Jerome, and the other hometown fellows I had grown to cherish, it was almost unbearable for me. I learned that after a 30-day furlough, J and the other soldiers in that select group would be headed to South Korea. They would all be subjected to a 13-month tour of duty and that, to me, sounded like an eternity.

I was heartbroken, to put it mildly, but I withdrew a measure of refuge from my sincere and underlying hope that I'd, alternately, be sent to Korea also. Meaning, that when I completed my advanced individual training phase, I fully expected and prayed that I'd reconnect with Jerome and the other guys in a short while. I actually derived comfort from that anticipation.

Admittedly, I knew very little about civilian college life, but I imagined that A.I.T. was similar to it, but on a much smaller scale. Since my primary focus was on business precepts, I attended daily classes on every facet of it. I learned about expenditures, debits, assets, spread sheets, tax codes and you name it; every principle applicable to managing and mastering most business venues.

I took to business education like a fish takes to water and I thoroughly enjoyed it. Notably, out of everything I was introduced to during my rather compacted business training at Fort Leonard Wood, I ranked my learned skill with a typewriter as number one. Very seldom did boys enroll in typing classes while in high school (I surmised they considered it somewhat sissy-fied), but I quickly deemed it an invaluable skill. I, eventually, typed only 55 words per minute, but I made very few mistakes. (Incidentally, far beyond my army career, it was a skill that enhanced my entire life).

Unlike my basic training experience, which was conspicuously prolonged by the T.R.O. component, my 'second eight' practically flew by. I stayed busy, studied hard, went to a lot of movies, regularly wrote upbeat letters to my mother and J bi-weekly, but, surprisingly, made no new friends. That was somewhat out of character for me, but due to a certain factor, it was understandable. There were very few black soldiers in my class, none in my assigned barracks, so I was practically invisible. Although I was spared overt racist remarks (I occasionally heard the "nigger" term whispered from Caucasian mouths), but I was not subjected to any kind of harassment. I, nevertheless, felt isolated and read quite a bit.

To one of my white barracks mate's credit, however, I wasn't able to pigeon-hole all of my Caucasian classmates. Pvt. James Hancock, who bunked right next to me, always cordially said hello to me, asked me how was I doing and, on one occasion, accompanied me to the Post Exchange (PX) and downed a couple of glasses of beer with me. I couldn't speak for Pvt. Hancock, but that was the first time I had cordially interacted with any person who was racially different from me. And I was 18 years old at that time.

Naturally, I was overjoyed when graduation day came. I was proud of my overall performance regarding school (I was ranked 6th out of 57 students) and I enthusiastically looked forward to my ensuing transition. To me and my mind-set, that meant that I would soon be travelling to South Korea where I would, in time, be reunited with Jerome and my newly found family of friends. I was pleased and bubbling with anticipatory excitement.

Unfortunately though, my transition meant something entirely different to Uncle Sam. Instead of being sent to Korea, or to any other overseas designation, I was scheduled to remain stateside. To be specific, I was slated to go to 'Fort Sam Houston,' which was located in San Antonio, Texas. To say I was taken aback and severely devastated is a vast understatement.

When I was handed those pertinent orders, I confess to breaking down and crying unashamedly. Any onlooking observer would have instantly assumed that I was in deep mourning. And just so happened, my barracks sergeant, a middle-aged black man named A.J. Allen, was on hand to see me. I was sitting on my footlocker, staring down at my written orders when he spoke to me.

"What's the matter with you, Harris?" he frowningly asked me. "Talk to me."

Shaking my head, I could barely contain my composure before I was able to respond. "I - I was expecting to be sent to South Korea, Sarge, but they're sending me to San Antonio, Texas instead, a place called Fort Sam Houston. And I hate it, absolutely hate it!"

The onlooking noncom seemed to be visually dumbfounded. "Are you fucking shittin' me, Pvt. Harris?" he spoke. "You want to go to fuckin' Korea, that goddamn hell-hole? Have you lost your cotton-pickin' mind, boy?"

"No, my friends are in Korea, Sarge," I pitifully replied.

"Harris, I don't give a shit if your grandma's over there!" the sergeant yelled. "Harris, you'll make new friends. Son, you don't know how lucky you are. Why Fort Sam Houston is like the country club of the whole goddamn army! It's like sop duty!"

In actuality, I could not be consoled, no matter what Staff-Sgt. Allen said or emphasized. "I don't care about any of that, Sarge, none of it," I argued. "I just wanna be with my friends, that's all."

As he stood before me, shaking his head in disbelief, Sgt. Allen came to the conclusion that he was fighting a losing battle. "Look, kid," he suggested, toning down his rhetoric, "you go ahead and go to San Antone, give yourself time to get adjusted to your assigned unit there. And I mean - a fair chance, Harris. Then, if you still can't . . . live without your buddies . . . Friends come and go all the time, Pvt. Harris. But, if you're still hell-bent on joining them, joining them in hell, I might add, then you can put in a formal request to be transferred to South Korea. As a United States soldier, you have a right to put in a '1049' for an overseas transfer."

"A 1049, that's what I need?" I responded, perking up a little. "I'll do that, Sgt. Allen. I thank you for telling me about it."

"Like I suggested, Private, take the time to get squared away in your new unit," Allen reemphasized. "Give yourself a fair chance. Who knows? You might have a fuckin' bird's nest on the ground. So, don't be hasty. Think long and hard about it. Will you do that, just as a favor to Sgt. Allen?"

Stifling my tears, I smiled in sincere gratitude. "I'll do that, Sarge," I vowed, "and I appreciate you. Thanks for taking the time to speak to me."

"Well . . . I only hope I've talked some sense into you," the noncom replied, taking the time to firmly shake my hand. "Best of luck to you, and take care of yourself."

Back in late August and early September when I spent a couple of weeks in Saint Louis with J and the other guys, I was officially convalescing from my bowel obstruction surgery. After finishing up my recycling period, I went directly into my 'second eight' phase. When I was scheduled to go to my newly-assigned home base (which, in my case, was Fort Sam Houston, Texas), I was afforded my first traditional and bonafide leave.

To my heartfelt regret though, the leave I was granted was after the Thanksgiving Day holiday and five days before Christmas. Therefore, after a casual and leisurely vacation in Saint Louis, I boarded a plane out at Lambert Field and arrived in San Antonio on December 20, 1962. Just so happened, that was exactly six months after my formal army induction.

Although the 20th was also a couple of days shy of kicking off the official winter season, it wasn't cold in San Antonio. In fact, the temperature was in the low 70's. Although I climbed aboard the flight in Missouri, wearing my military overcoat, I definitely did not need it when we finally touched down in Texas.

I wasted no time hailing a taxicab for the impending trip to Fort Sam Houston.

When I informed the cabby that I was headed to the 24th Evacuation Hospital on the army post (that was my specified unit), he rather proudly said he knew exactly where it was. The man was Hispanic (Mexican, maybe), middle-aged, friendly and apparently a veteran taxi driver. He didn't actually tell me that, but when he claimed he was equally familiar with the general layout of the not-too-distant air force bases too (Kelly, Randolph and Lackland), I kind of assumed he was. At any rate, he drove me directly to my new company. Not surprising to me, he also knew to pull up in front of the unit's Orderly Room.

As I retrieved my duffle bag and proceeded to pay him, he seemed to be itching to say something to me. He had a puzzled frown on his face. Admittedly, I was momentarily uneasy. Upon gesturing with his hands somewhat, he spoke, "Soldier, can I put a crazy question to you? Why do they do you people like this?"

I was instantly resentful. "What do you mean when you say "you people?" I asked.

Right away I realized the cab driver and I were not on the same page. He replied, "You know - you soldier boys, and the air force boys too. Why do they do it? Christmas - it is not even a week from now. Why could the military bosses not wait and send you guys here to the lonely post - after the holidays are gone? That, to me, is jest a leetal crazy, a leetal loco!"

I responded with laughter. "Do ya' know what, Sir?" I injected. "It's a leetal crazy and loco to me too. But there's a right way, a wrong way and then there's the army way. Believe me, you have to be a little crazy yourself to figure it all out."

At that moment, the cabbie smiled himself and then opted to shake my hand. "Well, young man, you try to make the very best of it. Try and be happy, and have a very merry Christmas too."

"And I hope the same for you, Sir, you and your family, both. Have a happy New Year and thanks for the ride too."

A very short while later, after I signed-in at my new company and was issued my bedding supplies by the Orderly Room clerk (obviously, my arrival was anticipated), I promptly proceeded to my nearby billets. Across the adjacent street, and catty-cornered to the O.R. itself, was an elongated walkway Standardized barracks were situated on the walk path's left and right extremes (three separate structures on each side) and my assigned domicile was the second one on the left side. Although my new post was much more attractive than Fort Leonard Wood (more scenic and more greener as well), the billets were apparently designed by the same, uninspired architect. Meaning they were quite drab and archaic looking.

Actually, I was neither surprised or bothered by the appearance of my new home. (All I had to do was to reflect back to the accommodations I was subjected to in Benton Harbor, Michigan and Sturgeon Bay, Wisconsin). What irritated me from the word say-go was the eerie emptiness of the place. I had figured that the majority of the soldiers would be on Christmas and New Year's leaves (San Antonio's airport was overflowing with assorted military personnel when I came through it), but I didn't think all of my new barracks mates would be gone! However, when I entered my assigned dwelling, there was absolutely no one downstairs and, if someone was upstairs, they were awfully still and quiet. Since my covey-hole was on the first floor, I took the initiative to flip up the light switches on both sides of the billets, hoping that, to some degree, it would help relieve my feeling of aloneness. Sadly, it did not.

Now, in my early army days and certainly prior to them, I confess that I hosted little, if any, affection or high regard for Caucasian people. Centering around the "nigger" insult that came from the mouth of that little five-year-old white boy (back when I was only twelve) and continuing all the way up to the two-faced deception of Capt. Hensley at that holding company, I harbored a deep-seated contempt for white folks in general.

Furthermore, since I considered myself to be a student of logic and a great believer in righteousness as well, when it was evident to me that most Caucasians loathed black folks for the mere sake of hatred itself (skin color was their primary focal point), I was in total awe of them. In a certain sense, they were like aliens to me!

However, in all honesty, the aforementioned was not the full extent of my utter distaste for white people. Unlike the majority of blacks, or Negroes, I knew, I was acutely aware of my people's age-old history in America (slavery, Jim Crow, the lynchings, all of it) and I deeply abhorred the blatant injustice of it all. Therefore, I didn't remotely understand the so-called "white race' and as time marched forward, I hosted little desire to want to know any of them or to understand them either. And if that made me some kind of reactionary bigot or begrudging racist (meaning, my rapidly-growing tendency to paint all Caucasians with the same, broad brush), then so be it! Although it was totally contrary to Christian doctrine, I was resolved to live with it!

Significantly, the foregoing thought pattern was almost ever-present on my mind on the maiden afternoon I arrived at Fort Sam Houston. However, my ruminating did not crop up out of the clear, blue sky. Instead, it came to the forefront when I proceeded to sign my name on the log-in sheet inside the Orderly Room, just a short while earlier. To be specific, it was when I noticed a type-written name, just above my name on the incoming roster. Although it wasn't exactly news to me (or comforting), 'James

Hancock,' whom I knew from Fort Leonard Wood, was also being assigned to the 24th Evacuation Hospital. Owing to my official orders, I was fully aware of it.

~

Earlier on that particular afternoon, in addition to issuing my bedding supplies and pointing out my assigned barracks, the company clerk provided me with a special meal ticket. He also informed me of the serving times for breakfast, lunch and supper, and then told me exactly where the eating facility was located. He specified the 'Brooke General Hospital' and said if I walked out the rear door of my new home and continued directly westward, I'd shortly converge on the designated hospital. "It's only a 10 or 15-minute hike," he said.

When 4:30 P.M. rolled around (the supper period would begin at five), I was quite hungry and very intent upon embarking on that predescribed foot-journey. But when I took the time to secure, both, my wall and foot-lockers (I, of course, had unpacked and emptied my duffle into those lockers), I was slightly startled. Reacting to the incoming footsteps on my right extreme, I quickly looked in that direction to scope out the pertinent individual.

Since it was early evening, I was actually poised to address a soldier who already resided in the barracks. However, although my distractor was sort of entering into uncharted territory himself, he and I needed no formal introduction. Fact was, it was Private E-1 James Hancock and upon sighting me, he immediately paused (similar to me earlier, he was toting his duffle and bedding supplies) and smiled at me like I was his long, lost best friend or somebody.

"Hey, Hancock, how you doing, guy?" I asked, seizing the initiative to speak. "I kinda expected you some time later tonight. It's good to see you."

"And I'm glad to see you, Harris," Hancock replied as he perused the immediate area. "But I wasn't so sure you would feel the same way about me. Not really."

Since I had never had a cross word with Pvt. Hancock, I was puzzled by his remark. "But why - why do you say that?" I questioned.

Although I was slightly irritated, Hancock did not respond to my query right away. He spotted a vacant bed that was just two spaces away from my area (the bunk next to me was neatly made up, indicating that it belonged to another soldier), then walked over to it and dropped his bedding issue atop it. He even relieved himself of his duffle bag before turning around to address me.

"Remember, Harris?" he spoke. "I was on hand that day you were talking to Staff-Sgt. Allen. You were so disgusted and so upset. You know, when you found out you were being sent here to Fort Sam Houston - instead of Korea like you wanted? I felt so sorry for you. And I thought - you'd still be mad and pissed off about it, that's all. Are you still upset?"

"Oh - I'm dealing with it," I stated. "But I wasn't mad at a - real live person, and especially not at you, Hancock. Why would I be pissed off or upset with you? You didn't have nothing to do with my assignment orders."

Hancock flashed an understanding grin at that point. "Harris, you looked like you were mad at the whole world that day," he mused. "And I happened to be part of the world too. I was tempted to tell you I was being sent here too, but I was sure that wouldn't mean nothing to you, wouldn't make you feel better. Like I said, I felt real bad for you."

I took a moment to reflect back. "I imagine I did come across as a spoiled brat that day," I admitted. "I wasn't really mad though, just indescribably sad and feeling sorry for myself. But it had absolutely nothing to do with you, Hancock. And I am glad you're here, happy as hell to see you."

"And that goes double for me, Harris. It's nice to know at least one person when you come to an entirely new place. We can, maybe, help each other out. And that'll be fine with me."

"The same with me, Hancock," I congenially responded.

Starting with dining together on our maiden day at Fort Sam Houston, Texas, James Hancock and I spent a great deal of time with each other for the next couple of weeks or so. We continued to eat meals together, drank beer at the Post Exchange together, attended movies in each other's company and even spent, both, Christmas and New Year's together. Even in the wake of my prejudgment baggage (though I kept my feelings under wraps), I actually liked and enjoyed interacting with Hancock and he seemed to sincerely like me too.

As it would go, however, after the holidays went by the boards and our fellow soldiers gradually returned to their roost (in their case, the 24th Evacuation Hospital facility), our relationship slowly normalized.

In essence, without any overt begrudgement on either of our parts, Jim Hancock simply forged alliances with fellow white soldiers while I began to bond more and more with black troops. Right in line with that well-known analogy that, "Birds of a feather flock together," I had to admit that our rather brief and diminished relationship was actually atypical of normal, polarized American people.

Being the friendly and outgoing fellow I was (my mom often said I never met a stranger), I soon found myself in the company of a whole slew of Negroid companions. Just from being quite familiar with a popular card game called 'bid whist' (which was a pastime I regularly engaged in as a teenager), I frequently interacted with older black soldiers. Then, when it came to guys around my age, I was always up to accompanying them to almost any and everywhere they asked me to go. So, in spite of my putting in that 1049 request for a transfer to South Korea (despite Sgt. Allen's sincere advice, I did that within two weeks of my arrival at Fort Sam), I was still open to novel friendships.

Out of all the new friends I made in the 24th Evac., there were two guys I came to favor almost instantaneously. One was five years my senior and the other young man, even though we were the same age, happened to be newly-married. They both, however, were draftees. The 23-year old's name was Nathaniel Johnson, he was from Lackawanna, New York; and the other boy, Daniel Williams, hailed from Detroit, Michigan. While they were completely diverse personality-wise, they both had a real knack for making me laugh.

For example, since I almost never ate breakfast (that was an entrenched carry-over from my childhood), I was a notorious late-sleeper during weekends. 'Nate,' who resided on the second floor of my barracks, was well aware of my slumbering preference and loved to tease me about it.

Usually, I did get up in time to eat lunch with, both, Nate and 'Danny,' but my pal, Nate, didn't always wait until I rose on my own accord. As I laid on my bunk, still trying to sleep, I could hear his voice as he stood nearby, looking down at me. As he mimicked the gruff voice and manner of a hard-boiled, veteran drill instructor, he traditionally delivered a prolonged verbal critique, which, of course, was comically aimed at me. Often, our mutual friend, Danny, would be standing alongside of him.

Without even a glint of a smile on his face, Nate would say something like, "I have seen some sorry-ass soldiers in my day, but this one here takes the proverbial cake. Lyin' there like a goddamn 'Sleeping Beauty,' bombs droppin' all around, American soldiers being killed and maimed on the battlefield, and here he lies sleeping like a friggin', sissyfied candy-ass! How do they 'spect me to win this here war? When they keep shipping me lazy, good-for-nothin' and deficient 'cruits like this one? Makes me wanna puke, jest lookin' at him! Why I've seen tougher lookin' soldiers at the goddarn Wac Detachment! What's this man's army coming to?"

As usual, in the middle of Nate's amusing and mock tirade, I would emerge fully awake and in the throes of consistent laughter. However, I certainly wasn't the only one who found Nate comical. Danny and every soldier in the immediate vicinity would be chuckling, but not Nate himself. He would remain in character and retain his serious expression. That was, until I opted to sit up and say something in retaliation to his foregoing insults.

"Mark my words," I would smilingly say, "they are going to commit you to the looney bind someday, and probably sooner than later. And when they carry you away in a straitjacket, Nate, I ain't gonna say a word. In fact, I'm gonna sign your butt in!"

My buddy, Nate, was great with comeback remarks. "Well, I don't mind them taking my butt in," he countered, "as long as they leave the rest of me alone. 'Harry,' git the hell outta that bed! It's almost lunchtime."

To my joy and great fortune, Nathaniel Johnson was a perennial, fun-loving jokester. He got a kick out of, occasionally, throwing hand-grenades at select individuals. Of course, not real, live grenades, just imaginary ones! Such as, he would actually be talking to a person (looking as if he was sincerely absorbed in the ongoing conversation) and then, when the discussion ended and the other party proceeded to walk away, Nate would conjure up the make-believe grenade, pretend to pull the pin with his teeth and feign tossing it in the direction of the departing soldier. Then, as he threw up both of his hands, he would make an explosion sound with his mouth.

Oftentimes, I would be in the immediate vicinity to observe him and no matter how many times I saw him implementing his little joke, I would virtually crack up in laughter. However, I did come to worry about him sometimes, and essentially because of 'who' he chose as an unsuspecting foil for his tomfoolery. Although he frequently subjected his jovial antics to fellow enlisted men, he, sometimes, behaved similarly when it came to noncoms and a few officers too. In those cases, I was worried he would eventually be caught in the act. Nate, though, didn't seem to care.

Although my pal, Nathan Johnson, had a rather bizarre and inexhaustible sense of humor, my other intimate comrade, Dan Williams, would tickle my funny bone by occasionally verbally degrading my hometown, which, of course, was Saint Louis, Missouri. Without ever setting foot in St. Lou, he loved focusing on the criminal activity that plagued my native city. Admittedly, Saint Louis was newsworthy when it came to a variety of criminal acts but, similar to a lot of people I came to know, Danny thought East St. Louis was a part of St. Louis proper. I schooled him on the fact that it was actually a city in Illinois, but that meant absolutely nothing to him. He teasingly suggested that my city should drop the word Saint in favor of changing it to Stain instead. Citing all the shootings and killings that were occurring in urban Saint Louis during the 1960's, Danny was alluding to the word 'bloodstain.'

Similar to the way I reacted to Nate's ongoing teasing and absurdities, I took Dan's taunting in stride as well. He, just like Nathan, was basically a nice guy and was very caring. In addition to kidding around, he liked to pick my brain about a hodgepodge of subjects and seemed to be quite interested in some of the reading materials I possessed also. In fact, he and I were discussing my reading prowess when he casually divulged that he had not graduated high school. Almost instantly, his admission didn't set well with me.

Seizing on that very confession, I became a constant and unrelenting nag to my friend, Danny. Upon vowing to assist him in whatever studies that prevailed, I encouraged him to pursue his G.E.D. After all, the army offered free and comprehensive classes right on post. Therefore, and to his own enthusiastic credit, Danny jumped into the learning process full-scale and a couple of months later, as I proudly looked upon him, he earned his high school equivalency. Even at present, I can still recall the look of gladness and accomplishment on his face, and on my face as well.

Just as I revealed previously, Daniel Williams was practically a newlywed. He had married his long-time sweetheart and talked about her very often. In fact, he reflected on his wife so often and with so much adoring enthusiasm, I came to feel like I actually knew her. And according to my buddy, it was just a matter of time before I would come to meet her in the flesh. In essence, Dan had signed the papers for 'off-post lodging' and he looked forward to 'Valerie' (that was his wife's name) eventually coming to San Antonio to join him. Meanwhile, as Danny bunked just five areas from my assigned cubbyhole and our relationship deepened and virtually solidified, we continued to interact daily. As I did with Jerome and Nate, I grew to think the world and all of him.

CHAPTER TWENTY-NINE

IN LIEU OF DIPLOMACY

When I made the decision to join the military service, I called myself adopting a new, improved attitude. I vowed that I would shun fighting of any kind (unless, of course, I was in a war zone) and I would make a valiant attempt to walk away from all volatile confrontations. However, in less than three months of my transplant to Fort Sam Houston, I found myself yielding to a familiar adage that was put forth by my beloved mother, Ruby. She urged me to, "Never, ever say what you won't do."

Unfortunately though, there was one particular factor I completely overlooked when it came to my newly-adopted stance regarding physical violence. I, along with the fellows I ran with while in high school, labelled it the "Bogarting quality." To be precise, it was acutely derived from actor, Humphrey Bogart's gangster persona and was simply a synonymous term for blatant 'bullying.' Therefore, when it occasionally reared its ugly head, it was practically impossible for me to remain silent and somewhat submissive. It became more and more clear to me that some people could be unreasonable beyond reason itself and I never came to understand that.

Admittedly, I have never been a fan of rigid, unyielding rules. (As strange as it sounds, I am pretty sure my feelings dated back to my father and my 'Cisco Kid' days). Then again, there are some rules that are based on fairness and common sense. Such as, since soldiers are traditionally rousted from their beds at 5:00 A.M. during most weekday mornings (and, sometimes, earlier), it seemed appropriate to designate 10:00 P.M. as the official 'lights-out' hour. It was the army way of life in Fort Leonard Wood and was the same way at Fort Sam Houston. The greater majority of my fellow soldiers were in compliance with that rule.

Evidently though, there was one 24th Evacuation soldier who wasn't a fan of that set regulation. But to the direct point, he was totally defiant of it! Even when the ceiling lights were turned off at the stipulated time and the majority of the men were already in their bunks, the fellow I'm speaking of would enter the barracks (sometimes, as late as two o'clock in the morning) and turn the lights on. Then, he would slowly undress himself for bed, but instead of retiring for the night, he would come up with a book to read. A few nearby soldiers would protest, and especially soldiers who were assigned to his side of the billets, but the guy would respond with a nasty remark or just ignore them. Seemingly, Julio Garcia's cry was, "Hooray for me and the hell with you."

To my total disadvantage, I am not only a very light sleeper, but my hearing seems to become keener at night also. So, continuous snoring and other unpleasant nocturnal sounds often kept (and keeps) me awake. All in all, sleeping in a barracks in the company of nine or ten other soldiers was an ongoing struggle for me. Thankfully, with the help of a set of ear plugs, I was able to cope with the irritating sounds.

Naturally, I had no legitimate gripes with my fellow barracks mates and their unconscious slumbering habits. (Danny even told me that I, sometimes, grinded my teeth). However, when it came to a soldier who obviously had no regards for universal barracks rules, then compromise on my behalf went completely out the window. To me, it was bad enough that Garcia turned the lights on at all hours during the night, bad enough, too, that he took his sweet time getting undressed, but when he elected to read a darn book - that took the proverbial cake! Quoting my mom once again, "Enough is enough and too much stinks."

Pvt. E-2 Julio Garcia occupied a lodging area that was catty-cornered to my across the aisle living compartment. He was around 20 years old, of Mexican descent and was stockily built, if not obese. He was one of the many soldiers who returned to duty after the New Year's holiday and since only three weeks had passed by, I hardly knew him. Actually, except for Daniel Williams and James Hancock, I barely knew any of the first floor residents. Specifically, there were three other fellow black soldiers, another Caucasian youngster, Garcia and two Puerto Rican young men assigned to the ground floor.

However, in spite of not having any kind of personal dealings with Garcia, I had made a single assessment of the guy, and one that was not at all complimentary. Although he, basically, kept to himself and was somewhat docile during regular, daylight hours, he appeared to be altogether different at nighttime. That's because he appeared to have a drinking problem. Quite often, when he entered the barracks during his early-morning appearances, he would be reeking of the smell of strong alcohol. He wouldn't be sloppy drunk, but, similar to my Uncle Major, he displayed a mean streak.

It was evident that Garcia was spoiling for a fight during those particular occasions and that's why the other soldiers weren't more adamant regarding the ceiling light issue. I, too, didn't want to get into a brawl over the matter but, after holding my tongue during several foregoing episodes, I concluded that it was about time to address the problem. I was hoping to avoid a physical confrontation. Plus, I wasn't at all sure I could handle the guy (with me weighing a buck-forty, he certainly was heftier than me), but I thoroughly believed one thing: No matter what, after the fisticuffs, Garcia would know he had been in a fight and, oftentimes, that alone would bring about a change of heart.

To be entirely frank, I had my eyes trained on Pvt. Garcia from the very moment he entered the barracks. It was around 1:45 in the morning. I saw the soldier hit the light switch, watched him as he removed his civilian garb and spied him as he retrieved a book from his wall-locker too.

Merely minutes afterwards, while wearing only my underwear and house slippers, I climbed out of my bed and then converged on Garcia's lodging area. That's when he lowered his book and angrily shifted his eyes towards me.

"Are you planning on turning the lights off, any time soon?" I asked him. "They're supposed to be off at ten o'clock and you know that. Here it is, almost two in the morning and here you are reading, my man. I don't think you're being very fair."

"Well, you know what I think?" was Garcia's reply. "I think you best take your little boney ass back over to your own space where you belong. I think you should mind your own damn business!"

Although I calmly said, "Alright," I immediately headed for the light switch on the far wall. I flipped it down and returned to my assigned area. Naturally, my foregoing action didn't set well with Garcia. Although it was then quite dark inside the billets, I could hear him making his way over to the same wall switch.

He pushed it back up, took a moment to defiantly mug me, and promptly retraced his steps back to his cubby-hole.

However, I was just as stubborn as my Hispanic adversary. In addition, I felt I had <u>right</u> on my side. Therefore, in spite of the silliness of the episode, I soon walked back to the light switch and doused the lights again. Even upon doing it though, I could hear Garcia strolling towards my position. I remained offside the light switch as my adversary angrily flipped it back to the 'on' position and, in turn, I switched it back 'off.'

"Let the fuckin' lights alone, Harris!" Garcia demanded, illuminating the barracks once again.

Growing tired of playing the silly game, I turned the lights off one more time, saying, "The lights are staying off, fella. Don't turn'em back on again!"

"Fuck you, you nigger-punk!" Garcia shouted, forcefully hitting the switch for a fourth time.

Actually, I was already fed-up with indulging in the 'lights on-lights off' contest with my Mexican antagonist, but the spontaneous racial slur spurred on my subsequent action. As I pivoted sideways with my left shoulder, I delivered a blunt left fist to Garcia's face and, then, a follow-up right cross and he reeled backward. However, although he appeared to be stunned, he did not fall. Instead, as I assumed a boxing stance, readying myself for his retaliation, he instantly rushed me. With both of his arms outstretched, he apparently favored wrestling over traditional fisticuffs!

In the midst of the ongoing battle between Garcia and myself, the majority of our first-floor barracks mates woke up and looked on from their respective bunks. In all probability, they had no idea of what was going on. But at that particular moment, I had my own concerns. With Garcia's arms locked extremely tight around my waist, I fell back upon the barracks wall and tried desperately to break his grip. Grimacing in severe pain, I struck my opponent several times in the back and side of his head, but that didn't seem to faze or deter him. His enwrapment was crushing and fixed, and he seemed intent upon breaking my back!

Now, I never considered myself to be a dirty or vicious fighter and, in actuality, I never, ever wanted to seriously injure or maim another person. However, I had to break Garcia's hold. I was in excruciating pain! So, when I solidly kneed Garcia in his groin and then (after he severed his grasp) followed through with an uppercut blow to the same, exact private area, I was explicitly fighting in the name of mere survival and sheer physical relief. In my opinion, I had no other option!

As I stood back, trying to cope with my own terrible pain, I was momentarily inclined to punch Garcia one more time. But, upon seeing my opponent writhing in probably even greater agony than mine, I could not bring myself to do it. However, I ended up doing something that was entirely unorthodox in itself. I held out my hand, offering Garcia my assistance and, to my surprise, he readily accepted it. He firmly grasped my hand, allowed me to help him stand erect and, then, to gingerly escort him to his nearby lodging area.

"I'm sorry I had to do that, Garcia," I almost ashamedly said, steadily assisting my former opponent as he painstakingly seated himself on his bed. "But you came close to breaking my back. "You're a real strong dude, Garcia, as strong as a darn ox!"

Although he was tenderly grasping his aching groin and trying to catch his breath as well, Julio Garcia practically willed his self to speak. "I'll be alright, Harris," he softly told me. "I just need some . . . some shut-eye. And you can - turn out the lights now too. Okay, Harris?"

I stood still for a prolonged minute, looking down at Garcia with eyes of wonder and sincere sympathy. And in his state of subdued calm, I felt almost doubly sorry for him. Then, I decided to honor his foregoing concession. I proceeded to walk down the aisle, switched the lights off and returned to my lodging site. For I, too, was yearning for a few hours of restful slumber. Unfortunately though, there were only a <u>few</u> hours left for it.

 Although it's more than evident that I managed to live beyond my 'light switch brawl' with Private E-2 Julio Garcia, my poor back pained and agonized me for days on end afterwards. In the final analysis, was it worth it? Though many of my billets mates praised me in memory of it, I wasn't quite sure, but I imagined it was. From that morning forward, the barracks lights were turned off at the stipulated time and my former adversary and I established a cordial relationship.

 In all probability, even if my Mexican associate wanted to forge a closer bond with me (which he did not), I would have, more than likely, nixed the alliance. Although I was able to laugh about it later on in my life, I was somewhat begrudging in the short aftermath of that barracks scuffle. In knowing that white America did not have much love or affection for Mexican and Hispanic people either (which was similar to their age-old and overt hatred of black folks), I absolutely resented Garcia calling me a "nigger-punk."

 In retrospect, a Caucasian cop had once called me a "punk" while a little 5-year-old white boy had addressed me as a "nigger" when I was only 12, but it was the first time those two slurs were angrily mixed together. Maybe, Julio Garcia was under the impression that 'his' people were superior to Negroid people, but I certainly didn't think so. However, despite of all the foregoing,

I still had the ability to cordially co-exist with the guy and with any other so-called 'minority' who came my way.

When I seriously take out time to reflect back on that early-morning, physical skirmish that pitted me against a bullying and unreasonable barracks mate, I still struggle with a certain degree of wonderment. For a number of days after the confrontation, I was practically showered with praise and compliments, and especially from soldiers who slept near Garcia's lodging space. They could and should have pushed back on Garcia's "Bogarting" conduct before I even came into the picture. "Nip it in the bud" was an advocation I learned from my Uncle Bill and it was certainly applicable to Garcia's former behavior. According to quite a few of my fellow soldiers, it was ongoing before I was sent to Fort Sam Houston. Therefore, although I eventually shrugged it off, I was somewhat resentful of my barracks mate's foregoing inaction.

I don't know what it is, but every time I start doubting myself, thinking I had made a misstep, something occurs that tends to water down my resolve or knock me back to square one. And those were my exact sentiments when, on a Saturday afternoon, I was in the company 'Dayroom' and patiently awaiting my turn to play a game of pocket pool. Up until that time, I had watched three other soldiers fall to quick defeat at the hands of a skilled and rather braggadocious black fellow named 'Taylor' and (although I expected the same fate) I was still anxious to compete. Then, finally, I was up next.

Just as Taylor proceeded to down the 'eight ball' and I stepped forward to grab the cue stick from the defeated player, 24th Evac's official mail clerk (a white PFC by the name of Gregory McIntosh) walked through the entrance door. And before I could rack up the pool balls, which was traditional for the incoming challenger, McIntosh boldly declared he was going to play next. I, naturally, begged the difference and immediately informed him I had the 'winners.'

Not that it was remotely relevant, but I didn't much like the mail clerk from the moment I met him. But I was not alone in my feelings towards him. He was an abrasive loud-mouth and a know-it-all; an obnoxious white boy who thought he was notches above regular soldiers, and especially men of color. Maybe, his job as mail-clerk fed into his inflated ego but it didn't impress me. So, when he opted to 'steal' my turn on the pool table, I felt he needed to reconsider and I told him so.

"Well, you can play next, Harris," he casually stated as he wrapped his hand around the pool stick I was holding. "This won't take long."

Being a lefty, I was tightly clutching the stick with my right hand. "You're not taking my winners, man, and you best let go of this stick too," I firmly stated. "Just who the hell do you think you are anyway?"

McIntosh actually appeared to be incensed, just like he was in the right. "Goddamnit, let go of the fucking stick, Private!" he shouted. "Let it go, damn you!"

Only fractions of a second later, I yielded to PFC McIntoshes' demand. I let go alright - but with two solid and consecutive fists to his face. Then, when he relinquished his hold on the cue stick, I bluntly cracked him on the head with it too. Actually, I was intent upon hitting him again, but the soldier named Taylor cautioned me not to do it. However, it wasn't due to his concern for the mail clerk, but because he was fearful I'd break the pool stick. I gave in to his plea and halted my aggression.

As a round of loud and spirited applause was rendered by the majority of the onlooking soldiers, the foregoing fight (if it even could have been called that) was essentially over. As McIntosh collected himself and rather sluggishly turned and strolled back out the same door he had recently walked through, I was astounded!

I realized that Gregory McIntosh felt humiliated in the wake of the joyous clapping, but I was momentarily taken aback myself. I thought, after all the PFC's mouth and his brazen attempt to try and intimidate me (and flaunt his rank at me as well), he had no desire whatsoever to retaliate. He was, in my estimation, a classic, everyday bully, but obviously was one who was void of real conviction.

Although PFC McIntosh displayed a badly bruised black eye on the Sunday following our Dayroom fracas, I was informed that he didn't attribute his injury to a run-in with me. From my understanding, he told his close-knit buddies that he had been attacked by a gang of civilian thugs outside a San Antonio proper nightclub. Frankly, I could have cared less. All I know is, that after our bizarre confrontation, he and I never exchanged another cross word. To me, that was a good thing.

Just from being a black teenager living in the city of St. Louis, Missouri, I met and interacted (and, sometimes, locked horns) with a whole slew of Negroid bullies. In all honesty, I believed as a youngster just as I believe at present, that far too many of my fellow black folks are guilty of self-hatred and, sadly, they aren't even aware of it. (I am thoroughly convinced that is why there are so many killings in the black community, and especially in the inner cities). Oddly though, I could count on one hand just how many black bullies I encountered during my entire army career. Maybe, a military environment fostered a certain degree of maturity and, maybe (as Uncle Tomish as it sounds), Negroes behave more civilly in the presence of our white counterparts. Whatever it was, black camaraderie seemed to flourish in an army setting.

As I admitted though, I came into contact with a few 'homeboy' bullies while in the army and I was just as turned off by them as I was by Garcia and McIntosh. The so-called brothers I'm alluding to may have been the same skin color I was, and they might have personally treated me respectfully, but I didn't remotely like their ways or their actions. Using fear and intimidation to gain submission or leverage is a technique I truly disdain.

If there was such an individual as a 'premiere bully,' then a young soldier named William Grant had to be him. A native of Philadelphia, PA., he had the stature of a body builder, he was haughty, arrogant and was a braggart as well. He claimed he had several years of college under his belt, said he had pledged a fraternity ("frat") while there, and often talked about his adoring fiancee who still resided in "Philly." In addition, he often tossed around a bunch of 'fifty-cents' or lofty words but, although I never called him on any of them, many of the terms (though they were real words) were frequently out of context.

In my opinion, Private Grant relished talking over the heads of younger soldiers, and especially fellow black ones. But despite his foregoing flaws and foibles and the fact that I secretly peeped his hole card, I gradually grew to like him. I'm quite certain it had much to do with turnover and attrition.

It seemed for a while that every time I looked around, two or three soldiers were moving out of my home barracks. Some of them were being reassigned to neighboring billets, or were being transferred to other army bases, or being sent overseas, or were being discharged. Within four months' time, I bade farewell to individuals such as James Hancock, Julio Garcia and even my close-knit friend, Daniel Williams. Regarding Danny's departure, however, he was still accessible to me and he and I were as tight as ever. Dan and his wife, Valerie, were, then, living off-post.

Almost instantly, when William Grant moved into my barracks and selected a bunk that was located directly across from my assigned cubby-hole, I became aware that he and I had something quite in common. Although I wasn't particularly proud of my feelings, but we both had a marked distaste for Caucasian people in general. And just so happened, when Pvt. Grant arrived on the scene, soldiers of the Caucasian persuasion had become the predominate race on my barrack's first floor.

Quite contrarily though, Grant and I were not on the same page when it came to our viewpoints about race co-existing. Totally unlike me, Grant seemed to be bent on intimidating and antagonizing them. That's why he made it a point to strut around the first floor, showcasing his rippled bare-chest and flexing his muscles. He obviously felt our white counterparts were envious of his physique and, in time, I came to believe he was right on the money about his feelings.

However, Bill Grant's aggravating actions towards Caucasian soldiers did not remotely set well with me. Sure, I had no affection for white folks collectively, but I elected to stay away from them as much as humanly possible and talk to them when it was necessary. In my heart, I knew it was wrong to harbor such unfriendly and unsavory feelings but I had had my fill with racial bigotry and animus.

Down deep, William Grant's feelings regarding white soldiers paralleled mine but he wasn't, in the least, standoffish like me. Instead, he chose to interact with them, almost on a daily basis. But it proved to be a total sham on Grant's part, a virtual charade and I feared that rough waters laid in-wait ahead.

Therefore, when I entered my barracks one Saturday afternoon, fresh from eating lunch, and observed our barracks 'jack-leg' barber engaged in the task of cutting William Grant's hair, I knew right away that things were going to quickly go awry. Because the amateur barber was a white soldier named Ralston, I could almost feel the tension in the air. And it came to the forefront when a flustered Ralston voiced a sudden complaint.

In a state of hysteria, the barber said, "I told you 'fore we started, Grant, I ain't never cut a color'd kid's hair! I ain't no fuckin' good at it!"

It was obvious that Bill Grant was just as anguished as Ralston was. He sat in a chair, holding a mirror in his right hand, as he responded to his barber's previous statement. "Well, you gonna do a better goddamn job than this, Ralston, you skinny-ass motherfucka!" he yelled. "Git it right - goddamn you!"

As Grant sat in that chair, repeatedly viewing himself in the hand-mirror, I was inclined to laugh, but I did not. Actually, Grant's head did resemble that of a plucked chicken but I didn't want to make a bad situation even worse by extracting amusement from it. However, I had to remove myself from the barracks because I couldn't take much more.

When I physically flew the coop (or exited the billets), it was 1:20 P.M. Then, when I returned later, after watching an entire full-length movie on the television in the company dayroom, it was 3:45 P.M. And to my complete surprise and wonder, PFC Ralston was still frantically protesting and, as crazy as it was, was still working on William Grant's head as well! As I staved off my laughter one more time, I opted to get the hell out of that billets and the immediate vicinity as well. That hair-cutting episode was one of the most bizarre and comical scenes I had ever observed.

Due to the fact that I spent most of the evening with Danny and Valerie Williams on the day of that rather 'absurd' haircut incident, I never knew how long it played out or its final outcome. (However, immediately afterwards, William Grant took to wearing his fatigue cap indoors was quite a spell). But despite of not being personally involved in that episode, I didn't think well of Grant in the aftermath of it. Although I continued to cordially speak to him, I made it a point to keep my distance from him. I cannot help myself, I never liked or understood blatant meanness.

In actuality, I was content in being standoffish when it came to Pvt. Grant. The guy had so many negative traits I disliked in people. His misusage of words didn't bother me so much, neither did his lofty bragging, but when we worked together at 24th Evacuation's warehouse, he would behave in a manner that irked the hell out of me and other observers too. I doubt, however, if my personal irritation was of the same mind-set as my fellow soldiers, and especially the white ones.

For the sake of clarity, working in the company warehouse was a necessary prelude to spending about a week in the wilds of a place known as 'Camp Bullis.' Since we were a mobile field hospital, we often went there to set up and hone our medical operative skills. In essence, similar to an efficient stationary hospital, 24th Evac. was poised to medically aid and assist military personnel in or near a combat area. And since practical application and precision simulation was at the forefront of our mission, we were compelled to spend almost two weeks out of each month in the field. (Admittedly, I had never been a fan or lover of outdoor activities or living, so I secretly hated it).

THE LONG AND WINDING ROAD

As I previously mentioned, the day prior to convoying out to Camp Bullis was spent at the company warehouse. In fact, the entire day saw a good number of 24th Evac. soldiers loading up two and a half ton trucks and other army vehicles and, then, collectively readying ourselves for a week's stay in the field.

It was during those warehouse preparatory periods that I observed an embedded peculiarity in Bill Grant. The loading specifications for each military vehicle was documented on paper. Therefore, it was just a matter of physical execution and hard work. And without the presence of a single noncom or an officer, the soldiers would dutifully follow the written instructions and load the trucks accordingly.

Apparently though, some individuals very much need on-hand supervision and William Grant fitted that profile. While the vast majority of the soldiers were busily laboring and pulling their load, Grant would be defiantly standing around, casually observing the ongoing work process and, sometimes, audaciously reading a newspaper. He would practically do nothing the entire workday and, displaying a rather smug expression, was confident that no one would say anything to him about his behavior.

In all honesty, William Grant's laziness and staunch defiance wasn't the primary reason I was contemptuous of him. I was intent upon fulfilling my work role, no matter how many shirkers were amongst us. However, Pvt. Grant displayed another vexing and head-scratching action, and one, in my opinion, that was like shooting himself in the foot.

Just let one of 24th Evacuation's officers, or, perhaps, Sgt-Major Walker show up and presto - like magic, you would observe an entirely different William Grant! Similar to the fictional Superman darting into a telephone booth, Grant would swiftly cast off his fatigue jacket and, with his muscles bulging, would single-handedly pick up a GP-large size tent, if one was still available. And he would continue his feats of strength, quite certain he had impressed the onlooking superior, until that particular person would finally leave the vicinity. Then, as soon as the superior had made his retreat, Grant would casually dust himself off, slip his fatigue jacket back on and become a stationary statue once again. He would leave me and a number of surrounding enlisted men shaking our heads in amazement. Oftentimes, similar to the hair cutting memory, I caught myself laughing.

Frankly speaking, I wasn't angry or resentful of Bill Grant in the wake of his bizarre and deceitful actions when we labored at the company's warehouse. Actually, I was upset with him for his lack of intelligence and insight regarding the matter. I believed he totally underestimated the soldiers who were witness to his warehouse shenanigans, and especially the Caucasian soldiers who practically hated his guts! I asked myself, did Grant really think the onwatching young men would keep silent about his blatant deception? Did he honestly believe they would shy away from informing 24th's noncoms and officers of his staged and phony antics? Well, if he did, I maintained, he was certifiably nuts!

Eventually, I decided to leave Pvt. William Grant to his own devices. However, as it came to pass, my barracks mate from Philadelphia wouldn't allow me to. Though it practically bowled me over, after almost two months of being a staple dweller in my home barracks, Grant became the reincarnation of the departed Julio Garcia. No, he didn't become a Mexican overnight, but he did come to doggedly insist upon keeping the billets lights on well after ten o'clock P.M. during weekdays, similar to Garcia. Contrarily though, instead of citing reading as his driving motive, he attributed his craving for overhead illumination to his beloved fiancee. He claimed that "late evening" inspired him to write her a rather lengthy letter.

Well, I denounced the foregoing rationale as a "crock of crap" and reasoned, instead, that he was trying to personally provoke me. I imagined that someone had informed him about my former physical confrontation with Pvt. Garcia and because I had become somewhat cool towards him, he wanted to get under my skin. I honestly believed that.

Originally, I tried to cope with the novel development by merely ignoring it. But after three nights of saying nothing, observing Grant as he sat atop his bunk and busily writing in a tablet, I decided to tackle the problem head-on. I spoke candidly on the evening of the fourth day and made sure no one heard our conversation. In fact, except for a white soldier who was asleep at the far end of the billets, Grant and I were the only individuals on the ground floor of the dwelling.

"Grant, did anyone tell you about me and a dude named Garcia?" I began. "You know, about me and him having a fight about the ceiling lights, the barracks lights?"

Apparently, Bill Grant was completely unaware of what I was talking about. He noticeably frowned, questioning, "You cats had a fight about the lights, Harris? For real?"

I shook my head affirmatively, then said, "I should have tried to reason with Garcia, but I didn't. And that's why I'm trying to reason with you, Grant. You're what people describe as an "imposing figure," a fellow who's muscle-bound, strong as all get-out, and you scare the devil out of a lot of the dudes around here, and especially the fay boys."

Grant showcased a rather suspicious face at that juncture. "So, what are you getting at, Harris?" he asked as I remained sedate.

"I'm just saying, man, that when it comes to the barracks lights being on after 10 at night, especially when it comes to weekdays, workdays, I am totally against it," I stated. "I'm saying - that if it comes to a fight, I mean - between you and me, I imagine you'll probably be the victor. But you'll know you were in a fight. But, Grant, even in winning, you will still be losing."

"And why is that, Harris?" Grant asked, seemingly grinning.

"Simply because I'll report it to the higher authorities, to the First Sergeant or to the so-called "brass," maybe," I casually stated. "Then, we might fight again - and I'll have no recourse but to report that too. So, it'll be a kind of lose - lose proposition to you."

To my surprise, Pvt. Grant laughed aloud. He then asked, "And you wouldn't give a care if dudes called you a snitch, huh?"

"No, Sir, not even remotely," I replied. "Grant, I don't give a darn about what most people think of me, and I never have. I can't live by other people's standards."

"And you would really squeal on me, Harris?" Grant quizzed.

"I wouldn't enjoy it . . . but I would. Like cowboy star 'Wild Bill Elliot' used to say, "I'm a peaceable man," but I'd be compelled to report you. After all, a man has to do what he has to do. Yeah, I'd squeal on you, if that's what you wanna call it, but only if I have to."

Strangely, William Grant took a moment to check his wristwatch. "Wanna have a cup of tea with me, Harris - or coffee?" he congenially asked. "I'll buy. Might even spring for a sandwich - and some fries. You game?"

For the first time since our talk got underway, I issued a grin. "The last time I turned down a free cup of coffee, I was wearing diapers," I joked. "Gimme a minute to square away my area and we can go."

At that point, Grant and I briskly shook hands, I wasn't at all certain that my words had a positive impact on him, and I wasn't even sure he would bow to my wishes on that <u>very</u> night, but, still, I felt good about addressing the matter. In the final analysis, whatever came out of our discussion was up to my comrade from Philly. As he and I set out for the snack bar, I hoped for the best but the ball was in his court.

***

As it turned out, the face-to-face conversation I had with William Grant reference the barracks lights were only moderately fruitful. If I was in my billets at 10 P.M. on weekday nights, which was the official 'light turn-off time, Grant would obligingly cut off the ceiling lights. However, if I was not in the barracks at that particular hour, my newfound friend, Bill Grant, would still pen his letters. Then again, he would congenially dowse the lights <u>if</u> I showed up. Therefore, for a very lengthy period, I was frequently encouraged by a number of my first floor barracks mates to retire for the night when ten o'clock rolled around. Oftentimes, even when I wasn't in the least tired or sleepy, I would accommodate them. Incidentally, Pvt. E-2 Jared Ralston, our company's jack-leg barber, was my chief prodder.

CHAPTER THIRTY

GRIN AND BEAR IT

In addition to intensely disliking those trips and mock maneuvers in the woods of Camp Bullis, there were two other military activities that I absolutely loathed while soldiering in the 24th Evacuation Hospital. One was pulling 'kitchen police' duty (KP) three times per month and the other one was having guard duty quite frequently.

    Pulling KP simply meant laboring in the Headquarters mess hall facility all day. And 'all day' in army vernacular purely meant rising at 4:30 a.m. and working almost continuously until 7 p.m. in the evening. While I did a credible job mopping floors and washing dishes and pots and pans, I wasn't very good in a particular area of food preparation. Military personnel consumed a whole lot of potatoes, so soldiers assigned to mess hall duty seemed to be forever engaged in the task of peeling them. Of course, I was one of those soldiers, but I was rather inept when it came to the peeling procedure.

    To be more precise, I was positively awful at it! I'm not sure if it had something to do with my being left-handed or not, but when I started off with a potato that was the size of a major league baseball, it was as tiny as a lemon when I got through with it. Almost every time, the in-charge mess hall sergeant would hit the ceiling. Acting like I committed a federal offense, he angrily criticized me, accusing me of "mutilating" or "massacring" his potatoes! Then, he would switch me to a different chore. Although I would assure him that I wasn't "killing" his potatoes on purpose, his reassignment was always cleaning what was called the 'grease trap.' Ordinarily, that was a punitive measure but the mess sergeant claimed it was not and insisted that he wasn't mad at me. Not for a minute did I believe him and I, alternately, carried a grudge for that sergeant and his damn potatoes too.

Although there was somewhat of a 'saving grace' when it came to pulling 24-hour guard duty (two hours on and four hours off), I hated the very thought of its premise. Every now and then an assigned soldier would be charged with guarding an important and valuable military site but, most of the times, the applicable enlisted man would find himself assigned to what was deemed a "dummy area." Operating from the well-known military adage, "Yours is not the reason why, yours is to do or die," so-called guards would consistently march around an essentially vacant area and all under the guise of mute and strict discipline. Being specific, don't ask any questions, just follow the orders you are given.

For example, a few times I found myself protecting a virtual empty lot that was covered with only white rocks. There I was, with my rifle resting on my shoulder, continually marching around a site that was, seemingly, of no real value at all. There were no buildings, no fellow human beings, no equipment, absolutely nothing! I opted to ask the sergeant in-charge a question once and he became a little upset with me.

I asked him, "Sarge, should I be on the lookout for the notorious rock burglar or what?"

Although I was obviously joking, the sergeant was not amused. Looking quite serious, he countered with a reply that I had become quite familiar with. "Harris, don't be a wise guy. Jest play the goddamn silly game, will you?"

As I alluded to priorly, the "silly game" known as guard duty had a kind of saving grace to it. While there were only three designated areas that required guarding, seven soldiers were selected to pull the duty. Since two men were assigned to each site, that meant there was one man too many. However, that was by design and not due to error. In light of a component called 'supernumerary,' one of the assigned soldiers did not necessarily have to fulfill their guard role. In fact, unless one of the specified six soldiers became ill or an unforeseen emergency cropped up, the so-called supernumeral could spend the entire twenty-four hours inside the guard shack, relaxing, watching TV and, essentially, what we called, "cooling his heels."

However, in order to snare the coveted supernumerary title, a soldier had to emerge well-deserving of it. Pitted against the other six soldiers, he not only had to be impeccably dressed (starched fatigues and spit-shined boots), he had to be a virtual whiz when it came to military protocol and regulations and be able to recite the chain of command with the utmost precision. It was a no-nonsense competition that was conducted by the officer-in-charge and it required precise and snap responses. And I was well up to it, I thought.

Now, although I was cocky enough to believe I would emerge victorious whenever I participated in a supernumerary contest, I actually only won four out of nine times. Of course, I was quite disappointed when it came to every one of the five defeats but I wasn't particularly upset or disgruntled in the short aftermath of them. I wish I could claim I was a benevolent and congenial loser, but that would be a stretch of the truth. Since the supreme victor of all of those competitions happened to be a dear friend of mine (namely Nathaniel Johnson), I took my defeats in subdued and calm stride.

The supernumeral contest, in itself, was relatively simple. A senior officer, usually a lieutenant or a captain, would judge the seven competing soldiers on their dress attire and then engage in a 'question and answer' process. To me and my fellow soldiers, it was SOP (standard operating procedure).

However, during one of those simplistic and standard occasions, when Nate and I were deemed as the two, competing finalist, something went terribly awry. The official questioner, Capt. Austin Greene (who was 24th Evacuation's newly-installed company commander), was saddled with a dilemma of his own making. Strangely enough, our C.O. could not come up with a question that would stump and, subsequently, eliminate me or Nate from the ongoing contest.

For instance, the officer quizzed us on the Chain of Command and my buddy and I responded correctly. He went on to military rules and regulations, then military protocol (including the Code of Conduct), and even dabbled into military history and, still, Nate and I precisionly rattled off those correct answers as well. Then, finally, after the passing of a half an hour or so, Capt. Greene gave up in sheer frustration and exhaustion. Although it was unorthodox, he proclaimed us co-supernumerals and, alternately, left one of the designated guard sites essentially unsecure.

As it turned out, nothing significant or noteworthy occurred at the unmanned location (probably, the dummy area), but our company's ranking noncom, Sgt-Major Frank Walker, was quite livid about the happening. On the following morning, he took the initiative to summon, both, me and Nate to his Headquarters office and proceeded to chew us out soundly. Although my fellow supernumeral elected to remain silent throughout our dual-headed 'dress down' (the Sgt-Major even suggested that one of us should have decried our Commanding Officer's solution), I managed to piss off Sgt. Walker even more when I posed a particular query to him.

"But, Sir," I spoke, "what about Capt. Greene's role in the matter? After all, he's our superior and we're just enlisted men."

As he cast eyes of anger, I am certain the sergeant branded me smart-alecky, but, momentarily, he seemed to be at a loss for words. Finally, he said, "Pvt. Harris, don't git on my goddamn bad side. Don't be a fuckin' wisenheimer. You need to git out of my damn face, both of youse. Git out of here, both of youse!"

As Nate and I executed dual 'about-faces,' I could not resist smiling. And when Nate and I vacated the building, it was apparent that my friend noticed my smirk too.

"Alright, Lionel Harris, what's with that shit-eating grin?" he smilingly asked.

"Nate, I know this sounds kinda weird, but all of a sudden something that my mother once told me just popped into my mind," I responded. "Ya see - my mom once worked in a Jewish-owned clothing store, back in St. Louis, and she told me several times. Most of the customers were Negroes. She said - every now and then, when 'colored' customers got into heated arguments with the Jewish owner or one of the salesmen, they resorted to a common tradition. My mom said when Negroes pissed them off, they would pull the customer's file folder and jot the letters 'SLN' right next to the man or woman's surname."

"I could probably guess, but what did those letters really mean?" Nate questioned.

"They stood for "**S**mart **L**ittle **N**igger," I replied. "So I imagine, by now, old man Walker already pulled my personnel file and wrote those letters next to my name. I can see him doing it right now."

My friend, Nate, practically guffawed at that juncture. "Well, I don't know about that, Harris," he stated, "but I am positive your name's near the top of Walker's shit list. Boy, I thought he was gonna bust a gasket! Good thing his ass didn't have a firearm! He'd have shot you, Harris."

"And probably would have blew you away too, Nate!" I joked.

~~~

In retrospect, after my buddy, Nate, and I were ordered to appear in front of Sgt-Major Walker, I never knew for sure if he proceeded to defame my military file or place my name on some kind of 'shit' or 'hit' list. But in less than a week after that 'chewing out' happening, I was thrown an unhittable curve. Without even consulting me, I was informed that I had been enrolled in something called 'Medical Records School.'

To say I wasn't even remotely happy or receptive to being enrolled in the 'Medical Records School' (in fact, I wasn't aware that such a place existed), was putting it lightly. I was not anti-school or disinterested in higher learning either, but after attending business administration school, I figured I was finished with educational enhancement for quite a while. Plus, since I was still holding out hope for an overseas transfer to South Korea, I felt as if I had been thrown a major league curve ball.

Although I was all but certain that my dissent would fall on deaf ears, I was still intent upon making my underlying feelings known. Therefore, after 'bravely' subjecting myself to the gruff, verbal wrath of Sgt-Major Walker (He spewed out something crude like, "Remember - your little ass is grass and the army's the fucking lawn mower!"), I was, then, permitted to plead my case to our Company Commander, Capt. Greene. However, the captain was much more pleasant during our meeting and was somewhat complimentary as well.

"PFC Harris, it seems to me that you should feel honored to have been chosen to attend med. records school, and be very proud of yourself," the officer smilingly spoke. "Your barracks sergeant, the First Sergeant, and even Sgt. Walker — they all felt you were the right pick for the task. And I haven't known you for long, but I think you're the ideal soldier for it too, young man. And ya' know what? I am sure, positive, you'll excel and make us all proud."

    Although I acted appreciative, I was actually feeling sad inside. Going to medical records school would give me a distinction I certainly did not relish. Upon graduating from that school, I was fearful that my military future would be mired in gloom, tedium and redundancy. Fact was, although I had no affection whatsoever for outdoors activities, I could almost count on spending a great amount of time in the woods of Camp Bullis. 24th Evacuation Hospital was a field unit and I was sure my schooling would be used in that particular setting. Therefore, in spite of Capt. Greene's upbeat and flattery flavored attempt to put a positive spin on the school issue, it would, alternately, render 24th Evac. a more proficient mobile army hospital. In essence, upon graduating from the school, I would be regarded a valuable asset. Not personally, but in the eyes of my company's superiors.

    On a positive note, to my utmost joy and good fortune, the school I was scheduled to attend was located in the Medical Training Corps. area (MTC). And although that training division was spread out over a rather large tract of land, my home barracks was situated only two city blocks from the school site itself. And with the help of my friend, Danny Williams, and a large and sturdy dolly, I was permitted to move my footlocker and two wall lockers to my newly-assigned billets.

    However, when I stopped in at my new unit's Orderly Room and proceeded to sign in on the registry book, I was somewhat alarmed. There was a column on the sheet that asked for the soldier's birth place and I wasn't thrilled in light of the birth states

I observed. There was Alabama, Mississippi, South Carolina, Illinois and even my home state, Missouri.

In addition, and further to my onsetting agitation, none of the applicable surnames resembled that of a black individual's last name. Not a Jones, a Jackson, a Johnson, a Smith or even a Harris was in the mix. Then, I thought - "Hell, there's a brother named 'Ogelthorp' in 24th Evac., so, maybe, I'm just guilty of being stereotypical." But, to my dismay, I wasn't being stereotypical after all. Other than myself, there was only one other Negroid soldier in the entire 'cycle.' The other brother's name was Dexter Parsons, he was assigned to a different barracks and he hailed from Tulsa, Oklahoma. And I learned all of that over a two-week period, well after I had settled-in at my novel billets.

I wish I could report that my settling-in procedure was smooth-sailing and without fanfare, but I can't. After Dan and I placed my civilian wall locker inside my new barracks and, then, went back to retrieve my military wall locker, we immediately returned to find the first locker setting upside down. As a cluster of silent and smug-faced white soldiers stood in the rear of the barracks, staring defiantly in our direction, Danny and I looked at each other in marked disgust.

My friend shook his head in exasperation. "Harris, you don't deserve this foul-ass bullshit!" he loudly remarked, making sure our observers heard him. "Why the fuck they sent you here - to deal with a bunch of racist crackers, just pisses me off! Man, I hate - hate leaving you here with them - hate it with a damn passion. It ain't right. Harris, it ain't!"

As I reached out and patted Dan on his shoulder, I forced a smile in an effort to try and calm him. "Kiddo, they ain't worth getting upset over," I said in a casual manner. "They're just typical, bigoted white boys. Racism is in their blood and hatred - it's a way of like with 'em. But I'll - handle it. I'll be alright, Danny."

Heavy concern marred my comrade's face. He stared angrily at our Caucasian onlookers, then suggested, "How 'bout I go back to the company, gather all the brothers up, and we can come back and turn this motherfucker out? Man, you don't have to put up with this bullshit."

I shook my head in disagreement. "And what would that accomplish, Dan?" I asked. "It'll just make a bad situation even worse. I love you for your concern, but, sadly, I have to live with these dudes or, at least, co-exist with them. Either way, I'll be alright."

"Well, I'll be worrying about you, Harris," Dan said. "All the time you're here, I'll be worrying about you. Tell you what: Let's go on and set your two wall lockers up, and you can stay here while I go back and grab your footlocker. But I'll tell you, Harris, if they fuck with you while I'm gone, they gonna have hell to pay. I kid you not, man."

"I'll be okay, Danny," I assured my friend. "They're basically a bunch of sick cowards. I doubt if they'll make a move right in front of my face. But I don't want you to worry, especially about me. I'm a survivor."

"Okay, survivor," my comrade smilingly replied. "But if you need a fucking knife or gun, I can get in touch with one if you want. Cut one of these motherfucker's throats or bust a cap in their ass, and they'll leave you the fuck alone. Hell, Harris, you ain't did nothing to their honkie asses. I'm serious, man! Gimme the word and I'll get you a piece!"

Dan purposely raised his voice when he issued the foregoing statement, making sure our white observers heard him. So, I was actually playing along with him when I remarked, "I'll let you know on that, kiddo, but I'm hoping it won't come to that. I was sent here to attend school, not to hurt or kill some s.o.b."

Minutes later, after Dan assisted me in turning my 'civie' locker back upright, he walked out of my barracks with the dolly in tow. As he returned to the 24th Evac. to pick up my footlocker, I stayed put, straightening up my wall lockers, making up my bunk and squaring away my assigned cubbyhole. Then, upon my friend's return, although he offered to stay around for a while, I talked him out of it. I reminded him that it was nearing supper time, and since he was "an old married man," his wife, Valerie, was probably waiting for him to come home. We hugged, shook hands and he was soon on his way.

To be perfectly honest, from the very second I noticed the southern birthplaces of my soon-to-be schoolmates, I came to a behavior consensus. It was my intent to say little of nothing to my Caucasian associates and I hoped they would behave similarly. Though it would be totally contrary to my basic character, I was prepared to go through the entire school cycle without any of them uttering a single, solitary word to me and vice-versa.

In light of the recent locker prank, I instantly realized that my planned strategy was a mere pipe dream. While I personally viewed racism and bigotry as nonsensible and barren of reasonability, I knew I was dealing with hate-filled Caucasian young men who were diametrically and historically opposed to my assessment. Therefore, within a few moments, I emerged silently scolding myself for being totally unrealistic and somewhat stupid as well!

And it was at that particular juncture, as my inner feeling of stupidity and frustration graduated into a resurgence of anger, I was prompted to make my next move. As if I was on a mission or something, I proceeded to my military wall locker, sought out my entrenching tool and casually tossed it on my bed. Then, as I opted to lie supine on my bunk (and right next to that shovel), I tried my best to relax and regain some semblance of composure.

In reality though, I was almost itching for one or two of my would-be antagonists to come forth and confront me. I could actually visualize myself, fiercely wielding that shovel and putting a serious and devastating hurt on any and every hateful white boy who elected to challenge me. In my seething silence, I was loudly crying, "The hell with medical records school, the hell with my damn field unit, the hell with the United States Army and doubly hell with the entire Caucasian race!"

In just a matter of minutes, however, as I stared aimlessly straight ahead and found myself struggling with the ongoing intensity of my marked anger and fury, I came face-to-face to one of the on-hand white soldiers. Frankly, I was thoroughly poised and combat-ready to counter whatever nasty remark the guy hurled my way but I was, alternately, taken aback and quite ill-prepared as well in wake of the soldier's wide smile.

"Before you go out and break ground for a grave plot," he jokingly said, "I was hoping to talk to you, PFC Harris. My name is Kevin Brenahan and . . . "I'd like to shake hands with you."

I immediately rose to a seated position prior to uttering a single word. "And why would you want to do something like that, Pvt. Brenahan?" I suspiciously asked.

The soldier's grin never waned. "Well, we got this strange habit back home that people do when they meet somebody for the very first time," was the soldier's reply. "It probably don't make good sense, but it's kinda in our blood. Well, at least it's in my blood."

Although I tried to remain serious as I chose to come to a standing position, I, too, was smiling at that point. "And where, pray tell, is 'back home' for you?" I asked. "Where are you from?"

"I was born and raised in Davenport, Iowa. And what about Mr. Harris?"

Instantly, I was no longer upset and I felt somewhat relaxed also. That prompted me to say, "Aw, <u>Mister</u> Harris is somewhere in Chicago, he ran off when I was just a kid. But his second son, Lionel - me, I originally hail from St. Louis, Missouri. Glad to make your acquaintance, Kevin Brenahan."

The young man stepped forth, offering me his hand as we stood, smiling at each other. "I love a fellow with a sense of humor," he stated, firmly grasping my hand. "So, I am pleased to meet you, Lionel Harris - from St. Louis, Missouri. Have you got plans for dinner? It's about that time, ya' know."

I glanced begrudgingly in the direction of the young men who were still milling around in the rear of the billets, before saying, "Maybe it's best for me to stay here, at least for the rest of the evening. No telling what your . . . buddies might do if I leave my stuff here, unguarded."

Brenahan became serious at that moment. "A low-life scumbag named Cantrell did it, messed with your locker," he stated. "He's a class A asshole, but he left right after he did his dirty work. Your lockers and stuff will be alright."

Naturally, I was still quite reluctant. "Easy for you to say, Brenahan," I said. "And suppose this Cantrell character returns before we make it back here?"

For some reason my new acquaintance took a moment to glance back at the bystanding soldiers. "Irving, come up here for a minute, would you?" he yelled out. As the sought out young man walked towards his summoner and me, I had no inkling of what was on Brenahan's mind. He put his hand on Pvt. Irving's shoulder, stating, "Irving, this is PFC Harris, he's a friend of mine. Harris and I are going to grab ourselves some chow. Now, if Cantrell or any other 'cruit fucks with his shit while we're gone, tell them nicely - that I'm gonna come back and kick the holy cow shit out of them. You don't have to do nothing, Irving, jest tell 'em what I said. Okay, good buddy?"

"You've got it," Pvt. Irving quickly responded. "Over and out, Brenahan."

As the Irving kid turned about and walked off, I was completely in awe of my newfound friend's actions and words. To say I was curious and perplexed was a stark understatement. However, before I could address Kevin Brenahan about my feelings, he turned his attention to me. "Better secure your lockers, Harris," he suggested, "and don't forget your entrenching tool over there. Hell, we might have to dig a few graves after all, before the evening's done."

A short while later, as Pvt. Kevin Brenahan and I left the barracks and headed for the post exchange (PX) which was located in the Medical Training Corps. complex, I was actually intrigued by him. I wanted to get to know him; wanted to know about his background, his thoughts and viewpoints and, specifically, where he was coming from when he candidly spoke to the soldier named Irving. In essence, I was anxious to pick the guy's brain.

During our relatively short stroll to MTC's main Post Exchange, Kevin Brenahan and I, basically, engaged in light-hearted small talk. However, after ordering a large pepperoni-sausage pizza, along with french fries and a couple of steins of beer, we seated ourselves at a table across from each other and embarked upon a free-flowing, but in-depth discussion. Grinning from ear to ear, I could not refrain from asking my newly-found friend a rather comical query.

"Kevin Brenahan, are you from the planet 'Uranus' or somewhere?" I asked him. "I mean - are you even a being from this solar system? You have my word, I'll keep your secret, my man."

Apparently, Brenahan and I were on the same wavelength and he responded accordingly, but with a measure of sadness. "I'm afraid not, Harris," he spoke. "Just like you, I'm from the planet Earth. But my pop - now he might be some kind of alien. He's a fire and brimstone minister, Protestant, and he would have knocked my lights out if'n he had heard me a while ago. Rev. Marcus Brenahan can't stand a dirty mouth and he raised up me and my sister, driving that thought into the both of us. It's funny - you join the service, and everything you learned as a kid, it flies right out the darn window. There was a time, Harris, I didn't even think about using a swear word. Hard to believe, ain't it?"

I sat, smiling and shaking my head negatively. "Not at all," I replied. "Cause believe it or not, you're preaching to the choir. I came into the army myself last year, almost never using a curse word, never. Some of my childhood friends used to call me all kinds of profane names, trying to make me lose my temper, but I never did. Then, after hookin' up with Uncle Sam, I woke up one morning, cussing like a drunken sailor. It's everyday barracks language, and you fall prey to it. So, don't beat yourself up about it, Kevin. And can I call you Kevin?"

"Sure you can - as long as I can call you Lionel. And what about your pop - Lionel?" Kevin asked. "You said he's in Chicago. What does he do there? And how many sisters and brothers do you have?"

After telling my comrade about my MIA father, and then about my mom and four brothers, I soon guided our conversation back to Kevin's clergyman dad. Precisely, I wanted to know if his foregoing actions in our barracks was in some way connected to his father's religious teachings. Kevin answered affirmatively and even quoted something from the Holy Bible like, "If you see the son, then 'sometimes,' not always but quite often, you see the father also." He also added, "My pop taught me and my 'sis' about the perils and evils of racism and all the other isms."

"Kevin, I find that refreshing," I remarked. "Up 'til now, I've been under the impression that all white parents drum into their kids that they're superior to - people of color, to put it nicely."

My companion displayed a reflective smile. "And there's that word again," he mused, "the one my father always warned me about. The word 'all.' According to my pop, Harris, Lionel - when people resort to that word, they're opening up to bigotry galore. All colored people are lazy, shiftless and sex-crazy, all Jews are greedy and born cheats, all Mexicans are . . . well - you get my drift, Lionel. No, sir, all white parents aren't racist and bigots, just the ignorant and godless ones."

I nodded my head in joyous agreement. "Do you know what, Kevin Brenahan?" I spoke. "I haven't known you for a good hour yet, but I think you oughta be in somebody's college. What led you here, guy, to Uncle Sam's army?"

Brenahan emitted a grin, but it soon faded. "My pop was grooming me to attend the seminary, sorta follow in his footsteps," he divulged, "but I wouldn't go along with him, Lionel. Broke his heart a little . . . but he'll get over it, hopefully. But what's your story, fella? You're a PFC, so you've been soldiering for a while. Out of all the guys in your company, why did they decide to enroll you in medical records school? It's not a punishment, is it? You know - why did they throw you in with a bunch of southern rednecks?"

As I reached for a second slice of pizza, I chuckled for a moment. "I guess I'm just plain-old lucky," I kidded. "I was told I should feel honored when I was selected out of the blue, but I never felt that way. 'Yours is not the reason why.' But back to you for a minute, Kevin. What about that threat you made, the one involving the dude named Cantrell? Do you expect some kind of retaliation?"

"Cantrell is a loud-mouth, overweight, hateful bully," was Kevin's rather angry response. "I tangled with him a couple of days ago and he got the worse end of our scuffle. Harris, he came into the dayroom, and me and some other soldiers were minding our business, just watching television, right? This bold ignoramus goes over, doesn't say a word, and just switches to another channel! As if we weren't even there!"

"I well-know the type, Kevin," I injected.

It was more than apparent that my comrade detested the mere memory of what he was telling me. "Well, one thing led to another," he continued. "I switched the channel back to the movie we were watching, and the fool took exception - like $\underline{I}$ was in the wrong! I beat him like a bass fiddle, Harris! I mean - Lionel."

"Like a bass fiddle?" I teasingly asked.

As we sat, looking at each other, Kevin and I, both, burst into laughter. It was more than obvious that we enjoyed being in each other's company.

CHAPTER THIRTY-ONE
MY WORLD IS A BETTER PLACE

When Kevin Brenahan and I returned to our assigned barracks on my first day in our new 'learning' environment, despite not mentioning it to my novel friend, I was actually surprised to find my lodging area still intact and untouched. The dwelling was practically filled with white soldiers at the time, but since none of them proceeded to approach me (not a casual hello or a hostile remark either), I behaved similarly. Ideally, if the white boys didn't bother me, I had no real desire to bother or interact with them either.

However, the 'co-existing' stalemate lasted only about ten days. After daily classes got underway and test scores became a matter of record, I emerged somewhat conspicuous and undeservedly unpopular. Simply from getting stellar grades as a student, I was subjected to a whole gamut of ugly and bigoted under breath remarks. And from time to time, I would enter my home billets and discover my footlocker standing on end or be turned completely upside down atop my bunk. No soldier had the balls to step forward to claim responsibility, but Kevin and I suspected it was the actions of multiple culprits, and not the burly bully named Cantrell.

After seriously mulling over my dilemma, I realized my fate was essentially left up to me. I figured I could either 'dummy down' and regain my invisible status or I could do my level best scholastically, buckle down, and incur the childish wrath of my racist, white peers. Of course, I chose the latter option and no matter what was thrown my way as a discouragement, I resolved to do it in grand style. It was my primary intent to become the 'outstanding soldier of the cycle' and I vowed to pursue that coveted goal with a passion.

While I did not consider myself as intellectually superior to my Caucasian classmates (or the other Negroid student), I did believe I had a clear advantage over most of them. I was disciplined (since I only associated with Kevin Brenahan, I had a lot of free time on my hands), I was highly motivated (I almost savored being labelled an SLN by my white peers) and, borrowing a made-up word from my cousin, Frank, I was blessed with a great rememory. Therefore, when it came to every facet of the schooling process, whether it was medical terminology, disease symptoms, record maintenance and hospital principles and precepts that were unique to field operations, I excelled. My grades continually stayed in the 90's and only a single white boy, an Indiana native named Jordan Olson, emerged as a formidable opponent. Pvt. Olson posted test scores in the high eighties and mid-nineties, but he never bested me.

After taking at least ten exams, with the results and rankings being posted on the company bulletin board each time, the class was given what was deemed the 'final examination' in the middle of our eighth and last week. That test, of course, touched upon every and anything we were taught from day-one and it was challenging and quite lengthy as well.

In fact, it took nearly two hours to complete, but afterwards, I was confident and almost certain I had 'aced' it. After all, I had studied four days for it.

Unfortunately though, I didn't match the test, like I first thought. I did score a 97, however, and that was more than exemplary, I felt. Then, when I learned that Jordan Olson did ace the exam, although I was somewhat suspicious, I was not overly concerned about the news. I reasoned that if every test score mattered and the principle of 'average' came into play, my scholarly performance would still rise above Pvt. Olson's. I figured I would be awarded the top soldier of the cycle prize for sure.

Well, if I lived in a different world or universe, I would have certainly proceeded to snare that impressive award. But, since I resided in a sphere that was infamous for 'unearned white privilege,' a world that unashamedly tosses honor and fair-play out the nearest window, and one that traditionally discriminates against peoples of color, Pvt. E-2 Jordan Olson was officially celebrated as the "Outstanding Soldier of the Cycle" and I, in turn, was ranked number two. And since I felt soiled and defecated on in the aftermath of it, it instantly occurred to me that that was keenly appropriate.

Although I was highly upset over the foregoing act of biasness, I didn't officially protest it or stir up any waves about it. Instead, I said, "Screw medical records school and all the racist white folks" and looked forward to the future. I had a single and pressing desire on graduation day and it actually overshadowed my dashed hopes and ire regarding the biased oversight. I desperately wanted to physically remove myself from the immediate vicinity of the school and I was intent upon making a speedy and deliberate retreat. In fact, I had rose earlier on that particular morning and had picked up a large dolly from my home unit which, of course, was the 24th Evacuation Hospital.

However, there was something that weighed heavily on, both, my mind and heart. I thought about a young soldier named Kevin Brenahan, a special guy who I regarded as a saving grace and a tangible blessing from God. And, soon, sadness consumed my very being. When I was selected to attend that MTC school, irrespectful of what awaited me, I felt somewhat disenchanted with the Supreme Being. But, on graduation day and many, many days prior, I applauded God and thanked Him for his gracious favor. For He wasn't compelled to usher Kevin into my life but I was awfully glad He did!

By the time I got around to bidding my final farewell to my friend and intimate cohort, Pvt. Kevin Brenahan, my former begrudgment regarding the award slight had almost magically dissolved entirely. My world had become a much better place with Kevin in it and I longed to tell him so. Even when he attempted to assume some degree of blame for the award fiasco (apologizing as if he had personally played a role in it), I told him that the matter wasn't even worth talking about and he was no way connected to the travesty. I begged him not to try and identify with a group of hate-inspired bigots.

"Lionel, you talk like you understand their racist chicken shit," he replied, displaying a flustered face. "But I sure as hell don't understand it! How do those evil bastards even sleep at night? They actually gave that fuckin' Olson a copy of the final test! Did you know that shit? And all because they didn't wanna have a colored soldier as the friggin' soldier of the cycle. That goddamn Sgt. Iverson did that, and he calls his self a damn instructor! Man, can you believe that foul shit?"

Although I was appreciative of my cohort's fury, I stood smiling in the face of it. "Kevin, to me and countless black dudes who look like me, it's just the same old soup warmed over," I calmly responded, "but, Kev, I don't want <u>you</u> to lose sleep over mess like this. Forget about those people, the hell with all of 'em. But this - this is <u>our</u> time, and it's not a good time for me. Because, Kevin, I absolutely hate having to say goodbye to you, hate it with a passion."

Just from glimpsing the sorrow in his eyes, my friend was now able to divorce himself from his anger. He produced a smile, saying, "Lonnie, I'm gonna miss the hell out of you. I wish I could just . . . stuff you into my duffle bag and tote you right along with me to Fort Benning, Georgia. Your common sense, your deep feelings, and that weird sense of humor of yours, man-alive, you have constantly warmed my heart and made my day, every day."

I froze for a prolonged minute, trying to get a grip on my emotions and marvelling over Kevin's warmly spoken words. "Leave it to you to steal my thunder, kiddo," I teasingly spoke, "speaking the exact words that I should be saying to you. But I want you to know something, Kev. Do you recall when we talked about race relations that day? When I kinda bared my soul, confessed to you that I was forever straddling the fence between Dr. Martin Luther King and Malcolm X? You know - violence up against non-violence?"

"Yeah, I remember that discussion, and I ended up telling you that I understood your feelings, your reasoning and I still do. And especially in light of the crap you just went through."

Although I was feeling somewhat full inside, I forced out a smile. "Well, kiddo, all because of you - I am more confused than ever now," I stated. "And that's a positive thing, a good thing - and with no downsides to it. If God Almighty was to come to me and speak, saying, "Try and hold on, Lionel, be patient and persevere, and I vow to someday send you a dear and wonderful friend who, in essence, will be a carbon copy of a young Christian man named Kevin Marcus Brenahan, I would derive comfort and joy in anticipating that promised 'someday.' Kev, from my very first day here, all the way up to this second, I thank the living God for you. And I'll pray . . . pray that you never change. I dearly love you, and knowing myself, I always will."

Though I became verbally choked up towards the end of my lengthy speech, I was genuinely surprised by my friend's reaction. He was shedding tears when he said, "Boy, just look at me . . . and you're supposed to be the cry-baby in our relationship. Ya' know, Lionel, besides my pop, I've never met anyone who's as sincere and honest as you are. You always say what you mean, and mean what you say. Please, please stay that way."

It was hardly a surprise to me, but my true self emerged at that point. Similar to my close comrade, I, too, was profusely weeping. However, neither of us seemed to be ashamed of our actions, just deeply sorrowful. We, then, huddled together in a firm, heartfelt embrace and, alternately, stood apart, fondly looking at each other.

Not more than five minutes later, my beloved friend, Kevin, and I went through the motions of putting the finishing touches on our emotional farewell. We engaged in a hearty handclasp, hugged again momentarily, wished each other good luck and a bright future, and then went our separate ways. Kevin and I parted with the intent of keeping in touch with each other, but, unfortunately, we failed to do it. I guess we both allowed the demands and toils of life to distract us and that was no less than a crying shame in itself. I can't speak for Kevin but, to me, he still remains tenderly tucked away in my heart.

To be quite frank, when I finally returned to my home unit, the 24th Evacuation Hospital, I fully expected to be subjected to a series of field maneuvers in the wilds of Camp Bullis and since

I was now wearing the hat of a 'medical records specialist,' I was also certain I would be working harder than ever before. However, to my surprise and great joy, I was only half-right. Field excursions still took place but when we were not out in the wilderness, I was assigned a role that was more suitable to my formal schooling.

Serving in what was specified as an O.J.T. capacity (On the Job Training), I worked 8:00 a.m. to 4:30 p.m. shifts at Brooke General Hospital's 'Registrar Office.' In addition to being the site where official hospital records were kept, the facility dealt with every facet of hospital administration. From a patient's admission to his or her final disposition (ergo: discharge or transfer), the Registrar maintained a paper trail and any and everything pertinent to one's hospital stay.

The term 'Registrar,' however, was not solely the name of the physical office itself. It was also the official title of the select man who was in charge of it and, throughout my time there, he was a full (or bird) colonel named Simpson. And from the moment I made the colonel's acquaintance until the final second I left his office, I admired the man greatly.

Colonel Simpson, the official 'Registrar' was tall and slender (about 6'-2"), deeply tanned (of course, he was Caucasian), cordial but essentially business-oriented, and was forever dressed immaculately with glistening low-quarter shoes. When the man walked, he appeared to proudly strut and, in my opinion, even when he wheeled his automobile, he seemed to be in an 'attention' mode. In my personal assessment, my distinguished boss was an officer prototype.

In reality, I liked most of my co-workers at the Registrar Office. Incidentally though, they were not all army personnel. There were a number of civilian employees (G.S. status) on hand and even a couple of air force enlistees working there too. Although professionalism and cordiality was the primary order of the day, I actually bonded with two of my army counterparts at almost rapid speed.

One of those soldiers was a black buck sergeant named Alexander Gray (actually, he was the only fellow Negro there) and the other fellow, a PFC Thomas Preston, happened to be white. Although Sgt. Gray was a long-time staple at the records facility, Pvt. Preston, on the other hand, was also an OJT pupil and was attached to the 250th General Hospital. That unit, too, like 24th Evac. was a field company and was, in fact, located right next to my assigned company.

Now, in spite of my underlying bias towards Caucasians in general, I must admit I liked Preston from the very first day I met him. He was a happy-go-lucky sort; always smiling, always friendly and pleasant and if the guy had a prejudiced bone in his body, he was a master of disguise. He treated, both, Sgt. Gray and me with the utmost respect and seemed to genuinely relish being in our company.

Notably, in a relatively short while, Alex Gray and I emerged gleefully reciprocal when it came to our feelings. We virtually savored having Tom Preston around us. And within a single week of working together, uncannily similar to my former relationship with Kevin M. Brenahan, PFC Preston and I dropped our last names and behaved as if we had known each other for months, if not for many years. We worked in congenial concert, ate lunch together, attended movies together, generally hung-out together and, soon, Preston chose to call me 'Barry' (which was my middle name and what I preferred over 'Lionel') while I found comfort in calling him 'Tommy.' And if you were but a casual observer, I am sure you would have thought that Tommy and I were lifelong friends. And to our mutual delight, we felt that way too.

Job-wise, Tommy and I were not restricted to just paperwork in our office environment. We did our share of standard filing and streamlining medical records, but we were, alternately, assigned to a more prominent and far-reaching role. Operating under a premise called 'Line of Duty Determinations,' we were charged with personally interviewing recently injured and hospitalized military personnel and recording their responses (or verbal accounts) in verbatim.

Oftentimes, functioning as a team, Tommy and I would find ourselves in the confines of Brooke General Hospital, or at the Beach Pavilion Medical Center, or even at the mental facility known as Chambers Pavilion. And while visiting any one of those medical sites, we would interview select patients at great lengths, and all in an official effort to record the service member's recollections and stories.

Without biasness and embellishment, my partner and I were intent upon churning out detailed and well-crafted written accounts of what military personnel had recently endured and suffered. To be more specific, me and Tommy were charged with producing official reports that were concise and void of conjecture. In addition to dotting all of our *i's* and crossing all of our *t's*, it was vital that we address all the 'whos,' the 'whats,' the 'wheres,' the 'whens,' and, sometimes, the relevant 'whys' and 'hows' when it came to every case and my close-knit friend and I came to excel in our dual-headed capacity. Garbed in our khaki uniforms, all Tommy and I needed was a pencil, a writing pad and an empathetic spirit. And taking the liberty to speak for my affable cohort, we both epitomized the latter trait.

Since Thomas Preston and I were personable and compassionate, we were quite adept in our interviewing roles and when it came to composing and typing up the informational affidavits, we were just as proficient. And although it might sound as if I'm tooting our collective horn or being braggadocious, that was not the case. Our esteemed boss, Col. Simpson, sung praises to us as well.

Unfortunately, there were a couple of downsides to ascertaining those official reports, or affidavits. One dealt with fatalities; when complications arose and armed services personnel would succumb to their relevant injuries and Tommy and I were affiliated with the loved ones they left behind. Coping with the deaths of young men and women who weren't even as old as us, and realizing that we had even met some of their family members, was downright heartbreaking. That was when I happily learned that we were both creatures of deep sentiment.

However, there was, yet, another aspect of the Line of Duty mechanism that rained havoc on our collective emotions. Since Brooke General Hospital was renowned for having a superior and top-notch burn ward (maybe, the best in the entire nation), Tommy and I were compelled to meet and converse with seriously-burned soldiers also. That meant dealing with the putrid smell of burnt flesh, paired with the smell of counteractive antibiotics and ointments.

In reality, the odor alone was difficult enough to cope with, but when we found ourselves directly dialoguing with one of those victimized souls (in some cases, their faces were monstrous looking), it was, oftentimes, an exercise in emotional restraint and endurance. No matter how sorrowful or empathetic we felt, we were intent upon keeping our deep feelings in check and conduct our interview in a professional, no-frills manner. In essence, we were expected to treat burn victims with a degree of normalcy, regardless of our suppressed feelings of sympathy or the disfigurement status of the respective interviewees.

To say the very least, the foregoing was a very tall order, and especially when it came to an emotional and empathetic guy like me. Regretfully, I rushed out of the burn ward and threw up in the middle of my first interview session. I was ashamed afterwards and quite upset with myself as well. Soon, however, I vowed to <u>never</u> do such a thing again.

But that pledge, too, was easier said than done. I eventually learned to cope, but only by adopting what I identified as a 'visionary technique.' Whenever I faced a burn patient, I simply imagined I was talking to one of my beloved brothers and was soon alright and firmly committed to the task that was before me. As I said, I never again loss my composure.

Even as I was skilled at doing my job at the Registrar Office, I was just as proficient in juggling my various friendships too. In addition to interacting with Tommy Preston, I still occasionally ran around with Nate Johnson, sometimes drank coffee with Bill Grant and still spent a great deal of time with Dan and Valerie Williams. On most weekends, in fact, I could be found at the off-post residence of the Williams couple.

During those weekends (essentially Saturday evenings), I also tagged along with Dan and his wife to the Enlisted Men's Club. Located on the army base and frequently called the 'Snake Pit,' it was a facility for dancing and social mingling and was a popular hang-out for numerous soldiers, with the majority of them being black or Negroes.

To me, the Snake Pit was a throwback to my basement dance days, replete with current and yesteryear recordings and I enjoyed it to the virtual hilt. I simply could _not_ dance, although I tried to (Robert and Charles Harris had tried their level best to teach me, but it was to no avail) but I enjoyed watching others, and especially my two married friends. Standing or sitting on the sideline and observing Val and Danny out on the dance floor was like watching Fred Astaire and Ginger Rogers on the silver screen, but with exaggerated flair and more rhythmic style. The two of them were magical! They obviously spent a lot of time practicing their in-synch moves, their precision-turns and snappy steps, and onlooking observers (and they were numerous) would assume they had been skillfully choreographed. My friends from Detroit were just that impressive!

Frequently, my friends Danny and Nate, both, would encourage me to get out on the dance floor (my buddy from New York was also a good dancer), but I was mostly resistant. I was fair and felt I could 'get by' when it came to slow-dancing with a young lady, but, admittedly, I was pretty lame and awful when it came to 'bopping.' That was a version of fast-paced dancing wherein the boy and the girl (while holding hands and facing each other) would continually step-in and, then, step-out in almost perfect timing. Sadly (and weirdly), my problem was that when the girl was stepping in (coming forward), I was habitually stepping out or back. I, sometimes, joked that I could probably walk my female dance partner home like that.

My good friend, Dan, could not begin to understand my problem but, during one occasion, I tried to explain it to him. I told him that I plainly did not have rhythm. Although I had long-heard that all black people were born with rhythm but (as Kevin Brenahan would say) I was conspicuously omitted from that all. And if I wasn't black, I wished someone had informed the racist white folks I had dealt with throughout my young life. Still, I longed for Danny to fully understand my dilemma.

Being quite sincere and adamant about it, I put it to him in an alternate way. "You know how you go to church on Sundays?" I asked him. "And a gospel song is being sung by the choir, and the congregation too? Everybody is clapping, and in perfect unison, right? Ya' know what, Danny? If I don't closely watch the people standing near me, and I kid you not. Man, when surrounding people's hands come together and make the clapping sound, my hands are always out! I don't hear what other folks hear, I guess. And I don't know why . . . but I've always hated it! It's frustrating!"

Dan grinned in stride, and then mouthed one of his patent sayings. "Well, Harris," he remarked, "no matter what, my friend, you are still my nigga, even if you don't git no bigga." Although I wasn't at all thrilled with the 'nigga' term, and no matter what context it was used in, I didn't really mind being Danny's whatever. He was like a prized brother to me (similar to Jerome, Kevin Brenahan and Tommy Preston) and I grew to regard Dan's wife, Valerie, as the sister I never had.

Valerie Williams's feelings for me seemed to be genuinely mutual. She delighted in having me in her company, enjoyed having me over for dinner and truly savored my close-knit relationship with her husband. But I loved her even more, and mainly because she adored Dan so very much.

In retrospect, it may seem odd to a number of people I came to know over the years, but in a bizarre way I felt indebted to my father, Melvin V. Harris. Solely because of him, I was never dazzled or impressed in the wake of an individual's physical attractiveness. I certainly wasn't blind so I knew when it came to women like Dorothy Dandridge, Lena Horne and even Marilyn Monroe and Elizabeth Taylor, they were considered to be beautiful. Also, when I reflected upon men such as Adam Clayton Powell, Tyrone Power, Errol Flynn and even my old man, himself, I realized that such men were deemed handsome as well.

However, from dealing with my biological dad and then recalling that my spiritual father had once ousted a handsome and so-described "beautiful angel" down from the realm of heaven (who was, in fact, Satan incarnated), I learned to not be overly impressed by an individual's physical attractiveness. In addition, when I proceeded to think about some of those misfortunate and infirmed patients in Brooke General's burn ward, I agreed wholeheartedly with a popular adage. Without an iota of doubt in my mind, I was positive that, "Beauty is only skin deep."

Still, I realized that the vast majority of people neither shared my personal assessment or my philosophical insight. Therefore, when I acknowledge that Valerie Williams was, firstly, extremely pleasing to look at and, secondly, was a thoroughly nice and kind-hearted young lady (with the latter being my personal focal point), I was well-aware that my platonic feelings were not shared by the majority of my fellow soldiers, especially the older men.

Mrs. Daniel Williams turned a lot of male heads when she frequented the Snake Pit (even in the presence of her husband), but to Val's credit, she never flirted with her oglers or seemed to be remotely distracted by them. Maybe I could have been painted with a 'naive' brush, but she seemed to have eyes only for Danny. And although Dan, too, was no slouch in the good looks department, and turned a few female heads himself, he appeared to be just as devoted to his wife. In my opinion, it was a marriage made in heaven.

Although I was quite young during my military days, I truly believed I had an innate knack for reading people. I prided myself in surmising what certain individuals were thinking and also felt adept at detecting a person's underlying desires and motives. So, I was hardly ever surprised by what people did, or were capable of doing. And to be sure, that was my thought pattern in the short aftermath of a particular incident that established Valerie Williams and myself as two of the principal players in it.

Not that it was positively crucial to the forthcoming remembrance, but just so happened the woods of Camp Bullis was the site of the opening scene. If I had my rathers on the day I'm on the verge of recounting, I would have been behind my desk at the Registrar Office, but since my position there was still considered to be 'temporary' and was an 'OJT' status, I remained susceptible to being involved in regular field exercises. Again, I detested those outdoor treks but, regretfully, I had no say in it.

However, even in my ongoing loathing for those trips out to Camp Bullis, I never resorted to trickery or any measure of deception. It never occurred to me to feign some illness and go on sick-call. Therefore, just one day into a week-long stay out at Bullis, when I came up with the worst toothache I had ever had in my young life, it was definitely not a staged ploy that was aimed at removing myself from the field excursion. My pain was so severe and agonizing that it actually made my head throb. To be precise, it was a surging wisdom tooth that was accompanied by a nagging cyst.

As I indicated, it was day-one of the field trip, and although I did not conjure up my condition, Sgt-Major Walker behaved as if I did. Though my jaw was swollen and continually throbbing, he branded me a "faker" and said I should, "Tough it out and endure until the field exercise concludes."

But to my Company Commander's credit (who was Capt. Greene), the top sergeant was overruled. I was granted a sick-call status and was soon transported back to Fort Sam Houston and was immediately treated at the dental facility. Believe it or not, if Capt. Greene had not pulled rank on the sergeant-major, things could have gone very badly. In the throes of my excruciating pain, I could perceive myself becoming a deserter or worse. I could picture myself shooting Walker and, then, myself as well. Sure, afterwards I would have been labelled as "demented," "vindictive" or "certifiably nuts," but I would no longer be riddled with unbearable pain. The foregoing is keenly symbolic of how I really felt that day.

Naturally, the forestated was mere conjecture and supposition. Nothing remotely similar to it took place and normalcy soon prevailed. Back at Fort Sam, after my bad tooth was extracted (and I thanked God for it) and I was given a liberal supply of pain medicine, I was "ordered" not to return to my former environment, Camp Bullis. And to me, of course, it was like being thrown into the fabled 'briar-patch.'

It was 9:45 a.m. when I left the dental office and although I was expected to stay in my company area, I took a two-and-a-half-hour nap but did not relish being alone in my billets when I woke up. And that's when I decided to spend the rest of my day with Valerie Williams, fully aware that I had left her husband out in the wilderness of Camp Bullis. I entertained no doubt whatsoever that Val would not welcome my company.

Thankfully, I was right on the money about my friend's better half. Valerie was not only glad to see me but after I told her about my toothache ordeal, she immediately offered to prepare me some chicken noodle soup. I declined, saying, "Maybe a little later," and held up my packet of meds, adding, "These are all I need right now."

Shortly, Valerie and I sat down on the living room sofa and casually conversed, although Val occasionally loaned her attention to the on-playing television set which was tuned to some soap opera. But that certainly didn't bother me, not in the least, because I was content and happy in the wake of being far away from Camp Bullis. Although the lower portion of my face was still slightly numb and my medicines had rendered me a bit woozy, I was doing exceptionally fine at that precise moment in time.

However, as an old adage states, "All good things must come to an end," and that was my exact sentiment when, within two hours of being at the Williams home, an unexpected, loud knock originated from the domicile's side door. Due to my antibiotics,

I had actually yielded to slumber once again. So, when I was awakened by the knock and instantly faced my hostess, it took a few moments to get my bearing. An expression of total surprise marred Valerie's face.

"I can't imagine who the devil that is, Harris," she spoke. "Except for my honey and you, I don't know a single person in this state. Plus, don't nobody know where we live at. Let me see who the dickens that is. And why would they come to the side door?"

"I don't know - but let me get the door," I suggested, climbing to my feet. "Even a salesman would come to the front door."

A minute later, as I stood at the rear door and peeped out its miniature window, I became instantly miffed and disgusted as well. Standing on the other side of the door was a tall, black soldier by the name of Ogelthorp. He was a specialist-five, a long-time member of my assigned unit (24th Evac.) and, most relevant, I had sized him up as a rather slick and unsavory character. I softly divulged his name to Valerie and after she acknowledged she didn't know him, I then proceeded to open the door.

"Harry - my main man!" he cried, showing what we called a 'shit-eating grin.' "Whatchu doin' here, fella?"

Shaking my head, I gazed at the specialist with eyes of absurdity. "Danny Williams and I are tight, we're like brothers - and you're well-aware of that, Ogelthorp," I cheerlessly responded. "So, a more suitable question is - what brings you here, my man? Huh?"

Spec-5 Ogelthorp didn't even opt to answer my query and behaved as if he hadn't even heard me. Instead, the man grinned even wider, acting like he had stumbled upon some novel revelation. "Oh, I got it, Harris - you little ol' devil you. Danny-boy is out in the field, and you are on the scene and layin' in the cut like old Yuccapuck! Didn't know you had it in you, ol' buddy. Well - I'll be on my merry way, 'cause I know three's a damn crowd. But you got the best go, Harry, you ol' slick rascal, you. So long, boy."

With that, Olgelthorp, who was still smiling, promptly made an about-face and then strolled briskly away. It was at that point that a curious Valerie Williams came forward and attempted to spy her now-retreating visitor. However, it was not until she rushed to the front door and observed Ogelthorp climbing into his automobile that she realized she <u>had</u> seen him before. She frowned in resentment as she looked my way.

"I have seen that nigga before, Harris," she informed me. "Danny introduced him to me at the Enlisted Men's Club last Saturday night. I didn't like the way he looked at me then, like a hungry, mad dog! Wonder how he got our address? Harris, I am so glad you are here. I sure wouldn't have let his ass in, might have even called the police. The nerve of his black butt!"

I stood, nodding my head in compliance. "Val, if he ever comes back, talk through the door to him," I spoke. "Tell his ass you're gonna call the cops and Capt. Greene, our company commander too. And if that don't get his attention, threaten to get in touch with his darn wife too. That'll fix his butt, a lousy-ass snake."

"Harris, you mean to tell me he's married?" Val asked. "He has got some nerve, a mangy, low-life dog!"

Although Valerie Williams was highly upset over Spec.- 5 Ogelthorp's foregoing gall (and she had a right to be), I certainly was not. I knew far too many men who were just like him.

"Unfortunately, Val, this old world is full of two-legged dogs like Spec.-5 Ogelthorp," I stated. "They go through life, screwing up other people's lives. That's the sad, sick world we live in, I'm sorry to say. But it's up to people like us - you and me and Danny - to make our world a better place."

CHAPTER THIRTY-TWO
ABNORMAL, BUT CONGENIAL

During mid-summer of 1963, my friend and coworker, Thomas Preston, met and fell deeply in love with a young civilian lady of Mexican descent named Angela Mendoza. 'Angie' was a native of San Antonio, she was around nineteen years old and was quite attractive. (I emphasized the word civilian because a WAC detachment, or Women's Army Corp., was located at Fort Sam Houston also).

Notably, Tommy's newfound love resided a couple of miles on the outskirts of Fort Sam itself and I eventually became familiar with the terrain that led 'to and fro' Angie's residence. And in a relatively brief time, as the months progressed, I came to know Angela's mom and dad as well as her younger sister and little brother too. To my delight, her family grew to like me a great deal and I, naturally, reciprocated their affection.

In almost double time, Tommy and Angie came to the consensus that they were "in-love" and became passionate and sexually active. Although they didn't flaunt their intimacy or even mention it to me, they didn't seem to mind my surmising they were. On weekend nights, either a Friday or a Saturday, they would trek up to the not too distant parade field on post, scope out a secluded area beneath the stationary viewing stands and, then, make love. I didn't stoop to spying on them but since they carried a large blanket along with them on those outings (and no picnic basket), I didn't have to be Sherlock Holmes or Charlie Chan to deduce what they were doing.

Of course, the couple would have the same blanket in their possession when they would stop by my barracks and wake me up in the early morning hours. On each occasion, just like clockwork, I would almost dutifully climb out of my bunk, take a quick wash-up, and throw some clothes on. Then I'd join the waiting lovebirds outside and the three of us would journey to Angela's house. Never did I balk or complain in light of that reoccurring foot-trek and my two companions were always appreciative of my congeniality. It was no big deal to me. After all, I grew to cherish Tommy and Angie more and more with the passing of each day.

In marked contrast to Thomas Preston, I wasn't sexually active and was inexperienced and naive in that area as well. I was, in fact, what people called a "virgin," but, unlike a lot of guys, I didn't really care who happened to know it. I wasn't afraid of sex per se but I was very fearful of its frequent by-product, which was a flesh and blood baby. To me, having a child out of wedlock was like driving a nail into your forehead!

Admittedly, I was once in love, or 'in lust,' with a young lady but I never dreamed of impregnating her and producing an innocent child and, plus, I was practically gun shy when it came to marriage and its all-too-frequent by-product, which was divorce.

Almost always the mother would be awarded custody of the child and I couldn't see myself being deprived of hugging and kissing my baby goodnight. That was a parent amenity I secretly craved.

Goes without saying, but my biological father was very much afoot in my viewpoints regarding children and marriage too. When it came to the financial component (child support), I realized, like my old man, I could always pack up my duds and flee to a different state too. But since I harshly criticized my dad's foregoing actions, I could not picture myself doing likewise. In my estimation, that would be the epitome of hypocrisy!

Not surprising, I was subjected to a few crude and hateful comments about my virgin status and my sexual-orientation as well ("Harris and Dan Williams are screwing each other," "Harris is in love with that white boy," or "Harris is a queer" and the likes), but I wasn't remotely upset about them. I always believed that most people habitually judge others from their personal perspectives (ergo: If an individual doesn't think and behave exactly like them, then that person is grossly wrong.), and, sadly, many of their embedded perspectives have played havoc with their personal lives or have even led to their ruination.

Those are my sentiments when I think of guys who jump into the sack with every girl who submits to them. They recklessly help produce unwanted and needful offsprings and, alternately, assumes a 'hands-off attitude regarding the kids. I was always in awe of that kind of callous and repetitious tragedy, always! Furthermore, in my estimation, if being so-called normal means wandering through life with a 'devil may care' attitude (behaving irresponsibly), then I relished being considered abnormal and an enigma too!

Towering well-above most 'good qualities' I lay claim to, I have always prided myself in being considerate and congenial. Meaning, if someone I care about wants me to accompany them to a band concert, a ballet or even a symphony (which are three events I truly dislike), I would grin and bear it and go along with them. Occasional sacrifice and compromise are almost vital when it comes to close-knit, long-lasting relationships and I believe it wholeheartedly. Therefore, on one Saturday evening when I tagged along with my buddy, Nathan Johnson, to the Snake Pit and my comrade practically begged me to indulge him in a certain venture, I reluctantly gave in to him.

Earlier in the evening I'm recounting, as Nate and I sat at one of the tables, drinking our beer and savoring the DJ's nostalgic record selections, we were approached by two civilian-status black women. And when I identified them as women, it wasn't mere happenstance. Neither of them was unattractive or decrepit, but they weren't spring chickens either. They, both, had to be in their late twenties or early thirties. Being that Nate was now 24 years old, he wasn't remotely bothered by the pair's ages, but since I was only 19, I wasn't at all comfortable with those ladies. However, as the evening wore on and I persistently slow-danced with the woman named 'Minnie' (her friend was 'Rosie' or Rosemary), I began to relax somewhat. I am sure the beer-drinking helped.

Notably, Minnie and I were out on the dance floor when she elected to behave quite bold and risqué. All of a sudden, she firmly cuffed my right butt cheek! And she did it as she said, "I would sure like to see more of you, young Mr. Harris."

I was somewhat startled and embarrassed as well. And I surmised that my buddy, Nate, knew how I felt too. He and Rosie were out on the floor too, dancing right next to me and Minnie and he was noticeably tickled. For he had observed my dance partner's hand.

"Did you hear me, soldier boy?" Minnie reemphasized. "I would just love to see more of you."

Of course, I knew right off what the woman meant, but I chose to play dumb. "Aw, you probably will see more of me," I replied, smirking widely. "I come up here almost every Saturday night. You can show up here again, I guess."

My dance partner responded with laughter. "You are a real character, Mr. Harris," she cried. "Boy, you know darn well what I mean, what I'm getting at."

As I mentioned, I knew exactly what was on Minnie's mind. However, I had no intention whatsoever of acting on her sexual craving. After all, I hadn't even known her a good three hours!

I was adamant about my innermost feelings. Shortly, however, my comrade, Nate, opted to take me aside and speak to me in private. And when he did, I soon found myself in the throes of a quandary that I had not anticipated. My pal, on the other hand, seemed clear-headed and somewhat pleased with himself. He retrieved a packet from his pocket before speaking.

"I used to be a boy scout, Harris," he joked, passing me a packaged condom. "Being prepared has always been my motto. Look, man, I know you're a damn puritan or studying for the darn priesthood or something, but you gotta help me out. I'm pleading with your young ass."

I responded with subdued laughter, asking, "What's this, a darn rubber?"

"No, it's a friggin' balloon, Harris. Sure it is! Look, man, these two bitches are hot to trot. Minnie's about ready to rip your clothes off and rape your young ass. Harris, they live in a two-family flat; one downstairs and the other upstairs. They got a ride outside and they want us, both of us. But that's the deal. Rosie will give it up, but only if Minnie gets her man - you. Minnie's fuckin' stacked, really I want her - but I'll git my rocks off with Rosie. So, what do you say?"

I frowningly balked. "Nate, you're asking me to do something I don't wanna do," I stated.

"Come on, Harris, don't let me down here," Nate argued. "You can go to confession tomorrow, say ten Hail Mary's, whatever, but don't disappoint me like this!"

For a prolonged moment, I was poised to say "No," and, in my heart, I was leaning towards nixing the idea also, but I forced myself to be agreeable. I couldn't bring myself to refuse the little 'hound dog' who stood before me, practically panting. All kidding aside, I didn't want to damage our ongoing friendship. Therefore, I half-heartedly gave in.

In less than an hour, after bowing to Nate Johnson's plea (it was well past midnight by then), I found myself inside Minnie's first floor apartment. We were sitting together on the woman's living room sofa and engaging in continuous tongue kissing. I became sexually aroused and was on the verge of retrieving my condom when Minnie reached down and unzipped my fly.

As I said before, I was totally inexperienced when it came to sexual encounters, but I was momentarily freaked out in light of Minnie's aggressive behavior. Being naive, I was under the impression that the male partner was the primary horny one. However, at the precise moment when the woman reached inside my pants and grabbed a hold of my erect penis, we were both suddenly startled.

I immediately looked up, as did Minnie, and there near the hallway (and less than five paces from our location) stood a sleepy-eyed little girl. She was wearing only panties, no top garment, and she couldn't have been over ten years old!

"Momma, my throat - it still hurts bad," the child pitifully complained. "I don't feel so good, not at all."

As my erection instantly subsided, Minnie was visually upset. She fused at her daughter, saying, "Agnes, jest take some more medicine! You know where it's at. You jest wanna be damn nosey, that's all. Take yo' little butt back to bed 'fore you go and wake up the other kids. Go on now."

I was already feeling shameful and uneasy when the little girl appeared, but when my female companion referred to the "other kids," I was downright taken aback. "You've got more kids, Minnie?" I questioned. "How many?"

"Shit - I got nine little crumb-crunchers," the woman proudly announced. "But they still be sleep in there, and they know not to come in here like that. Agnes, she knows damn better not to do that shit! She can be a little bitch sometimes."

Well, I am reasonably certain my female partner said something similar to the foregoing, but I couldn't swear to it. My mind was still stuck on the number nine.

"Minnie, you've got nine children?" I asked in sheer amazement. "And you wanna jump in bed with me? I'm sorry - I can't do this."

Instantly, my companion was severely pissed off at me. "Can't do what?" she spoke. "Boy, I don't want no bed action anyway, jest some head action. Shit - I got too many damn kids already. Jest lay back, relax and enjoy it all."

At that point, I proceeded to climb to my feet, straighten up my clothes and carefully zip my fly back up. "I . . . I can't do this," I restated, "and I gotta get outta here. It's not right. I never should have come in the first place. Never should have let Nate talk me into it."

Minnie, who was still seated on the couch, was facially furious. "Well, then take your lame-ass outta here then!" she emphasized. "I believe you're a goddamn punk anyway. Git the fuck out, ya' young, stupid-ass junior flip!"

I wasn't, in the least, ruffled by the woman's verbal attack. In fact, I was smiling as I walked over to the front door and threw the latch. I, then, looked back at my irate hostess and teasingly replied, "How does that old saying go? 'Sticks and stones may break my bones, but' . . . Well, you get my drift. Goodnight, Minnie - maybe we'll see each other again."

"Not if I see your little stupid, punk-ass first!"

In actuality, I was in an emotional daze when I left out of my would-be sexual partner's first floor flat. I thought about ringing Rosie's doorbell, but soon changed my mind. Although we had been transported over to the flat via Rosemary's automobile, I didn't want to cut short Nate's visit due to my problems. Besides, when I reminded myself that 'Birds of a feather flock together,' I thought, maybe, Rosie had a <u>tribe</u> of kids too. I certainly didn't want to wake any of them up.

Minutes later, as I chuckled to myself in light of my foregoing supposition (of course, I might have been right on track), I went on and descended the dwelling's front steps. However, my grin quickly abated. Since I didn't pay much attention to the outdoor terrain during the drive over to the flat, I had no idea where in the hell I was. I was in a part of San Antonio proper that I wasn't remotely familiar with.

I embarked upon my foot-journey at that juncture, not even knowing which direction was the correct one. (Of course, I couldn't accomplish anything by just standing in place). Therefore, upon committing myself to a continuous and leisurely pace, I began to walk, then walk some more and, then, walk a great distance farther and, eventually, converge on an area that would, subsequently, reveal my bearings to me. And thanks to the directions that were provided to me by a Mexican-American man I met on the street (I purposely made reference to Angie Mendoza's neighborhood), I finally found my way back to Fort Sam Houston. From start until finish, approximately three hours had gone by since I started my foot trek.

Naturally, I was exhausted, bone-weary and anxious to jump into my sack when I entered my home barracks on the morning of my rather bizarre ordeal. However, I was reconciled to the fact that my former actions were most appropriate and morally right. Although I had my regrets about the episode and would long-remember it as well, there was a lesson I learned from it too. Even when a person strives to be accommodating and congenial, they will, sometimes, find themselves kicked to the curve. Sometime the word "No" is most appropriate too.

Later on in that particular day, and much, much later (around two p.m., in fact), I found myself trying to explain my early-morning behavior to my friend, Nate Johnson. He had spent the whole night with the woman named Rosemary (as well as a large chunk of the succeeding hours) and Rosie had recently dropped him off about a block away from our billets. My friend anxiously shook me awake, smiling in burning curiosity and anticipation. But just from sighting his devilish expression, I instantly knew I was about to engage in a verbal exercise in futility.

Before Nate uttered a single syllable, I questioned, "Nate - man, did you have any idea that Minnie had nine darn kids? And if you did, it would have been nice if you had pulled my coat about 'em!"

Always the humorist, Nate responded with a grin. "Nine fuckin' kids?" he remarked. "Yeah, Rosie did mention to me that the bitch didn't like odd numbers. Said Minnie was dead-set upon making it an even ten. Damn, Harris, how the hell would I know about that kinda shit? Plus, what . . . what difference do it make, huh? They sho' as shit ain't your kids or your responsibility!"

I looked at my buddy with eyes of absurdity. "One of the kids, a little girl, walked in on us when her momma had her hands inside my pants! Suppose Minnie had had my thing in her mouth at that time, like she wanted?"

Suddenly, Nate's eyes lit up. "Your dick? A head job, Harris?" he excitedly asked. "I knew I should have been the dude with Minnie!" For a moment Nate was laughing almost hysterically, but then he stopped and turned serious. Still, he was joking when he asked me, "You didn't try to put the rubber on at that point, did you?"

I hopelessly shook my head, trying desperately not to join my crazy comrade in his state of merriment. "I knew from the get-go, that I shouldn't have said nothing to your nutty butt!" I grinningly said. "You little degenerate, horny bastard."

"Hey - don't confuse me with my daddy, whoever the motherfucka was," was Nate's retort. "Tell me more, Harris, go on. This is damn interesting!"

Moments later, as my friend's mirth was on the decline, I was quite disheartened. I realized Nate was seldomly serious about most matters, but I still wanted him to understand my viewpoint. "I feel so sorry for those children," I sadly told him. "I wonder if they even know who their father or fathers are, and how many different ones there are. It's a crying shame what adults do to children in this world, especially black folks."

To my surprise, Nathaniel Johnson turned serious at that moment. Maybe, he was influenced by my joyless face. "Lionel Barry Harris, you cannot save the whole goddamn world," he spoke. "You're a nice, decent kinda dude, but you're setting yourself up for a real bad fall, and a lot of naggin' headaches and heartaches along the way. And I'm gonna hate not being around to, like you say - 'pull your coat' from time to time. Boy, if you don't make some changes in your life, I'm so afraid the world's gonna knock your head off."

I sat still for a time, seriously soaking in Nate's heartfelt advice. "Well - I can't see myself changing, Nate," I stated. "I guess I've seen too much . . . too much foul and poison water running under the bridge. But I thank you for your advice, my friend. You really sounded sincere, for a change. And I'm sorry for running out on you . . . earlier this morning. But I was in a real tizzy, like I was suffocating inside of Minnie's apartment."

Nate displayed an understanding smile. "Hey, ace-boy, I had _my_ fun, and all through the friggin' night. Harris, I'm just damn happy you made it back to the barracks safe and sound. I was worried about your ass. Did you hike all the way back here, hitchhike or what?"

"I walked all the way, but like I said - I had to get the hell out of that woman's house. I couldn't stand being there a minute longer."

My friend sat, smiling. "Oh well, Harris," he spoke, "as they say, 'All's well that ends well. At any event, I'm glad to see you."

CHAPTER THIRTY-THREE
THE DEEP SOUTH

In being a native black St. Louisan with a modest travel history that included such locales as Benton Harbor, Michigan, Sturgeon Bay, Wisconsin and Indianapolis, Indiana (which was the site of a childhood summer vacation), I had never set foot in any infamous state that was commonly referred to as the "deep south." However, I was exposed to quite a few white soldiers who called that region 'home' and I wasn't happy to interact with the majority of them. In fact, I came to loathe quite a few of them. And as peculiar as it might sound, I deplored them even more for forcing me to bring my begrudgment to the forefront.

Of course, I did not have to physically cross the so-called 'Mason-Dixon line' to be aware of church burnings and bombings, police brutality, lynchings, Jim Crow, voter-suppression, the Ku Klux Klan (the KKK) or any of the age-old racial atrocities that were commonplace in the south. I was always race-conscious (back in 1955, I had seen that grotesque photograph of Emmett Till in Jet Magazine), was an avid reader who was acutely attuned to current events (especially news stories about race), and was keenly cognizant of the history of America.

Therefore, in the declining days of June of 1963 when I learned that my assigned company, the 24th Evacuation Hospital, was scheduled to play a participatory role in a mammoth military operation in Greenville, South Carolina, I emerged depressed and somewhat disgusted too. (At that particular time, I was still mourning the early June murder of Medger Evers and miffed in the wake of Gov. George Wallace disallowing black students to attend the Univ. of Alabama as well). So, to put it mildly, I despised the very thought of it!

'Swift Strike II,' which was what it was called, was slated to consume most of the month of July and a good portion of the proceeding month of August too and, to me, that sounded like an eternity. To be completely candid, a one-week field exercise was _way_ too long in my opinion.

Of course, regardless of my personal feelings or any other dissenter's protest, Swift Strike II was going to be implemented and thousands of soldiers would participate in the massive undertaking. To be precise, it was inevitable and well-underway even before minor subordinates (or 'peons'), such as me, were apprised of the time factor and the specific role we would play in the venture.

After becoming reconciled to the upcoming operation, there was one thing that consumed my mind. I was well-aware that Dr. Martin Luther King's 'March on Washington' was on schedule to take place on August the 28th and it was my greatest intent (by 'hook or crook') to be parked in front of somebody's television set when that historical event took place. And since Swift Strike II was slated to end during the waning days of August, I extracted solace from knowing I'd be back in Fort Sam Houston, Texas prior to Rev. Dr. King's planned march.

In spite of that singular saving grace, however, I was still somewhat repulsed by the thought of spending a substantial amount of time in the so-called "deep south." In the 1950's and '60's, owing to television cameras and news outlets, I was visually made aware of the various southern states that openly declared war on citizens of color and I was always deeply saddened, outraged and awestruck by it all. Therefore, in heartfelt homage to those vivid atrocities, I was resolved to live my entire life without <u>ever</u> setting foot on southern soil. And that declaration, to me, practically epitomized my disdain for Swift Strike II and its specified, southern setting known as Greenville, South Carolina.

As I pre-stated, Swift Strike II was a mammoth, enormously expensive, awesome and rather mind-boggling exercise. It incorporated military personnel who numbered into the thousands, tons and tons of supplies, equipment and vehicles, and required a collective soldier perseverance that was a daily challenge to, both, physical and mental stamina. With the winning of the simulated '<u>war</u>' at the forefront (the red forces versus the blue forces), there was no regard for human weariness or tedium, no regard for rest and sleep periods and, seemingly, no concern for adverse weather conditions either.

In reality, a support unit such as the 24th Evac. was subject to be deployed to an overseas arena in virtually a moment's notice and that certainly came into play in Greenville, SC. We were expected to operate and function according to standard field hospital regulations, and in spite of soldier's gripes and grumblings, we were made to cope with an array of 'staged' but not so improbable problems, which were designed to increase our efficiency.

One of those orchestrated problems was especially irritating, taxing and pointlessly redundant in the estimation of myself and my fellow soldier cohorts but, obviously, our official superiors didn't share our assessment. Frequently, the soldiers of the 24th would spend five or six hours erecting and setting up our specialized outdoor medical facility, replete with an Admissions and Disposition Office and various components of medical sustenance and, in less than an hour later, we would be bombed.

Simply put, an enemy helicopter would hover over our hospital site, dump a few bags of flour-like substance upon us and we would be 'knocked out' of commission. Then, practically minutes after the air assault, we would collectively pack up our tents and equipment, load everything back on military trucks again and convoy to another selected camp area.

However, to the shared chagrin of enlisted men and noncoms too (what I perceived as adding 'insult to injury'), our labor and toil was far from being over. Upon converging on the chosen site, and without so much as a 15-minute break, we would start up the set-up process anew. To the powers-that-be (who were, of course, the officers in charge), it didn't matter how hot and humid it was, how rainy or stormy it was, or even the lateness of the hour, they were resigned to the goal of rendering our field hospital operational and viable once again. And even if it angered, displeased or even killed us, the soldier work force.

During one of those occasions, despite it being pitch-black at the time, we were ordered and expected to maintain almost total silence and erect tents with only the aid of illuminated tent stakes and wooden mallets. But although we prodded along and eventually accomplished our set-up mission, quietude was virtually impossible to maintain. Boisterous outcries of profanity, complaints and groans were periodically heard. Of course, being accidentally struck on a finger or hand with a wooden hammer probably accounted for many of those verbal outbursts.

Again, since I disdained outdoor exercises in the state of Texas, and surely hated the large-scale operation that transplanted me in the state of South Carolina, I emerged appreciative of what I deemed as a few 'silver linings' when it came to the affair. Due to the fact that the 250th General Hospital was also included in the Swift Strike II endeavor, it meant that my close-knit comrade, Tommy Preston, was somewhere in the not-too-distant vicinity also. And since I hung out with Danny Williams on a daily basis as well, I withdrew a degree of joy from looking forward to the conclusion of the military undertaking. Upon being aware that we would be awarded an 'administrative break' prior to boarding a plane and being air-lifted back to San Antonio, I looked forward to spending some quality time with both of my cherished friends.

As I previously stated, participating soldiers knew beforehand that Swift Strike II would last a month and a half, at best. Living amidst the southern boondocks of Greenville, I not only grew tired of swatting at mosquitoes, flies, bees and a large array of crawling and flying bugs I had never laid eyes on before (and that included the strange looking animals that were common to the region), I disliked the taste of c-rations and k-rations as well. Sure, I could self-describe myself as an 'unhappy camper' and a soldier who, sometimes, balked at playing the so-called 'silly game' also, but I could not quite get used to eating food substances from heated up metal cans that were dated all the way back to year 1952. I didn't openly gripe about it though. I felt that if my fellow soldiers could cope with and adjust to the various displeasures, then so could I. Still, it was an ongoing struggle to me.

Finally, Swift Strike II came to a rather subtle and lackluster end. We were informed that our side, which was the red forces, had won the mock war. (I wasn't positive, but I imagined that our side had dropped more and larger sized bags of white flour during war). And just as we were promised, the participating troops found themselves on the administrative break afterwards.

According to Sgt.-Major Walker, it would be four or five days before we would reboard the military airplanes that had originally transported us to South Carolina. The nearest large city to our campsite happened to be Augusta, Georgia and since we were given access to continuously rolling shuttle buses, many of my soldier comrades grouped together and went to town. However, for troops who weren't so adventurous or were lacking funds, our unit provided entertainment and recreational pastimes right within our designated camp.

A couple of makeshift dayrooms were erected (GP-large tents), organized sports activities got underway and, at nightfall, a gigantic white-colored screen appeared in our midst and a mixture of theatrical movies were screened back-to-back. Goes without saying, but the latter amenity was right up my personal alley. However, since it, too, involved an outdoors setting, I wasn't exactly gung-ho about it. Sitting on the ground in a large field was somewhat like being at a drive-in theatre, but minus an automobile.

For the first few days, everything was going relatively fine and smooth. I hadn't gone to Augusta and had not hooked up with Tommy either, but Danny and I had sat together in the evenings, playfully talking and teasing each other and viewing the featured flicks under the stars. In fact, we had seen, both, 'Seven Ways to Sundown,' starring Audie Murphy and 'Lonely Are the Brave,' with Kirk Douglas, a couple of times and was on the verge of memorizing the dialogue of each film.

Then, on the morning of the third day, a happening cropped up that slowly came into focus and proceeded to render me depressed, outraged and somewhat awestruck as well. However, I wasn't alone in my feeling of disenchantment. Since the roots of the episode sprung forth during our regular morning assembly (or formation), it was immediately a matter of common knowledge.

Additionally, since the gist of the happening came from the mouth of 24th's rather vociferous Sergeant-Major, there was zero doubt that the man's verbal message was vague or remotely misunderstood. Walker was standing upon an elevated platform when he addressed our company.

"I have a taste of good news to share with you men on this fine and illustrious morning," he smilingly began, "and I'm sure you'll be well-pleased . . . *most* of you, that is. There's a large country-club located just due west of our camp! About a two or three-mile hike, I'd venture to guess! It's called 'Grayson Manor' and it happens to have an enormous clubhouse, a good sized golf course, four tennis courts, horse stables, and one of the hugest swimming pools in the entire Greenville vicinity! And as a courtesy, the manor's owners are graciously allowing us, the soldiers of the 24th Evac., to enjoy its facilities, but . . ."

Due to the outburst of soldier cheers and spirited applause, the sergeant was instantly drowned out at that precise point and I was almost positive that no soldier, myself included, was able to make out the end of his last statement. Even in light of the ongoing merriment amongst the ranks (men were joyously shaking hands and slapping backs), I was acutely aware that Walker had uttered the word "but" and I smelled a rat. I feared the noncom was on the verge of divulging something that was negative and, although I hoped my suspicions were wrong, I was doubly afraid it had something to do with race as well. Minutes later, after all the hoopla and gaiety had subsided, I learned that my skepticism was not at all ill-founded.

In an effort to regain order and quietude, the top sergeant held up both hands and began to speak again. He returned to his foregoing speech, saying, "But, unfortunately, we are all aware of where we are. We're in the deep south, for God's sake! And the south has its way of doing things. They're tryin' hard to change down here, trying to be a little more race friendly, more humane, but they're a very stubborn and contrary bunch! What I'm trying to say is ... well, our colored troops were not included in that invite! I tried my damndest to reason with the club's owners, but I was ..."

As cries of uproarious protest and marked grumbling erupted throughout the assemblage, mostly from the lips of black soldiers, I was literally stewing in anger. While fellow Negroid soldiers were cussing in outrage and many of our Caucasian counterparts were excitedly on board with the 'separatism' factor, I, for one, had heard more than enough. I looked into the dejected eyes of Danny Williams (he was standing right next to me) and soon opted to push my way through the buzzing crowd with the sole intent of vacating the immediate area. However, an incensed-face Sgt. Walker took rapid exception to my retreat.

"PFC Harris, where the fuck do ya' think you're going, you little shit?" Walker shouted out. "Git your little ass back in formation, mister! And right this goddamn minute!"

When I turned around to address the top sergeant, not only was I filled with anger, tears were building up in my eyes. Shaking my head negatively, I yelled, "No, Sir, fuck a goddamn formation, Sgt.-Major! You should have called this ... gathering in secret! Should have sent invitations out to all the white boys! We have <u>all</u> been busting our balls out here for over a month, but you got the nerve to discriminate when it comes to us, the Negro soldiers? This is not 1943, Sgt.-Major, it happens to be 1963!"

Walker was facially furious at that juncture. "I'm ordering you to rejoin the fuckin' formation, Harris," he reemphasized, "and I don't want no more of your goddamn lip!"

As tears streamed down my cheeks, I was not intimidated by the top sergeant. "Do what you want to me, sergeant, but I'm returning to my quarters," I replied. "But I'm not putting up with this shit!"

Before Walker could muster up a return response, my friend, Danny, spoke up. "Wait up, Harris," he called out, "I'm going with you, man! Like you said, fuck this lame, sorry-ass bullshit!"

In the midst of catching up with me and affectionately slinging his arm around my shoulder, Daniel Williams incurred the verbal wrath of Sgt. Walker too. The top sergeant threatened both of us with disciplinary action (to be precise, an Article 15), but we jointly ignored him and continued our withdrawal. Then, something purely unexpected took place, and something that made me especially proud. One by one, and then in clusters, fellow black soldiers began to defiantly break formation also.

I was sincerely taken aback and heartened by the development. Not so much in the wake of Danny's actions, but certainly in regards to the blanket support of men who actually looked like me and Dan. Then, momentarily, I was shocked even a notch further. As a single Caucasian soldier broke ranks and boldly aligned himself with the ongoing boycott, I was genuinely heartened by it. The young dissenter's name was 'Jeremy Lockhart' and he happened to be a longtime, second-floor dweller in my assigned barracks back in Fort Sam Houston. Lockhart hurriedly proceeded to converge on my and Danny's position and when he did, he instantly issued some words that were not only compatible with his recent actions, they managed to further uplift my sagging spirit.

"You are totally right for doing what you're doing, Harris," he spoke, "and so are you, Williams. Sometimes, I find myself ashamed of being white my own darn self. I am really sorry about all of this, guys. It ain't right and Sgt. Walker knows darn well it ain't right too."

Although I was still a bit tearful, upon entertaining a certain perspective, I smiled and briskly shook hands with my newly-found Caucasian associate. "Quiet as kept, Lockhart, I'm sometimes ashamed of being black myself, my man - but today is not one of those times. It took a ton of nerve for Negro soldiers to do what they just did, and especially career and veteran soldiers. And I'm proud of you two dudes too. But I'm sure, too, Lockhart, that you'll be given a hard time by a lot of fellow white boys. So, feel free to hang-out with me and Danny, here. Cause I appreciate you to the max, fellow."

"And that's ditto for me too, dude," Danny chimed in.

As it eventually turned out, unless it was cleverly carried out in a state of concealment and secrecy (like I previously suggested), it appeared that no soldier from our company, neither white, black or other, partook of the invitation to Grayson Manor. Although Dan Williams, myself and, of course, Jeremy Lockhart, coped with a heavy degree of resentment and disdain from the majority of our white comrades, we were also praised and appreciated by the Negroid soldiers who were amongst our ranks.

In fact, partly owing to the accolades and words of encouragement I received from fellow black soldiers, it managed to make my swiftly-levied and aftermath punishment much more palatable and tolerable as well. On the fourth day of the administrative break, since I was branded the 'ringleader' of the formation upheaval, I was ordered to pull a ten-hour kitchen police (KP) shift in the field mess hall.

However, I not only took my penance in subdued stride, I proceeded to work diligently, void of verbal protest whatsoever and had no feelings of regret or remorse. On the contrary, I was quite proud of my previous actions.

But I felt pleased and secretly thankful too. In knowing that, both, Daniel Williams and Jeremy Lockhart had escaped Sgt.-

Major Walker's craving for retribution, I felt fortunate. The top sergeant also threatened to bust me back down to private E-1 but, apparently it didn't fly or he had a change of heart.

To my great joy, day number five of the leisurely break period started off with a feeling of anticipatory promise. Finally, I was able to connect with my other cherished friend, Thomas Preston. In fact, Tommy sought me out and showed up at the 24th Evac. encampment shortly after our morning formation. We hung out until early afternoon, he and I and my staple buddy, Dan, too; and after the three of us had eaten lunch together at the unit mess facility, we decided to do something that none of us had, yet, to do.

The three of us had remained within the perimeter of our respective units and had never gone to town. And since we did have a little money to our credit and I was told that there were two movie theaters located in downtown Augusta, Georgia (Danny and I were tired of Kirk Douglas and Audie Murphy), I suggested that we try those movie houses out.

Prior to leaving the vicinity of the camp, however, we were approached by Jeremy Lockhart and he asked if he could join our party. I said "yes" right away. "The more the merrier," I congenially added and, both, Danny and Tommy were in quick compliance. Even as I completely relished the companionship of my trio of friends, I excitedly looked forward to viewing a decent, first-run flick. I hadn't seen one in a very, very long time.

After riding in a shuttle bus (all four of us, garbed in dress-khaki uniforms), our group eventually found ourselves standing in the middle of downtown Augusta. It wasn't much of a downtown area for a city, I thought. "Nothing to write home about," as my dear mother liked to say. But the two movie theatres were there, just like I was priorly told. One movie house was featuring 'Billy Budd,' a filmed version of a Herman Melville novel, and the other offered 'A Gathering of Eagles,' which starred Rock Hudson.

I was actually trying to persuade my comrades to go see the Hudson film when I noticed the hostile stares from various Caucasian passersby. Sure, I knew we were on southern soil, but I couldn't quite figure it out! The four of us were wearing our military uniforms, we were all clean and well-groomed, we were minding our own business and we were not, in the least, behaving in a rowdy way! What the hell was it?

I thought - maybe they are not used to seeing black and white soldiers interacting with each other. But I soon dismissed that deduction. After all, Fort Gordon wasn't too far away. I mean, I couldn't fathom total segregation on, of all places, an army base!

Virtually minutes later, it became crystal clear to me that I should very well have been wearing my fatigue work outfit rather than my dress khakis. Not that my buddies and me would have been more presentable and acceptable to our white observers, but because it would have acutely defined my foregoing state of mind. In essence, in being so very naive, it would have been most appropriate for me to be wearing the color green. Like some kind of epiphany, that was my precise thought when my three cohorts and I went to place our fare down on the ticket booth counter in anticipation of viewing 'A Gathering of Eagles.'

"I am so, so sorry, young men," spoke the lady inside the booth, "but ya' see . . . I don't know where ya'll hail from but . . . colored soldiers can't go to this here theatre. And I hate to tell you guys, but not the one up the road neither. Like I said, I am so sorry, boys. And ya'll look like real nice boys too."

Although I and Danny and Jeremy were momentarily speechless, obviously Tommy wasn't. Grimacing with absurdity, he remarked, "Ain't that a crock of shit? Shit-fire, what's wrong with the people down here? I can't believe this crap!"

"One thing about it," tossed in a disgusted Danny Williams, "I can't hardly wait to find my ass back in San Antonio. I'm sick and tired of these goddamn crackers down here!"

In the midst of Danny instantly 'begging the pardon' of our white comrades, I was calm and collected. (I had grown almost unshockable when it came to racial prejudice). Inwardly, I was just as incensed as my three comrades were, but I suppressed those feelings as I posed a certain query to the rather nervous ticket agent.

"Miss, could you, maybe, point out, or direct us to the . . . <u>colored</u> part of town?" I asked. "Can you instruct us how to get there?"

The woman responded with a frown but went on to respond to my question. "Well, ya' take that there road there," pointing towards her right extreme, "the one right on the right. Walk about a mile, or a mile and a half, maybe. And ya'll will sooner or later come to a railroad track, and ya'll will jest about be there. Ain't too, too far from here. But you cain't hardly miss it, boys."

I cordially thanked the lady and, after we retrieved our money, I spoke to my still somewhat upset buddies. "Let's try the <u>Negro</u> portion of town," I stated. "Maybe grab a beer or two. At least, we'll all be together. Come on, guys, just shake it off. Forget about southern racism and ignorance, it ain't even worth getting hot and bothered over."

As the day went on, in less than an hour after the exasperating movie fiasco that took place in downtown Augusta, Georgia, I found myself (and my trio of companions) in the throes of, yet, another deep south revelation or eye-opener.

Although I later deemed myself unbelievably stupid and a notch greener that I had originally saw myself, I was under the impression (or engrained mind-set) that oppressed, southern black folks were, both, docile and subservient when it came to their

Caucasian oppressors and I was clearly and emphatically proven wrong. Maybe I had been exposed to too many motion pictures that depicted that premise, but it wasn't necessarily so. Me and my three cohorts rather crudely learned it wasn't.

In less than two city blocks, after me and my group strolled pass the ticket agent's pinpointed landmark (which was the railroad tracks), we not only found ourselves in a black-populated part of Augusta, we were collectively happy to site the local tavern. And as I assumed the role of a wise and confident leader (acting as if I was familiar with the area), I wasted no time entering the bar. And, instantly, as I came face-to-face with the nearby bartender, I cordially began to speak.

"Hello, Sir, me and my friends are new to Augusta," I smilingly stated, "and we walked quite a distance to get here - so can we bother you for four, large draft beers? Or a pitcher, if you got it?"

Behaving as if I was speaking a foreign language, the man behind the bar completely ignored my request. Instead, he angrily focused on Jeremy Lockhart and, then, Tommy Holland, and stated, "Boy, we don't serve no white motherfuckers in here! What's the matter with you, nigga? Where you from anyway? Get 'em outta my place and take your black ass wid 'em!"

For a second I was dumbfounded, and then I was highly pissed off. "That's exactly what I fucking need right now," I disgustedly cried out, "a racist-ass black brother who hates white folks just like they hate us! "Why you bigoted-ass sonofabitch! Man, you need your damn head busted!"

Although the fiery-eyed bartender was anxious to reply to my verbal assault, a foreign voice came forth and abruptly snared the floor. Alarmingly though, the interceding voice rang familiar. And when I looked to my left extreme, which was were the remark originated from, I realized that my ears were not playing a trick on me. Rapidly converging on my position, was

Mst.-Sgt. Ellis Ruomo who, in spite of being of Nigerian descent, was the ranking noncommissioned black officer in my assigned unit. And, apparently, he was just as angry and out of sorts as the man who was standing behind the adjacent bar.

"PFC Harris, who the fuck do you think you are?" he irately singled me out. "And where do you think you are? You are down in the prejudice, racist south right now. You were lucky not to have ended up in the stockade or - Fort Leavenworth yesterday, Harris! That stunt you pulled, it was pure insubordination. Good thing Capt. Greene spoke out in your behalf. The top sergeant was out for your damn blood, and I kid you not, young man!"

I stood silent, downhearted and almost flabbergasted at that point. However, I was able to totally dismiss the sergeant's foregoing criticisms and almost beggingly asked him, "Sgt. Ruomo, is there anywhere down here we can go? I mean - just to stay together?"

I guess I appeared to be somewhat pitiful in the eyes of the master-sergeant, because he managed to calm himself and spoke in a soft manner. "Look, PFC Harris, you and Williams can stay put here," he proposed. "I'll smooth it over with Mr. Mason, the owner there. But your white amigos, they can't stay here. They will just . . . have to move on, that's all."

Jeremy Lockhart offered up a suggestion at that juncture. Turning to Tommy, he proposed, "Preston, why don't you and me head on back to the downtown area? After all, we don't have a whole lot of choices left."

Tommy was staunchly resistant to the idea. He fondly looked at me, replying, "Naw, that won't work, Lockhart. I'm staying with Barry, no matter what. Maybe, we should take the shuttle back to 24th's campsite."

"That may be your best bet," Ruomo injected. "You can grab a bus back to Greenville or, if you guys are totally against splitting up, you all can catch a shuttle that's headed for Fort Gordon, Georgia instead. The boarding point is located a little ways from downtown Augusta. That's a good solution to the problem, I suspect."

Throughout the ongoing dialogue between me and Mst.-Sgt. Ruomo, the man behind the bar kept a cheerless eye on the proceedings. Looking over at him, I could only imagine what he was thinking.

"We're gonna head out of here in just a minute, Sgt. Ruomo," I spoke, "but there's something I need to say first." I turned to the bartender, saying, "Sir, I want to sincerely apologize to you. I was as wrong as two left shoes when I came into your place, and I'm truly sorry for my disrespect and stupidity. I had no right to speak to you the way I did . . . and I'm honestly sorry about it."

The man Ruomo referred to as "Mr. Mason" soon relaxed and issued a smile. "It's okay, young blood, and I hope the rest of your day goes much better than this," he responded. "I really do, PFC. But, son . . . where are you actually from?"

"I'm from St. Louis, Missouri," I grinningly replied, "and my friend, Danny - over there, he's from Detroit, Michigan. And . . . in case you're wondering, one of my white buddies is from Louisville, Kentucky and the other one's from Oklahoma City, Oklahoma. And they're real nice guys too."

Taking a moment to cast somewhat censuring (if not, condemning) eyes at my two Caucasian comrades, Mr. Mason remarked, "Well - I'll take your word for it, young blood, but the jury's still out on the case. You guys - take it slow though, all of you."

In the aftermath of our trying and traumatic beginning on day number five of the administrative break (within the confines of the region called 'the deep south'), the late afternoon and evening hours went quite well and relatively smooth for me and my multi-discriminated against group. Adhering to the plan what was essentially put forth by Sgt. Ellis Ruomo, my companions and I proceeded to climb aboard the shuttle bus headed for Fort Gordon, Georgia and, upon arriving at our military destination, we congenially socialized.

After eating our share of pizza, chili dogs and french fries at the PX snack bar (not to mention the continuous flow of ice cold beer we indulged ourselves with), we topped it all off with viewing an enjoyable movie that, fortunately, had not been seen by any of us.

Sitting alongside each other in that theater, eating our popcorn and candy and drinking our soft drinks, we were collectively engrossed by the filmed version of H.G. Wells's 'The Time Machine' (which starred Rod Taylor) and it managed to chase our residual disenchantment and blues away.

In spite of what me and my friends were subjected to earlier in the day, it is a consolidated memory in time that I have always savored and have vividly relived from time to time. While I can't speak for any of my comrades who were with me that day, in my personal opinion, the living God was amongst us throughout our ordeal and beyond. I felt <u>His</u> presence.

CHAPTER THIRTY-FOUR

A TOPSY-TURVY EVENT

Although many Caucasian soldiers regarded me as somewhat of a villain or a spoiled sport when the 24th Evacuation Hospital returned to Texas soil (of course, they blamed me for depriving them of the Grayson Manor outing), I didn't lose any sleep over their ill-feelings. However, despite of pulling punitive kitchen-police duty for my defiant conduct, I was proud and unrepentive of my actions. I felt I would behave similarly the next time.

Admittedly though, I was ponderous and anxious when it came to Sgt.-Major Walker. Since he and I had locked horns before (the supernumerary episode), I didn't perceive him as a person who forgives and forgets. Surmising that I was high on the top sergeant's 'shit-list,' I entertained little hope of ever obtaining a higher rank.

In spite of my being 'on guard' for my noncom nemesis, I was actually on an emotional high when I returned to San Antonio turf. Not because I was overly fond of my Texas setting, but solely due to the specific date of our return. It happened to be August

21st, and a week later the Rev. Dr. Martin Luther King's well-publicized 'March on Washington' was scheduled to take place.

When that anticipated day arrived on the scene, I, along with numerous men in military uniforms (whether they were black, white, Hispanic, Asian or other), came together and watched the televised proceedings in the company dayroom or tuned into it on the radio.

All in all, the servicemen around me appeared to be attentive and receptive as well. But speaking for myself, I was virtually bursting with racial pride, emotionally-charged and, occasionally, tearful in the wake of it all.

In addition to being uplifted and totally mesmerized by Reverend King's speech, I could not refrain from mentally revisiting Augusta, Georgia. After all, it was a very fresh, enlightening and impactful memory. I could still visualize the dejection and outrage in Danny Williams' eyes (standing outside that downtown theatre), still distinctly taste my personal grief, and all in the name of age-old racism and the ever-present desire for white supremacy, while I, simultaneously, marvelled the profound and inspiring words of Dr. Martin Luther King Jr.

I sat in reflective silence inside that dayroom, intently watching that unprecedented and historical event and thoroughly digested and savored every, single minute of it. But, in its aftermath, I was still a realist. I was warmly heartened by Rev. King's rather superlative 'dream' and was truly impressed by the minister's sincerity too.

However, I had been bathed in the scalding waters of racial biasness and I could not refrain from branding Dr. King's vision as a virtual pipe dream. In reality, the good reverend was imploring our white oppressors to cleanse their hearts and minds of engrained and entrenched hatred and I could not see or even imagine white people collectively doing such a thing, not in my lifetime and, maybe, not in the lifetime of my children either. I was only 19 years old and the foregoing was the state of my mind in the summer of 1963.

With all of the forestated said, however, in spite of my pessimistic opines, I was not the person I once was. I wasn't even the same begrudging boy who took the military oath 14 months prior. My underlying regard for Caucasian people was no longer explicitly anchored in distrust and disdain. Thanks to young white men like Kevin Brenahan, Thomas Preston and, most recent, Jeremy Lockhart, I was obliged to vanquish the collective "all" from my future vocabulary. Instead of advocating that all Caucasian folks were bigots, racist and hate-mongers, I took the initiative to say most.

Certainly, I realized that Jeremy, Tommy and Kevin were stellar exceptions, and not the rule itself. Seemingly, the three of them ascribed to Rev. Dr. King's "content of character" premise and proceeded to look beyond surface skin color. And I realized, too, that I was somewhat of an oddity myself. I was not only aware that very few individuals valued friendship the way I did, I was almost positive that few of them were as outwardly demonstrative as I was either.

In my heartfelt affection for my friends, I often hugged them, encouraged them, sympathized with them and verbalized my love for them also. And in retrospect, if any of them felt embarrassed or uncomfortable as a result of my overt conduct, they never complained to me about it. In fact, all of my friends, J Smith and Dan Williams very much included, seemed quite reciprocal. Without a doubt in my mind, I knew they all loved me back.

In actuality, when I really take the time to concentrate on racial hatred and bigotry, or any prejudgment that's rooted in superficial differences, I immediately think of the beauty that resides in true friendship. And since I regard it as so precious and so hard to find and retain, I emerge feeling genuine pity for individuals who elect to shun or keep it at bay in the name of surface biasness and prejudgment. I recall having those exact feelings when I sat in 24th Evacuation's dayroom, watching the March on Washington back in August of 1963, and I thank God for enabling me to maintain those sacred sentiments throughout my life. I credit Him for rendering me completely void of inhibitions. I feel blessed by it.

***

With the memory of the historical civil rights spectacle so vivid in my mind, paired with my subsequent return to the Registrar's office when September of 1963 got underway, I considered myself as a serene and relatively 'happy camper.' (Pun-wise, my happiness had a great deal to do with my not being in a camp setting, Bullis included).

In addition to being back in my work groove with Tommy Preston and Alex Gray, I spent leisurely time with Danny and Valerie Williams, participated in a 'bid-whist' card playing tournament at the Post-Exchange club (which was reminiscent of my teenaged years), wherein my partner and I won two cartons of Marlboro cigarettes - for him, and I even rooted loudly for Jeremy Lockhart at the same recreational facility. My buddy, Jeremy, fashioned himself as a singer and competed in a talent contest and, although he wasn't awarded the top prize, he did a credible job anyhow. I delighted in being his number one supporter.

***

Now, if I were a person who could shut out the world, or an individual who was self-centered and unmindful of world happenings, I am sure (back then and now) that anguish and mental turmoil would be substantially minimized in my life. But to me, it would be like removing wet from water. Even before enlisting in the army, I kept up with news events and after my personal baptism on southern soil and my assessment of the famed March on Washington as well, I was almost obsessed with daily news happenings.

Even as I kept a watchful tab on the ongoing actions of Rev. Dr. King, I closely followed the life of Malcolm X too. I was completely fascinated by the opposing philosophies and strategies of the two black leaders. And, sometimes, in spite of admiring King's nonviolent efforts to achieve racial equality, my emotional sentiments, occasionally, lined up with the ones advocated by Black Muslim leader, Malcolm X.

Sorrowfully, the latter unsettling mindset was representative of my personal feelings when, on Sunday morning, September the 15th, the world was apprised of the horrific bombing episode at Birmingham, Alabama's '16th Street Baptist Church.' While almost 200 Negroid worshippers were attending church services, a massive explosion rocked the building's foundation, and abruptly ended the lives of four, little black girls and injured 19 other people as well. Then, in the ensuing aftermath of that horrendous and evil-inspired act, as riots of grief and anger broke out, two black teenaged boys were also killed.

Alternately, I posed a rather soul-searching query to myself: "How could people of color possibly reckon with, let alone - love, individuals who, apparently, have neither fear or respect for God Himself? People who, seemingly, have no sense of decency whatsoever?" Although I wished so much to invest in Martin Luther King's Christian principles, I surely could not denounce or criticize the violent and retaliatory viewpoints of Malcolm X. My heartfelt lament for those six innocent children and their grieving parents in the southern city of Birmingham, Alabama would not allow me to.

Sometimes, when I struggled with the world's brutality and callousness, I would tell Dan Williams that, "The world is too much with me" and he would sympathetically agree, and then give me a very wise perspective. He said I worried about too many people and too many <u>issues</u>, and especially about situations I could not do anything about. He smilingly branded me "uptight" and said I should try to "loosen up." I was in lock step agreement with him, there were certainly things that were well-beyond my control, but, as they say, "A leopard can't change his spots" and I, sure as hell, couldn't stop being me either. I guess I was stuck with being <u>me</u>.

Every now and then, in spite of always striving to do the righteous thing and focusing on a sense of fair play, something occasionally pops up that proceeds to turn your life topsy-turvy. In October of 1963, all was quite well with me. Employing many precepts, I learned in medical records school, I was at the top of my game during field maneuvers and in my office role in the on-post Registrar's office as well. Within the framework of both of those diverse venues, I felt greatly appreciated and well-liked by the majority of my coworkers and my on-site superiors alike. Also, when it came to my off-duty life, since I regularly interacted with my favorite people; Tommy Preston, Danny and Val Williams and Jeremy Lockhart as well, I felt like I was in seventh heaven.

Regretfully, my heartfelt feeling of euphoria was abruptly and, certainly, unexpectedly interrupted. Owing to a single but rather major development, and one that brought forth a boisterous protest from my staple nemesis, who was Sgt.-Major Walker, my state of mind was swiftly transformed from calm serenity to clamorous confusion. Although it was somewhat bizarre, the development I'm alluding to got underway around 1700 hours on a Thursday evening.

I deemed it bizarre because it transpired after the regular workday had concluded and, additionally, in light of the top sergeant's involvement in the matter. Ordinarily, Walker would be long-gone from the company area during that particular time of day. Therefore, from the moment I recognized it was Walker's voice originating from my barracks intercom, summoning me to the Orderly Room, I was instantly alarmed. I suspected right then and there that something was direly wrong.

Then, only five minutes later, when I walked into the O.R. and came face to face with the fiery-eyed noncom, it became crystal clear to me that whatever was afoot was even worse than what I originally thought it might be.

At that time, Sgt. Walker was inside his office, sitting at his desk and practically staring daggers at me. To put it mildly, he was pissed and furious with me and I was absolutely clueless as to why.

Almost immediately, upon tossing military protocol completely out the window, the man gruffly addressed me, stating, "You know what they call people like you, Harris? A goddamn snake in the fuckin' grass - a slimy, brown-nosing night crawler! You think you're so goddamn clever, don't you? You little snot!"

I was not only totally confused, I was equally upset as well. "Sgt.-Major, I have no idea what the devil you're talking about! What the hell's the matter now?"

"Do us both a fuckin' favor, Harris, drop the damn innocent act," Walker barked. Then, upon grabbing a sheet of paper from atop his desk, he added, "We send your ass to medical records school, permit you to work at the Registrar's office - and you turn right around and stab us in the goddamn back! Should have busted you down when I had a mind to! Ever hear of the words 'loyalty' or 'honor' and something called 'esprit de corps'?"

Even as I stood rigidly, frowning, I was still very much in the dark. "Maybe - if you take a moment to calm down, Sgt. Walker, and stop calling me out of my name, then, maybe, you'll be able to tell me what the hell you're squawking about?" I softly said. "What is it?"

"Calm down - my ass!" the sergeant yelled. "I'm talking about this shit, you little brown-nosing bastard! Had your nose so far up Col. Simpson's ass, he finally caved in. Gave you exactly what you wanted, huh? And you come in here, pretending it's fucking news to you!"

In his ongoing frustration, Walker angrily shoved the sheet of paper towards me. Then, without even bothering to get his permission, I picked it up and perused it. To my personal surprise (regardless of the noncom's foregoing suspicions), it was an official transfer order and it specifically had my birth name on it. To be more precise, the document indicated that, as of October 21, 1963 (which was the forthcoming Monday), I would be reassigned to the 250th General Hospital.

At that particular moment (although it was entirely unbeknownst to Sgt. Walker), my initial surprise was actually trumped by instantaneous relief. For a fleeting second, I was afraid that my long ago transfer request for Korea was now being honored. (After all, J and my other hometown comrades would be stateside once again come November 1963).

Alternately, I looked sternly in the face of the sergeant-major and upon placing the transfer order back on the noncom's desk, I offered, "I know I'm probably wasting my breath, Sgt.-Major, but up until this very moment, I didn't know anything about this, nothing whatsoever."

"That's a crock of amalgamated bullshit, PFC," snapped Walker, "and you know it - goddamn you!"

I stood, smiling to myself but not really concerned if the top sergeant believed me or not. "You're right about one thing, Sgt.-Major," I remarked. "I don't have an ounce of loyalty or love for 24th Evac. Thanks to this unit, I learned first-hand about racial bigotry and unfairness. I endured it in that precious school you like to throw in my face, down south when Swift Strike II ended, and right here, where we're at odds this evening. No, Sir, I don't feel I owe this company anything."

Walker sat at his desk, practically smoldering in disdain in the wake of my frankness. "All you goddamn color'uds are alike, ya' know? Always blamin' your fuckin' shortcomings and . . . deficiencies on the white man. With you boys, it's always race prejudice. You all need to man up, all of your black asses!"

Glaring back at the top sergeant in firm defiance, I calmly shook my head. I'm sure he expected a verbal reply from me, but none was forthcoming. Truth being told, I highly resented his ugly remarks but, after all, he was still my military superior.

However, in a moment's passing and as tears formed in my eyes, I opted to speak. "Unfortunately, Sgt.-Major Walker," I softly spoke, "I have trouble seeing the shortcomings you see in me, but I do see my <u>black</u> <u>ass</u>. And I'm afraid ... as a whole, that's what the Caucasian race only sees too. But there's so much more. Can I ... can I go now, Sir?"

I guess it was my day for surprises because when Walker remained silent, I was somewhat shocked. He then waved me off, dismissing me and displaying an expression of regret. And for a fleeting moment, just a fraction of a minute, he seemed poised to, maybe, issue an apology. Of course, that did not happen but from that evening forward, I seldomly laid eyes on him again.

THE LONG AND WINDING ROAD

When the forthcoming Monday morning arrived on the scene, in compliance with the official transfer order, I quietly and somewhat somberly took up residence in the nearby 250th General Hospital complex. Notably, my new dwelling location placed me directly across the road from 250th's Headquarters facility.

It was a bittersweet transition for me, however. Although I relished the infrequency of field exercises when it came to my new unit, I would sorely miss being in the company of, both, Danny Williams and Jeremy Lockhart as well. (At that particular time, Nathan Johnson had fulfilled his 'draft obligation.' Actually, he had mustered out of the service in the middle of the Swift Strike II (venture). And, additionally, I would no longer be a tangible deterrent to Bill Grant's bullying persona. Meaning, Grant might resort back to writing love letters in the wee hours of the night. But, on the brighter side, and a real plus to me, Tommy and I would share the very same unit.

~

Prior to my physical move from 24th Evac. to the 250th General Hospital (the Friday after Sgt. Walker crudely informed me of the transition, in fact), my mind was practically awash with wonder and intrigue. As an active duty soldier, I knew I was at the mercy of the United States army, but I still longed for an explanation regarding the sudden change.

In reality, I knew I was but a tiny minnow in a vast lake but I still concerned myself with the 'why' of the happening. I yearned to know what prompted my unexpected transplant and since Walker had offered up Col, Simpson's name during our verbal confrontation, I decided to take my queries directly to the office of the Registrar. Following military protocol, I opted to speak to Master-Sergeant Benjamin Bartels who was the head military honcho, serving under Col. Simpson himself.

"The Registrar is very pleased and highly impressed with your overall performance here, PFC Harris," the bespectacled sergeant stated. "The colonel often sings praises to you, young man, and you should be very honored by it."

"I am, Sgt. Bartels," I responded, "but I'm a bit curious about it too. I mean - why the sudden transfer?"

"Well, the Registrar and I - we tried our damndest to get you over to the Ameds company, get you completely exempt from field duty. But we ran into a gosh darn snafu - and when we did, we had to recoup and then go with the 250th General. So, you'll still have to put up with those confounded field maneuvers from time to time, but nowhere near the frequency you dealt with when you were still in 24th Evac. Are you upset with us, PFC Harris? 'Cause I guess we could undo what we did, if you wish."

I smiled with absurdity. "Well, I'm not that upset about it, Sarge," I joked. "It's just that it happened so darn fast, and without any heads-up."

"And that was Col. Simpson's decision," Bartels told me. "He didn't want to run it by you, git your hopes up high, and then have them dashed to hell. Bottom line is this, PFC Harris: The old man has a great deal of faith in you. So, please, don't disappoint him. 'Cause if you do, then you'll have yours truly to contend with. And, sometimes, I can be a genuine ogre. Am I coming across loud and clear, PFC?"

"Certainly, Sgt. Bartels. I'll do my level best to live up to Col. Simpson's expectations, and yours too. And thanks, Master-Sergeant, and please thank the boss too."

"You are quite welcome, PFC Harris," Bartels smilingly replied. "Just continue doing what you've been doing and I'm certain we will all be tickled pink about it. Well ... maybe not you,

PFC being a colored kid and all. I'm just ribbing you, Harris - just being a little lighthearted. Don't mean to offend you."

Since the noncom seemed somewhat pleased with himself in the wake of his off-color dig, I was also in a jovial mood. "That is very, very witty, Sarge," I grinningly remarked. "And I'm firmly aware, too, that you can sometimes come across as a genuine ogre. Quite often, actually."

Although Bartels feigned an expression of resentment, he laughingly responded, saying, "Hey you best watch your step, young man. And at this point, you are dismissed. Afternoon, PFC Harris."

As I turned and proceeded to walk away, I could still hear Bartels snickering. I was well-pleased by his congenial behavior. After pre-assessing him as somewhat stern, rigid and markedly business-like, I now knew he had a sense of humor. And that, to me, was a pleasant and admirable revelation.

CHAPTER THIRTY-FIVE
THE AWFUL NOVEMBER

Although I felt blessed in the wake of my relocation to the 250th General Hospital in the fall of 1963, I cannot report that my life there was serene and smooth-sailing, neither for me nor the vast majority of my fellow soldiers either. On the contrary, a rather ferocious tornado touched down within only two weeks of my transfer and brought forth a rather widespread and lingering devastation.

Oddly enough, that twister had a given name and, almost instantly, my company peers and I were hard pressed to pronounce the name without adding a profane adjective to it. 'Captain Kyle M. Rutkowski' was the tornado's surname and regardless of his nationality, he certainly was not a Polish joke.

In fact, in a remarkably short while (I'd say in about 30 minutes at tops), the officer was almost collectively perceived as an out-and-out egotistical, mean-spirited and braggadocious bastard. Without the slightest doubt in my mind, if 250th General's new and incoming company commander was remotely a man of his words, that was the precise take-away he was aiming at. The captain made no bones or excuses about being viewed as an <u>A-number one</u> asshole.

Now, I wish I could recall verbatim what our new company commander said on the November afternoon he addressed 250th General as an assembled unit, but I can't. And I could not gauge my fellow soldier's feelings either (although most of them appeared to be severely perturbed), but, personally, I found myself suppressing laughter. While I was almost positive that none of the soldiers in the formation would align themselves with my mirth, my thoughts were momentarily elsewhere.

In being an avid and longtime movie-goer, I was almost sure I had seen the captain on the big screen once upon a time. And if I had not, I stood silent, surmising that he surely belonged in the movies. The man's diction was perfect, his demeanor was stalwart and his remarks seemed to be carefully scripted, just as if it had been penned by a veteran screenwriter.

Admittedly, I was initially somewhat suspicious also. Things seemed to be out of kilter. For instance: In the brief aftermath of our Commanding Officer's rather lackluster introduction of Capt. Rutkowski, he wasted no time withdrawing from the assembly and retreating to the adjacent Headquarters facility. And although Lt. Col. Mathis was, sometimes, described as "a man of few words," I was wary of him being a man of <u>no</u> words. Something was awry but it wasn't mere happenstance, it was by design. That became clear when Capt. Rutkowski addressed the group.

"As the C.O. mentioned, gentlemen, my name is Captain Kyle Rutkowski," the officer proudly spoke, "and much like many of you men who stand before me this afternoon, I enlisted in the United States army as a green, snot-nosed and wet-behind-the-ears recruit. I was 18 years old and, like most of you, I didn't know my ass from a hole in the ground. But unlike the majority of you men, I am dedicated, a quick-study and an excellent soldier. I was so excellent and impressive, in fact, that I was bestowed a battlefield commission during wartime. And I'm here to tell you, gentlemen, although you may dismiss me as a braggart and blowhard, I am the best soldier, the best damn officer - pound for pound, you have ever seen!"

There was, of course, a grumbling in the ranks at that point, but our incoming company commander took it all in stride. He didn't miss a beat, loudly inserting, "And in my being the very best you have ever seen, gentlemen, it is my primary goal, if not, obsession, to make this deficient, sorry-ass company, yes - meaning you sorry-ass soldiers ... to transform you people into the best field outfit the world has ever laid eyes on! I believe wholeheartedly, gentlemen, in grueling hard work, and whether it be on-post, in the boondocks of Camp Bullis or in a actual war zone!"

As, yet, another undercurrent of jeers and mumbling emerged from the assembled troops, Rutkowski was still unmindful of the unrest. He resumed his oration, saying, "And I assure you, gentlemen, you will not like me very much either! I'll even venture to say you'll <u>hate</u> my military guts. But guess what? I don't give a rat's ass about being liked or loved by any of you! I wasn't assigned here to win a goddamn popularity contest!"

Pausing momentarily to purposely cast eyes at a 1st. lieutenant who stood amongst us, the captain went on with his address, inserting, "And this goes for seasoned noncoms and subordinate officers alike - I expect and demand 150 percent performances from each and every one of you men, with no exceptions! No one gets a pass in this outfit and you can take that to the bank! So, shape up, do your damndest to stay in my good graces, or - I will personally see that you are swiftly shipped out. Meanwhile, gentlemen, I wish you a good day and this formation is now history. You are now, hereby, dismissed!"

THE LONG AND WINDING ROAD

Although I was truly hoping (if not, praying) I would not have to resume dealing with the wilds of Camp Bullis, Texas until the upcoming year of 1964 (and especially since I was told that was the driving factor behind my October transfer), I was obliged to play an active role in 250th General's 'next to last' field excursion for the current year. Another outing was scheduled for December but I was exempt from it.

I suspected the November exercise was the brain child of our incoming company commander and since I was informed that our unit had recently welcomed two, new fresh-faced 2nd lieutenants (both of them, white), I anticipated that the November excursion would be rather frustrating, exhausting and filled with simulated challenges which were relevant to military hospitals in outdoor settings. And since Capt. Kyle Rutkowski was the chief orchestrator of the field problem, I was positive our company would collectively be subjected to a continuous, exasperating 'hell on earth.' Unfortunately, my assumption proved to be correct.

To be perfectly honest, when I was still an official member of the 24th Evacuation Hospital, and essentially when it came to that massive Swift Strike II endeavor, I felt the 24th's overall performance in the field was somewhat substandard and had a lot of room for improvement. Of course, in being a neophyte or a lowly peon, I made it a point to stay on the sidelines and keep my mouth shut. I had a number of ideas and suggestions (or innovations) but I stayed mum, just the same. I recalled the assertion, "There's the right way, the wrong way and the army way."

Now, whether I accredit it to maturity, a sudden metamorphous or my ever-present feeling of being esteemed and valued by my boss, Col. Simpson, I wasn't the same soldier I was back in July. I felt confident in almost running the field Admissions and Disposition Office (A&D) single-handedly, I was cognizant of all the principles, regulations and printed forms that rendered the field operation efficient and smooth-sailing and, shortly, I found myself displaying a talent that even I was not aware of.

Although I instantly viewed it as absurd and unfair as well, Capt. Rutkowski elected to assign the task of erecting the all-important GP-large tents to the two novice 2nd lieutenants and, in spite of being afforded the necessary man-power, the officer-duo had no idea what they were doing. However, I had had plenty of practice while soldiering in the 24th and thanks to a few short-cuts I had learned, I taught the two officers to pitch tents in record-time. They were truly appreciative of my assistance too, and especially since it had nothing to do with my official job.

When I wasn't playing the role of an unofficial advisor to lieutenants Morrison and Sanders (that was the duo's names), I was serving as an understudy and administrative assistant to a staff-sergeant named 'Harold Kurn' (who also happened to be my barracks sergeant) and he and I hit it off extremely well. In fact, if an observer wasn't the wiser, he or she might have thought that the two of us (similar to me and Tommy) had worked alongside each other for a prolonged period of time. To our mutual delight, we gelled from the very moment we met. And that was applicable to, both, our on-post relationship and the one we formulated in the boondocks of Camp Bullis. In a real sense, Staff-Sgt. Kurn and I emerged as the official Registrar team in the field.

I traditionally strived for excellence in every job I had held and my efforts were no different when it came to excursions to Camp Bullis. I was cognizant and familiar with every and all official forms that were vital to mortar-base 'general hospitals' (which was our model), I kept them in plentiful-supply and I implemented and maintained a comprehensive record on every 'mock' (and, sometimes, real) patient who was treated at our makeshift facility.

In addition, since Harold Kurn emphasized that Lt. Col. Mathis was a "real stickler" for administrative propriety (and I assumed Capt. Rutkowski was likewise), I was adamant about crossing all the 't's' and doting all the 'i's' on every document that was generated and handled by our office. Sgt. Kurn applauded me for my efforts.

Naturally, I was well-pleased by the verbal accolades that were extended to me by Staff-Sgt. Kurn. In what the army called "quick-time," I also found myself endeared and deeply appreciative of him as well - and in spite of him being a white man from the south.

However, when I reflect back on the entirety of that November field exercise, I must acknowledge that I wasn't the only participant in the venture who was deserving of high praise and a pat on the back. In my viewpoint, and in spite of being roundly criticized and degraded by the majority of the enlisted men, the noncoms and the junior officers who were subjected to the week-long exercise (although those gripes were understandably muffled and whispered), our newly-installed company commander was worthy of kudos also.

After throwing every simulated problem at our unit (dilemmas which were explicit or unique to a general hospital in a field setting), the captain proceeded to guide us through those mock trials (or tests) with an efficiency that was indicative of his multi-year experiences. Furthermore, when he verbally critiqued those episodes, alluding to all the relevant 'pros' and 'cons,' he not only dissected the solutions he applied to the situations, he cited the military precedent and protocol as well.

While I could not speak for my fellow soldiers who stood alongside me during the evening formations, I was personally impressed with the man. He may have been abrasive, braggadocious and somewhat rough around the edges, but he knew his stuff. When he priorly told our company "he was the best damn officer, pound for pound, we had ever seen," I didn't wholeheartedly buy into his boast, but I was in awe of his leadership skills. If 250th General suddenly found itself in the midst of a combat arena and I was still assigned to it, I would relish having an officer like Capt. Kyle Rukowski in charge. To me, that was giving credit when it was due.

Every now and then (but infrequently, thank God), a happening plays out that not only takes you completely by surprise, it boggles and astounds one's senses. That acutely described my feelings when, on November 22, 1963, I was summoned to the telephone at my on-post workplace, the Registrar's Office. Since I hardly ever got a call during work hours, it was an oddity in itself, but when Alex Gray informed me that the caller was Danny Williams I was downright alarmed. And my alarm was escalated further by a subsequent remark that was made by Sgt. Gray.

"Your boy sounds kinda pissed or ... really upset about something," he frowningly whispered. "Even sounds like he's crying, Harris."

I grasped the telephone, staring into Gray's face. "What's up, Danny?" I asked. "Naw, we don't have a radio on here. What? What? Are you serious, man? Aw hell, Danny! When did it happen? Alright - thanks for calling. I'll git back to you later on. Okay - okay."

Upon hanging up the phone, it seemed like everyone in the immediate vicinity was looking at me. I'm certain it was due to the severe anguish in my face and the tears that were instantly welling up in my eyes too. I started to speak but the bystanding Tommy Preston addressed me first. He had trailed me over to Sgt. Gray's desk.

"Barry, what the hell's the matter?" he asked. "What did Dan Williams say to you? What?"

I struggled with uttering a reply. Then, finally I said, "They shot President Kennedy in Dallas, Tommy. Danny said they shot John Kennedy! It's on the radio, he said!"

From where I was standing at that particular moment, I could see Master-Sgt. Bartels and Col. Simpson casually conversing in the Registrar's office. And even as my surrounding coworkers frantically sought out radios and erupted in a state of awe and chaos, I was intent upon apprising the pair of the situation. Not only was I aware of the colonel's fondness for President Kennedy, I knew the Registrar housed a television in his office as well. Tossing military protocol to the wind, I confronted my two bosses unannounced.

"PFC Harris, what's the meaning of this?" asked an indignant Sgt. Bartels. "You know better than to barge into the colonel's office without permission!"

Although I was cognizant of Bartel's angry words, I was unmindful of them and faced the colonel head-on instead. "Could you turn your TV on, Sir?" I asked. "They say . . . President Kennedy was shot in Dallas. I don't know how serious it is, but he was wounded, they said."

I could not help myself, I was openly crying when Sgt. Bartels spoke, "Are you kidding me, Harris? Who's this they you're talking about? Why that's fuckin' incredible, Harris, unbelievable!"

Looking as if he was stricken, Col. Simpson was momentarily speechless. He glared at me almost aimlessly, then spunned around in his swivel chair and promptly switched his television set on. Then, as he casually signaled for me to take a seat, he and I and Sgt. Bartels sat, watching the awful proceedings coming in from Dallas, Texas. And we remained in that office, intently watching, and with hardly a single word exchanged between us, until it was, alternately, announced that the sitting President of the United States, John Fitzgerald Kennedy, was, indeed, dead!

Even as our fellow coworkers outside the Registrar's office loudly wailed in indescribable lament and outrage (Tommy Preston and Alex Gray, included), I sat, still weeping profusely and without shame, and so did an emotionally-shakened Master-Sgt. Bartels.

However, Col. Simpson, totally dissimilar to both of us, was wearing a rather stern and stoic expression and remained dry-faced and emerged verbal also. "What a sick and perverse world we live in," he mused. "Here's a splendid man, serving his country without any semblance of monetary payment and some cold-hearted monster comes along and cruelly snuffs his life out. That is terrible, just simply horrific."

Taking a moment to seek out the tear-saturated face of his second-in-command, he went on to say, "Sgt. Bartels, our workday is over as of now. Please take a moment and apprise the staff of my determination. I'd appreciate it."

"I'll take care of that right away, Sir," spoke the sergeant, climbing to his feet. "On the double, Colonel."

"And that, of course, goes for you too, PFC Harris," the colonel spoke further. "And thanks for alerting me. I'm sure you're heartbroken about it. And I can assure you, I deeply feel your pain."

Although I failed to say it, I was thoroughly inconsolable at that moment. "But, Colonel, what will become of our country now?" I asked. "Where do we go from this point on?"

My officer boss seemed to give serious and reflective thought to my queries and, then, calmly issued a reply. "We will get through this tragedy, my young friend, we'll have to," he stated. "Lyndon Johnson will be sworn-in as our new president and commander-in-chief - and by nightfall, I'll venture to guess. And we'll survive this, we always do. You might even bet on it. But . . . who would have ever thought in this day and age, that such a horrible act of violence could actually happen? Who could fathom it?"

※

Now, I don't know exactly why; label me young, naive, overly-optimistic or just plain-old gullible, but I was somewhat soothed by Col. Simpson's positive viewpoints. Even as he struggled to comprehend the assassination in Dallas, Texas, the officer didn't feel defeated or hateful. Instead, he spoke of resilience and survival. And before long, as I proceeded to get a grip on my emotions, and even in the midst of observing the ongoing mourning of my Registrar coworkers, I, too, was able to see the proverbial light at the end of the tunnel.

Less than ten minutes later, with my close-knit friend, Tommy, walking alongside me (of course, he, too, was absorbed in grief), I left my workplace that afternoon with a deep sense of optimism. I credited my state of being to the words voiced by my esteemed boss and I felt compelled to pass them on to my lamenting <u>brother</u>, hoping they would uplift and inspire him too. However, I never knew if they managed to do the trick. All I knew was that I withdrew a measure of solace from the colonel's parting words and I prayed they soothed Tommy also.

Unfortunately, but not so surprisingly, there were numerous people in America and around the globe, too, who were neither appalled nor grievous in regards to the horrific murder of President John F. Kennedy in Dallas, Texas. (Just so happened,

Black Muslim leader, Malcolm X, was one of them). However, the greater majority of the people in the United States and the world at-large were virtually prostrate in sincere grief. Owing to the various media outlets, it not only weighed heavily on the hearts and minds of millions of fellow Americans, it played havoc with the psyche of most of the free world also.

I had heard selective people claim (most of them, Caucasians) that assassination and violence was contrary to the American way, but I staunchly begged to differ with them. With the memory of the killing of Medger Evers fresh on my mind (that was only about six months prior to the Kennedy murder), along with the ever-present violence in the southern regions of the U.S., I had no idea what they were talking about. Malcolm X had advocated that violence in our country was "the American way" and I was inclined to agree with him in late November of 1963.

However, when the Muslim leader made reference to the Kennedy slaying, mockingly saying, "The chickens have come home to roost," I found myself denouncing his coldness. Still though, it occurred to me that if Medger Evers had been a white man, or those six children in Alabama had not been black, they probably would have been still living and breathing as well. And that was the plain and ugly truth of the matter.

But, in looking back, I could not entirely divorce my personal lament from that of my Caucasian counterparts. Just from being amongst them, observing their faces of despair, made my heart ache even more. One thing about it, being in the armed services at the time of the Dallas tragedy was bad enough but being an active duty soldier in the state of Texas during that exact period was close to hell. In addition, due to the fact that John and Jacqueline Kennedy had landed at San Antonio International just a day prior to that fateful tragedy, was doubly sorrowful and agonizing for military personnel stationed at Fort Sam Houston and the uniformed men and women who were assigned to the surrounding air force bases as well.

In regards to the soldiers who converged on the numerous dayrooms that were located throughout Fort Sam Houston (and I was certainly one of those servicemen), merely watching television was an exercise in heavy morose and tortuous repetition. Over and over again, we were granted a visual account of the events that surrounded the shooting, they continually updated us on the condition of the Governor of Texas (John Connally was wounded in the episode), they flooded the airways with a myriad of prominent people and celebrities (all of them, intent upon voicing their heartfelt condolences and words of encouragement) but, worst of all, at least, for me, they periodically highlighted filmed footage of a lively and vintage John F. Kennedy.

In addition, as collective TV viewers, we were apprised of Lyndon B. Johnson's formal oath of office, were, eventually, informed of the shooting of Dallas police officer, J.D. Tipit, and were, subsequently, made aware of the arrest of the alleged assassin, a man who was identified as Lee Harvey Oswald; essentially everything and anything that was even remotely connected to President Kennedy's gruesome murder.

Speaking for myself, sitting in complete silence inside that dayroom, I was almost mesmerized by the continuous news footage. Even though the room was almost overflowing with fellow soldiers who acutely shared my grief and sense of hopelessness, I felt completely alone and desolate, an individual living on the outskirts of time. I sat there but a little while longer and then took a few minutes to reflect on the entirety of the day. I concluded it was a God-awful day, so why not conclude it? And with that I climbed to my feet and headed to my barracks, which was across the street.

CHAPTER THIRTY-SIX

BRIGHT TOMORROWS

As I sat practically 'ringside' in the TV room inside 250th General's recreational facility (traditionally called the 'dayroom'), I was still in the throes of depression and deep mourning as I intently watched the news footage coming out of Dallas, Texas and Washington D.C. Since I was privy to an on-playing radio in my home barracks, I was aware that Lee Harvey Oswald, who was considered the lone triggerman in the murder of JFK, was scheduled to be transferred to a so-called "more-secure" facility on November 24th (just two days after the assassination) and I wanted to observe that event. That's why I sat, physically camped out in front of the television set on that particular morning.

However, not in my wildest imagination or nightmare, did I anticipate seeing what I saw and was, alternately, made to come to grips with that day. In real time (live, and in black and white), as John Kennedy's alleged killer was being escorted down a corridor by a team of law officers, a bystanding man darted in front of the prisoner (and the TV camera) and shot him pointblank! And although instant Pandemonium broke out, even as the on-hand lawmen frantically scrambled to apprehend the brazen shooter, I will never forget the look of excruciating pain on Oswald's face.

The shooter, who was later identified as 'Jack Ruby,' fired a bullet into Oswald's abdomen and was immediately taken into custody.

Later on, JFK's accused murderer would be pronounced dead, Jack Ruby would be carted off to jail and I, along with a multitude of eye witnessing Americans, were adrift in a state of indescribably shock. I, of course, could not speak for others who had viewed the event (I did recall one of my fellow soldiers shouting, "What the fuck!"), but I eventually hearkened back to something Col. Simpson said in the immediate aftermath of the Kennedy slaying itself.

To be precise, the Registrar remarked, "Who would think, in this day and age, that such a thing could occur?" And I concluded on that very day, if I lived to be a hundred years old, that those words alone would always describe my personal take on that most vivid incident. And unless it was depicted on the silver screen and was fictionalized, I prayed that I would never, ever witness anything like it again.

Not long after the televised shooting of Lee Harvey Oswald, and even before the somber funeral of President John F. Kennedy got underway, one of my barracks mates made some rather crude statements that not only momentarily took me aback, they served as an instant jolt to my memory. Referring to the shooting of JFK's _alleged_ assassin (Oswald's guilt was still undetermined), the soldier bitterly asserted, "I'm glad that that fucking Oswald is somewhere burning in hell, but if Jack Ruby had blown his goddamn brains out, like he did to the President, then my Thanksgiving would be the best I ever had! That little sonofabitch Oswald should have been born dead!"

During all the ongoing furor and excitement, I had completely forgotten about the upcoming Thanksgiving holiday. It was only two or three days off and, in spite of not being in a festive mood (I was almost certain that was a universal mind-set of most Americans), I still had a great deal to be thankful for. I was in good health, my family and many friends were doing relatively well and, despite our fallen chief executive, our country was basically at peace.

Therefore, even in my state of suppressed mourning and anxiety, I felt blessed and singularly fortunate. Personally speaking, I could in no way rationalize the horror of the last two or three days, but I was able to extract a measure of solace and refuge from something that the Rev. Dr. Martin Luther King Jr. had said during that very year. He had spoken of, "Transforming dark yesterdays into bright tomorrows," and as idealistic and ambitious as it might have sounded, I honestly believed I had the capability and fortitude to do such a thing. Maybe, not on a large scale, but certainly on a small and significant one.

Actually, I hosted that ambitious feeling well prior to the double murders in Dallas, Texas. But, afterwards, as I emerged dazed by the swiftness of foreboding evil and sinister acts, I became more adamant about it. In less than a minute's passing, it was keenly clear to me that tragedy could strike in the blink of an eye and a dear and cherished loved-one (yours, mine, anyone's precious loved-one) could cease to live and breathe forever, I reasoned. And regardless of an individual's station in life (from an esteemed John F. Kennedy down to a despicable Lee H. Oswald), we are all susceptible to an unpredictable fate.

Therefore, in being acutely aware of all the foregoing suppositions, it seemed to me that people, in general, should always strive to be more endearing and more appreciative of each other. Our recently-slain President had once declared, "We are not here to curse the darkness, we are here to light a candle" and when I mingled those words with Rev. Dr. King's desire to "transform dark yesterdays into bright tomorrows," I felt exhilarated and emboldened too. In the waning days of November 1963 those were my heartfelt feelings and I sincerely hoped, with God's spiritual help, it was a viable and sustainable mantra. Only time would tell.

To state that I was glad and grateful to see November of 1963 go by the boards was probably a cliché acknowledgment when it came to the majority of Americans in the aftermath of the Kennedy assassination. For me, the only saving grace in regards to the entire month was having Thanksgiving dinner with Dan and Val Williams, and being informed that the couple was expecting their very first child. Due to that joyous announcement, we even engaged in a toast to a "most splendid and beautiful future." Those, by the way, were specifically my words because I thoroughly adored children. In fact, I deemed them as priceless and ultimate gifts from God Himself.

Without so much as being asked by the expectant parents, I took the liberty of appointing myself as the godfather of the forthcoming baby and since Valerie quickly seconded the motion, I considered it a done deal. In addition, I jokingly told Danny that he had no 'say-so' in the matter whatsoever and to just stay out of the way and keep quiet. Danny, taking it all in stride, shook his head in amusement and mild exasperation as well.

However, just as the countdown to the Williams couple's birth due date got underway, two other novel revelations came my way. Notably, they both happened to involve my other cherished comrade and staple coworker, Tommy Preston. Since my eyesight was 20-20 at the age of 19, I wasn't remotely shocked when I was informed that Angela Mendoza was almost five months pregnant, but I was surprised (and, admittedly, hurt too) when Tommy apprised me of the fact that he and Angie had taken marriage vows. No matter how simplistic or brief their wedding ceremony was, I would have loved to have been present during it.

～

The dawning of December of 1963 lifted my spirits somewhat. I was already scheduled for Christmas leave (from December 21st through the 3rd of January 1964) and since a recent letter from, yet, another beloved and endeared friend (namely, Jerome or J) had indicated that he would also be in Saint Louis during much of the same time period, I was thrilled and overjoyed.

Jerome was on the threshold of finishing up his tour of duty in South Korea (the same applied to his high school buddies who had gone with him there) and, then, after the upcoming leave hiatus would officially conclude, he was slated to remain stateside at a military installation called the 'White Sands Missile Range,' which was located in New Mexico. I had made it an express point to communicate bi-weekly with J by mail for the last year or so and I longed to see him again.

When I reflected back on my close-knit friend and homeboy, Jerome, exclusively, I must admit it always managed to warm my heart and lift my spirits. Specifically, I could still vividly visualize him as he frantically ran back and forth to my assigned barrack's latrine during basic training, still see him gingerly placing hot towels on my bare and agonizing stomach and still, somehow, empathizing with his feeling of heartfelt pain as he gave way to profuse sobbing.

However, in spite of the poignancy and pathos of that unforgettable, bygone memory (and it remains prominent in my heart), I found it difficult (if not, impossible) to separate or distance my affection for Jerome from my other cherished companions. I absolutely loved interacting with, both, Danny and Tommy as well. But to be frank, and I know this will strike some people as looney and strange, but I have never been able to stifle or vanquish my love for people, not way back when or at present. I feel I am incapable of doing it.

I don't always regard my rather bizarre but innate mind-set as a fulfilling virtue (in fact, it is, sometimes, discouraging and heartbreaking), but it has tremendous staying power. For instance, (till this very day), I have never stopped loving and cherishing individuals such as Robert, Charles, Woody, Larry, Willie, Walter and all the other 'fellows' either. So, I go through life, missing and holding people dear who may, or may not, know just how much I treasured them.

However, I never felt cursed or disadvantaged in the wake of my unexplainable personality trait (or disorder). Similar to my long-time penchant for not being in synch with musical beats heard by others, it was a condition beyond my control. Good or bad, I perceived it as part of my biological make-up.

Sitting aside my 'now and then' tendency to examine and self-analyze myself, I was still joyously poised and looking forward to being reunited with my buddy, J, come Christmastime. I had excitedly anticipated the upcoming trip; both physically and mentally. Thanks to my monetary winnings from a barracks poker game at the start of November (it took place in my former billets in 24th Evac.), I had purchased a round-trip airplane ticket for the undertaking and, in addition, had saved up nearly $300 for spending money (which was darn commendable for a PFC who was sending $40 per month home). So, I considered myself 'good to go.'

A writer by the name of 'John Steinbeck' penned the words, "The best laid plans of mice and men, sometimes, go astray," but I ascribe to the notion that, "Greed, sometimes, prompt men and women to be dumb and foolhardy." Unfortunately, the latter revision acutely applied to me and my subsequent feelings on December 19th, 1963, which was just two days prior to my boarding a plane for St. Louis, Missouri. My analogy grew directly out of my involvement in a five-card stud poker game that took place inside a 24th Evacuation barracks. In fact, it was the same billets where I emerged a 'winner' in November.

At six o'clock in the evening, as I readied myself to carry a load of clothes to the adjacent laundromat (it was less than two blocks from my assigned barracks), I was approached by a fellow soldier from my former unit. Not that it was relevant, but PFC Foster and I only casually knew each other and we did not consider ourselves friends. In fact, in spite of us being Negroes, our singular connection was occasionally engaging in monetary poker games, and that was exactly what prompted him to seek me out at my home-barracks in 250th General.

According to Foster, there were three other soldiers who were itching and waiting to gamble back at his assigned billets and he invited me to join the assembled group. Not that it was relevant either, but one of those soldiers in-wait happened to be Specialist 5 Ogelthorp, who was the same obnoxious <u>noncom</u> who had audaciously paid an unannounced (and certainly, unwelcomed) visit to the off-post home of Valerie Williams, fully aware that her husband was in the wilds of Camp Bullis. Therefore, since I considered him a two-legged dog, I didn't like him at all.

Well, against my better judgment, paired with a yearning for more money, I decided to participate in the gambling competition. Ogelthorp, grinning like a slick con-artist, acted like he was pleased to see me, deemed me a 'stand-up dude' to a player I didn't know, and even claimed I was sorely missed in the 24th Evac. Hospital.

I suspected he was being phony and insincere, so I accepted the man's praise with a grain of salt and, soon, the five of us (the assembled players) got down to cases. And that, of course, meant playing five-card stud poker for monetary stakes.

Although it could be viewed as rather unorthodox and unusual, but as very young children, one of my first cousins (his name was Gerald) had taught my four brothers and me how to play multiple games of poker. And over the years, I grew to believe that I was quite proficient at it. Meaning, I felt that I knew when to retain and play the cards that were dealt to me and knew, too, when to give up on a hand and discard it as well. However, my skilled instructor failed to teach me how to be consistently lucky when I competed.

Moreover, cousin Gerald didn't apprise me of how I could ward off what I considered 'buzzard luck' during those gambling session either. As the evening wore on, I was dealt one hideous and deficient hand after another and even when I received a hand that I felt was worth sticking with, I was bested time and time again. It was downright uncanny and bizarre! If I had a 'straight,' an opposing player would have a 'full house,' when I displayed a 'full house,' someone would come up with a 'straight-flush' or even 'four-of-a-kind,' and one time when I confidently laid down 'four nines,' Ogelthorp smilingly produced four jacks! And if that wasn't <u>buzzard</u> <u>luck</u>, then what is? I felt, not only was it not my darn day, I had been evilly cursed!

Finally, after stupidly losing an excess of 160 dollars (I kept returning to my nearby barracks and retrieving additional money), I gave up and decided to go and wash my dirty clothes, which was what I should have done in the first place. (As they say though, "Hindsight is 20-20). Then, as I withdrew from the poker game,

Spec. 5 Ogelthorp had the urge to throw a dig at me as I walked off.

"Hey, Bro," he yelled, "if you run across a few mo' bucks, you come on back to see us. Most likely we'll still be at it. Maybe, your luck will change, Harry. I mean - who knows, buddy?"

Well, I mentally beat up myself throughout my time at the laundromat, couldn't help it. I once had ample monies to buy a few inexpensive Christmas gifts and now it was halfway gone. Then, after a short while, I decided to plunge a little deeper into my <u>fool</u>-<u>pit</u>. After drying my clothes, I dropped them off at my billets and soon returned to the ongoing poker game in 24th Evac. It was still going strong, although a new face had replaced one of the old ones.

To be candid, from the very moment I reentered the poker competition, my luck changed for the best! However, that statement alone was putting it mildly. All of a sudden, I could not lose! After winning 8 out of 10 hands consecutively, I'd lose one or two hands, and then go on a long tear again.

In actuality, it was the exact reverse of earlier, when I couldn't buy a decent and decisive hand. At that point, it appeared I couldn't pick up a losing or even mediocre hand. I was literally winning money "hand over foot," pot after pot and, finally, three hours later, I had won <u>all</u> the money. As my four opponents displayed long faces of dejection, and especially Specialist E-5 Ogelthorp, I had won a whopping $1,297.75.

Naturally, I wasn't braggadocious or arrogant about my good fortune or uncanny change of luck when it came to that lengthy poker game, I was extremely thankful. In addition, I was sympathetic to the losers and so much so that I agreed to do something that is sort of an unwritten taboo in the world of gambling. Over the years, I had been advised (if not, <u>warned</u>) to never loan any portion of my winnings to defeated contestants.

Reason why: Recipients of such unsecured loans have a tendency to regard the money in question as their own. Of course, the money involved would no longer be theirs, but they would proceed to almost begrudgingly think it was.

The requestor of the loan, in my case, was none other than Specialist Ogelthorp. With the utmost sincerity, he 'politely' begged me to loan him my 'loose' change and although it could have been a meager amount, it wasn't. Mostly, in half dollars, quarters, dimes and nickels, it totaled up to $247.85.

Exhibiting a degree of humbleness, I had never witnessed before (especially in him), Ogelthorp remarked, "Look, Harry, you know I'm a married man, right? With a little tot crawlin' around the crib. Bro, if I go home with empty pockets tonight, my old lady will jump in my shit. Brotherman, she'll skin my ass alive! So, why doncha let me hold on to your change, borrow just the coins, old buddy?"

"Ah - I don't know about that, Ogelthorp," I responded, immediately wary of the proposal. "I mean, you know, I'm a little skeptical. When - when will you pay me back, guy?"

"Well, you know I'm still working my part-time gig, working for the cleaners and all," was the noncom's reply. "I'll probably be able to throw it out to you . . . maybe, in a couple of weeks or so. Pay you all your money back, Harry. Come on, Bro, ya' know I'm good for it."

I was certain that Ogelthorp was at least being honest about his extra job. Being a long-time employee of an off-post cleaners, the specialist was well-known throughout Fort Sam Houston. He would go to assorted barracks around the post, collect soiled clothing from numerous soldiers (fatigues, khaki uniforms, civilian attire and the likes), and return them in a dry-cleaned or laundered state. Notably, I had personally used his services from time to time in the past.

After momentarily mulling over Spec. 5 Ogelthorp's request, I caved in and congenially agreed to it. (Actually, although the specialist didn't know it, I was 'all-in' when he mentioned "the little tot crawling around the crib"). Upon counting up my loose change, I then presented it to Ogelthorp. I also informed him that I'd be away on leave for the ensuing two weeks, telling him he could repay me in mid-January. Evidently, my Christmas spirit had already kicked in.

CHAPTER THIRTY-SEVEN
A STORYBOOK LIFE

Out of all the Christmases I celebrated in my 19 years, the one in 1963 was the most enjoyable of them all. Thanks to my gambling winnings in the middle of December, I had the means to buy gifts for my closest friends, a few relatives and my immediate family as well. I even bought a present for my stepfather, William.

Additionally, I was able to see an array of first-run movies (the comedy 'It's a Mad, Mad, Mad, Mad World' was amongst them), I made it a point to visit my favorite kinfolks and a few of the 'fellows' such as Woody and Larry and, to my great delight, my prized comrade, Jerome, was in my company during most of those outings. And although I had no qualms about voicing my heartfelt feelings to J in person, his physical presence, paired with me seeing and interacting with my mom and my quartet of brothers once again, was the single-best gift I could ever hope for. Of course, upon being fair and accommodating to Jerome, we spent quality time with his former high school classmates too. Many of them were fresh-back from their tour of duty in South Korea also.

In reality, when it came to the 'gift-giving' premise, I never placed a premium on being awarded a tangible thing, but I placed a great deal of value in meaningful and endearing relationships. In fact, I thought nothing of encouraging my brothers to bypass me during the traditional 'gifting' process and asked them to purchase a present for my soldier buddy, Jerome, instead. A couple of my <u>bro's</u> reluctantly adhered to my request and when I observed the look of joy on J's face on Christmas day, it was well-worth my 'smallish' sacrifice. I wasn't trying to be noble but, to me, my dear friend's happiness was <u>my</u> happiness.

Now, even as a teenager and a young man serving in the armed forces, I always felt I had an innate knack for reading people. Therefore, when it came to my unabashed affection for Jerome (although I knew it was genuine and innocent), I well - knew that some onlooking individuals were capable of affixing a negative connotation to our close-knit friendship. Of course, I couldn't speak for J, but since I regarded myself as a free spirit and totally uninhibited, I didn't concern myself with what people thought of me, let alone of my relationships with others. Similar to 'The Shadow' from my early radio days, I was aware that "a great deal of evil lurked in the hearts of mankind." And that was a dilemma an individual had to wrestle with, it wasn't concerning to me.

Personally, I always entertained good thoughts (not sometimes, but <u>always</u>), I was an eternal optimist, I treated everyone with the utmost respect and I adored and actively sought out congenial and kind-hearted individuals. That was my primary and main thrust in life and I was never overly concerned with what people thought of me. I could never find time for it.

However, in being a guy with deep empathy, I would not get upset when people asked me about any of my past or ongoing relationships and that included the bond I had with Jerome. Admittedly though, my rather candid responses to those kind of queries had much to do with the identity of the questioner involved. For the most part, it had to be a person I esteemed and respected.

For certain, my dear mother fell into that select category and she rather 'diplomatically' voiced her concerns shortly after she and I had watched a couple of movies together at the Fox Theatre one evening during my ongoing leave. At the time, we were in the middle of a meal at a restaurant, and one that was very near the movie house.

"Duke, I wanna ask you something, and I know how sensitive you are about things?" Ruby began. "I don't wanna hurt your feelings or rain on your parade, but it's about Jerome, your ace-boon-coon."

"Why? You don't like him?" I asked, jumping to a conclusion.

"Aw - Jerome, he's nice enough, and I like him, I do," my mother remarked. "He's real mannerable, easy-going and everything. And he seems to care a lot about you too. Most of your running buddies were pretty nice boys. They just kept you in a lotta hot water, all those darn fights they got you into."

I sat, smiling and shaking my head. "Come on, Mom," I said. "I told you before, most of the times it was me. I was always protective of my friends, even Alonzo - and, sometimes, me and him would fight each other. I had a lot of anger in me, a real bad temper, and I'm sure it had a lot to do with the old man, my AWOL father. But . . . that's another subject. What - what about J?"

My mother displayed a reflective grin. "I told William it might be an Indian thing, since we have some Cherokee in our bloodline."

I was truly puzzled. "Ruby, I don't have the foggiest idea of what you're talking about," I smiled. "You lost me somewhere back on the Indian reservation. What are you trying to say?"

"Well, I don't know if it applies to the Cherokee tribe, but they say - when a person saves an Indian's life, then the Indian, turns right around and devotes his life to the person who saved him. And since you feel that J, or Jerome, saved your life in basic training, then . . ."

"Then I feel I owe my life to J?" I laughingly offered, finishing Ruby's thought. "Mother-dear, you are a real doozie! And you know you oughta stop watching all those dumb cowboy movies too!"

"I read it in a book, Mr. Smarty-Pants," my mother grinningly stated. Then, upon turning serious again, she questioned, "Then - what do you think it is, Duke? Can you put it into words, so I can understand? I mean . . . is it just friendship?"

At that juncture, I became somber myself. "<u>Just friendship</u>," I mused, seriously pondering my mom's query. "Well, saving my life is part of it, and remembering how he cried over me, it has a great deal to do with it too, I'm sure. Since I'm a creature of emotion myself, that had a lasting impact. Plus ... I never told you, knowing you would get upset about it. But remember when I came home on convalescent leave last year, and Jerome was on leave after basic too?"

"And what happened back then?" Ruby grimacingly asked.

Although over a year had gone by since the happening I was focusing on had occurred, I still wasn't comfortable telling my mother about it. "If you recall, at the time," I went on to say, "my stomach was still stitched up. Well - J attended an outdoor party with me in my friend Robert's backyard. And I know it was stupid, but the old Duke showed up."

With an expression of disgust, my mom deduced where my account was headed. "Don't tell me you were gonna fight some kid?" she quizzed. "Not with sutures, still in your belly?"

Momentarily, I'm sure I looked like a subdued child, a kid caught with his hand in the cookie jar. I nodded my head 'yes,' then went on to further explain, saying, "A couple of party-crashers were threatening to jump on Alonzo, and I mean just for the hell of it! And so, I got wind of it, and I tried to face-off with the dudes, stitches and all. I said I was being real dumb and stupid."

"Duke - Duke, when are you gonna learn some sense?" Ruby fused. "It wasn't even your darn fight, with your crazy, bone-head!"

"Yeah, I know, Ruby," I soon admitted. "But that's all in the past - I swear - I know better now. But, what I'm getting at is this: The fellows, Larry, Arthur and the rest of them, they were edging me on, kinda wanting me to fight. But, do you know what Jerome was doing? He was trying his best to hold me back, almost begging me to stop and, once again, crying his heart out! Meanwhile, the two guys who wanted to beat up Lonnie disappeared from the scene. And I ended up trying to console J, assuring *him* that everything was alright. Do you know what I'm saying, Ruby?"

Even in a state of gloom, my mother affirmatively nodded her head. "That you think of Jerome as a true-blue friend, a young man who sincerely loves you?" she replied. "I hope you are right, Duke. I'll even pray that you're right about your feelings. But, just remember this: You are a good person and I'm glad and thankful for having a son like you. I'm serious. You have a good heart and you have always given a hundred percent to people, and especially to folks you dearly love."

I sat in silence, actually deeply humbled by Ruby's foregoing comments. Then, she spoke further, stating, "I'm not here, trying to badmouth or throw cold water on your relationship with Jerome. I think he's genuine with his feelings and he's a real likable boy too. But, sometimes, Duke, when we put a person upon a pedestal, they eventually tumble down and, sometimes, very, very hard."

It was easy to detect the sadness in my mother's eyes. "Are we talking about J or my long-lost, wayward father?" I asked her.

"We're talking about your J right now?" my mom replied. "Your old crazy, conceited daddy placed his self on top of a pedestal. But... what I'm talking about is this: Sometimes people fall short of our expectations and when that happens, it can be heartbreaking and very sad. Again, I'm not trying to knock your friendship with Jerome, it might be the 'Real McCoy," but think of what the Bible says. It says, "Do not squander your pearls on swine." In other words, don't waste your goodness on undeserving people. Like I said, I'm not criticizing your best friend, and not saying he doesn't deserve you either. For some reason, you have always searched for a kind of storybook friendship and, maybe, a storybook life too. And I'm willing to bet it has a lot, if not, everything, to do with your childhood and our nightmarish life with Melvin. And I pray to God, Duke, I pray that the Lord will someday grant you the beautiful storybook life you dream of. I would love to be around to see it all."

In looking back, I never forgot what my dear mother said to me on our special movie-dinner date during the Christmas season of 1963. (To be quite frank, I never forgot anything she had ever told me). In Ruby's calm and discerning wisdom, she had come close to defining me as a man. To be sure, I didn't see the world as it really was, I saw it as it could and should be. It wasn't because I was naive or living in a fantasy or alternate world, I wasn't.

I simply and firmly believed that if I reached out for the best qualities in people (whether it be a man, woman or child) and then proceeded to nurture them without fear of criticism or reprisal, I could not only make a positive and lasting impact on the special individual involved, I could make a worthwhile contribution to the world around me. And although I was keenly aware that my aspirations and goals would be branded as extreme, ambitious and idealistic by the greater majority of the American populace, I remained adamant about my feelings.

Therefore, owing to the 'storybook' concept that my mother made reference to, I truly believed I could etch out a positive difference in the lives of most of the people whom I had the pleasure to interact with. And with my inner drive, which was actually emboldened by my mom's assessment, I was more determined and resilient than ever.

However, also piggy-backing on Ruby's rather intuitive words, I realized I would be susceptible to a sizable amount of heartaches, disappointments and setbacks along the way too. I had no idea what stood in-wait for me on life's long and winding road, but if I stayed my course, I was reasonably certain that my triumphs would greatly surpass my failures. And that would more than make my journey worthwhile and a pilgrimage of rare beauty. During the waning days of the year 1963 and the onset of a brand new year, I was anxious and joyful to resume the trip.

CHAPTER THIRTY-EIGHT

LOVE AND MARRIAGE

During my high school years (which was from mid-1958 to mid-1962), there was a particular song that was played on the musical airways. And although it wasn't an extremely popular tune (in fact, I might have been the song's biggest fan), it was especially meaningful to me in those bygone days and it instantly made an auditory resurgence in my mind in 1964. I liked the tune's melody and its lyrics, but I especially was fond of its title. It was called 'A Little Bit Wiser Now' and in spite of it being a yesteryear recording, it acutely captured my heartfelt feelings when the former year 'finally' came to a close.

As I recollected the momentous events during the outgoing year (the June slaying of Medger Evers, the 'March on Washington' in late August, the church bombing in Birmingham, Alabama in September and the assassination of JFK in November), I willed myself to extract a measure of solace from the belief that a newly-derived wisdom was very much in the offing. One thing was chillingly evident, I surmised (and an individual did not have to be a Rhodes scholar to deduce it), but similar to the televised shooting of Lee Harvey Oswald, and without any word of warning whatsoever, life can be altered dramatically and drastically and a person's world can be turned upside-down in the blink of an eye.

Therefore, if you were a human being who took life for granted or an individual who viewed the world through rose-colored glasses prior to 1963, then you were (or, at least, should have been) a different and changed person when the new year, 1964, arrived on the scene. In my estimation, unless you were sociopathic or essentially dead inside, you just had to be! And in a most poignant and sober sense, just as I concluded, you, too, were 'a little wiser now.' And with all my heart and soul, I sincerely hoped that the greater majority of the American populace was onboard or, maybe, even lock step with my feelings. However, only time itself would tell that story.

Meanwhile, in spite of my rather philosophical assessment and yearnings at year's end in 1963, life as I knew it went full speed ahead. In the short aftermath of my almost dream-like vacation in Missouri (it was a magical period that flew by much too swiftly), I arrived back at Fort Sam Houston, Texas on the evening of January the 3rd, 1964. With a heart that was virtually betwixt two worlds, I felt deeply downhearted when bidding farewell to my immediate family and Jerome back in my hometown and my melancholy would linger for many days afterwards.

Then, at the same token, I was upbeat and joyous when I was reunited with my military family on January 4th, the very next day. I was delighted to see, both, Danny and Tommy and their female mates also. And they too, each one of them, appeared to be genuinely glad to see me again. Within a two-week time period, even as I fondly reminisced my time in Saint Louis, it was as if I hadn't been away at all.

Although it was well-expected, a lodging change had transpired while I was away on leave. Since Tommy and Angie were now considered an "old married couple," they were residing together in a modest bungalow that was located on the outskirts of Fort Sam. The three of us, meaning, the Prestons and myself, were quite familiar with their new living area because, just so happened, we would pass by it when we would frequently walk Angie home in the wee hours of the morning. Due to mere coincidence also, the Preston domicile was less than five blocks from the home of Dan and Val Williams. I, for one, was thrilled in the wake of that factor.

In my observing estimation, the Preston newlyweds took to the marriage proposition like ducks take to water. Tommy seemed to enjoy the role of dutiful husband and expectant father, and he could hardly wait for his day to conclude at the Registrar's office, and alternately embark on his leg-journey to his off-post home. And, meantime, his bride would be at their domicile, cooking up a sumptuous, hot meal and virtually pining for his arrival.

Typical of young lovers, and despite Angie's state of pregnancy, the Preston couple seemed to be incapable of keeping their hands off each other. And even though I felt somewhat awkward at times (in fact, like a third wheel), I nevertheless was quite happy and comfortable in their presence. They appeared to be deeply in love with each other and that, in turn, increased my feeling of euphoria. In essence, I was happy because they were happy.

In actuality, my high regard for the Preston marital union, in spite of its newness, paralleled my long-held feelings for the Williams couple. Valerie and Danny weren't as demonstrative as my newlywed friends, but it was quite obvious that they, too, adored each other and were committed to the sanctity of their marriage. Being that I was a product of a broken and abusive home as well, I was practically awestruck and pleasantly enthralled by the ongoing marital relationships in regards to both couples. I was hopeful that their unions would last forever and a day.

Although I was quite aware of the adage, "Two is company and three is a crowd," I was a frequent visitor and dinner guest at the homes of, both, the Williams and Preston couples. I intently wanted to give them their space, not wanting to be a bother or that "third wheel" I mentioned priorly (and especially a wheel that was on a flat), but, seemingly, neither Danny and his wife, nor Tommy and Angie, viewed me as a nuisance or someone who was underfoot.

On the contrary, both couples seemed to relish my company and, occasionally, I found myself struggling with a rather odd dilemma. Sometimes I had to make a choice of <u>whose</u> house to go to. And since I dearly loved and enjoyed all four of them, that was a difficult decision for me to make.

Notably, although it had little bearing on where I chose to go during various evenings or on a Sunday afternoon, and especially as a dinner guest, I essentially knew beforehand just what kind of food would be on the table at each couple's house. Valerie was well-adept at preparing 'soul food' (fried chicken, pork chops, pig ears, greens, mashed potatoes, cornbread and the likes) and Angie, being right in line with her heritage, was skilled at cooking up some of the most delicious Mexican meals a person could ever hope for. And in both cases (and to my utter delight), whether I was at the Williams residence or the Preston domicile, there was always an ample supply of beer on hand. Admittedly, I personally made sure it was.

For a young, city-bred, black soldier who was single and had no immediate desire to be other than that, I realized that my married comrades didn't remotely understand me. They didn't appear to be suspicious of me though; neither of my underlying motives or my sexual-orientation. All they actually knew was that I wasn't like them and they did not exactly know why. In their youthful states of mind, and because they were happy and somewhat content in their respective marriages, they secretly longed for me to taste their ongoing bliss.

However, while I realized they were collectively sincere and well-meaning in their desires and hopes for me, I didn't come close to understanding or sharing in their enthusiasm. Vividly recalling my mom and dad's very erratic and volatile marriage (a union that Ruby deemed "nightmarish" in December of 1963), I viewed matrimony as a horse of a different color, mostly dark gray. It could be blissful in substance, I imagined, but it could also be catastrophic and ugly. Unfortunately, I had sat in a ringside seat for the latter.

Personally, to me, it was a virtual 'no-brainer.' Similar to me, most of my childhood friends and running buddies were so-called "products of broken homes." Other than Larry, Walter, Sherrod, Henry (or Moose) and the Harris brothers, the biological parents of the rest of us had either parted company, legally divorced each other or had never taken marriage vows at all (maybe, because they were already wedded to someone else) and we, as offsprings from those severed alliances, were essentially raised by our birth mothers.

Furthermore, and also aligned with my personal plight, the fellows who comprised that group (with the exception of Alonzo) were physically and emotionally estranged from their biological dads. And that, to a young man of deep sentiment like me, was a grievous and heartrending commentary.

While I wasn't so naive or idealistic to believe that there was such a thing as a 'perfect marriage' (except the ones depicted on TV series such as 'Leave it to Beaver' or 'Father Knows Best'), I could not help but desire it for myself. Even in high school when my sociology textbook exposed me to the "broken homes derive broken homes" precept, I dreamed of someday shattering that rationale. However, not only for myself, but for the sake of the kids I fully expected to one day be blessed with. For certain, I had no idea what the future actually held for me and, therefore, I left it up to God. But I was hell-bent on <u>Not</u>, with a capital N — not being a man, a husband or a father who would emerge MIA (missing in action) in a child's life.

When I seriously took the time to think about all of the foregoing, weighing all the pros and cons of the issue, I found myself gradually surrendering to something my mother had alluded to a while back. Maybe, I was on a relentless hunt for a "storybook life" and at the age of 19, I was just beginning my quest and I was not overly concerned with the length of my journey or the time it required. In January of 1964 I was comfortable in my skin, happy for and 'with' my friends (whether they were married or single) and thankful that the good Lord had made me <u>who</u> I was. No matter how others sized me up, I was exceedingly content and I wished and prayed that most others (not only my loved ones) felt likewise.

※

In spite of my personalized feelings about the institution of marriage (I regarded it as sacred, ultra-serious and a lifetime commitment as well), there were some uniformed individuals who didn't come close to sharing my heartfelt assessment. In fact, there were some military personnel who not only viewed the marital process as trivial, frivolous and marginal as well, they thought nothing of exploiting it.

Since there were certain amenities and benefits in place when servicemen and women took their marriage vows (special allowances such as free or discounted housing and monetary stipends) and, sometimes, they were consequential (if not the main thrust) to the marital liaison itself.

Although I kept my skepticism under wraps (and I hoped I was wrong), but that was my first impression when one of Tom Preston's long-time pals, a Cuban-American soldier named Mario Moran, rather quickly married his Women's Army Corps. (WAC) girlfriend. The young lady's name was Katherine Lester, she happened to be Caucasian and she, too, was stationed at Fort Sam Houston. I selected the word 'quickly' because it was like - one day, single and the next day, married.

Sure, the suddenness of the Moran-Lester marriage could have been innocent and legitimate too (even I was a believer of the 'love at first sight' premise), but when I became aware of the two-fold benefits that aptly applied to their union, my suppressed wariness escalated. Then, not too long afterwards, when I found myself in the actual presence of the newly-joined pair, I emerged more suspicious than ever.

However, it wasn't due to what I observed, but, moreso, it was because of what I did not observe. For instance, while I could plainly see and almost feel the intimacy of the Preston pair and, at the same token, delight in the look of mutual love in the eyes of the Williams couple, I found it difficult to detect an aura of genuine affection in regards to the recently-wedded Mr. and Mrs. Moran.

I wasn't aware of any book or pamphlet that specifically addressed itself to the post-behavior of newlyweds in general, so I wasn't exactly sure of what I expected to see. For certain, I was no expert when it came to matters of the heart, but when the state of matrimony came into play, I was on the lookout for something called 'romance.' And, in my opinion, it was not demonstrative or even slightly evident in the Moran-Lester liaison.

THE LONG AND WINDING ROAD

Regardless of my visual assessment of the marital bond between Kathy and Mario, it had little to do with my personal feelings about the two of them as individuals. In truth, I sincerely liked them both, and especially Mario. Prior to Tommy taking the marriage plunge, he and I and Mario had attended several movies together at the main theater on post. Notably, we had seen 'The Outsider' (wherein actor Tony Curtis portrayed 'Ira Hayes' of Iwo Jima fame), as well as the award winning musical, 'West Side Story.'

The latter film was enjoyable and quite memorable too, but not solely because of its entertainment value. It vividly stayed in my memory bank (in fact, it's still there) after the movie concluded. Instead of the three of us leaving the theater and behaving like we were 'normal' and modest movie-goers, we collectively strolled down the street, dancing, singing and frequently popping our fingers. Taking on the persona of the two rival street gangs depicted in the film (meaning, the Jets and the Sharks), we proceeded to unashamedly dance our way all the way back to our not-too-distant company area. For certain, we were acting silly and nutty but we really didn't concern ourselves with what others thought. For a short while we were revisiting our long-ago childhoods and, seemingly, enjoying it to a virtual hilt! As I alluded to, it was a happening I still treasure.

When it came to Mario Moran's bride, Kathy, I quickly developed a fondness for her too. Although it was the first time I had any social dealings with a white female, she and I hit it off right away. To my great delight, Kathy happened to be an enthused lover of music performed by black artists. And I'm not talking about some of them, but most of them! Black entertainers such as Jackie Wilson, Dinah Washington, Marvin Gaye, Ray Charles, Etta James, Smokey Robinson and Stevie Wonder. But, in addition to liking them, when I took the initiative to purchase a small phonograph player, Kathy was in possession of a lot of record albums by the aforementioned performers and would graciously loan them to me. That, of course, added extra icing to our friendship cake.

Above all else though (and in spite of what I did or didn't see at first glance), I came to cherish Mario and Kathy so much that I prayed their union would grow into a sincere and enduring love affair. In actuality, I wanted something for the Moran couple that I, someday, wished to have for myself; a lengthy and fulfilling marriage.

Admittedly (and in honest retrospect), whenever I incurred something good and special in my life, I yearned for people whom I held dear in my life to realize something similar. So, during many moments of isolation and solitude, I prayed that in addition to the novel marriage of Kathy and Mario, the Williams and Preston alliances would 'fundamentally' rival the marital union of my beloved and esteemed prototypes, Mr. and Mrs. John Harris.

In essence, I longed for my married friends (the Williams couple, the Prestons and the Morans too) to truly love each other, to have happy, content and God-fearing children and to carve out a home that was free of turmoil and strife. And as idealistic as it might sound, I didn't feel it was a pipe dream. It was feasible and doable, I thoroughly believed, but only if the husband and wife were 'mindful of and 'obedient' to Christian doctrine and were on the same, exact page. I acutely realized it would require a liberal amount of compromise and sacrifice, but, then, most worthwhile endeavors in life called for those two, hand in glove principles. All I knew was that I had once glimpsed it during my teenage years. It was a memory of rare beauty.

CHAPTER THIRTY-NINE
A FRIENDSHIP BEYOND COMPARE

In the wake of a rather unorthodox incident that took place in late January of 1964, I had a strong inkling that Danny Williams and his spouse had a pretty good chance of having a successful, easy-going and enduring marriage. To their credit, I had never observed them arguing or bad-mouthing each other and it was crystal-clear to me that they mutually respected and sincerely liked each other.

Naturally, Val and Dan loved each other but, to me, love and like were always two, different entities. For example, I knew parents who loved their children, but beneath the surface, they staunchly disliked their offspring's contrary and nasty ways. That was applicable to husbands and wives as well.

However, Valerie appeared to truly like Danny and he seemed to genuinely be pleased with her benevolent ways as well. In my opinion, when they verbally communicated and joked around too, it was concrete evidence of their reciprocal admiration for one another. And although I never verbalized my heartfelt assessment, I sat back and savored every minute of it.

The "unorthodox incident" I priorly referenced came into play as a result of a somewhat bizarre and almost freakish weather development. After eating dinner with the Williams couple on a Saturday evening, the three of us retired to the adjacent living room. Dan and Val sat side-by-side on their rather smallish couch while I sat alone in an easy-chair and the three of us soon became totally absorbed in an in-progress movie on television.

In actuality, we were intending to watch an old James Cagney movie entitled 'The Roaring Twenties,' but when the ongoing film snared our attention, we were content with loaning our attention to it. As it turned out, it, too, was another Jimmy Cagney gangster flick which was called 'White Heat' and, soon, we were collectively delighted to learn that we were actually in the midst of a Cagney movie salute.

Upon taking the liberty to speak for my two married companions, we were all content and happy at that particular moment in time, and especially us two guys. As Valerie climbed to her feet and took the initiative to close the Venetian blinds at the nearby windows (due to the incoming, bright glare), Danny and I sat comfortably in our seats and indulged ourselves in the task of drinking our frosty beers.

After all, what could Dan and me possibly complain or gripe about? Thanks to Val, we had virtually stuffed ourselves at the kitchen table, we had a liberal supply of brew in the fridge and, to Danny's _exclusive_ joy, he had four or five marijuana joints on hand too. Although I had recently teased him by calling him a "down-and-out druggie," he grinningly replied, "Okay - I'll drink to that, Harris, and thanks for the compliment."

Of course, much of the foregoing was par for the course, not too different from most of my visits to the Williams off-post residence. But what was different and off-kilter as well, in addition to being one of the coldest days I had ever spent in the San Antonio region, was that it was <u>snowing</u> outside! It hardly ever snowed in San Antonio, Texas! And those words were reflective of my immediate feelings when, at 11 P.M. that night, I stood to my feet and proceeded to look out the kitchen window. Although it was high time for me to embark on my hike back to Fort Sam, I was instantly amazed!

"What the hell? Man, look at this crap!" I yelled, fixating on the snowfall.

Reacting to my outcry of surprise, Valerie soon aligned herself with my boisterous feelings. She had hurriedly walked over and reopened the blinds when she remarked, "Harris we're not gonna let you walk all the way back to the post in this stuff! No - no, not tonight! You're staying put, right here with us. Ain't that right, Danny?"

"Well, Baby, if Harris didn't have sense enough to bring his sled along with him," Dan kiddingly spoke, "then I guess it's cool with me. I guess I can put up with him for another few hours or so. Are you game for it, Harris?"

Even as I laughed, I kept my eyes trained on the heavy snowfall outdoors. I was momentarily speechless. Since neither I nor my two companions were San Antonio natives, we would not learn until the next day that it hadn't snowed in the San Antone region for nearly seven years, but for the time being, I was prolongedly shocked.

"This is crazy!" I marvelled, shaking my head. "I didn't think it ever snowed here, and especially not like this."

Apparently, both, Val and Dan were waiting on my reply to Danny's previous invitation. Still jovial, Danny went on to speak to his wife, saying, "The dude's as drunk as skunk, Honey. He probably couldn't safely find his way back to Fort Sam anyway, snow or no snow. All that beer! Don't worry, Babe, he's staying here with us tonight."

Flashing a smile, Valerie seemed pleased. "Okay, it's a done deal then," she said. "You two are about the same size. So, I'll grab you a pair of Danny's pajamas, Harris."

I was somewhat hesitant. I didn't want to put my friends out, be a pain or bother, and I was on the verge of objecting. Then, I reluctantly changed my mind. Although their small sofa looked more like a love seat or settee to me, I soon entertained a viable alternative. Hell - for a single night, I could camp out on the living room floor, I reasoned.

"Alright, Val," I said, resorting to a jovial mood myself, "but I do prefer the PJ's with the feet attached to them. You know - the ones that come with the matching teddy bear?"

"Harris, you are so darn crazy," Valerie replied, chuckling along with her spouse. "Honey, what are we gonna do with your ace-boon-coon?"

"I don't really know, Baby," was Danny's response, "but I'll think of something for the dude, with his jive-time self."

As Valerie started to walk away, I detained her for a moment, asking, "Val, if you've got a couple of extra pillows, I'd appreciate them. That'll make the couch a little more comfortable - and I'll borrow a chair from the kitchen."

Val froze in her tracks and frowned as if I had insulted her. "You're not hardly gonna sleep on the little, tiny sofa, Harris," she spoke. "We gotta large-sized bed in our bedroom and it's big enough for all three of us. We won't molest you or nothing, I promise. Will we, Honey-bunch?"

As my jaw dropped, Dan grinned sheepishly. "Well speak for yourself," he addressed his wife. "The dude's awfully damn cute and when he puts those pajamas on, the ones with the feet in 'em, he's gonna be hard to resist."

Although we all found ourselves laughing, Val practically guffawed. Finally, when she calmed herself, she addressed me, saying, "Pay him no never-mind, Harris. The very minute his little fat head hits the pillow, he'll be out like a turned off light bulb. Smokin' all that dope, I just hope you don't get a contact high. The boy's completely harmless, just as gentle as a little lamb."

Though I decided not to make a major issue of it, I wasn't at all comfortable with Valerie Williams' proposal. It was unheard of, bizarre and unorthodox! However, she was adamant about me not sacking out in the living room and so was her husband, Danny. They both behaved like it was commonplace for two guys and a girl to sleep in a bed together! But, shortly, after they double-teamed me and practically browbeat me too, I reluctantly gave in. I figured, since it was perfectly agreeable with the three of us, then nothing and no one (other than an omniscient Supreme Being) really mattered. And since our select actions were completely innocent, benevolent and free of ulterior motives as well, it was likely acceptable in the eyes of God Himself. In essence, it was no human, flesh and blood being's business but the applicable trio - meaning, us.

Well, in less than a half an hour's time, as Danny opted to lay between me and his wife, the three of us were quietly sleeping together in the Williams couple's large bed. And, within mere moments, I was able to take it all in casual stride. After all, I had always regarded myself as an individual with few inhibitions. Therefore, sharing a bed with a male and a female, void of sexual connotations attached to it, was right in line with my basic nature. And one thing was for sure, it was a notch better than my childhood days. That's when I slept in a rather small bed, lying alongside two or three of my biological brothers.

Quite typical of me, I woke up the next morning, refreshed, energetic and in an optimistic and playful mood. Except for a single trip to the washroom overnight (which was beer related), I had slept peacefully through the entire night, and so had my two bed mates. Valerie, who rose before, both, me and her husband, was in the kitchen and busily cooking an aromatic breakfast while Dan and I took turns washing up and getting dressed for the day.

Then, after checking the weather forecast on TV, we sat down to Val's sumptuous meal and engaged in light and frequently amusing conversation. Like I mentioned earlier, I woke up in a playful and silly mood. Therefore, a little while later, after I insisted upon washing the dishes, my innate sense of humor came to the surface. I was staunchly intent upon remaining straight-faced when I spoke.

"Man, I can hardly wait to tell people 'bout how we all slept together in the same bed last night," I spoke in feigned delight. "I mean - it was so darn ... romantic!"

Val and Danny cracked up in laughter, but it was Valerie who came forth with a response. "Boy, don't you tell anybody about that!" she grinningly warned me. "Harris, don't make me have to hurt you, boy!"

Dan was trying to stifle his mirth when he spoke to his still-chuckling wife. "Don't worry, Baby, he's only yanking our chain. He ain't gonna say nothing to nobody about it."

I displayed my best deadpan expression at that point. "What? Why?" I innocently quizzed. "Don't ya'll think people will understand? I mean - it was all perfectly normal, right? What's the problem?"

Val tried to be serious, addressing her husband. "Honey, should I punch him or should you?" she questioned. "He's your goofy friend."

Danny actually walked over to me and lightly smacked my face. "Be for real, dopey," he told me. "Boy, you keep your damn trap shut. People won't understand and you know damn-well they won't."

Still, I stayed in character. "Ouch!" I cried, rubbing my jaw. "Are you two suggesting that it's <u>not</u> commonly done, like it's abnormal or kinda weird or something? Like the other thing I say to Danny and he tells me I shouldn't say it in public?"

Despite Val's continuous smile, she was somewhat puzzled. "Now - what's he talking about, Honey Pot?" she asked her spouse.

Dan seemed momentarily embarrassed and I just loved teasing him. "Tell her," I coaxed him, before I went on to divulge what I was referring to. "Every now and then I tell him that I love him, and I do," I addressed Valerie. "I have always felt comfortable telling the people I love - exactly how I feel about them. But - do you know what his response always is, Val? With his crude, ghetto self?"

Detecting the look of discomfort on her husband's face, Valerie was practically in stitches when she jokingly answered my query. "That he dearly loves you too?" she guessed.

"I ain't said that lame-ass shit to him!" Dan immediately protested. "And you know it too, Baby!"

"Well - tell her what you <u>do</u> say," I inserted, agitating my buddy further. "Go on, tell her! What is your classic response?"

As his wife stared at Dan, eagerly awaiting his reply, I, too, faced him down. Finally, he said, "Well, I tell Harris - don't love me, just like me. Love leads to screwing and he ain't gonna screw me. And I mean that, Baby!"

Val was unmistakenly sincere when she spoke. "Aw, Danny, that's not nice," she scolded her mate. "Shame on you! Harris, he does love you, talks about you all the time. 'Harris this, Harris that!' Danny, I'm surprised of you."

My good friend seemed flustered, and momentarily at a loss for words. Then, he spoke, singling out his wife. "Honey, you know I dig the dude, and to the very max," he said. "But I ain't gonna tell him I love him! How does that crap sound, coming out of the mouth of another hard leg? We ain't a couple of punks or flamin' fairies!"

Actually, I was at my taunting best, showcasing an expression of fake dejection and knowing all the while it would garner me a degree of sympathy from Val. It worked too, hearing what she said to Dan next.

"Honey-Pots, you shouldn't be ashamed of your heart feelings for Harris," she softly insisted. "And it doesn't make you a punk neither. I think it's kinda sweet, the way you guys feel towards each other."

My comrade glanced hopelessly up at the ceiling, more befuddled than ever. "Valerie, Harris knows damn-well I love him," he argued. "I just ... just say it in a different way, that's all. Like - when I tell him, 'You're my nigga, even if you don't git any bigger.' That's letting Harris know how I honestly feel about him."

Now, I grinningly perked up. "Aw, I git it now," I injected. "It's like when the white folks speak to lowly black folks in the deep south, right? Hey, nigga, fetch me a cold, glass of lemonade. Nigga, bend over and let me kick you in the backside. Lord knows I loves you dearly, my nigga. Is that what you mean, Danny? I mean - <u>nigga</u> is such a loving and endearing word."

Both, my buddy and his wife laughed for almost a minute, and so did I. Then, as Dan collected his composure, he kiddingly demanded, "Harris, git the hell outta my house! Boy, you ain't nothing but a damn shit-disturber! Comin' in here and causing confusion in me and baby's happy home. And I hope like hell you fall down in the damn snow on the way back to Fort Sam."

"Well, no matter what you say, fella," I playfully retorted, returning to the task of washing the breakfast dishes, "I still happen to love you, and that applies to you too, Val."

"And no matter what my honey says, Harris," Valerie replied, "we feel the same way about you, <u>both</u> of us."

Again, Dan sought out the ceiling. "Give me a damn break," he remarked. "I think I'm gonna come down with diabetes behind all this sugary crap."

"Well, I think it's kinda sweet, sugar or not, Baby," Valerie addressed her husband. "Pay Danny no never-mind, Harris, 'cause he doesn't mean it. Now, tell Harris you're just kidding around, Honey."

"Aw - Jesus, Val!"

In actuality, five hours would go by before I finally made my exit from the Williams residence on the particular Sunday I elected to recollect. However, just as the familiar saying goes, "All good things must come to an end" and it was high-time for me to return to my military home, which was a barracks at Fort Sam Houston. However, after rendering farewell embraces to, both, Danny and Valerie, my sense of humor instantly resurfaced. I was standing at the front door's threshold when I remembered a remark Dan had made that very morning.

"Oh - by the way," I spoke, cracking the door open. "Earlier this morning, Daniel Williams, when we were in the heat of our dispute, and you so coldly and boldly ordered me out of your house, I want you to know something."

"Uh-oh - here we go," Danny uttered as he and Val stood together, anticipating my punchline.

"I just wanted you to know," I continued my parting statement, "that I have been thrown out of many houses before, but none near 'bout this small. That has no reflection on you, Val - just my <u>nigga</u> there."

Even as he and his wife surrendered to laughter, Danny still mustered up a reply. "Boy, git the hell outta here - and right now!" he shouted.

"Yes, Sir, I am on my way. Thanks for a wonderful, enjoyable couple of days - both of you. And I still love you two."

"We enjoyed your company too, Harris," Val replied, "and you come back real soon. You hear?"

Throughout my somewhat chilly and rather gingerly hike back to post (I slipped several times in the snow), I was heartened by an almost surreal and soothing warmth inside of me. Spending the last 24 hours with the Williams couple made me exceptionally happy for them. They truly enjoyed one another's company, and although that seemed like a small and insignificant factor to others, in my personal feelings, it was vital to a strong and long-lasting marriage.

Thinking back, I had once coined a phrase from a biblical passage, and although it made people laugh, I was actually dead-serious about it. I said, "Man does not live by <u>bed</u> alone," but, unfortunately, a whole lot of people (and especially young people) held contrary views. Sexual gratification seemed to be at the forefront of far too many marital unions and, even as a virgin sitting on the sidelines, I couldn't imagine it sustaining an authentic, joyous and well-entrenched marriage.

Just being aware that Danny and Valerie thoroughly and unequivocally liked each other and relished one another's company, I was more than hopeful that their union would thrive and prolongedly last. To me, it was a marriage made in heaven!

CHAPTER FORTY

THE SAME OLD STORY

Although their obstetrician had told Angie and Tommy Preston that their baby would be born during the first part of April 1964 (somewhere around my birthday on the 3rd of that month), the doctor forgot to talk it over with the child involved. Thomas Preston Jr., weighing in at seven pounds and two ounces, made his grand debut on the world stage on March 17th, 1964. He was born at Brooke General Hospital after his mother was in labor for a whopping 12 hours.

Now, I don't know how Angela looked after the lengthy ordeal, but Tommy, on the other hand, was a complete mess! Every time I sought him out in the maternity waiting room (which was quite regularly), he looked like he had gone numerous rounds with boxing heavyweight, Sonny Liston. Severe worriment and the long and tedious waiting period had taken a mental and physical toll on the expectant father. Then, thankfully, the baby cooperated. The little guy came forth and everything was swell and dandy.

Personally, I fell in love with 'little' Tommy from the very second I saw him. He had beautiful ebony hair, sparkling brown eyes, a winning smile and was endowed with the attractive features of both proud parents.

I immediately complimented the couple on "a job well-done" and then made them laugh as I took the liberty to methodically check their infant's tiny hands and feet. I, then, addressed their shared wonder, informing them that I was emulating my own, biological dad. I was just making sure Tommy Jr. had all of his toes and fingers, I told them.

"But why, Barry?" Angie asked me.

Exhibiting a serious expression, but intent upon pulling the legs of the new parents, I quickly lied, alleging that my old man had actually left a couple of his babies in the maternity ward, solely because the newborns had failed his 'digital' examination.

Of course, Tommy instantly frowned, knowing I was fibbing, but Angie (lying in bed), apparently believed me. "Why would your father do such a thing, Barry?" she asked. "That's awful!"

As Tommy remained silent, I playfully pushed the envelope even farther. Speaking directly to Angie, I went on to explain, "Well, to my dad the baby would be an out-and-out fraud. I mean - the kid could be the spitting image of my old man, but if all of his little fingers and toes weren't intact, then it was like 'So long, been good to know you.' You see, Ang', my dad was very judgmental and conceited. To him, Harris babies, especially his kids, had to be absolutely perfect and physically fit and formed too. You know - like me?"

Shaking his head and laughing as well, Tommy had heard enough. Plus, I was on the verge of chuckling too. "Don't listen to him, Angie, he's just putting us on," he informed his wife. "Leaving a baby in a maternity ward. Barry, you oughta quit it!"

Angie also gave into laughter at that juncture, finally realizing I was just funning. "Barry, you really had me fooled," she announced. "Had me feeling sorry for you! I'm gonna stop believing anything you tell me!"

Actually, I wasn't quite through joking around. "Hey - don't be like that, Angie," I pleaded. "Once in a blue moon, I sometimes tell the truth. And don't waste your sympathy on me, I was lucky enough to pass my old man's test. Feel sorry my little brothers in the maternity wards. Hell - they're still there as we speak!"

At the conclusion of my absurd joviality and lying, all three of us (Tommy, Angela and me) were in a state of serene mirth. Our behavior was evidence of our shared inner feelings.

Although I poked fun at my father's yesteryear antics, his <u>real-life</u> habit of actively examining his newborn offsprings, I, along with the new daddy and mommy, were thankful that little Tommy was, seemingly, born unimpaired and healthy. In my viewpoint, there were far too many novel parents who were nonchalant and unimpressed that their offsprings were born without any physical or mental maladies.

As I stood inside Angie's hospital room, observing the doting parents and feasting my eyes on their beautiful little baby, I was totally heartened that Tommy and Angie, both, were aligned with my feelings. Quiet as kept, that was the underlying moral of my rather goof-ball story about my father.

Although I'm sure it's apparent by now, but I dearly and emphatically relished the memorable and wholesome times that I spent with the diverse array of people I came to love while in the military. However, in spite of virtually coercing those special folks to frequently laugh 'with' and 'at' me, I could not detach myself from a troubled and increasingly-dangerous world.

My most intimate confidants and loved ones (my family in St. Louis, in San Antonio, Texas and elsewhere) were faring relatively well during the early months of 1964, but I certainly knew better than to let my guards down. Practically shell-shocked by the catastrophic events of the previous year, I could not help fearing the calm before the storm. As my mother often said, "There's always something to take the spice out of life," and I was geared to cope with whatever it might be.

Though it might sound as if I was walking on the outskirts of pessimism and paranoia, my state of impending peril was not at all groundless. Keeping aware of the daily news, I was aware of apartheid in South Africa and the continuous racial atrocities in southern America.

In retrospect, 1964 was the year when Nelson Mandela was imprisoned in his native homeland (which, of course, was South Africa) and when southern United States senators filibusted the proposed civil rights bill in America. Also, it was the year when President Lyndon B. Johnson launched his so-called 'War on Poverty,' when Surgeon General Luther Terry released a report that directly linked cigarette smoking to cancer and other serious illnesses and when an earthquake measuring 8.4 on the Richter scale struck the state of Alaska.

However, in spite of anything and everything else that occurred throughout the entire world during 1964, what concerned me most (as a soldier in the army and a citizen too) was America's increasing involvement in the affairs of a Southeast Asian country named Vietnam. Personally, since this country seemed to be incapable of coping with its own age-old and deeply-rooted racial problems, who the hell were we to try to 'right' the 'wrongs' of a faraway, foreign nation? Furthermore, since the targeted country was filled with 'people of color,' I was acutely wary of America's sincerity. Therefore, I foresaw disaster in the making, and all in the name of a flimsy, deceitful and nefarious motive.

Meanwhile, in the immediate world around me, I was intent upon being reasonably content and happy. With a bevy of devoted friends in my life and a job that kept me busy and self-satisfied, my spirits were mostly high and I did my level best to uplift the morale of practically everyone around me. Incidentally, in the spring of 1964, when taxing field maneuvers were again sprinkled in with my standard work routine at the Registrar's office, that select everyone grew to include such individuals as second lieutenants, Rand Morrison and James Sanders and Staff-Sgt. Harold Kurn as well.

From day number one, when it came to my relationship with Harold Kurn (who, again, happened to be my barracks sergeant), I found myself recalling a well-known line from the 1940s movie 'Casablanca,' which starred Humphrey Bogart. In verbatim, the line was, "This may be the beginning of a beautiful friendship" and, eventually, our alliance proceeded to be just that. Working in close concert with Staff-Sgt. Kurn (who was officially my field supervisor), I was allocated the necessary latitude and leverage to set-up and run an outdoors 'Admission and Disposition' facility (A&D), along with an adjacent and supportive 'Registrar's office' as I personally saw fit.

And owing to my formal school training, paired with a hodgepodge of innovations and precepts I had honed while soldiering in my former field outfit (the 24th Evac. Hospital) and during my ongoing apprenticeship at the on-post Registrar as well, I felt confident and more than adequate upon tackling and handling any administrative problem that prevailed. And thanks to the work assistance from 2nd lieutenants Sanders and Morrison (in spite of me being a mere enlisted man, they graciously performed under my tutelage), it was an operation of sheer beauty! Admittedly, that was my rather spirited assessment, although I wasn't braggadocious or cocky enough to share it with my three Caucasian team members.

When it came to the 'race' issue (and whether we admit it or not, it is always an issue), I felt the jury was still deliberating when it came to my two officer pupils, but I viewed Sgt. Harold Kurn differently. Since he was middle-aged and had southern roots (he was from Atlanta, Georgia), I originally expected it would be 'the same soup warmed over.' Was I guilty of stereotyping? YES!

To be perfectly frank, Harold Kurn was the first adult white man whom I came to respect, admire and trust. He did not come across as the least bit racially prejudiced. In the field and out of it he treated me with professional courtesy and esteem. He praised me for my efforts during field ventures, valued me for my input and opinions therein, and, in a short while, seemed in total awe of my growing and almost endearing relationship with the lieutenant duo.

The latter realization became evident to me when the end of March came around and Sgt. Kurn had recently learned that I had been awarded a couple of 'letters of commendation' from the officer pair. Practically smiling from ear to ear, the sarge teasingly complimented me in regards to those written documents.

"Young fella, I'm hoping to be just like you when I grow up," he remarked. "To Lieutenants Morrison and Sanders, you are like the second coming of Christ! Those two young officers practically set horses by you! But you well-deserve their praise and admiration, and I've got to admit that."

I can't pinpoint the reason why, but I've always felt uncomfortable when people complimented me. "Come on, Sarge, I just believe in doing my job, and the best way I know how," I responded. "What's that old saying? 'A job that's worth doing, is a job worth doing well?' My mother drummed that into me and my brothers too. Plus, our lieutenant buddies are easily impressed. What can I say?"

"You're a modest little devil," Kurn remarked, still grinning. "I'll say that much for you. But you've got a great future ahead of you, young man. You oughta seriously think about making a career of it - because you got what it takes. You're a natural born soldier, Harris, you are."

―⁂―

While I was sincerely appreciative of Harold Kurn's faith in me, I never, ever pictured myself as a career military person. Since I was still signed up for a forty-dollar allotment, my monthly salary was less than two hundred dollars per pay period and I knew I could earn much more than that when I rejoined civilian life.

However, I never shared the foregoing narrative with my sergeant friend. My dear mother had always encouraged me to "never say never," so I wasn't about to turn thumbs-down on the sarge's suggestion. For I knew he meant well and I wasn't about to hurt his feelings or dash his hopes in any degree. Harold Kurn had almost ten years under his military belt, he had travelled to a slew of foreign shores (in fact, he was married to a Japanese woman) and his eyes practically sparkled when he talked about his immediate family. In essence, he was apparently happy and content.

Admittedly, most of the sergeant's re-enlistment rhetoric fell on deaf ears when it came to me. In addition to my too-frequent skirmishes with classic racism, I never really had a desire to go overseas (and that 'really' applied to my transfer to South Korea) and if field exercises would emerge commonplace to my suggested army career, I would have preferred to dig ditches or work in a coal mine instead.

However, when Staff-Sgt. Kurn casually invited me to have dinner at his off-post home, I came face-to-face to the authentic source of his surface and inner joy. He had a devoted and beautiful wife named 'Myoshi' and two of the cutest, well-mannered and adorable little kids I had ever laid my eyes on. The seven-year-old boy's name was 'Cornel' and his baby sister, 'Marla,' was but four.

After spending less than two hours with the Harold Kurn family, I silently retracted a thought I had previously had. Taking the liberty to imagine myself in the position of my noncom friend, I was quite positive that even I would be able to withstand the most strenuous and most aggravating field trek, and in the remotest locale - <u>if</u>, at the conclusion of the field outing, I would have a comparable and loving family awaiting me on my home front. Although the sarge never verbalized it to me, I truly believed the key to his ever-present good cheer, optimism and upbeat attitude was none other than his intimate family.

Myoshi Kurn was strikingly attractive and that, to me, was undisputable. And the children, with their Asian features, were as beautiful as a picture on a Hallmark card. But their physical attractiveness, all three of them, took a far second place to their individual conduct and actions. The sergeant's spouse seemed to have the greatest love and respect for her husband and while, both, Marla and Cornel clearly adored their dad, they relished his mere presence. Without being the least bit subservient or condescending, the trio appeared to collectively have a single goal at heart. From the moment Kurn entered the dwelling, they sought to please and cordially interact with him.

Whenever I went home with the sergeant (which grew to be almost twice monthly), I felt joyous and exhilarated in just being in Kurn's company. Seemingly, the guy was in his supreme comfort zone (his personal Seventh Heaven) and I was absolutely thrilled for him.

Just from being a guest in the Harold Kurn residence, I was treated almost royally myself but, upon observing the man of the house himself, I was truly envious of the sarge. Love and serenity was virtually at his fingertips and I could almost feel it.

In looking back to my high school years, the Kurn alliance was reminiscent of the marital union enjoyed by John and Florida Harris (Charles and Robert's mother and father) and that was exclusive and high praise in my book. And in spite of being on the outside-looking-in, it was my sincere hope and prayerful desire that the unions between Daniel and Valerie Williams and the one involving Thomas and Angela Preston as well, would, in so many exemplary ways, be similar in context and longevity too. In reality, I wanted something for my endeared married friends that I dreamed of, someday, having for myself also.

Even as I entered into a third close-knit friend relationship with a married couple, I still spent a lot of meaningful and quality time with my other cherished and intimate companions. Though I considered it to be just another day, Danny and Tommy made a big deal of my 20th birthday. A few days prior to it I had received a mailed gift from my mother and a nice card and letter from Jerome, but on the specific day itself, which was April 3rd, I was treated to lunch by Tommy and to a delicious dinner in the evening at the home of Dan and Val Williams.

While I appreciated all of their efforts and gestures (from my mom to my friends), there was a single and memorable birthday card that deeply impacted and touched my heart that day. The card was given to me by Tommy during our luncheon session and he pointedly told me he purchased it, specifically with me in mind. We had just finished eating our meal at the time and he insisted that I read it, right then and there.

Although the birthday card wasn't expensive, it struck a meaningful chord in me. It simply read, "I know a certain person - who's as nice as he can be. He's always nice to everyone, but especially nice to me." Then, at the bottom of the card it was signed, 'I love you, Barry. Your friend always - and a day, Tommy."

At that moment in time, I looked over at my comrade in solemn gratitude and he rather anxiously posed a query to me. "Whatchu think?" he asked. "Is it too darn dopey, or sentimental? Unmanly, maybe? Ang - she thought it was just right, appropriate. You know, for our special friendship?"

Since I was deeply touched, I was only able to halfway smile. I was trying to address Tommy's anxiousness in regards to the endearing words on the card when I said, "When I was a youngster, just a young boy, I ran across a poem. And it instantly hit home with me, and so much so that I went on to memorize it."

I froze for a moment, concentrating on what was in my heart. "I still recall till this very day what that poem said," I went on. "It was written by a fellow named Edwin Arlington Robinson, and it goes like this: 'I wish that I had known him then - that friend of mine. I did not even show him then - one friendly sign. But cursed him for the ways he had - to make me see - my envy of the praise he had ... for praising me. I would have rid the earth of him - once in my pride. I did not know the worth of him ... until he died.' And - that's it, Tommy."

My dear friend stared at me momentarily, then said, "That is so - so beautiful, Barry. It's really deep and meaningful."

I nodded my head affirmatively, thoroughly in agreement with Tommy's reply. "The name of that poem is "The Same Old Story," I told him. "Unfortunately, some people live an entire lifetime, failing to tell people how they truly feel about them. And oftentimes, <u>far</u> too many times, they wait until it's too late. Their loved one will be lying dead in a coffin, and they regret not saying three, little, simple words to them. 'I love you.' And that's why I often tell you, and Danny too, that I dearly love you guys. People like to say, 'Here today, gone tomorrow,' but like JFK last year, it's sometimes, "Here today, gone today.' I don't wanna ever come up short, Tommy. I don't care about what other people think - but I'm going to always let my loved ones know where they stand with me, always."

"And that's damn good advice, Barry," Tommy remarked, "and I totally agree with you."

Almost teary-eyed, I purposely held my birthday card up at that juncture. "Just like that poem I recited, I will always remember the wonderful words on here too," I vowed. "Because I think they kind of define me. I long to have people think of me like this, I crave it in fact, and especially when it comes to you, Tommy. I thank the living God for ushering you into my life, I do, because He wasn't <u>compelled</u> to do so. And I'll always be nice to you, and I'll always love you too."

Upon being somewhat misty-eyed himself, my dear comrade tried to flash a smile. "Hell's-bells, Barry!" he spoke. "You're about to make me lose my grip. But happy 20th birthday, guy. And like my card says, I love you very much too."

CHAPTER FORTY-ONE

A BIT OF MOTHER-WIT

"If you'll love my dog, then I'll love your cat."

Although I pride myself for having an exceptional memory, I have to confess that I do not know when or where I first heard the foregoing quote (or even who originally coined it), but I heartily agree with its basic premise. I've always put a great amount of stock in compromise and reciprocal fairness.

In homage to that viewpoint, since Tommy Preston was cordial, nice and respectful to Danny Williams, I was obliged to treat Tom's close-knit buddy, Mario Moran, likewise. That was the only way to go in my estimation.

To be precise, I had met and had interacted with Mario even before Tommy started 'dating' Angela Mendoza. At that time, I was still soldiering in the 24th Evacuation Hospital and my Cuban comrade, like Tommy, was assigned to 250th General. It was during the time, also, when the three of us, me, Tom and Mario, enjoyed the motion pictures 'The Outsider' and 'West Side Story' together at the main-post theatre.

In truth, I would have liked Mario Moran regardless of the 'dog-cat' analogy. He was always cordial and friendly towards me, he liked to laugh and joke around (which was right up my alley) and he could take what he teasingly dished out. For instance, when he elected to call me "Barrel" instead of Barry, I playfully countered by referring to him as "Ricky Ricardo" from the long-running 'I Love Lucy' TV sit-com. (In recollection, Ricky Ricardo was the Cuban bandleader played by Desi Arnaz on that show). Additionally, he was an avid beer-drinker like me and Tommy too. So, all and all we were a congenial trio when we hung out.

However, as the months passed by and, both, Tommy and Mario became almost preoccupied with the female gender (I was happy and content, sitting on the sidelines), I began to see a different side of Mario, and a side that wasn't very admirable. My mother had occasionally told me I was blessed with "mother wit," an inborn insight that was way beyond my young years, and whether she was right or wrong about her analysis, I even considered myself to be a keen observer but I wasn't so sure that my discernment was a genuine <u>blessing</u>.

Ever so often, when I was in the presence of Mario and Tommy's lawfully-wedded wife, who was Angie, I came to feel somewhat uneasy and awkward. However, my underlying feelings (and I kept them to myself for quite a spell) were not based on anything that was overt and tangible. It wasn't so much of what the pair said or did to each other, but was, moreso, how they <u>looked</u> at each other.

But what was so alarming to me, even after Mario had taken a bride himself (Kathy) and Angie had become a mother herself, the covert attraction between the duo still continued. In my heart, I truly believed Angie dearly loved her husband and vice versa, but I suspected that Mario lusted for Angie and vice versa too. Sorrowfully, it was like a merry-go-round, but one without Kathy being aboard it.

In spite of being practically all bottled up inside, I was adamant about keeping my silence and I hoped and prayed that

I would, eventually, be proven wrong about my sideline assessment as well. Down deep though, I knew I was right but I thought that, maybe, Angie and Mario would, somehow or someway, denounce or overcome their mutual attraction or, in my opinion, come to their moral senses.

Soon, however, I managed to come to my senses and back to the real world also. Nothing benevolent or miraculous was going to transpire, so I decided to 'horn-in' and tackle the problem 'head-on.' After shying away from speaking to, both, Angie and Mario, I persuaded myself to have a private, man-to-man discussion with my dear friend, Tommy. After all, he was the select individual whom I dreaded being hurt in the matter.

"Tommy, I don't wanna be what some people call a 'shit-disturber' or a trouble-maker," I announced, opening up our conversation, "and, believe me, kiddo, I've thought long and hard about this. Even prayed on it. But, Tommy, you need to keep a watchful eye on our friend Mario, and especially when it comes to Angie. Something's not right between them."

My cohort was immediately hurt and I felt awful detecting it on his face. "Barry - Barry, come on buddy," he spoke. "Ang' and Mario just like kidding around with each other, but they don't mean nothing by it. They don't mean me no harm, not at my expense. Look - Angie's my wife and she loves me friggin' to death. And Mario - he's like a brother to me, just like you. Barry, you don't have to worry about Mario. 'Cause you're more special to me, and I love you much more."

"Tommy, I'm not jealous of Mario Moran," I frowningly responded. "And that's not where I'm coming from, it's not. I'm only saying, telling you to be . . . to be more aware of how he acts around your wife. Tommy, all people are not morally good, or on the up and up. I might be all wet about Mario, might be reading him completely wrong! But I've seen far too much, Tommy, too much deceit and ugliness. And I hope I'm being ridiculous, being a hundred percent wrong! I just don't wanna see you hurt, that's all."

My friend displayed a smile at that moment. "Barry, it is so wonderful to have a friend, and a friend who truly cares about you," he marvelled. "But don't waste your energy worrying about Mario Moran. He's a born flirt, I give that to you, but he thinks of Angie as a sister, nothing more."

Tommy could see I was unconvinced, so he spoke further, saying, "Plus, Kathy's got his number and keeps an eagle-eye on Mario. Besides, Barry, I'm as cute as a button, and the apple of my wife's eye. My honey is absolutely crazy about me!"

Now, I surrendered to mirth. "Well, maybe, Angie's in dire need of a pair of strong bifocals," I joked, "but all I see is a conceited young guy with a large, apple head. And, maybe, since Angie's <u>crazy</u> about you - she's also in dire need of a shrink too."

Tommy sat, laughing at that point. "Now that's the Barry I've come to know and love," he responded, before turning serious again. "But don't give Mario a second thought, Barry," he added. "Mario values friendship too, just like you and me."

I nodded, sincerely hoping my friend was correct. "No matter how I come off here, Tommy," I offered, "I happen to like Mario Moran a lot, and I feel he genuinely likes me too."

"He does, Barry," Tommy insisted, "he thinks the world and all of you - respects you too."

Once again, I nodded. "I'm in no way jealous of him," I inserted, "and, believe me, I would love for you two guys to remain the closest of friends forever and a day and just like me and you. And I mean it, Tommy."

With God as my witness, I was being absolutely honest and candid when I pushed myself to speak to Tommy Preston in regards to his wife, Angie, and his close-knit buddy Marion Moran. I truly believed there was something off-kilter with the ongoing relationship between Angie and Mario. Otherwise, I would have continued to keep my feelings tightly under wraps.

I didn't extract comfort or a single ounce of pleasure from casting aspersions on either one of them (both, Mario or Angie), and especially when it meant causing emotional pain or anguish to Tommy. And it wasn't my intent to damage the relationship between Mario and Tommy either. However, when one visualizes an impending disaster on the horizon for an endeared loved one, then what should the caring observer do? Right or wrong, I was desirous of averting a problem.

In the aftermath of the frank discussion I had with my pal, Tommy, about the situation, I was quite sincere when I issued my final remarks. If my suspicions did prove to be groundless and misunderstood, I truly wanted all of our relationships to remain close and intact for many years to come. Goes without saying, I was never one who took friendship lightly or for granted.

Although it's much easier said than done, I took pride in not uttering cross or negative words to people I associated with on a daily basis. In fact, I never wanted to rain on the parade of <u>any</u> person, or even dampen their spirits. I figured that if an individual was already having a lousy or trying day before interacting with me, why should I say or do something that would make their day even worse? With that engrained mindset, I was definitely my mother's child. Ruby often preached, "If you can't say something nice, then don't say anything at all," and I bought into it lock, stock and barrel.

I knew in the eye sights of some folks around me, I was regarded as a rather rational, straight-laced and easy going young black man; a soldier who embraced certain morals and, sometimes, voiced strong opinions, but wasn't obsessed with implanting them into others. I spoke in earnest when I was asked my viewpoint, I didn't believe in sugar-coating a response, but I was bent on practicing restraint and civility, and even when someone managed to get on my bad side.

Sometimes, I would get upset and become disenchanted with individuals. However, my anger was momentarily fleeting. I thoroughly believed that ill-feelings, begrudgment and spite are a waste of precious time and energy. Plus, those strong feelings take a mental and physical toll on the person whose harboring them.

Significantly, the foregoing rhetoric happened to be my personal sentiments whenever my longtime associate and fellow poker player, Specialist 5 Ogelthorp, came to mind. Well after I had been on hand to 'bust' the noncom at Danny William's off-post home (when he paid a sneak visit to my dear friend's wife), I still could not bring myself to disdain and begrudge the man. To be honest, I knew far too many men who were like him, but still I distrusted and remained wary of the specialist.

More relevant though, Ogelthorp still owed me a sizable amount of money (to be exact, $247.85) and even in being cordial and civil towards him, I would occasionally ask him about it. But my requests were never fruitful. Although the noncom never became miffed or smart aleky either, he came up with every flimsy and asinine excuse under the sun, anything to put me off.

Well, in June of 1964, a whole six months after I had 'foolishly' made that loan to the specialist, I had all but decided to just write-off the debt as a lost cause. I figured that unless I caught up with Ogelthorp during a poker game and put a pistol to his head, my money was 'long-gone Chicago' or 'Gone with the Wind.' But, unexpectedly, something occurred that completely altered my resolve.

During the very last Friday in the month of June '64, I decided to just look-in on the traditional poker game that took place in the 24th Evacuation compound and that's when a certain opportunity presented itself.

After confessing to the assembled gambling party (of course, Ogelthorp was amongst them) that I was "broke, busted and disgusted" and was there only as a spectator, the noncom pitched me a legitimate and enticing proposal. He offered me a one-time job, and one that was directly connected to his part-time position at the off-post cleaning facility where he worked. In essence, if I agreed to indulge him in the matter, he promised he would pay me a sum of thirty dollars.

The specialist had a handful of printed-up laundry and dry cleaning bills in his possession and he opted to hire me, instructing me to go to a variety of surrounding companies (MTC, Ameds, the Wac Detachment, 250th General, etc.) and collect the money that was due on them. Then, he methodically schooled me on how to write up the receipts and how to record partial payments, and assured me that my entire foot-journey was within a four or five block radius of the 24th Evac. complex.

However, before I embarked upon my mission, my temporary employer seemed determined to say something specifically to me. As his fellow poker opponents sat in silence, rather anxiously waiting for the card contest to resume, Ogelthorp spoke with a candor that caught me by complete surprise.

"I don't mind telling you, Harry," he stated, "I cain't think of another soldier on this post, not even in the state of Texas - for that matter, no other dude I would even think of hirin' 'em to do this for me. I've always admired you, Harry - for your honesty and your integrity. Ain't many splivs like you. And like your buddy Williams said, 'They broke the fuckin' mold when they made your ass.' I ain't kidding."

Although my noncom associate sounded sincere, I wasn't sure he was. Regardless, I felt uneasy in light of his praise. That's why I jokingly said, "Just remember those words when I ask you for a job reference, boss."

Despite of being appreciative of Ogelthorp's stellar and unexpected compliments, I have to admit something. From the moment I committed myself to the short-term proposition, I had ulterior motives. From the very second the specialist placed the idea on the table, my mind was spinning with possibilities. Since there was so much money involved in the venture (and that was apparent to me, looking at the thickness of the stack of paper bills), I saw a chance to recoup most of the money that Ogelthorp had owed me for so long. From the get-go, I realized I was considering something that was a taste underhanded, but I was able to rationalize my actions anyhow. To me, there were major wrongs and minor wrongs, large sins and small sins, and I figured I could withstand whatever repercussions that would come my way. It's funny how you think and justify your actions when you're relatively young and, in my case, hurting for money.

At any event though, I craftily pulled off my scheme. I was holding over twenty-eight hundred dollars and carbon copies of all the 'paid' bills after completing my long foot-pilgrimage. That's when I extracted a wad of the carbon copy bills from the original stack (bills that added up to $240.00), carefully ripped them up and proceeded to count out the two hundred and forty bucks. At that time, I pocketed the specified sum and then returned to the site of the ongoing poker game.

Actually, marked guilt was already tugging at my conscience when I stood in front of Ogelthorp but when it became clear to me that the specialist was winning, and winning big, I was able to pep up somewhat. However, I would always wonder <u>if</u> Spec. 5 Ogelthorp would have been badly losing upon my return, would I have felt any different about my deceit? Who knows? Maybe, I could have retreated to, yet, another rationalization.

As it went that evening, Ogelthorp asked me if I had run into any problems and I replied, "No." Then, I handed him the money, along with the remaining copies of the bills, and he bowed out of the poker game to take the time to count up the cash I had collected for him.

The noncom was one of those individuals who liked to lick his thumb prior to counting money and I stood by patiently as he went through his figuring routine. As he completed his count, he frowned and soon embarked on a second count. Meanwhile, I stood idly by, calmly waiting with a bland expression on my face.

"Harry, old-buddy, are you sure this is right?" he asked, scratching his head. "Seems a little short to me."

Being a veteran movie-watcher, I knew exactly how to effectively act <u>indignant</u> and <u>insulted</u>. "Look, Ogelthorp, if you didn't trust me, man," I resentfully cried, "then you shouldn't have asked me to do a favor for you! I don't need this! If you don't wanna pay me, guy, just keep it and we don't have to deal with each other - ever again!"

"Simmer down, Harry, we ain't gonna be like that, Bro," the specialist responded, practically apologizing. "We ain't gonna fall out, not over a few bucks. Here - here's that thirty bucks I promised you, and I appreciate it, buddy. We alright? Hey - we ain't got no problem, Harry."

As I continued my 'Oscar' winning performance, the academy would have been proud of me. I pretended to be reluctant and hesitant when I accepted the thirty dollars. I took it, saying, "Yeah - we're alright, Ogelthorp. We're cool, no sweat."

Although my noncom benefactor invited me to "try my luck at the poker table," I promptly declined his offer. There was no way my conscience would allow me to do such a thing. To sit down with a man whom I had just 'swindled' (and that's how I actually regarded my actions) and behave in a normal fashion, was not in my make-up. My acting skills weren't that great, I figured.

Therefore, I left the site of the in-progress poker contest that evening, feeling guilty as hell! Believe it or not, the money I gained from that slick, deceptive venture wasn't at all worth the resultant mental anguish I incurred. However, the distinct lesson I learned from the happening was worth a truckload of money to me. In many respects, I alternately concluded, justice isn't always just, pay-back is not always fair and satisfying and rationalization can lead a person astray and leave them feeling guilty and tainted as well. Then, when I recalled hearing my mother saying, "Two wrongs don't make a right," my regret increased two-fold. Of course, I was grinningly able to rationalize my mom's wisdom at that juncture: Sometimes, the woman talked too much!

CHAPTER FORTY-TWO

THE WINDS OF CHANGE

Even in the throes of mentally berating myself in the short aftermath of the Ogelthorp deception scheme, my personal life did not grant me an uplifting refuge or any degree of salvation. On the contrary, it took a sudden and spiraling nosedive, and one that caught me by complete surprise. Although Valerie Williams was due to have her baby in just a matter of weeks, she firmly decided to return to her native home to give birth. And prior to the 4th of July holiday, Val was back in Detroit, Michigan and her husband, Danny, was, again, residing on post.

It seemed like a rather rushed and on-the-spot decision to me but I was, more or less, a minor spectator. And since Danny appeared to be perfectly on board with the idea, I kept my curiosity at bay. William Shakespeare was famed for writing the words "parting is such sweet sorrow," but, in my deep gloom, I found myself agreeing with a rationale that was once voiced by my former running buddy, Nathaniel Johnson. Nate often said "All goodbyes are not good and many farewells are not fair," and that's how I felt when I shared a final embrace with Valerie. Of course, when it came to my surrogate 'sister,' it wasn't a novel feeling for me. All of my young life, I sorely detested saying so-long to people I dearly loved.

As the summer months of 1964 practically flew by and ushered in the autumn season, despite of Valerie Williams' rather abrupt departure, I still spent a great deal of my leisurely hours and free time (especially weekends) with select married couples, and that included the Moran-Lester union. Notably though, Kathy and Mario would be frequent guests at the Preston residence when I interacted with them.

Without a doubt, I have always prided myself as a habitual or serial 'hugger,' an individual who is almost obsessed with uninhibitedly embracing fellow human beings, and especially people whom I'm truly fond of. And since I've always been totally daffy when it comes to miniature people (meaning children), I was virtually in a state of pure ecstasy when I visited, both, the Preston and Kurn residences.

In those two households I was granted the precious opportunity to prolongedly hold and cuddle a tiny arm-baby called 'little Tommy' on one day and, on a different day, to engage in an array of playful antics with Cornel and Marla Kurn. And, therein, I'd hug those kiddoes also, fully aware they would happily reciprocate my affection. And through it all, regardless of the respective parents who were on-hand, they, too, seemed in joyful harmony with my actions. Unbeknownst to them, their onlooking smiles heightened my feeling o euphoria. In the words of a song I had heard, "little things mean a lot" and those words were descriptive of the times I spent with the Kurn and Preston families.

When it came to my other prized and beloved comrade (who, of course, was Danny Williams), I realized there was a real void in his life after his wife moved back to Detroit at the beginning of July. I knew I didn't fit the bill as a substitute for his spouse (Dan confided to me that he sorely missed the intimate cuddling and the sexual contact he had enjoyed with Val), but I tried to be a good and steadfast companion to him nevertheless.

Danny wasn't much of a movie-goer, never was. Even when we were subjected to Swift Strike II, he wasn't gung-ho when it came to watching outdoor movies and wasn't enthused when it came to viewing a flick at that theatre in Augusta, Georgia. Being a congenial friend, he was trying to please me.

Occasionally, Danny would come over to my 250th General barracks, or I'd show up at his billets, and we'd go to our respective dayrooms to shoot pool or watch TV, or we'd head out to the Post Exchange and, sometimes, the Snake Pit where we would talk and hoist a few beers together, but other than those subtle pastimes, our interaction was limited. While I could not speak for Danny, personally I was quite unhappy in regards to our changed and sagging relationship. In being the sensitive and sentimental young man whom I was, my love and affection for Dan had never waned or declined in any way. Sadly, although I still considered myself "his nigga," the old Danny was MIA.

Sometimes, it was especially difficult for me to cope with Dan's morose and state of withdrawal. And then, when I noticed he was overindulging himself in his marijuana smoking, I came to worry about him even more. No matter what, I dearly loved my friend and I still relished having him in my life but, after a while, I began to emphatically look forward to the upcoming

November. Since Danny was a 'draftee,' he was scheduled to be discharged during that particular month. And although I well-knew I would be heartbroken to see him leave the state of Texas (and me), I silently longed to bid him farewell.

However, it wasn't all doom and gloom when it came to the first black and intimate friend I had made in Fort Sam Houston. During the third week in July, Danny and I celebrated the birth of his very first child; a six-and-a-half-pound daughter that he and his wife named 'Tiana.' According to my friend, his baby girl was born healthy and Valerie was doing great after the delivery.

When the proud dad hit me with the good news, I jokingly told him I had one regret. I told him "I would have liked to have been present during Tiana's birth - so I could have counted her little fingers and toes." Danny laughed and after presenting me with a cigar (one that I didn't know what to do with), Danny and I set out to 'paint the town red.'

Kicking back at a club located in downtown San Antonio, I filled my gut with one beer after another and Dan indulged himself with champagne and, then, wine, which he smilingly praised as "good pluck." Both of our heads were throbbing later on that evening, but it was a small price to pay. To look across the table and focus on an ecstatic and content Daniel Williams was like heaven to me. And for a prolonged time, as we laughed and reminisced our foregoing interactions with each other, the old Danny had magically resurfaced and I positively loved seeing him once again.

To my personal sorrow, however, the emotional high that prevailed in light of our 'fatherhood' celebration was rather fleeting. Not too long afterwards, instead of just yearning for his missing wife, Danny was also in the throes of anticipatingly seeing and holding little Tiana. He would habitually stare at the baby photos that Valerie sent to him, but they only served to escalate his longing. Understandably, he was a first-time and brand new father who dearly desired to hold and caress his baby in person.

Sometimes (and thank God they occur infrequently), we, as human beings, find ourselves coping with an unexpected happening that virtually knocks us for an emotional loop. Regardless of our social or monetary status, our age, our gender or racial origin, we are all susceptible of being blindsided by some devastating and, occasionally, life-altering event. And being an active-duty member of the armed forces clearly increases an individual's chance for a sudden pitfall or an instantaneous catastrophe.

During the closing days of August of 1964 a happening arose that, while commonplace to the United States military mechanism, practically knocked the socks off of my dear friend, PFC Thomas H. Preston, and everyone in his social and professional orbit. On or around the 10th of September he was due to be transferred to Southeast Asia, which, in plain-talk, was South Vietnam. It was an unforeseen development that shocked Tommy, Angie, the ranking officials of 250th General, Col. Simpson and all of our fellow employees who worked at the Registrar and, of course, myself who was not only taken aback but was downright outraged.

I despised the news from the moment I was told about it and felt it was unfair, ill-timed and somewhat callous as well. After all, Tommy was married and had a young child! I asked myself, "Why would the army just up and snatch a married man from his family when there were so many single men available?" I admit to being biased, but, still, I considered the transfer order to be cruel and void of compassion.

Of course, Tommy had similar sentiments. He realized it was his military duty to go to Vietnam (down deep, so did I), but he didn't want to go. As a father, he adored and doted over his baby boy, and I, as a friend who truly cherished them both, lamented the thought of that special bond being interrupted or severed in any way. In fact, I disdained the development so much that I came up with a plan to slightly alter it. Since Tommy and I were identical job-wise (we were the same M.O.S. actually) and were both ranked as PFCs, I was poised to go to Southeast Asia in his stead. After all, I was a single, unattached soldier with absolutely no baggage, except my duffle bag.

I was clear-headed and adamant about my remedy, And, soon, after emotionally selling my proposal to my very awestruck and reluctant comrade, Tommy himself, I set out to pitch my plan to 250th General's commanding officer, Lt. Col. Mathis. The C.O. himself displayed an expression of awe and absurdity as I pleaded my case before him.

"Are you fuckin' shittin' me, PFC Harris:" he frowningly asked me. "Why on earth would you want to do such a fool thing? That's plain lunacy, PFC! Hey - I'm a great believer in friendship. It's a precious and almost priceless commodity but, hell, friends - they come and they go."

"Not _true_ friends, Colonel," I calmly countered. "Thomas Preston and I are like the closest of brothers. We care deeply about each other. Colonel Mathis, the guy has a family here . . . and I don't have chick nor child. He _should_ be here with his family and that's the bottom line. Besides, what real harm would it do? Look - we have the very same M.O.S., the same job skills, we're both the same rank and we're even both the same age. Sure, we're not the same race, but I see that as immaterial. It has never stopped anything before. Sir ... I can't see a real problem with my request."

Seemingly, my commanding officer wasn't even hearing me at that point. He threw up his hand, signaling me to cease talking, and then lifted the receiver from his desk phone. I looked at him in sheer wonder as he quickly dialed a number.

I remained seated, grimacing as he spoke to his called party. "Captain Rutkowski, you got a minute or two?" he questioned. "Okay, would you step over to my office for a few minutes? It won't take too long. I wanna show you something."

Shortly, as the company commander came on the scene, I climbed to my feet, snapped to attention and rendered the traditional salute to him. Then, upon saluting me back, he uttered "at-ease," instructed me to retake my seat and turned his attention to Lt. Col. Mathis. And that's when our CO proceeded to address me again.

"PFC Harris, do us a favor," he spoke. "Give the captain a summary of why you're here. Tell him what you're hoping to do."

I tried my level best not to sigh, but I failed at doing it. I wasn't dumb enough to mention it to the colonel, but I resented him making light of my proposed actions. In sensing what kind of man Capt. Rutkowski was, I knew he would not remotely understand my viewpoints and I was nervous upon addressing the officer. However, I took a deep breath and went on to obey the colonel's foregoing command.

"My best friend, PFC Thomas Preston, received orders to go to South Vietnam a couple of days ago," I began. "He's married, resides with his wife off-post, and they have a five-month old little boy and I love all three of them. Captain, I'm requesting permission to take Tom Preston's place. In other words, to go to Vietnam in his place ... Sir."

Showcasing a sedate expression, the company commander took a moment to glance at Col. Mathis and then spoke to me. "That's rather incredible, PFC, if you don't mind my saying so," he remarked. "Quite dumb and stupid too but, nevertheless, incredible. PFC Preston's a white soldier, right? The young man who works with you at the post Registrar?"

"That's correct, Capt. Rutkowski but - so what if he is white or Caucasian?" I almost resentfully questioned. "We're still the best of friends. I'm afraid I don't understand. Sir."

I actually expected the company commander to go off on me, deeming me a wise-ass, but he didn't. He calmly stated, "According the Staff-Sgt. Kurn - your ETS is early next summer. He's endorsing you for a corporal's patch. Are you willing to piss away a promotion and extend your time as well? A deployment to South Vietnam would require you to extend your tour of duty. All in the name of your noble and unheard of sacrifice, or you willing to do that, PFC?"

I paused a moment, then replied, "If that's one of the prerequisites, Capt. Rutkowski, Col. Mathis - then I'm willing to extend my time. I'll do whatever it takes. Just instruct me on what to do."

At that particular minute, the demeanor of both officers was quite serious. However, the CO looked to the captain, seemingly wanting him to respond to my foregoing statement. The colonel himself looked dumbfounded.

Rutkowski asked, "Can I safely assume that you have talked this matter over with PFC Preston, your beloved, dear friend? And . . . is he gung-ho about it?"

I realized the company commander was being somewhat glib, but I played pass it. "Sir, we talked at length and Tommy, PFC Preston, was pretty resistant at first, but I showed the logic in it - to him."

"And, pray-tell, what is that <u>logic</u>?" Rutkowski rather smilingly questioned. "Explain the logic to us."

"Sir, like I told the colonel earlier," I replied, "PFC Preston is married, I'm not. He has a child, I don't. It's just that simple, cut-and-dried, Sir."

Apparently, Capt. Rutkowski wasn't satisfied with my explanation. "But is PFC Preston thoroughly aware of all the extenuating circumstances in the matter?" he quizzed. "All of them, PFC?"

"Well - most of them, Sir."

"And is he fully aware you'll have to extend your service tour of duty?" the captain injected, continuing his interrogation. "Is he, PFC?"

"To be honest, Capt. Rutkowski," I admitted, "until you brought it up, Sir, I hadn't even thought about it. But still, I'm willing to do it."

At that time, a smirking Col. Mathis chimed in with a remark. "And you don't wish to rethink or reconsider your self-sacrificing endeavor, PFC Harris?" he questioned.

I was still adamant about my desires. "I don't see it as self-sacrificing, Colonel, or noble," I respectfully took exception. "I see it as an act of true friendship."

To my surprise, Capt. Kyle Rutkowski appeared to be quite sincere when he remarked, "I only hope PFC Preston is worthy of your esteem . . . and affection for him, PFC Harris. But . . . we must deny your request. First and foremost, your dear friend is a United States soldier - and he has a military obligation. America is becoming more and more involved in that fracas in Southeast Asia and there will be thousands of young and old soldiers dispatched to that region. And they, just like your close buddy, Preston, will have to fulfill their military duty. Many of them will also be married and have families stateside too. And just like you and I and Lt. Col. Mathis, PFC Thomas Preston took a solemn oath to defend our country. So, again, I am sorry - but no."

I shifted my eyes to the CO in that instance, beseechingly hoping for a reprieve or some degree of reconsideration. Unfortunately, there was none forthcoming and the ranking officer opted to affirm that very fact when he spoke to me.

To be perfectly frank, PFC Harris," he divulged, "that was my decision - even before I summoned the company commander over here. I just wanted him to kinda behold you, to see someone who we seldom encounter in this day and age. I, too, hope your devotion to your friend is mutual. But no, PFC Harris. I'm not interested in setting such a precedent. So ... there you are, young man. I wish you the very best, wish PFC Preston the very best too, but ... our decision is irrevocable, etched into a pillar of stone. I bid you good-day, PFC, and I enjoyed talking to you. It was a real treat."

Momentarily, I was frustrated and visually hurt and downhearted, but I realized, too, that balking at my superior's joint decision would be futile and quite pointless. Therefore, I climbed to my feet, snapped to attention and rendered the customary salutes to both officers. And, then, with a heavy heart and a volley of tears falling from my eyes, I made my retreat from the Headquarters complex. At that juncture, I felt depressed, defeated and completely powerless.

CHAPTER FORTY-THREE
SOME THINGS NEVER CHANGE

Although I lived to regret it later on in my life, but during my high school years I wasn't grade-conscious. I strived to be slightly 'above' average, but I didn't much care if my fellow classmates made better grades than I did. It took Uncle Sam to fully arouse my competitive spirit. I, as well as the other soldiers in my midst, were consistently encouraged to 'best' or outdo other men in one area or another.

So, when the first part of September came on the scene (after the door was slammed shut on my sought after transfer to Southeast Asia) and I found myself seeking the rank of corporal, I knew it was absolutely crucial for me to brush-up and review 'anything' and 'everything' that was applicable to traditional military life and proceedings.

According to Staff Sgt. Harold Kurn (who was like my personal cheerleader), I, along with 15 other 250th General soldiers who wore PFC stripes, was scheduled to appear before a formal promotion board and respond to an entire spectrum of military queries and suppositions.

Unfortunately though, there wasn't a physical E-4 patch on-hand when the contest took place and all of the active participants were priorly apprised of that factor. According to board officials (which was comprised of veteran officers and a couple of high-ranking noncoms too), a list would be compiled and incoming stripes or patches would be, subsequently, awarded per the performance rankings of the 15 young soldiers.

To my total delight, but not so much - surprise (I knew I was blessed with an exceptional memory and I had studied extra-hard), I emerged as the number 1 candidate on that printed list. While I wasn't in the least bit haughty when I was informed of my top ranking, I must admit, however, that when the official list was posted inside the glass-encased bulletin board outside the Headquarters facility, I was bursting with a feeling of self-pride. Even in being extended praise and lighthearted teasing from my fellow troops, I was exceedingly happy.

In less than two weeks time (just so happened, it was in the somber aftermath of Tommy Preston's departure for Vietnam), a single corporal's stripe did come down the military pipeline. I was informed (off-the-record) of the development by the company clerk, a Spec.-4 Allan Swanson, and was even heartily congratulated by the same fellow.

Since I was still grappling with Tommy's departure, I was somewhere betwixt grief and glee at that particular time. I truly relished the elevated rank and I could certainly use the increase in pay that coincided with the promotion, but a pronounced and sizable portion of my heart seemed to have left town with my beloved friend. Although I tried, I could not quite chase away my inner sadness.

I soon came to learn, however, that there are some emotions that are capable of temporarily supplanting other deep feelings and they are almost impossible to fathom and cope with. That emotion lies between hatred and outrage.

Without any forewarning whatsoever, just like it was just and appropriate, the subject lone stripe was boldly awarded to the Caucasian PFC whose name appeared second on the compiled promotion list. And it hit me like a brick that was launched from a cannon!

To claim I was upset and infuriated would be a mild and very tepid understatement. I was immediately livid and almost ready to seek out an M-1 4 rifle and lock-and-load! To be perfectly frank, even at the age of 19 I had learned to neither be shocked nor surprised in regards to what white people were capable of doing. For I was keenly cognizant of their inhumane and racist history and I had been 'personally' scarred by their hate-inspired antics. But this affront was something else! It was totally uncalled for!

I reasoned, if those white men on that board were, in fact, racist (and they were well-aware that their respective hearts were racially biased and markedly discriminatory too), then why on earth didn't they simply award the top slot to the favored Caucasian candidate from the get-go? In keeping it under cover, no one would have been the wiser, not even me! To me, it was totally illogical, uncalled for and reeking of evil and I could not begin to wrap my head around it!

Then again, when I thought of the happening in-depth, it was typical of the greater majority of the white people I had dealt with during my relatively short lifetime. In fact, with the exception of Tommy Preston, Jeremy Lockhart, Kevin Brenahan and Harold Kurn as well, I regarded the entire Caucasian race as children of the devil. Collectively, for the most part, I had come to view them as creature's barren of any redeeming qualities.

Down-deep, I knew I was being harsh and somewhat cold-hearted too. The aforementioned exceptions weren't the only loving and fair-minded white individuals on the face of the earth and I well-knew it. The guys I mentioned had not cornered the market on Caucasian benevolence and goodwill. I was just in a passing state of anger and boiling frustration. I was in dire need of counsel from one of them though and since Brenahan was no longer accessible, Tommy was in a foreign land and Lockhart happened to be on a 14-day leave, I soon pleaded my case to Harold Kurn. After all, the sarge was the noncom who saw to it that I'd participate in the promotion competition.

As the old saying states, "Bad news travels fast" and that certainly applied to my decision to consult my close-knit friend and official barracks sergeant. He, too, was upset about the affair and assured me he had already voiced his protest to the powers-that-be, meaning, both, Capt. Rutkowski and Lt. Col. Mathis too. He "smelled a rat" he plainly admitted and encouraged me to follow the 'chain of command' while actively protesting the matter. "And don't you dare holdback, Lionel, loudly toot the damn racism horn every chance you get," he further advised me, "because I'm afraid it weighs very heavily on this shady bullshit too. I may be farsighted and a so-called white man too, but I sho' ain't fuckin' blind. This thing stinks to high heaven."

I was quite thankful in light of Harold Kurn's rather heartfelt candor and I viewed his advice as gospel. Therefore, in less than 48 hours after the stripe 'slap in the face' (and that's how I saw it), I was afforded the chance to officially launch my verbal protest while standing inside of 250th General's Orderly Room. Sgt. Kurn had arranged for me to speak to Master-Sergeant Arlen R. Davidson, 250th's 1st. sergeant.

Davidson was a tall and slim, freckled-face Caucasian man (maybe 6'4") and he spoke with a pronounced southern drawl. But, to be honest, although I was on the verge of observing my one-year anniversary of my transfer to 250th General, our interaction was quite limited. Since I worked fulltime at the Registrar on post, our paths seldomly crossed. In fact, I could count on one hand how many times we had engaged in a lengthy conversation (and that was when we were in the wilds of Camp Bullis).

As I indicated, I <u>stood</u> in the O.R. complex and although the top sergeant remained seated behind his desk and there was an empty chair on the other side of it, he didn't invite me to sit down. I found that odd but, as they say, "I didn't trip on it."

"Let's see here," he casually said, taking a moment to rifle through some papers atop his desk and, then, eyed my nameplate, "You're PFC Harris, right? A young soldier whose got a burr up his ass, right?"

If the sergeant was aiming to raise my dander, he nearly succeeded. "First-Sergeant, I don't really know what a <u>burr</u> is," I replied, "but I can assure you it's not up my backside - but I am Private First Class Lionel Harris."

The top noncom smiled, apparently pleased with himself. "You're claiming you suffered an injustice, right?" he asked. "Sayin' our company is persecutin' you, huh?"

I wasn't, in the least, intimidated. "I think the word is more like - discriminated against, 1st. Sergeant," I said. "Perhaps you can persuade me to see it differently, 1st. Sergeant."

Now, the top sergeant turned sedate and pulled open his side desk drawer. He retrieved a large notebook, questioning, "You believe you've been done wrong, being discriminated against - as you put it. Is that what you're claiming PFC?"

"Exactly, Sir - Sergeant. I can't think of nothing else. Perhaps you can enlighten me."

"Enlighten - that's a big word for a colored soldier," Davidson grimaced. "You been to college or something?"

"No, 1st. Sergeant, I just read a lot," I responded. "I also know words like 'biasness' and 'injustice.' They apply here too."

Presently, Sgt. Davidson looked somewhat peeved. "Well, are you familiar with a word called 'infractions?' It's a term we use when green and undisciplined soldiers fuck up from time to time. We keep tabs on 'em, in books just like this one. Will I find your name in here, PFC Harris?"

The book the sergeant was referring to was the one he had removed from his desk drawer. He began turning its pages as I responded to his last query.

"*If* my name's in it, Sgt. Davidson," I smugly said, "then it's something I was never told about. Tell me about it now."

While Davidson flipped the book's pages, I kept my eyes focused on the various names that were recorded on its pages. The greater majority of the names belonged to Negroid soldiers, not that I was surprised in the least.

Momentarily, the 1st. Sergeant seemed to be on the brink of panic. Then, he cried, "Oh, here it is! Leon Harris, right? Middle initial - S?"

"No, Sir. Lionel Harris. L-i-o-n-e-l and middle initial - B."

The top sergeant's visual search continued for another moment or two. "Well - I don't see you in here," he softly admitted, apparently disappointed. "Someone made a big mistake ... probably. I'll check it out, Harris, make things right. And I promise you - you'll get the next corporal's stripe, PFC."

Despite Sgt. Davidson's promise, and he appeared to be sincere about it, I wasn't even a taste satisfied with his resolve. I kept thinking about the number 2 white boy being awarded my corporal stripe. (When I was a child in grammar school, I was taught to regard number one as the urge to urinate and number two as a yearning to defecate and, therefore, since I felt 'shitted on,' I felt compelled to carry my protest further). That's when I thanked Davidson for his time and indulgence and respectfully insisted upon speaking to our company commander. Capt. Rutkowski was next in line regarding the chain of command.

Subsequently, my uphill climb to secure any semblance of justice and soothing satisfaction went rather sluggishly forward. And in spite of casual apologies, good-faith vows, patronizing back-slaps and even a few insults and threats I incurred along the way, I carried my official protest all the way up to the ultimate authorities at Fort Sam Houston.

Then, finally, after appearing before the Post Commander himself, I was awarded an E-4 stripe. However, my triumph was somewhat tepid, lackluster and bittersweet at best. I was promoted to the corporal rank alright but, after almost three weeks, another E-4 patch had come down the military pipeline. The number 2 white boy on the posted promotion list was altogether unscathed and had emerged with a one-month 'time-in-grade' advantage over me to boot. It wasn't even close to being fair, or just or aboveboard but, in reality, I happened to be a young soldier who had come into the world with a visible pigmentation problem. I, like millions of so-called 'Negroes' in America, was born with black skin.

In spite of being awarded stellar letters of commendation by two, different 250th General second lieutenants, despite of being considered as a valuable asset in the woods of Camp Bullis, Texas and regardless of the fact that I had been officially certified as the hand's-down winner of the E-4 promotion contest, the dark hue of my innate skin had managed to erase and nullify it all. I guess I could have deemed myself 'lucky' since my name was not scribbled on 1st. Sergeant Davidson's 'infraction' list.

Although my life in the United States army was a series of upswings and downswings (mostly, the latter), every now and then something would transpire that not only lifted my spirits, it managed to renew my faith in God and in humankind as well. While I was still stewing in anger and depression after the promotion ordeal, paired with my nostalgic feeling for the departed Tommy Preston, I was afforded an unexpected and heartfelt compensation that proceeded to take me aback.

On a regular weekday in mid-October of 1964 (less than a month after the stripe fiasco), I returned to my home barracks after completing an 8-hour shift at the post Registrar facility. Similar to my usual, everyday routine, I entered my billets through its rear extreme and walked towards the structure's front where my assigned cubbyhole lied. However, to my complete surprise and utmost shock, it was no longer there!

Oh - my former living area was <u>still</u> there alright, but with the exception of a metal bed-frame and a bare, folded-up mattress occupying the space, there was no tangible evidence that it was poised to house an incoming human being, not even me - who was officially assigned to it. I perceived it as a bizarre and mysterious phenomenon. After all, where the hell was my military-locker, my civilian-locker and my footlocker? Maybe, they all vaporized or vanished into thin air!

Before I jumped to another rather weird and crazy conclusion, my eyes soon focused on a written note that was taped beneath the nearest window seal. I, of course, walked over, retrieved it and was immediately somewhat relieved. However, it wasn't because of what was written on the note (I had not, yet, read it), but was solely because it had been signed by Staff-Sgt. Harold Kurn.

It read, 'Cpl. E-4 L. B. Harris. Before you go and blow a gasket over your missing stuff, please forgive me for having the gall to have them moved into your new home. Spec. 5 Galloway is now living off-post with his family and I feel you well-deserve his former cadre room! And I don't want no guff about it, young fellow. The cadre room key is in my mailbox in the Orderly Room. Also - I hope you enjoy my housewarming gift! (Over).'

Even upon pausing prior to flipping the note over, I smiled in warm appreciation as I savored my sergeant friend's signature. It was a kindness he went out of his way to do and I was deeply heartened by it. But when I finally turned the paper over, the words on it produced me to tears. It simply said, 'P.S. Lonnie, all white people are not bigots and racist!' Apparently, my barracks sergeant was emphatic about his message to me. And I was duly aware of it when he underlined the word 'all.'

While I was completely taken aback and caught off-guard by Harold Kurn's benevolent October surprise, whereby I was granted my own, private and solitary living quarters, I was further delighted and exceedingly grateful when I, subsequently, entered my room for the very first time.

Upon retrieving the specified key shortly after reading Kurn's note, I, soon, returned to my assigned barracks. (To be specific, the cadre room was off-side the front entrance of my billets and was less than 15 paces from my prior living space). I, then, unlocked the cadre room's door and, momentarily, stood back and practically feasted my eyes on the sergeant's 'housewarming' gift. However, in being a guy of sentiment, it was a 'heartwarming' gift to me instead. I was touched and speechless too.

To be honest, I was expecting to see a bath robe, a set of towels or a throw rug or something similar, but certainly not a 14-inch, black and white television set! And while it was not brand new, it was something that was right up my alley. I regularly walked over to the dayroom and watched the evening newscast, I loved viewing half-hour sitcoms, western serials and old movies that were shown on TV and, therefore, I felt like I had been thrown into the entertainment briar-patch - but one that was completely void of thorns! For sure, I was as happy as I could be.

CHAPTER FORTY-FOUR
DEJA VU IN SPADES

Just as my friend and barracks sergeant, Harold Kurn, indicated in his note to me, my 'missing stuff' was neatly placed inside my military quarters. Situated beyond my made-up bunk, and sitting side-by-side, was my footlocker, my army locker and my civilian locker.

My newly-assigned domicile, showcasing a shiny, recently-buffed out floor was about 12 by 12 feet and provided me (what I considered) a visual vantage point. Since my long-time billets set parallel to the three-fold Headquarters complex, the Orderly Room and the Dayroom respectively (located directly across the main street), it had a window that faced the aforementioned structures and another window on the left extreme which was approximately four paces from the barrack's entrance door.

Subsequently, after I procured a metal folding chair, a large hassock, a throw rug and a small table to set the television atop, it was 'home-sweet-home' for me. As I alluded to before, I was in my supreme comfort zone and loving every minute of it.

Of course, military life as I had come to know it, neither slowed down, accelerated or entered into a state of suspended animation in the immediate aftermath of my 'tainted' promotion or my personal saving grace, which was the unexpected awarding of my cadre room.

I, soon, returned to my authentic and regular old self; overly concerning myself with the world at-large, the current state of a strifeful and troubled America, the ongoing actions of a gung-ho and galvanized armed forces (the U.S. was becoming more and more involved in the conflict in Southeast Asia) and, most certainly, focusing on the well-being and peace of mind of so many people I dearly loved and cherished.

In the fall of 1964, whenever I thought about my South Vietnam-based cohort, Tommy Preston (which was quite regularly), I almost simultaneously focused on my other beloved friend, Jerome Smith, who was formerly based in another foreign region called South Korea.

Just so happened (not to the credit or fault of either of them), the two of them was racially different, were quite diverse personality-wise and, regretfully, did not know each other, but I could not differentiate the entrenched love and sincere affection I held for them. To me, Tommy and J were my non-biological brothers in, both, my heart and spirit.

When Jerome spent the better part of 1963 in South Korea, I was intent upon doing one, single, solitary thing. As a true and unwavering friend, I was hell-bent on writing him a rather lengthy letter practically every two weeks. But not aimless and rambling letters, but correspondence that was upbeat, inspiring and, oftentimes, jovial in nature.

Therefore, when Tommy was uprooted and then transplanted in Southeast Asia, I was dead-set on extending him a likewise courtesy. I was adamant about writing to him twice-monthly also and I was intent upon adhering to a format of lightheartedness and encouragement.

However, borrowing words that were made famous by old-time comedian Jimmy Durante, my letter-writing commitment was like "Deja vu all over again," but with a marked difference. J was in a country that was reasonably safe and peaceful and Tommy, on the other hand, was in a region that was volatile, stressful and on the verge of exploding into an out-and-out war.

In addition, since Tommy had left behind a wife and a baby son, he was direly in need of a special kind of uplifting and encouragement. I didn't know if I was endowed with the necessary writing skills, but I was intent upon doing my level best. I penned each letter, hoping to lift his spirits.

Although I was obliged to communicate with, both, Tommy and Jerome via the United States postal service (even J was stationed 500 miles away in the state of New Mexico), I still had a longtime and intimate friend in my immediate midst who owned a sizable portion of my heart.

For reasons I was unable to pinpoint (and it was not because I didn't address the mystery), Jeremy Lockhart emerged standoffish after I secured my corporal patch, but Danny Williams was still around, and was still assigned to the 24th Evacuation Hospital as well. In fact, he would, sometimes, come over and watch TV with me in my cadre room. And I truly enjoyed and savored those occasions.

Sadly, however, those <u>sometimes</u> became far and in between and for a man of deep sentiment (which, of course, is descriptive of me), it was heartbreaking and almost unbearable after a while. And that happened to be my solemn mind-set, when on a Saturday evening in early November 1964, I was determined to seek out my friend and spend some meaningful and quality time with him.

I initially struck out, however. When I went over to his home billets, I was informed by one of his fellow barracks mates that Dan had left an hour prior. But he speculated, saying he believed my comrade had gone to the Snake Pit. Then, he added too, "At least he was talking about going up there earlier this afternoon."

Like I said, I was adamant about catching up with my endeared friend. Therefore, the Enlisted Men's Club was my next destination. In actuality, I had not set foot inside the Snake Pit for quite a while, in fact, not since I was in the company of Danny and his wife. Sure, I was now an NCO but that was no big deal. Quite a few noncoms flocked there, and especially black ones. (It was where Spec. 5 Ogelthorp was introduced to Valerie Williams).

It was a Saturday night, the facility was jam-packed with military personnel (soldiers, WACs, etc.) and, of course, the music was blaring and rollicking. I immediately searched for Danny out on the dance floor, but he wasn't there. I, then, slowly walked around, physically circling the place, but, still, my friend was nowhere in sight. I even asked a select group of people had they seen him, but no dice there either. No one reported they had seen Danny, not a single person. So, after about twenty minutes, I had to give up. My friend was nowhere to be found and it was a disappointment I had to live with.

Admittedly, I was downhearted when I made my exit from the Snake Pit on that particular evening but I surrendered to mirth as I strolled forward and decided on an alternate destination. I know it sounds somewhat looney and bizarre on my part, but I found myself thinking of 'Tara.'

In the motion picture entitled 'Gone with The Wind,' <u>Tara</u> was the southern home (plantation and all) of Scarlett O'Hara. But, more significantly, it was the special site, or tract of land, where Scarlett withdrew her strength and resolve from, her personal place of salvation. And I could identify with her mindset. Because, in reality, my personal Tara was a movie theatre. Therefore, it was almost natural for me to head there after I left the EM Club.

It was a quarter after eight when I reached the theatre and laid my fare down at the ticket window. I figured the flick was already underway but since it was a movie starring Susan Hayward and John Gavin called 'Back Street' and I had already seen it before, I didn't mind not seeing it from its beginning. However, the ticket seller inside the booth, a young white girl, did seem to mind.

"Soldier, if you don't mind my saying it," she spoke, "I suggest that you come back tomorrow, see the movie from its beginning. You owe it to yourself."

"Well ... I appreciate your advice, Miss," I softly responded, "but ya' see - I've seen it before. Just passing some time. May I have a ticket?"

Although the ticket seller took my money and 'pushed' an admissions stub towards me, she was apparently not satisfied with my response. Rather begrudgingly, she said, "Well - I guess it takes all kinds."

After purchasing my refreshments, I soon entered the darkened theatre and sat in a seat that was located midway down the aisle. However, before I could fully focus on the movie screen and get my bearing regarding the still-unfolding storyline (in military jargon, I became 'dark-adapted'), I was almost stricken with a stark and severely-heartbreaking realization.

Sitting a mere six rows in front of my position was Daniel Williams, who, of course, was the focal point of my heretofore and fruitless quest! Under ordinary circumstances, I could converge on my friend and join up with him. But ordinary was a farcical and dismissive term in my rather censuring viewpoint. Danny was not alone! In fact, he was huddled up with a young, black woman and was passionately engaged in tongue-kissing her. Needless to say, his female partner was certainly not his wife.

To say I was extremely sorrowful and disenchanted was a very mild understatement. As I silently sat back in my seat, with my eyes fixed on the flesh-and-blood couple affront me instead of the celluloid lovers on screen (Hayward and Gavin), I could barely come to grips with what I was observing.

There sat one of my most beloved and intimate friends, a young man whom I had placed above so many others, an individual who appeared to be happily married and had recently became a proud father, and it was now crystal-clear to me that he was quite common and no different from most of the black men I had come to know in my life. And, of course, my own biological father was the leader of the pack.

Admittedly though, I could not blame anyone for my hurt and disillusionment but myself. My dear mother had once cautioned me about putting people upon a pedestal. Although we were talking about my relationship with Jerome at the time, she had pre-warned me about the disenchantment and regret that prevailed when a prized loved one fell from grace, and I casually shrugged off her warning. With my eyes still trained on Dan and his female companion, my mom's advice was virtually ringing in my ears and I felt like breaking down and crying.

In my uttermost anguish and as crazy as it sounds (and it would have been just that), I actually had to persuade myself to remain seated and inactive. For a prolonged minute or so, I entertained the thought of leaving my seat, advancing on Danny and his 'date's' position, and verbally berating him! I was tempted to tell him just how disappointed I was regarding his actions; angrily bawl him out about his infidelity and his lustful betrayal to his wife. But, soon, my common sense resurfaced and I gradually came to a personal consensus.

My ongoing despair and anger wasn't really about Valerie Williams at all, it was about me! Since Danny's wife was in Detroit, Michigan, it was unlikely that she was aware of her husband's unfaithfulness. So, I surmised that Dan was probably in agreement with the rationale that, "What my wife doesn't know about, cannot hurt her."

However, sitting in that darkened movie house and being eyewitness to Danny's amorous behavior was an insidious Deja vu for me. I vividly recalled my own dad's blatant philandering, and had long despised the very thought of those yesteryear episodes, so how could I cope with my endeared friend's deceit? And it was obvious to me, right then and there, that I could not!

When the featured movie finally came to an end, and I remained seated with tears in my eyes (in addition to being grievous regarding Danny's real-life actions, I was also weeping in light of Susan Hayward's tragic circumstances on the movie screen), I soon came face-to-face with my in-progress, departing comrade. Displaying a face of shock and sheer surprise, watching me as I rose to my feet, Dan told his lady he'd catch up with her and stayed back to converse with me. Naturally, we were both cheerless.

"Believe it or not, Harris," he rather nervously stated, "but all through that damn movie, man, I felt like somebody was watching me. But - what can I say? You caught me . . . doing shit I ain't supposed to do. And catching me doing something you absolutely hate. I'm sorry."

"Well - I wasn't watching you two alone," I replied. "A lot of surrounding eyes were looking at you two. Hell, Danny, you guys should have bypassed here. Should have headed straight to a motel or something."

My cohort tried to muster up a smile. "Kim - she's got her own place, and we're headed there now," he said. "Damn, Harris, I feel shitty about this, man. I sure didn't expect to run into you here."

The house lights were fully on when I replied, "Come on, kiddo, you know I'm a movie fanatic. Maybe that's it, Danny. Maybe, subconsciously you wanted to run into me. But you're a grown man, what difference does it make? You don't have to answer to me."

Seemingly, my friend's sadness plunged deeper. "Not on my life, Harris, did I want this to happen," he emphasized. "Harris, I want to . . . but I can't be like you. I wish I could, but I have needs, desires. No matter what you say, I didn't want this to happen - not in a million years! Man, a while back I remember you telling me you had seen this damn picture. I didn't expect to run into you here, and I hate it!"

I was set to respond to Dan's foregoing words, but I heard someone walking up behind me. I turned and it was my comrade's young lady.

"They're getting ready to throw us outta here, Baby," she told Danny. "Are you coming?"

Instead of taking the time to address his date, Dan spoke to me. "Can we, maybe talk about this tomorrow, Harris?" he asked. "I'll stop by your place, sometime tomorrow afternoon. Will that be okay with you?"

"I'll ... probably be there, guy," I stated. "Goodnight, Danny."

Waving goodbye, my comrade did not bother to introduce me to his date and I was glad. I had no desire to make her acquaintance. That was why I paused for several moments or so and then walked up the aisle behind them, staying silent. However, I was still close enough to the pair to overhear something the young lady said to Dan.

"Who in the hell is that nigga?" she rather angrily asked him. "And why is he lookin' so damn sad and shit?"

"Don't worry about him, Kim," was my cohort's response. "And don't call him no <u>nigga</u> either! He's my best friend."

To be perfectly honest, even when I told Danny Williams that I would "probably" be in my assigned barracks on the following day, I was reasonably sure I would <u>not</u> be there. I was scheduled to spend the early hours of Sunday with Angie Preston, Tommy Jr. and Angela's immediate family, and later in the evening, I was due at Harold Kurn's house for dinner. The latter event was almost routine and I truly looked forward to spending time with little Marla and Cornel Kurn.

Besides, in regards to meeting up with Dan, I could not see a resultant worth in it. It was more than apparent to me that my beloved friend and I were at an emotional crossroad and, even worse, an immovable impasse. I realized we were both adamant and set in our ways. Further dialogue and argument was fruitless, I believed, and I had to face the fact that I could not (and should not) impose my morals and life-long beliefs on Danny. In fact, I realized I could only make him more unhappy than he already was and I was not remotely inclined to do that. I loved the guy much too much and I had no desire whatsoever to make his life more worrisome and complex than it already was.

CHAPTER FORTY-FIVE

THE HIGH PRICE OF LUST

As a couple of weeks went by the boards, my once vibrant and priceless friendship with Daniel Williams remained estranged. Admittedly, I was the major party MIA in the matter and not my cohort from Detroit. Several times I was told that Dan had showed up in the 250th General area seeking me, but I was always elsewhere. Never did I return his visits and I didn't take it upon myself to phone him at Beach Pavillion either, his on-post work site. There was a time (which began after Danny had called me about the JFK shooting) when we talked daily during work hours.

Fact was, even as I grievously missed my friend and longed to see his face and hear his voice again, I could not bring myself to forgive him. Forgive him for what? I wasn't even sure! Maybe, for resurrecting bad memories of my womanizing father. Down deep, I knew I was grossly wrong and unfair in my ongoing begrudgment, but I couldn't seem to help myself. Although I never acted on it, I believed I would do well to seek out professional help.

However, less than three days later, I felt I was on the verge of getting a handle on things. Even without the aid of a psychologist or a head-shrinker, I tried to self-identify my personal demons. During my childhood when I played those repetitious extortion games with my old man, I now realized I greatly despised those deceitful episodes. And, then, to keep them bottled up inside me, to suppress them entirely, that was mentally damaging also. While I never regretted concealing those happenings from my mother (or my brothers), I should have discussed it with someone. After all, I was just an 8 or 9-year-old little boy!

Notably though, my self-analysis did not end with my forestated revelation. It had a common sense and universal addendum to it; and something that managed to give me pause and unseat me from my high horse. My heartfelt obsession to be diametrically different from my old man was 'my story.' It squarely set me on the narrow path to strive to be the man I longed to be; to be upstanding, forthright, compassionate, principled and fair-minded.

However, my story was not my friend Danny's story or anyone else's story. As close and tight as we were, I wasn't familiar with Dan's angels or his demons and I was basically unaware of his past and foregoing childhood as well. He seldomly reflected on it and I never pressed him on it either. Who knew what he had gone through? I didn't!

All I knew for sure was that Danny was not perfect, and neither was I or anyone else I had ever known (not even my mother, Ruby, or my Uncle Bill). And I knew, too, that my intimate cohort had a personal story of his own. Therefore, my Epiphany was, then, complete (and that's what I deemed it). To me, it was an inspiring rationale that was bequeathed to me from a Higher Authority and it was urging me to be, both, forgiving and more discerning also.

In the short aftermath of my two-part self-analysis process, which was directly spawned from my fractured friendship bond with Daniel Williams, I was joyously anticipating reconnecting with my missing comrade; whereby I'd beg his pardon for being so judgmental, assure him I still loved him and firmly hug him too, and whether he liked it or not.

Just so happened, I was grinningly thinking about that embracement intent when something totally unexpected occurred. As I sat alone on my bunk in my cadre room, I looked up and there, standing in my doorway, was Specialist-4 Mario Moran. I was momentarily startled.

"Hello, Corporal E-4 Barrel Harris," was the words that came out of the mouth of my Cuban comrade. "Long time, no see."

Mario had entered my room and was firmly shaking my hand when I climbed to my feet and smilingly replied, "Well as my mom likes to say, 'You're a sight for sore eyes, Mario.' How the devil are you? And how's Kathy doing?"

Almost instantly, my visitor's mood altered. With a frown on his face, he addressed my query, saying his wife was "doing fine" but, then, he softly asked, "Mind if I close your door, Barry?"

I was reduced to a state of wariness as I watched Mario shutting my door and I, soon, retook my seat on my bed, quizzing, "This is really not a social visit, Mario, is it?"

"Not quite," my comrade sadly admitted, taking the liberty to sit across from me on my hassock. "I've honestly missed seeing you, being with you too - but I needed to talk to you about something."

Now, I was on the offensive and suspicious as well. "And does it have anything to do with Angela Preston, one of your best friend's wife?" I questioned.

"Old Barrel, a guy who gets right down to cases," Mario mused. "That's why I've always had great respect for you, ya' know? Plus, you're a true-blue friend, the kind people dream of having someday. The kind . . . I would love to have."

Suddenly, I was tearful. "Exactly - where are we headed here, Mario? You've got me on needles and pins here. Why don't you just come out and say it?"

Tears were in my visitor's eyes too when he divulged, "Angela... Angela's pregnant, Barry. We found that out a couple of days ago."

While I absolutely, direly hated the context of Mario Moran's admission, I could not hardly say I was shocked or surprised by his news. My crying intensified when I said, "I was hoping and praying it wouldn't go this far. I wish I could understand, wish I could find some sympathy for you, Mario, but I can't."

"Are you saying ... you guessed what was going on between me and Angela, Barry?" Mario asked.

"Not guessed, Mario - but knew," I sternly replied. "And it's been going on for quite a while now, even when Tommy was still on the scene. Ya' know, Mario, I don't consider myself a bonafide Christian, I've even slacked off on attending church services lately, but I still remember certain passages in the Bible. One was like - "If thine eye offends thee, then pluck it out." I guess I'm saying - if you knew you were attracted to, or lusted for another man's wife, and especially for the wife of a guy you considered a dear friend, then why didn't you force yourself to withdraw from the relationship. Or did you care one iota about Tommy?"

True remorse was on Mario's face when he stated, "I really love Tom Preston, Barry, and I always thought he loved me too. But ..."

"But you love Angie more," I inserted, finishing my comrade's statement. "But you're married too, Mario. Did your vows mean anything to you? And where's Kathy in this sordid mess?" I waited but Mario stayed silent in his remorse.

"It's not like you didn't have options, Mario," I spoke further. "You had a wife of your own, the Wac Detachment is right up the road, there's a red-light district in San Antonio proper and, hell, Mexico is less than a hundred miles from here. Outside women galore. But you had to have Angie, right? And don't think I don't blame her, she's no angel in this crap!"

"But don't blame her, Barry - please," Mario said. "I'll take full blame."

I shook my head, insisting, "But you didn't rape her, Mario. She was a willing participant. Boy - the things people do to each other. But let me ask you this: Is Angie considering having an abortion? That's a way out."

Now, I don't know what words I expected to hear coming out of my comrade's mouth, but they certainly weren't, "<u>No</u> - you know we're both Catholic and we don't believe in abortion."

"Well - Jesus!" I cried, shaking my head again. "Ya' know, Mario, people piss me the hell off wearing religion like it's a damn coat! 'I'll wear it today, but I'll leave it at home tomorrow in case I decide to indulge or wallow in sin.' Were you and Angie Catholic when you guys decided to jump into bed together?"

Of course, I didn't really expect a rebuttal or a reasonable response. Concentrating on my comrade in his ongoing silence, I could not help feeling somewhat sorry for him. "Forgive me, Mario, for climbing upon my soapbox, man," I spoke, "And sounding like I'm 'holier than thou.' I have no right to pass judgement on you - or Angie. I'm just venting and a little frustrated. Sorry."

Mario mustered up a faint smile at that point. "You don't have to apologize, Barry," he said. "I well-deserve a good bawling out and an ass-kicking too. And I appreciate it from you. Like I said, I truly respect you. But this is what I wanted to ask you? Should Angela and I write and tell Tommy about our . . . sins? The baby and all?"

I was abruptly taken aback at that juncture. "Naw, Mario, not <u>naw</u> - but hell naw!" I angrily objected. "I don't care if a priest writes the letter, or the Pope, or even if Ernest Hemingway himself writes it! Don't do that boy like that, Mario - please don't! If you have any love, any affection whatsoever - left in your heart for Tommy, then shield him from that horrendous heartbreak! He doesn't deserve it, and no good could possibly come of it. Please, I'm begging you - wait till he comes home from Vietnam - please!"

Mario Moran sighed in a semblance of relief as he slowly climbed to his feet. "That's why I came to you, Barry," he declared. "To get some sound advice, and from someone with a clear and sensible head. Thanks, Barry - thanks for hearing me out. I'll get outta here now."

My retreating comrade advanced to my door but, momentarily, paused to speak to me once again. "Do you hate me, Barry?" he questioned. "I couldn't really blame you, if you do."

"The term hate is much too strong a word, Mario. I've never hated anyone in my entire life. But I can't say I like you very much at this moment in time and that makes me very unhappy and sorrowful too. I'm sorry for me, sorry for you, sorry for Kathy, sorry for Tommy and Angie too. And I'm especially sorry for the innocent, unborn child in this matter. I don't foresee a happy ending for him, or her - and that breaks my heart. But, at the present time, my heart aches and crumbles for a boy who's faraway in South Vietnam."

"Tommy has always had a good friend in you, Barry, the very best," Mario stated. "I just hope - that someday you will come to forgive me. But, until then - I guess I'll be seeing you around, Barry."

"You take care of yourself, Mario. Yeah - I'll be seeing you around."

In the brief aftermath of Mario Moran's impromptu visit, I was depressed beyond belief. I withdrew no solace from knowing I had been correct about my long-held suspicions regarding Angie and Mario. I had sensed the carnal desires between the pair and I tried to throw a monkey wrench into it. I forced myself to speak to Tommy about it, but without any success. Momentarily, I regretted not speaking to the two lovers who were directly involved, and especially after my Vietnam trade-off had met with failure. I sincerely believed that - <u>if</u> my dear friend would be permitted to stay stateside (and in the arms of his wife), his physical presence would, alternately, stave-off the ongoing liaison.

However, I well-deserved being called 'naive' and somewhat 'stupid' prior to the revealing meeting between me and Mario Moran, because I never gave the pregnancy issue a credible thought. Out of all the scenarios I imagined and reckoned with, I never gave serious thought of an innocent child being tossed into the equation, not ever!

Like I told my guilt-ridden and remorseful comrade, Mario, during our rather emotional powwow, I couldn't foresee a happy ending in the matter - not for the expected baby or anyone else who was involved in it. And that happened to include me - because I always knew (not felt) I would be a forever player in the life of Thomas Preston and, he, in my life. And there was no doubt in my military mind about it!

Shortly after the downhearted and heavy-laden Mario Moran stopped by my 250th General cadre room, wherein he virtually poured his heart out to me, I found myself reflecting on something my mother once shared with me. After losing one of her older brothers (Major) to the entity known as 'death,' she soon, a mere two weeks later, dealt with the sudden passing of, yet, another elder brother named Harvey. I was deeply troubled by the unfairness of the happening but Ruby took it in philosophical stride, telling me, "Sometimes sorrow comes in pairs; one terrible tragedy right on the heels of another tragedy." She uttered those words emphasizing the importance of prayer in an individual's life and, as always, I marvelled at her resilience and uncommon faith.

Personally, I wished I could have bottled up some of my mother's inner strength, or have heeded her sincere advice about the need and power of prayer. Because when I met up with Danny Williams (which was less than 24 hours after Mario's visit), perhaps I could have seen a glimmer of light or hope at the end of the proverbial tunnel, instead of converging gloom and imposing darkness. Similar to my recent meeting with Mario, Dan and I spoke alone in the privacy of my cadre room.

"I can't, for the world of me understand why you're so pissed off at my ass, Harris," Danny remarked. "A person would think that I killed somebody or something!"

"To me, man, it's almost as bad," I countered. "Look at it this way, Danny. Suppose that girl you're fooling around with, suppose she comes up pregnant? What do you think will come of it? What'll happen to your marriage to Valerie?"

My cohort was visually flustered. "Come on, Harris, you're being silly right now. Kim's not pregnant, and I'm not gonna git her pregnant either. And my wife, hell - she's a thousand damn miles away, and she'll never, ever hear about my dealings with Kim! I ain't stupid, and for your information, I do believe in protection, Harris! There's such a thing as a condom, you know? Harris, I'm just doing my thing! What real harm am I doing? Especially since Val doesn't know about what's going on."

I shook my head in despair. "Danny, you're like most dudes I've known," I argued. "You really think you're in control, don't you? I believe you. If you claim you use a condom, I honestly believe you do - <u>most</u> of the time. You know I'm inexperienced when it comes to sexual matters, but I'm not stupid either. A baby can crop up anytime, and a single sexual romp could produce one. So, Kim is in the driver's seat, most women are, not you. Danny, in less than a couple of weeks time, you'll be back in the arms of Val. You'll be able to hold Tiana and the whole smear. You don't wanna carry some kind of ... social disease home to your wife. It can happen, ya' know?"

All I knew for sure was that I was making my comrade more frustrated. "But you're thinking about the worst case possible, Harris," he grimaced. "Guy, it ain't that damn serious! I mean - I love Valerie to death, and she ... she loves the hell outta my ass too. I wouldn't jeopardize my marriage with Val, I wouldn't. Plus, like you say, I've got a beautiful baby girl back home, and she's just waiting for her daddy to get there."

It was becoming more and more apparent to me that I was waging a losing battle. "Can I ask you something, Danny?" I asked my friend. "Once you return to Detroit and you, God forbid, learn that Valerie has been messing around on you, could you deal with it? Say ... Val has a boyfriend and she's been having sex with him since she's been home, what would you do? How would you feel?"

My companion acted as if I was being absurd. "Come on, Harris, my baby wouldn't fool around on me, but ... you know damn well how I'd feel. I'd be mad as hell, and really hurt! But the girl loves me ... like nobody's business. And I trust her completely."

"Unfortunately, she can't trust you, right?" I inserted. "Dudes always get me - with their double standards. You know what, Danny? I've been waiting for you to hit me with that classic, age-old line. You know, when dudes say, 'A man's gonna be a man?' That always works, makes a guy feel comfortable and righteous about him fooling around."

Obviously, I struck a sensitive chord with my comrade. "And what do you know about it, Harris?" he almost angrily asked. "You admitted to me you're still a virgin, and ain't never screwed a woman before. How can you miss something you've never had before? And I'm not taking a pot shot at you, I'm only saying, man."

Although Danny curtailed his verbal retort, I took it in calm stride. "But I never told you that I didn't have cravings, or sexual desires," I told him. "But, think back. Do you remember when I shared that confession with you? It was right after that incident with the woman named Minnie, the bold and loose momma of those nine kids? You recall that, Dan?"

"Well - I vaguely remember it, kinda. I know you were depressed about it, kinda upset."

"Yeah, well I get upset and depressed every time I think about those kids," I angrily went on with my story. "All children deserve a loving mother and father in this world and, at least, when they first come into this world. I get so damn sick of adults screwing over kids like that, and especially in the black community!"

"Shit, Harris, honkies do the same goddamn thing!" Danny snapped. "We ain't the only ones!"

My companion hit my anger bone. "And I give less than a flying damn about what white folks do, Danny," I argued. "It don't make it right or fair! Then again, a lot of the times white folks have the financial means to take care of their out-of-wedlock babies, their darn mistakes! But little black babies - they enter the world starvin' for food and love too! And they don't deserve that bullcrap! No newborn child deserves it, Danny, regardless of the race factor."

"And, Harris - man, I totally agree with that shit too, every bit of it. And I'm gonna be a good father to my daughter, the very best I can possibly be. But, still, I'm a man, a man made of flesh and blood. And you ... you might accuse me of copping out, say I'm hiding behind that old saying too, the one you hate so much, but there's some truth to it. Harris, I have sexual needs and most dudes have 'em, and I need a woman every now and then! I can't be like you, man, I just can't!"

Upon looking at my anguish-filled comrade, I felt almost exhausted. "And what am I, Danny?" I quizzed. "A freak of nature, an alien, a being from another dimension? What?"

For a prolonged period, and with a volley of tears in his eyes, my friend glanced downward and seemed to seriously mull over my question. Finally, he replied, "Harris, I don't know <u>who</u> you are, I honestly don't. Man, I think you have tried so damn hard, and so damn long - to <u>not</u> be like your old man ... that you have become like no one else I have ever known. I'm not trying to criticize you, Harris, or say it in a ugly way - but, Harris, you're not like most people, not normal people. Harris, you are aware of that, aren't you?"

I really didn't intend to follow suit, but upon watching my friend weep, I was also reduced to tears. (Of course, there was no surprise to that development). I remarked, "I guess that kinda summarizes our relationship, huh? You don't remotely understand me, and I ... I don't want you to be like the greater majority of dudes I know. I want a friend who stands above other guys I've known, someone who's upstanding and, I guess, outstanding too. And you hit the pin on the head, Danny, a friend who's completely opposite my father. A friend I can believe in, brag on and admire."

It wasn't my goal to offend or hurt my companion, but I could see and feel I had done just that. Wearing a face of severe sorrow, he stood and prepared to leave my cadre room. "I am sorry, Harris," he said. "Sorry I disappointed you and let you down and I guess, I know . . . I'll always regret it. I'll miss the hell out of you, man - just like I've been missing you. And believe it or not, Harris, I do love you, I truly do."

Unable to harness my own tears, I opted to climb to my feet when Danny paused at the door and, then, looked back at me. Although inwardly I suppressed a strong urge to walk over and embrace him, I stood still instead, admitting, "And I love you too, Danny."

In the not-too-distant aftermath of my piggyback and emotional-draining meetings with Mario Moran and, then,

THE LONG AND WINDING ROAD

Daniel Williams, my heart practically shut down. I felt like a lifeless and wandering zombie. I fulfilled my work duties at the Registrar's office with my usual proficiency and remained professional and congenial with my co-workers and superiors alike, but, essentially, I was just going through the motions. Neither my heart or mind was in it and only when I retreated to a movie at one of the theaters on post, did I obtain any semblance of peace and serenity. I was in an emotional funk.

Actually, my antisocial behavior did not help the situation either. I not only made it a point to stay clear of Angie Preston (I knew I could not face her, void of an expression of condemnation), I also kept my distance from the Harold Kurn family. I surely wasn't upset with the sarge, he hadn't done a darn thing to me, but I didn't want to drag him into my hovering morose. And that included his wife, Myoshi.

To a certain degree, I was self-torturing myself. By avoiding Tommy's wife and Harold as well, it naturally meant I would be estranged from Tommy Jr. and Cornel and Marla Kurn also. My arms longed to hold them and my lips ached to kiss those kids.

In essence, I didn't want to communicate with a living soul. I guess I derived a measure of solace from stewing in my sorrow and self-pity and I didn't wish to infect others, and especially innocent bystanders. So, I chose to keep to myself, to read assorted books or watch TV in the lonely confines of my cadre room and hoped that my somber state was just a passing phase.

And I dealt with other side-effects also. It was a period when I could hardly sleep, when I could barely eat and, for the first time in my young life, when I was void of my desire to drink beer. I seriously believed that during the time I'm recalling, I truly needed some kind of psychiatric help. Seemingly, I had lost perspective and real purpose in my life.

Now, in harkening back to my early church-going days, I had heard that from time to time "God steps in right on time," and while that belief was somewhat debatable, it acutely rang true to me when I was a 20-year-old corporal in the United States army. At the very height of my weighty depression in the autumn of 1964, when I was beginning to think there was no end or escape from my ongoing and overbearing funk, I was subjected to a most bizarre and unexpected distraction. Without any prior warning whatsoever, I was summoned to 250th General's Headquarters building, and was assigned a very somber and unorthodox mission that not only displaced and superseded my self-pity, it would greatly change and enhance my entire life.

Standing before Lt. Col. Mathis, 250th General's commanding officer, I was ordered to escort the remains of a deceased young soldier to Chicago, Illinois. I had no idea <u>why</u> I was selected for what the CO described as a "rare honor," or <u>if</u> I could decline the mission - <u>if</u> I wished to. Seemingly, however, it was an assignment that was set in stone. When the ensuing Monday arrived on the scene, I was expected to actively pursue the undertaking. And without delay or protest, that's exactly what I did.

THE BEGINNING

"THE LONG AND WINDING ROAD"

EPILOGUE

"The good that you do, will come on back to you - and it don't cost very much."
>IT DON'T COST VERY MUCH
>Spiritual sung by
>Mahalia Jackson

"The evil that men do lives after them."
>From JULIUS CAESAR
>Classic written by
>Shakespeare

As far back as my high school years, maybe even farther back, I tried to live my life with the above two quotes very much in mind. Thanks to my mother, the first quote was endorsed to me in verbalization and in song, and the second one, a virtual soliloquy was derived from the literary prose of famed dramatist, William Shakespeare. I've always considered both quotes to be wise and teeming with truism.

In the latter days of November 1964, after fulfilling my memorable and mournful mission to Chicago, as well as enjoying my abbreviated vacation in St. Louis shortly afterwards, I returned to my military home in Fort Sam Houston, Texas.

Although I had left San Antonio under a haze of anguish and mental duress, I returned to the region with an entirely different mind-set. No longer was I in the doldrums because I felt disenchanted with the world at-large, or because I had temporarily lost faith in God and in people.

In fact, when I seriously thought about my entire <u>escort</u> venture (it's opportune timing, it's unexplained origin and my select role in the operation), I came to see and applaud God's divine influence in the matter. I was at my wit's end when it came to my entrenched begrudgment towards my biological father (my suppressed anger was severely marring my own well-being and was weighing heavily on my relationships with others), and seemingly I couldn't sink any further into my bitterness. Therefore, it was high-time for me to address my dilemma, or bring it into focus, and God "made" the way for me.

From the moment I saw and interacted with my father, something became clear to me that I should have known well-prior to our reunion. I am totally incapable of hating people! Not only that, but upon knowing people for a certain number of years, "good" memories seem to come rolling in and supersede the adverse ones. My old man had behaved badly, he had committed acts that were cruel and almost diabolical when he was still around, but my memories of him weren't all bad. In being an individual who was, and is blessed with an exceptional memory, I recalled him tucking me in bed when I was sick, kissing me, hugging me and crying over me as well. And the poignant memory of the latter emotion, the weeping factor, came hurdling back to me when he opened the door at his Prairie street apartment in Chicago.

However, I cannot credit my denouncement of hate and forgiveness of my dad solely to benevolent reflections. A sizable amount of sympathy and empathy entered into the matter also. I had long believed that my father sorely-missed and grieved over the five sons he had abandoned in the city of St. Louis and upon spending quality time with the man, I realized I was correct.

Seemingly, my old man was a self-absorbed alcoholic, he lived on the outskirts of despair and, both time and strong drink had taken an adverse toll on his physical looks. He was no longer the "pretty man" he deemed himself and I felt somewhat sorry for him.

Most notably, after interacting with my dad during my rather impromptu trip to Chi-town, I emerged clear-headed, refreshed and optimistic when I stepped back upon Texas soil. Prior to embarking on my mid-west journey, which allowed me the time to wrestle with and soundly defeat my childhood demons I had foolishly severed my intimate and precious friendship with Daniel Williams.

Behaving like both, judge and jury, I had convicted my endeared cohort of being <u>like</u> my errant, biological father. And that was not fair, I was grossly in error, and I came to realize I owed my wonderful friend a sincere and heartfelt apology. I could hardly wait to ask Dan to forgive me.

However, upon looking back, that was exactly my inclination prior to my back-to-back emotional meetings with Mario Moran and Danny Williams himself. That was at the very beginning of November of 1964.

Admittedly, I have had many regrets during my long life. However, very few of them had the intensity and endurance of the remorse I incurred in regards to my close-knit comrade from Detroit. On several occasions Dan had told me that his ETS (Expected time of separation) was the 30th of November, less than a week after the Thanksgiving holiday, but little did I know he would be allowed to muster out prior to the holiday.

Therefore, when I arrived back at Fort Sam Houston, I entered my cadre room, hurriedly unpacked my duffel bag and, then, rushed over to Danny's 24th Evac. barracks. Sadly, though, I was too late. According to one of my pal's on-hand billets mates, Dan had already been discharged and, as the soldier put it, was, "Back in '<u>Hitsville</u>' or good ole Detroit, Michigan by now." (That's what they called 'Motown' in those days).

To put it lightly, I was deeply hurt, disappointed and quite angry too. But not angry at my departed companion, but at myself. I had acted foolishly, arrogantly and immature as well and I immediately came to the conclusion I had been served 'my' just desserts. But even in being downhearted and remorseful, I was able to cling tight to a very comforting and very soothing saving grace. I sincerely loved Danny and his wife, Valerie, also (in fact, after all the years, I still do), and I withdrew a heartrending degree of solace from surmising that the two of them were back in each other's arms again in the state of Michigan. I know I've always been a dreamer and somewhat of a romantic, but that's a comforting vision that remains forever fixed in my mind.

Upon refocusing on the last days of November of 1964, even as I became reconciled to the sorrowful truism that I had managed to personally dismantle and nullify my precious and almost sacred friendship with Daniel Williams, I was hell-bent on resecuring my relationship with the Harold Kurn family and was equally determined to spend a great deal of leisurely time with Angela Preston and little Tommy Jr. as well.

In addition, I recommitted myself to the task of writing regular upbeat letters to Tommy Sr. in South Vietnam (twice monthly, to be specific) and I kept that up until, firstly, I was discharged from the army in June of 1965, and, secondly, until Tommy, himself, returned safely home to the United States and, subsequently, was separated from military service a few months later. I thanked the living God for keeping my friend well and out of harm's way while being in a volatile war zone.

Unfortunately though, in an indirect way, Thomas Preston was somewhat of a casualty of that ongoing and escalating war. And so was his spouse, Angela, and the children they went on to have together. The couple eventually added a little girl to their union when they returned to civilian status but owing to a particular circumstance, their marriage was on a downhill slide from the very second they were reunited stateside. Sorrowfully, divorce was looming and almost eminent.

Although the child that was fathered by Mario Moran lived only six months (to Tommy's credit, he loved the little guy) the deceitful story behind the baby's conception lived on. Eventually, Tommy and Angie dissolved their marital union, Tommy went on to enter into a second marriage and, then, start a new family and, just as I had priorly predicted, I was a consistent and intricate part of it all. Thomas Preston and I have remained close-knit friends for nearly 58 years (just two years shy of six decades) and our love and affection for each other has never withered or subsided. In, both, my heart and mind I have always regarded our enduring relationship as a special gift from God Himself.

As a reader of this book, no one will remotely be surprised to learn that I have had a lifelong fondness (if not, love) for various 'quotes' and 'adages' - and especially ones that are borrowed from an array of motion pictures. Therefore, when I reflect back on my yesteryear comrade named 'Mario Moran' and divulge that whenever I recall him, I, simultaneously, remember dialogue that was extracted from a 1960's movie entitled 'The Carpetbaggers,' it should not come across as altogether weird and bizarre to anyone.

When I revisit Mario's lustful affair with Angie (which culminated into the birth of a flesh-and-blood baby), I automatically reminisce some words that were voiced by actor Alan Ladd in that celluloid feature. Speaking to the main character (Jonas Cord Jr.), he said, in essence, "Draw your gun, aim straight ... but don't hit any innocent bystanders."

To my genuine regret (and to Tommy's forgiving regret also), I never knew what became of my Cuban cohort, Mario Moran, after my army hitch concluded. And to be perfectly honest as well, I never wished that he suffered repercussions or any ill-effects in the aftermath of his adulterous actions. However, just think of how many innocent bystanders were 'hit' in the wake of his devil-may-care behavior. Starting with his wedded-wife, Kathy, there was the remorseful but complicit Angela, her husband, Tommy, the Preston couple's two biological offsprings and, most certain, the child that sadly passed away.

So many times, whether a man or woman's actions are adverse or benevolent, they affect a whole gamut of people. That is the classic and ultimate 'domino effect.'

Although I have always described my love for people as 'insatiable' and seemingly 'everlasting' also, I well-know that my feelings are rare and not of the norm (and I am not patting myself on the back because I've suffered a great deal of heartache, disenchantment and sorrow along my life's lengthy path). In addition to that, it is also a rarity to become acquainted with like-minded individuals too. Therefore, in reporting that my once vital and intimate friendship with Jerome (or J) lasted an excess of 30 years and, then, withered on the vine, there is little remorse or sadness attached to my admission. Far too many vivid and wonderful memories come to mind.

Digressing back to the year 1965, I was not only awarded my buck-sergeant patch (E-5), but Jerome and I spent our respective 21st birthdays together. Since my close comrade was stationed about 500 miles from San Antonio (specifically, the 'White Sands Missile Base' located in New Mexico), J journeyed to Fort Sam Houston in February of that year (the 22nd and several days afterwards) and I in turn, travelled to White Sands in the ensuing April (the 3rd, with a couple of days tacked on to it).

(Despite the relevancy here, Black Muslim leader Malcolm X was assassinated one day before J's 21st birthday (which was 1965) and three years later, April 4th, 1968, Rev. Dr. Martin Luther King Jr. was murdered. That happened to be one day after my 24th birthday).

Returning to the year 1965, however, when J and I made it a point to celebrate our 21st birthdays together, I presented J an attractive, bluish-colored jersey (or sweater) and, on my special day, my friend gifted me my very first typewriter. Over half a century has passed since those days, but the memory of our twofold commemorations in 1965 remain forever etched into my brain.

Since my relationship with Jerome lasted for decades (all through the duration of his marriage and all), he and I delightedly gave each other an array of tangible gifts during that period. Significantly though, none of the presents or tokens we gifted each other came close to rivaling or surpassing the intangible gift that was an outgrowth of our once vibrant friendship. Sometimes, a single person can serve as a conduit in bringing forth an outstanding and, occasionally, a more enduring relationship.

Although I've been eternally grateful to God for installing J into my life in the first place (I know there was a time he loved me as much as I still love him), I am equally thankful to the Lord for ushering Jerome's oldest son, Patrick into my love orbit as well. "PJ" or "Pat" is in his 50's at present, but my affection for my godson still grows with each passing day.

Whenever I focus on terms such as 'outgrowth,' 'conduit' or 'by-product,' I automatically think about my biological father, Melvin V. Harris. I almost traditionally search for the proverbial 'silver lining' in various matters (and oftentimes I've found it) and inadvertently owing to my birth father, I perceived one in the autumn of 1964. I fell in love with my kid-brother Keith during my somber mission to Chi-town and my affection for the man lives on till this very day.

People casually mouth the term 'half-brother,' but since Keith is not considered one of the 'little people' (formerly known as dwarfs and midgets), I loathe the term. In fact, I have always loved <u>all</u> of my brothers with the same sincerity and intensity.

As I mentioned occasionally, my ETS was in June of 1965. In spite of being well-aware of that fact, however, it did not discourage Staff-Sgt. Harold Kurn from trying to entice me into reenlisting in the military service. Practically 'dangling' a E-6 stripe in my face (Hell - I was just promoted to sergeant E-5 in early March!), my fellow noncom was almost relentless in his prodding and coercing. But in the final analysis, his efforts were fruitless. I was a staunch and stubborn naysayer and nothing (absolutely nothing) could have changed my mind. Superseding the meager monthly pay salary was the ever-present racism factor.

Although I felt badly when I said "No" for the <u>final</u> time to Sgt. Kurn (that was the 19th of June, the day prior to my ETS), I complimented him for his persistence but emphatically told him I would <u>never</u> don a military uniform again. And with the word 'never' still reverberating in my ears, I sincerely thanked him for taking me under his wings. I thanked him for the latitude he allowed me during our numerous field exercises out at Camp Bullis, for his help and support when I tackled classic racism, for his audacious decision to provide me my own cadre room, for all the dinner invitations he extended me and, above everything else, for sharing his wonderful and adoring immediate family with me.

With the latter factor searing so warmly in my heart, as I visualized the sarge, Myoshi and little Cornel and Marla in my mind, I told my sergeant friend, "Harold, I will forever cherish and love you and your beautiful family and no matter where my life takes me, you four guys will always be with me, tucked safely in my heart." And, true to course, I made that statement with tears streaming down my cheeks. That occurred on the 20th day of June, only a couple of hours before I boarded a Greyhound bus headed for St. Louis, Missouri.

My beloved mother Ruby had advised me several times before I reached my manhood (I turned 21 on April 3, 1965) that I should refrain from uttering the word 'never.' She said when an individual opted to invoke the term never (not only me, but other people as well), they were setting themselves up for a rude awakening. "Never say never," my mom would tell me, "because when you do, it will likely come back to bite you on your butt."

LIFE GOES ON but, unfortunately, so does death! In mid-July of 1965, which was less than a month after I was discharged from the United States army, my childhood cohort and former running buddy, Alonzo (or Lonnie) was fatally shot while exiting a basement dance on a Saturday night.

Reportedly, no one seemed to know the underlying circumstances that led up to the shooting or even <u>if</u> Lonnie was the intended target of the unknown killer. Personally, all I knew (or surmised) was that my long-time comrade had gotten married, was the father of a baby boy and, at the age of 22, was somewhat out of place at a festive event that usually drew teenagers and youngsters who still attended high school. In my opinion (and I was still grievous of my friend's untimely demise), Alonzo <u>*should*</u> have outgrown teenage parties and should have been home with his wife and little boy. Of course, <u>*fate*</u> has little respect for words like 'could have,' 'would have' or 'should have.' Therefore, my opinion was somewhat moot.

No matter how anyone felt about the tragedy (me included), the fact was that my childhood comrade was indeed dead. I especially took Alonzo's death hard because there I was, praying so intensely that Thomas Preston would return home safe and unharmed from war-torn South Vietnam and Lonnie, who (again) <u>*should*</u> have been out of harm's way in the good ole U.S.A., was lying dead in a stateside morgue. Life is totally unpredictable but it can be so cruel and callous sometimes.

Garbed in my military dress uniform during Lonnie's subsequent funeral (since I had grown quite a bit during my three years in the armed services, my civilian wardrobe was virtually nonexistent), I spent a substantial portion of time with Alonzo's mournful loved ones in the aftermath of the somber ceremony. Naturally, it was reminiscent of my escort mission to Chicago back in November of the previous year.

Although I was initially shocked and appalled by Lonnie's violent demise, I wasn't awestruck by it in the least. To be perfectly candid, the killing of young men was almost routine or commonplace in the black community (I believed in the 1960's as I believe today that African-Americans, as a race, are victims of self-hatred.), but upon observing the devastated faces and the grievous behavior of Alonzo's biological mother and stepfather, his biological father and stepmother, his paternal grandmother and his young widow as well, I longed for the guilty shooter to <u>behold</u> what he had actually done.

Admittedly, I have always been philosophical and I'm a perennial cry-baby too (I make no excuses about that), but still I earnestly wished the drive-by murderer had been in the social mix. Because then, and only then, would he have realized just how many people he had callously slain by firing a single, fatal bullet, and how many innocent people's lives he had shattered and had, all but, destroyed.

Maybe the perpetrator would feel nothing, I further pondered; no remorse or sorrow whatsoever, but I somehow didn't believe he would be that callous or cold. However, at any event, I still wished the man, or boy, was on hand to observe the terrible results of his violent actions. I have always wondered that when a person commits such a horrendous and diabolical deed, do they truly believe that their future life should be trouble-free and smooth-sailing? I often think about that.

Well, as the familiar saying goes, life goes on. And I went on to live and enjoy my life, for the most part, after my military hitch had gone by the boards. I remained a dedicated and devoted son to my mother Ruby; spent a great deal of time in the company of my esteemed uncle, Bill Strickland; occasionally interacted with my childhood friends and relatives alike (especially Pauline and Frank); dedicated myself to making an impact and positive difference in the lives of every youngster I happened to meet and eventually got married and tried my level best to raise and nurture three upstanding children of my own.

Thus far, in the year of 2021, in spite of incurring my share of tragedies along the way, I have been afforded a blessed, charmed and relatively happy life. In so many, many ways, the Lord up above has been sustaining and good to me. After 28 years of marriage, I lost my beloved wife Gloria in 2007, I'm in great health as I approach the young age of 77 and I still regularly interact with devoted and loyal friends I've known for decades on top of decades and, notably, one of them is Thomas Harold Preston. We have been the best of friends for an excess of 57 years. Now, if that's not a sacred blessing from the Supreme Being Himself, I remain open to fiercely debate it! Throughout my rather lengthy life, I've learned to identify a blessing when I see one.

THE END (Of)

"THE LONG AND WINDING ROAD"
By Lionel B. Harris

CPSIA information can be obtained
at www.ICGtesting.com
Printed in the USA
LVHW080003260322
714464LV00002B/3